MONTGOMERY COLLEGE LIBRARY
GERMANTOWN CAMPUS

The Mode
and Meaning of
'Beowulf'

MARGARET E. GOLDSMITH

The Mode and Meaning of 'Beowulf'

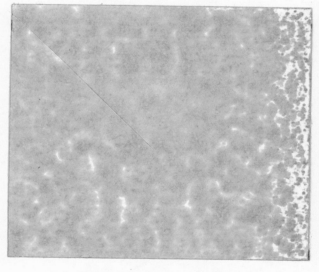

THE ATHLONE PRESS
of the University of London : 1970

Published by
THE ATHLONE PRESS
UNIVERSITY OF LONDON
at 2 Gower Street London W C 1

Distributed by
Tiptree Book Services Ltd
Tiptree, Essex

Australia and New Zealand
Melbourne University Press

U.S.A.
Oxford University Press Inc.
New York

© *Margaret E. Goldsmith* 1970

0 485 11110 1

78489490

Printed in Great Britain by
WESTERN PRINTING SERVICES LTD
BRISTOL

To Hugh, Neil and Michael

Preface

This study had its tentative beginnings more than twelve years ago, when I first examined the curiously ambivalent treatment of the treasure hoard in *Beowulf* in the light of Hrothgar's 'sermon'. Family responsibilities gave me little leisure to do much research at that time, but even desultory patristic reading convinced me that I was uncovering, not simply the unifying theme I had set out to find, but an extended allegory. My first conclusions were incorporated in 'The Christian Theme of *Beowulf*', written in 1958. By coincidence, this article appeared in print in the same year (1960) as Father M. B. McNamee's paper '*Beowulf*—An Allegory of Salvation?'. It was natural that bibliographers and others should class the two articles together, though our approaches and conclusions were quite different. My intention had been to find an underlying principle of coherence which would explain the choice of story material and the emphases observable in the various tales; McNamee on the other hand, like Cabaniss in 1955, had separated the element of religious symbolism from the other elements in the composition and magnified it in ways which upset the balance of the poem.

McNamee's work taught me much, though I disagreed with his critical methods. I realized that I knew very little about patristic modes of thought and their expression, and that my own paper had been much too superficial. I also became convinced that any interpretation of *Beowulf* must test every part of the poem against the beliefs known to be current at the relevant time about man as a social, political and spiritual creature.

In the years since 1960 I have been trying to find out what can be known or reasonably assumed about the thought-world of a literate Anglo-Saxon of the seventh or eighth century, and re-assessing the values implicit and explicit in *Beowulf* as a product of that world. This book is the result of that enquiry. It is offered as an essay in historical criticism, and I have used the past tense

Preface

throughout in referring to religious doctrines, even those which are still held by many people today, because I have no covert propagandist intent and no wish to use the poem as an instrument of sectarian controversy.

I believe that I have been able to demonstrate that the hypothesis that the author of *Beowulf* had received the religious education of his time best accounts for the attitudes of the poem and its complex character. I hope that I have also shown that *Beowulf* is the first great medieval allegory of human life and death based on the beliefs of the Western Church.

I was fortunate while my theories were in the making to be able to exchange ideas with my then colleague J. E. Cross (now Professor of English Language at Liverpool). His friendly, knowledgeable, and often sceptical comments were both constructive and challenging. I owe a special debt also to S. J. Tester of the Classics department at Bristol, who has helped me unravel knotty points in the Latin texts and has kindly read and suggested improvements in the translations I have made for the book. I also wish to thank Susie I. Tucker and I. B. Bishop for helpful suggestions made in conversation, and J. Farrell, sub-Librarian of Bristol University, for his generous advice and assistance.

This study naturally leans upon the work of many outstanding *Beowulf* scholars and critics, and I would particularly name Professor C. L. Wrenn, who taught me to read Old English poetry with his own enthusiasm. But above all the book owes its existence to my husband Hugh, without whose encouragement and constructive criticism it could not have come to fruition.

University of Bristol,   M. E. G.
July 1968

viii

Contents

Abbreviations

The following shortened forms of titles of books, periodicals, etc. are used throughout the footnotes and the practice of the notes generally is to omit details of publication if the work cited is listed in the Select Bibliography.

ASPR	Anglo-Saxon Poetic Records Series
ASS	*Acta Sanctorum Bollandiana*
(Bede) *HE*	*Historia ecclesiastica gentis Anglorum*
(Bede) *Ep. Ecg.*	*Epistola Bedae ad Ecgbertum Episcopum*
Beiträge	*Beiträge zur Geschichte der Deutschen Sprache und Literatur*
Brodeur, *Art*	A. G. Brodeur, *The Art of Beowulf*
Brodeur Studies	*Studies in Old English Literature in honor of Arthur G. Brodeur*
CSEL	*Corpus Scriptorum Ecclesiasticorum Latinorum*
CL	*Comparative Literature*
CCSL	*Corpus Christianorum Series Latina*
Continuations	*Continuations and Beginnings: Studies in Old English Literature*, ed. E. G. Stanley
Deanesly, *Pre-Conquest Church*	Margaret Deanesly, *The Pre-Conquest Church in England*
Dobbie, *Beowulf*	E. v. K. Dobbie, ed. *Beowulf and Judith*, *ASPR* IV
Donahue, *Traditio*, 1949–51	Charles Donahue, '*Beowulf*, Ireland and the Natural Good', *Traditio*, 7 (1949–51)
Donahue, *Traditio*, 1965	Charles Donahue, '*Beowulf* and Christian Tradition: a reconsideration from a Celtic Stance', *Traditio*, 21 (1965)
Godfrey, *AS Church*	J. Godfrey, *The Church in Anglo-Saxon England*
Gregory, *Moralia*	*Sancti Gregorii Magni Moralium Libri, sive Expositio in Librum B. Job*
Kenney, *Sources*	J. F. Kenney, *The Sources for the Early History of Ireland*, vol. 1, *Ecclesiastical*
Klaeber, *Angl.* 1912	F. Klaeber, 'Die Christlichen Elemente im *Beowulf*', *Anglia*, 35 and 36 (1912)

Klaeber, *Beowulf*	F. Klaeber, ed., *Beowulf and the Fight at Finnsburg*
Laistner, *Thought*	M. L. W. Laistner, *Thought and Letters in Western Europe, A.D. 500–900*
Magoun Studies	*Medieval and Linguistic Studies in honor of Francis P. Magoun, Jr.*
MGH	*Monumenta Germaniae Historica*
MGH AA	*Auctores Antiquissimi*
MGH Ep.	*Epistolae*
MGH Ep. Kar.	*Epistolae Karolini Aevi*
MGH Ep. Mer.	*Epistolae Merowingici et Karolini Aevi*
MGH Poet.	*Poetarum Latinorum Medii Aevi*
Ogilvy, *Anglo-Latin Writers*	J. D. A. Ogilvy, *Books known to Anglo-Latin Writers from Aldhelm to Alcuin*
PG	J. P. Migne, ed. *Patrologia Graeca*
PL	J. P. Migne, ed. *Patrologia Latina*
Rankin, *JEGP*, 1909	J. W. Rankin, 'A Study of the Kennings in Anglo-Saxon Poetry', *JEGP*, 8 (1909) and 9 (1910)
von Schaubert, *Beowulf*	Else von Schaubert, ed. *Heyne-Schückings Beowulf*
Sisam, *Structure*	Kenneth Sisam, *The Structure of Beowulf*
Sisam, *Studies*	Kenneth Sisam, *Studies in the History of Old English Literature*
Tolkien, *Monsters*	J. R. R. Tolkien, *Beowulf: The Monsters and the Critics*
Whitelock, *Audience*	Dorothy Whitelock, *The Audience of Beowulf*
Wrenn, *Beowulf*	C. L. Wrenn, ed. *Beowulf*
Wrenn, *OE Literature*	C. L. Wrenn, *A Study of Old English Literature*

1   *An Approach to the Critical Problem*

The central critical questions about *Beowulf* arise from its peculiar structure, the discontinuity of its narrative, and its abrupt
changes of tone. The author has made no open statement about
its signification, and no early reference survives to show how it
was regarded when its language was still current. No matter
what modern efforts are made to illuminate it, the poem is likely
to remain somewhat enigmatic, because of the nature of its
diction and its narrative method. Old English poetic diction is
inherently imprecise; it takes its colour from the context of the
whole work and the wider context of the poetic tradition; both
nebulous now, but then in common daylight for an initiated
audience. A different cause of bafflement is that the author of
Beowulf composed in chords reverberant to that audience, but
now dead sound. All general studies of the poem have in some
measure to fill in the silent intervals in the composition, but there
is no unanimity on how this should be done. It has seemed to me
best to proceed by way of a consistent hypothesis about the
author's outlook and the milieu in which he worked. The hypothesis was made after consideration of tendencies in the poem
itself and in the corpus of Old English literature as a whole.
It brings *Beowulf* fully into the tradition of edifying poetry
born of the marriage of native wisdom and Mediterranean
learning.

Professor J. C. Pope is typical of one school of scholarly
opinion in the reservations about *Beowulf* implied in this observation about *The Wanderer*: 'The author of *The Wanderer*, in
a more radical way than the author of *Beowulf*, seems deliberately to juxtapose the new mode and the old, to exhibit both
the strength and the limitations of the old, and to suggest a
synthesis dominated by the new.'[1]

It is my purpose to show that the tensions in *Beowulf* between

[1] J. C. Pope, 'Dramatic Voices in *The Wanderer* and *The Seafarer*', *Magoun
Studies*, p. 171.

secular and religious elements, between old and new values, are as deliberate and radical as they are in *The Wanderer*. Pope separates and distinguishes two speakers in *The Wanderer*, the one 'belonging to the conservative aristocratic world in both life and poetry', the other a man who 'has moved into the sphere of Biblical and patristic learning, with some flavour of classical philosophy'. These two imagined men, whether or not distinguishable in the fiction as Pope maintains, are of course facets of the author himself. Both the loneliness of the wanderer and the aloofness of the thinker are understood and created by the poet; he belongs to both worlds. Pope continues, 'And the darkness of spirit that has come over both these characters has different roots and leads to different conclusions'.[1] This perception is valuable, but the reader of the poem must go on to harmonize those conclusions, or alternatively to draw new understanding of human life from his inability to do so.

If Pope's observations are applied to *Beowulf*, it can be seen that most of the characters in the fiction suffer and endure like the wanderer, but in the outright philosophical statements of the author and sometimes in the wisdom expressed in the speeches of Hrothgar and Beowulf are found the 'pensive melancholy' which 'comes from the knowledge of other people's losses and the prospect of the general doom'.[2] The balance of the two worlds is quite different in *Beowulf*, but they are nonetheless both there to be reconciled, or to be more clearly understood in their relationship to each other.

I believe that the Christian poet's purpose was to examine the values of the heroic world as they appear when set against the whole history of mankind from Genesis to the Apocalypse.

Beowulf had not customarily been looked at in this way in modern times, before I published my theory of the Christian theme of *Beowulf* in 1960,[3] though Professor J. R. R. Tolkien had gone a long way in that direction in his highly influential essay, '*Beowulf*: The Monsters and The Critics'. The reasons for the origin and persistence of other ideas about the nature of the poem require mention, as does Tolkien's own halt in a mid-way position.

---

[1] *Magoun Studies*, p. 171.   [2] ibid., p. 172.
[3] 'The Christian Theme of *Beowulf*', *MÆ* 29 (1960), pp. 81–101.

An Approach to the Critical Problem

Like all *Beowulf* students of the last thirty years, I owe a great debt to Tolkien, who taught us to read the poem with imagination, as he had done. He gave us the key to understanding in his recognition of two special elements in the work: the 'fusion-point of imagination' which lies in the references to Cain, and 'the memories viewed in a different perspective'[1] which give the poem its depth. The first part of his now classic essay indicated some of the preoccupations which had blinded *Beowulf* scholars to the essential unity of the poem, and to these I need not revert. Another impediment *not* discussed by him was, I am sure, the belief that the hero of the poem was created as an ideal exemplar. Since Beowulf did not speak and behave at all points like a Christian prince, it was difficult to escape the conclusion that his creator had a somewhat limited or confused idea of Christian living. This conclusion did not accord with the unmistakably Christian language and thought of Hrothgar's long speech of admonition to Beowulf in lines 1700–84, and most critics, Tolkien included, agreed that at least part of the speech must have been added to the composition by a later hand. Finding this view unsatisfactory, I began to work with the assumptions that Tolkien was right about the poet's historical perspective (which implied that Beowulf was a noble pagan) and about the importance of the references to Cain (which led me into research concerning the traditional relationship of 'Cain's kin' and the Dragon) and that Tolkien was wrong to exclude Hrothgar's admonition from his consideration of the fusion-points between the heroic and the Christian worlds (which led to a study of the evolution of the figure of the heroic spiritual warrior). These researches disclosed that Hrothgar's admonition could itself be used as a key to unlock the symbolic meaning of Beowulf's life, involving as it does the right use of kingly power and wealth, which seemed to me to be a central concern of the poet, largely disregarded in Tolkien's interpretation. When I had satisfied myself that my original assumptions had been justified, in that I could now provide self-consistent answers to the critical questions raised by the text, I proceeded to draw inferences concerning the possible existence of different kinds of hidden meaning latent in the poem, such as I had recently come

[1] Tolkien, *Monsters*, pp. 261, 263.

to recognize in the Old English *Rhyming Poem*,[1] a little-understood work which has a good deal in common with Hrothgar's admonition.[2] There were indications that Tolkien's largely intuitive belief that Beowulf was in some sense a type of mankind fighting against the powers of evil might be substantiated by covered allusions to Adam in the latter part of the poem. By these stages I have come to my present view that *Beowulf* is a Christian allegory of the life of man.[3]

I am not unaware that the search for allegorical meaning in both medieval and modern works has sometimes produced highly subjective and precariously based interpretations.[4] *Beowulf* has had its share of these, and the more outstanding among them are critically reviewed in the course of this book. The criteria I would apply in evaluating criticism of this sort are of two kinds: historical and structural. The non-literal meanings proposed must be shown to be consonant with ways of thought contemporary with the composition of the work. They must also be shown to reinforce the structure of the whole composition, not throwing it out of balance or making otiose any major part of it. Because I regard these two criteria as necessary critical guide-lines, I have applied them to my own theory in subsequent chapters. Chapter 2 is concerned with ways of thought current during the period in which *Beowulf* was composed and, presumably, performed.[5] Chapter 8 relates the whole structure of the poem to the theories developed in the intervening chapters about the poet's view of life and death, the hero and the king, man and God.

The subject of this study may seem to some to call for an *apologia*, particularly to those who admire and accept the fundamentalist approach of Dr Kenneth Sisam. His book *The Structure*

---

[1] See Goldsmith, 'Corroding Treasure: a note on the OE *Rhyming Poem*, lines 45–50', *NQ*, May 1967, pp. 169–71.

[2] The similarity of *schema* in the two passages was pointed out by G. V. Smithers, 'The Meaning of *The Seafarer* and *The Wanderer*', especially pp. 8–10.

[3] The meaning I attach to the word 'allegory' will be discussed in Chapter 3.

[4] For a general demonstration of the weaknesses of some criticism of this sort, see M. W. Bloomfield, 'Symbolism in Medieval Literature', *MP* 56 (1958), pp. 73–81.

[5] For discussion of the question of dating the composition, see pp. 16ff. below.

of Beowulf deals some shrewd blows at 'conjectural interpretations', which must be parried. He has preferred

the plain meaning of the text because it is present in the mind of any attentive listener or reader who understands the language. Some of the words and some of the names carried associations for Anglo-Saxons that are now lost. But they would vary from person to person; they can seldom be guessed at with a fair chance of being right; and it is questionable whether they are necessary for the enjoyment of *Beowulf*, where so much is explicit.

He also utters the warning that conjectural interpretations 'are a channel for importing into the poem ideas that may never have occurred to the Anglo-Saxon poet and his audience'.[1] Perhaps few scholars would go as far as Sisam does in denying that the poem depends on 'silences, dark hints or subtle irony',[2] but his plea for 'the plain meaning of the text' can be speciously attractive until one asks oneself what the 'meaning' of a poetic text consists in, and whether there is any way of reading the poem (or any poem) which may *not* import into it 'ideas that may never have occurred to the poet'. Even if we knew the poet in person, we should still have to 'conjecture' what his poem meant. Our remoteness from the Anglo-Saxons only makes more apparent the problem of any reader facing any poem, the difficulty of 'understanding the language'. The more we know of an author's life and upbringing, the more we can hope to share the mental experience recorded in the language of the poem, and the more we can know of what he has left unsaid. It hardly needs to be stated that 'associations' vary from person to person in every period. No one of us can, even theoretically, expect to re-create the author's *Beowulf*, or even Klaeber's or Tolkien's *Beowulf*. The 'plain meaning' is a figment. We do, of course, distinguish for practical purposes between lexical and contextual meaning of words, and Sisam's 'plain meaning' might be thought to be the concatenation of glossary definitions which gives us our first inkling of what *Beowulf* is about, but reflection will show that in an allusive poem like *Beowulf* what is left unsaid is intended to be filled in by the reader; a second or subsequent reading will be coloured by the recollected matter as

[1] Sisam, *Structure*, p. 60.   [2] ibid.

much as by the plain text. If the older poetry had been composed, as much modern poetry has been, in personal language and private images, the author's meaning could 'seldom be guessed at with a fair chance of being right', but since the Anglo-Saxon poet does not speak as an individual, but as the spokesman of his social community, using conventional language and public images, there is some hope that by studying the conventions and themes of his art, the beliefs and *mores* of his society, in whatever monuments remain, we may make some valuable guesses to fill out the skeletal text. It seems to me self-evident that a more satisfying reading will be produced when the reader's mind is stocked with as much of the relevant contemporary material as can be gathered together after this lapse of time. 'Relevant' in this context means 'apt to deepen the meaning of the words of the poem'; it can only be tested against the reader's understanding of the whole work. The word 'contemporary' raises the large question of the limits of time within which we should look for comparative material; this matter will be debated more fully below.

All serious literary art contains an element of moral suasion, more or less concealed according to the conventions of the *genre* and the skill of the artist. In *Beowulf* as in other Old English poetry the moral intent is unmistakable. It is sometimes plainly stated—*swa sceal geong guma gode gewyrcean* (20)—but it also inheres in almost every part of the narrative, in the choice of characters as exemplars, and in the choice of incidents picked out for amplification. The puzzle *Beowulf* presents is the co-existence in the poem of conflicting moral attitudes, which may be explained in different ways. My own explanation, that the conflict is part of the scheme of the poem, reflecting different facets of the author's own view of life, has already been stated; my reasons for regarding it as more probable than the other possibilities must now be given.

There are, broadly speaking, two other possible explanations. One is that two or more authors were involved in making the poem we know. The other is that the author was a rather ignorant person whose attitudes reflect misapprehension and confusion rather than conflict.

Let us examine these possibilities in turn. There existed at one time a theory that *Beowulf* was a substantially pagan poem revised by 'a monkish interpolator'.[1] This view is now out of favour, because the dissemination of Christian vocabulary throughout the work and the nature of the supposed 'revision' itself militate against it. The strong argument which led me away from this theory is the great improbability that an ecclesiastical reviser whose purpose was to make the poem more edifying would have done his work with such restraint, to the extent of avoiding all reference to Christ and the church and of refraining from a homiletic ending.

A more subtle theory of multiple authorship is held by many scholars. The extant poem is regarded as the culmination of a series of orally preserved entertainments about the hero Beowulf and his adventures, formed by several successive singers.[2] The poem is thought to have developed by dilation and accretion, the extant form representing one dictated version of a well-known story. The degree to which the final version is thought of as either *extempore* or fixed and memorized depends on the pre-dilections of the critic holding the theory. The pre-literary history of the poem is quite outside the province of this study, but the stage of committal to writing is interesting and important. At that point in time the poem began its life as a literary artefact, either through the co-operation of an illiterate *scop* and a clerical scribe, or through the collaboration of a clerical thinker and an illiterate craftsman in verse (the Cædmonian situation), or through the single effort of a literate poet. The first of these possibilities, which can be designated the 'singer theory', is not, to my mind, a serious contender without a supplementary theory of substantial revision (which would be open to the same objection as the older interpolator-theory), for the simple reason that the minor stories are not presented as

[1] A classic instance of this view, now brought back to general notice through its inclusion in L. E. Nicholson's *Anthology*, pp. 1–21, is F. A. Blackburn's 'The Christian Coloring in the *Beowulf*', first published in *PMLA* 12 (1897), pp. 205–25.

[2] See F. P. Magoun, Jr. 'The Oral-Formulaic Character of A-S. Narrative Poetry', and R. P. Creed, 'The Making of an Anglo-Saxon Poem', *ELH* 26 (1959), pp. 445–54. For a general account of the controversy, see A. Bonjour, *12 Beowulf Papers 1940–1960* (Geneva 1962), especially pp. 136–49, and pp. 151–172.

entertainment in the way one would expect of a professional story-teller; the complete subordination of the bearers of the great names of the heroic world and the concentration of secular material within one small sphere of interest seem to me clear signs that the poem was not put together with the enjoyment of the *heorðwerod* as its guiding principle.[1] If any major reorganiza-tion of the composition was made after its literary history began, the reviser would have needed the purpose, the skill in versi-fication and the restraint in preaching which I would postulate as the requirements in our third kind of author, the learned poet, and to a 'reviser' of this calibre the title of 'the *Beowulf* poet' would not be inappropriate. The 'singer theory' in its bare form must, I think, be dismissed.

The second type of collaboration I envisaged would be a more actively shared process of composing in which a scholar pro-vided the plan of the work and wrote it down (or had it written) from the lips of a man trained in the traditional poetic tech-niques, who used his material along the lines suggested to him. Cædmon, as we know,[2] acquired great skill in verse-making, but being unable to read was fed with subjects from the Bible by his teachers, from which he made excellent poems. However, Cædmon was a special case. His great age when he received the gift of song would have made the learning of his letters imprac-ticable. Among the many who imitated him we may suppose that the majority were monks who saw in Cædmon's divine gift a sign that English poetry might be dedicated to God's service. In the absence of more positive evidence for such collaboration, the simpler explanation of a literate poet is to be preferred.

There are, of course, certain difficulties in the way of accept-ing the theory that *Beowulf*, substantially as we have it, was the work of a man trained in a religious school, but I think they can be explained away.

The theory would be damned from the start if it were true, as Professor Magoun unguardedly said, that 'lettered poetry is never formulaic',[3] since *Beowulf* obviously displays this quality

---

[1] For a contrary view see Sisam, *Structure*, p. 10.
[2] See Bede's account, *HE* IV, 22; Plummer I, 259.
[3] F. P. Magoun, Jr., loc. cit., p. 446.

throughout. It would also be difficult to maintain if it were true that monks were shut off from recitals of heroic poetry, or if ecclesiastical authors in general condemned and shunned it. There is, however, a great deal of evidence that these three propositions are untrue.

Professor Schaar has, I think, sufficiently answered Magoun's assertion,[1] though he himself, one may judge, leans rather too far in the other direction when he detects a number of literary borrowings between one Old English composition and another. On the general issue, however, he very clearly states the case for the lettered poets:

> There is some internal evidence pointing to a literary, a lettered, origin of at least a certain group of formulaic Anglo-Saxon poems, those composed by Cynewulf and some of those associated with him. Thus some weight must be attached to the occurrence in these poems of reminiscences of various classical, patristic, and apocryphal texts; reminiscences which occur, so to speak, outside the framework provided by the main sources. The foreign influence on such passages is recognisable, even if it is sometimes difficult to suggest the source with absolute exactness. Such allusions are most naturally explained on the assumption that the poet composed his work in the 'lettered' way, drawing on certain definite literary originals. It is less probable that the author derived such isolated passages from 'texts read aloud and/or expounded to him in English'; or that the 'lettered singers' saw fit to insert them now and then in the course of their performances; or being organic parts of the poems, that they were later interpolated by monastic scribes. They seem conditioned by the literary activity in monastic learned centres.[2]

Schaar's conclusions are drawn from the Cynewulf poems and *Guthlac*, *Phoenix*, and *Andreas*: on these he says that nothing forces us to conclude that they are the work of singers dictating to others or to themselves. 'But there is something to be said for the assumption that these works were composed in the ordinary way by poets who probably had access to MSS in English and Latin, and who probably worked in monastic communities.[3] Schaar himself is non-committal on the status of the *Beowulf* poet in this

---

[1] C. Schaar, 'On a New Theory of OE Poetic Diction', *Neophil.* 40 (1956), pp. 301–5; cp. also J. J. Campbell, 'Learned Rhetoric and Old English Poetry'.

[2] Schaar, op. cit., p. 303.   [3] ibid.

9

respect, as are other scholars, because this author does not betray precise knowledge of Latin texts; but in view of the demonstrated existence of lettered Anglo-Saxon poets, the onus falls upon supporters of the 'singer theory' to show why the simpler proposition is untenable. I doubt very much whether further research into the 'formulaic' and other phrases used by the *Beowulf* poet would end the controversy, because we do not know to what extent, if at all, a literary education might modify formulaic composition; valid comparison between different poems is scarcely possible because of the differences in subject matter, some subjects being well supplied with traditional stock phrases, others obviously less so. The inherited diction must have been adapted for Christian courts and there is no clear line beyond which we can distinguish a new method of composition. No doubt the lettered poets were content to use what was serviceable in the technique of their unlettered fellows.

In view of the preservation of *Beowulf* in writing, there is a natural presumption that the poet was in some way connected with a religious house. Is there any sound reason for thinking that such a man as the poem reveals could *not* have learnt to read and write in a monastic school? There is no means of finding out how *scopcræft* was handed from one poet to another; the Old English techniques are not difficult to understand and imitate, and eager listening would probably be the apprentice *scop*'s main requirement. Some young men must have entered monasteries already proficient in this art, and the monks of that day were by no means enclosed within their walls; opportunities might well arise while journeying to listen to secular songs and tales, and even in the monastery itself diversions of the sort were not unknown. The decree of the Council held at *Clovesho* in the Canterbury diocese in 747,[1] which forbade religious houses to allow performances by poets and musicians within them, is strong evidence that Hygbald's Lindisfarne was not uniquely reprehensible in enjoying secular entertainments.[2] It seems a fair inference that a recitation of *Beowulf* would have been well received in some eighth-century monasteries, and that an

---

[1] Haddan and Stubbs, *Councils*, III, 133; adduced by Sisam, *Structure*, p. 62 n.

[2] For Alcuin's famous letter, see *MGH Ep. Kar.* II, 181.

audience largely composed of monks need not have been ignorant of the cycles of heroic stories which lie behind its allusions. Professor Whitelock's comment on Alcuin's disapproving letter to Lindisfarne applies of course only to one time and place, and that a good deal later than the date most scholars would assign to the appearance of *Beowulf*: 'Nothing in the letter in which he reproved the monks of Lindisfarne for their interest in songs about Ingeld suggests that this taste was pandered to in monastic scriptoria.'[1] It would be quite unjustifiable to assume from this letter that all churchmen, even in the reforming days of Alcuin, would have disapproved of edifying poems like *Beowulf* (in which Ingeld has a minor and not very creditable role). If we look back a generation or two there are signs that vernacular poetry was not despised by the Christian writers of the day. Moreover, the apparent influence of *Beowulf* upon the religious poem *Andreas*,[2] which most scholars accept, argues that *Beowulf* was heard or read by hagiographers. The more uncertain relationships between *Beowulf* and the *Visio Pauli* of the seventeenth *Blickling Homily* is another pointer to the likelihood that *Beowulf*, or its author, moved in religious circles.[3] Perhaps the most impressive evidence comes from the lives of Aldhelm and Bede: as is well known, William of Malmesbury preserves a tradition, transmitted through King Alfred, that Aldhelm composed admirable songs in English, as well as his considerable Latin compositions.[4] Bede himself is credited with a little song in the native measure, though some have doubted whether he composed it, or merely quoted it;[5] either way, it argues acquaintance with and pleasure in vernacular poetry on the part of one who rarely left his monastery at Jarrow. This is not unexpected from a man who clearly saw the importance of using English to teach religious truths to the laity and those who knew no Latin.[6] He writes with evident approval of Cædmon's

---

[1] Whitelock, *Audience*, p. 20.

[2] The recent account of *Andreas* by R. Woolf, 'Saints' Lives' in *Continuations*, pp. 51–3, argues strongly that *Beowulf* was a model for *Andreas*. K. R. Brooks, ed. *Andreas* (Oxford, 1961), regards it as likely but not proven (following Whitelock), Introduction, xxvi.

[3] The possible relationship is discussed more fully below, in Chapter 4.

[4] *Gesta Pontificum Anglorum*, ed. N. Hamilton (Rolls Series, 1870), v, 336.

[5] See *ASPR* vi, cvii.   [6] Bede, *Ep. Ecg.*, Plummer, i, 409.

verse compositions and the wave of religious poetry they stimulated; he naturally rejoiced that Cædmon could not waste his gift on trivial songs,[1] but one hesitates to say that he would have disapproved of serious poetry like *Beowulf*. I can find no real obstacle to the assumption that the author of the poem had received instruction in a religious school, or had at the least been grounded in the Faith by a teacher from such a school; nor do I find any reason to think that *Beowulf* would have been unknown in monastic houses in the century or so after it was composed; though it hardly seems likely that it was put together for a monastic audience.

There remains the curious matter of the author's silence about the central truths of Christianity, which some attribute to his ignorance or failure to grasp them. It is evident that I do not accept the views of Dr Sisam and Professor Whallon that he only partially understood the new religion. Sisam's view is that the author was not concerned with religious questions, but that he remembered some outstanding Bible stories, those which 'stick in the minds of children'.[2] I find it hard to believe that a man with the moral sensibility and wide historical interests which *Beowulf* reveals would have disregarded the rest of the history of man as the Christian teachers presented it. Still less can I believe with Whallon that we have here an author whose lessons, beginning with the story of creation, had reached an abortive end with the Flood.[3] Missionaries are not normally so slow to get to the point. If we do not accept that the *Beowulf* poet's silence about the redemption of man was due to simple ignorance, some better explanation must be found.

I do not find it difficult to offer a reason. Salvation is outside the scheme of the composition: to introduce Christ or Christ's congregation into the world of the characters would be to place the issue of the fate of the righteous heathen at the heart of the poem. Clearly the author did not want this. Critics who know the poem well give contradictory answers to the question, 'Was Beowulf saved or damned?'[4] The truth is that this question,

---

[1] Bede, *HE*, Plummer, I, 259.   [2] Sisam, *Structure*, p. 75.
[3] W. Whallon, 'The Christianity of *Beowulf*', especially pp. 87 f.
[4] See E. G. Stanley, '*Hæthenra Hyht* in *Beowulf*', *Brodeur Studies*, pp. 136–51, passim.

like the sometime critical problem 'Was Hamlet mad?' has no answer, because the author of the fiction chose not to give unequivocal indication either way. We are not on this account prevented from using Elizabethan theories about madness to illuminate Hamlet's behaviour, or inhibited from discussing the apparent doctrinal laxness of the *Beowulf* poet as a piece of evidence about his attitude to life; but such discussion cannot clear away the doubt. I follow Tolkien in finding in the poem 'a Christian English conception of the noble chief before Christianity'[1] (though I do not agree with his distinction between Hrothgar and Beowulf in respect of their religious attitudes) and it seems to me natural enough that the author, while not arrogating to himself the power of the Judge, should wish to hint that Beowulf's manifest virtues merited recognition after death.

The theory I have propounded to account for the mixture of material in the poem and this equivocal attitude towards the hero and his *dom* is that the giant- and dragon-slaying, the court scenes, the subsidiary stories, and the Christian and gnomic statements, bear a purposed relationship to each other, such that the combats and rewards usually glorified by the *scopas* are called in question. *Beowulf*, I believe, was in its day a disturbing poem, in that the predictable pattern of the hero's victorious progress through dangers to posthumous fame was interrupted and darkened by tragic stories of faithlessness and inherited enmity, so that the hearer could not rest confidently in the assurance that all in the end would be well. The treasure piled about a corpse is the most memorable of the recurrent images of transience in the poem, and Beowulf's own surpassing achievements are depicted in a perspective of history which emphasizes that their beneficent results are short-lived. By this means the poet, while not disparaging the hero's excellent qualities, displays the weakness of unregenerate man in face of the evils which beset human kind, and reveals the worthlessness of rewards which a man must leave against his will.[2]

---

[1] Tolkien, *Monsters*, p. 270. On the religion of the characters in the poem see Chapter 5, below.

[2] See Augustine, *De Libero arbitrio*, ed. W. M. Green, p. 73, 13–14: 'Nemo autem securus est in his bonis quæ potest invitus amittere'; cp. also p. 187, below.

His motive in illustrating the transience of earthly grandeur is obvious enough; it is a familiar strain in Old English Christian poetry. In Beowulf, a man is celebrated who is neither saint nor Christian king, yet has much in common with both of these, and this unusual concept of a hero requires explanation. In Chapter 7 I examine this concept and its realization in the course of the poem; the central point of my argument is that Beowulf displays or is credited with every good human quality in his public career (his private life is not the poet's concern) but is lured as he nears death by the illusory solace of personal glory and great wealth. In his person, man is on trial: in God's service he can conquer all his enemies, but until the moment of death *manncynnes feond* will endeavour to snare him with these lures. The effect of the poem, as it appears to me, is to show that the intellect, strength and courage of a great man derive from God and are given to serve God and his fellowmen; such strength and courage when used for personal ends or gain can lead to consequences violent in their beginning and ever more tragic in their ramifications. Since this theme is discernible throughout the poem, becomes explicit in Hrothgar's homily to Beowulf and rises to a climax in the hero's last fight and hollow victory, it is reasonable to think that a single author's mind conceived and moulded the present shape of the composition.

The first major problem of procedure to be faced when I began my study was that of setting boundaries for the collection of illustrative material. In the absence of any direct information about the date and provenance of the final substantial redaction of the poem, it was necessary to set some limits of probability within which to work. I have in the preceding pages spoken of 'the poet' or 'the author' and I have stated my conclusion from the discernible motive outlined above that one shaping mind was responsible for the structure of the composition; I must now address myself to the difficult task of making my initial hypothesis—that *Beowulf* is the work of a poet who had received a Christian education—more definite, by considering his status, and when and where he might have lived. It is to be understood that by 'the poet' I mean the man whose mode of composing the poem I have been discussing, the man who committed *Beowulf* to writing in substantially the form now extant.[1]

I have already indicated my dissent from Sisam's view that he was a professional entertainer. The factor which, more than any other, inclines me to believe that the poet was a monk or a cleric is the authoritative tone of the work, which passes moral judgment upon kings and denounces the faithless. The poet is tutor as well as entertainer of his audience. Sisam tends to overemphasize the broad appeal of the poem to the king's retainers whom he regards as the main intended audience. He contends that delicate effects discovered in the poem by modern critics are modern inventions, on the grounds that the poet's audience

should not be thought of as learned in legendary history or theology, and quick to interpret any difficulty of expression or allusion. Bold rather than delicate effects would suit them best. A good poet will not be limited by the power of appreciation in his immediate audience; but to be successful in the conditions I am assuming he should not neglect a main part of them.[2]

One might counter this argument by making an analogy with, say, Elizabethan plays written for public performance before an audience largely composed of illiterate and not specially intellectual people. The best playwrights were not afraid to include subtle effects because the groundlings would fail to appreciate them: they addressed themselves to the nobility, as I think the *Beowulf* poet clearly does, and put in plenty of vigorous action to please the crowd. *Beowulf* in its present form has none of the marks of popular entertainment; the characters and their pastimes are aristocratic and no interest whatever is shown in any menial activity.[3] The one category of person whose special interests are evident throughout the poem is the ruler.

---

[1] The only reasonable course a critic can take is to assume that the unique text is reliable; I recognize the possibility of scribal alteration of words or phrases, but my argument rarely hangs upon the choice of individual words; where it does it is admittedly more tentative. Anyone who insists that some passages are later interpolations must disregard some of my observations about date and schooling and read my interpretation as applicable only to the 'revised' text, which presumably was read entire at some period before the end of the tenth century.

[2] Sisam, *Structure*, pp. 9–10.

[3] The point is made by Wrenn, *Beowulf*, p. 42. The dubious *þeow* (2223) and the dead *feormynd* (2256) hardly constitute exceptions.

And since a king would be in a position to inspire or commission a work of this kind and would also have the power to ensure its preservation for posterity, the hypothesis that *Beowulf* was composed by an educated poet for the pleasure and edification of a king seems to fulfil all the conditions.

Anyone who attempts to go further than this by identifying the king in question is guessing unashamedly. The few kings who are known to have had scholarly or religious leanings are naturally candidates for the role of royal patron, but the benefactor could as easily be someone little-known. I have no new evidence to offer on this question; I confine myself to some observations about the relative value of current opinions.

Whitelock's properly cautious survey of the possibilities in the last chapter of her book[1] is a useful reminder that it is the unsatisfactory state of modern knowledge of the English kingdoms during the relevant period which has led to the favouring of the one most is known about, the Northumbria of the age of Bede. I quote an important piece of her argument:

For a lay company to be so steeped in Christian doctrines, a considerable time must have elapsed since the acceptance of Christianity. This is still more certain if the terminology of Christian vernacular poetry has become so familiar that it can be used in a generalized and weakened sense; for, if we are to believe Bede, it was not until late in the seventh century that the native poetic technique was first applied to religious subjects.[2]

Her two points, that the poem is steeped in Christian doctrines and that Christian terminology is used in a weakened sense within it, are significant and well substantiated in the course of the book. The argument, however, involves two uncertain elements, the nature of the 'lay company' for whom the poem was composed, and the supposition drawn from Bede's story of Cædmon. The first of these has already been mentioned,[3] and one may suggest that the intimates of a religiously-minded king might understand and appreciate the doctrines in the poem at a time when great tracts of the kingdom were largely untouched by the gospel. I suppose that by the time a generation

---

[1] Whitelock, *Audience*, pp. 99–105.   [2] ibid., p. 21.
[3] See above, pp. 12 and 15f.

of men had passed through the first English schools the church was sufficiently well-established in the foremost religious centres for the dissemination of ecclesiastical words to begin. The supposition that English Christian poetry began with Cædmon has behind it the authority of Professor Wrenn, yet he himself admits the doubtfulness of this generally accepted dogma when he writes 'It is tantalizing indeed that St Aldhelm may well have been a slightly earlier Anglo-Saxon poet than Cædmon, and yet that we possess not even one line of his native verse'. He speaks of the literary aims of Aldhelm as being

to combine ecclesiastical with literary culture, to make the Anglo-Saxon Church employ fully the literary arts which were necessary to the proper handling of the Bible; and to direct the nascent literary art into ecclesiastically desirable channels. This is true of his work for Latin. No doubt the same principles guided his vernacular poetry, of which we can now only catch memories.[1]

Bede does not appear to have known any of Aldhelm's vernacular poetry,[2] which gives us little confidence that he could make an authoritative generalization about the beginnings of Christian poetry in English. His religious purpose in describing the consequences of Cædmon's miraculous vision would lead him to stress its effect on other poets, and also to say that his imitators did not come up to his standard because his gift was from God. A great deal has been read into the phrase *post illum*;[3] it does not appear to me to exclude the possibility of Christian poetry earlier than Cædmon in other areas of England. Further modifying Whitelock's conclusion is the possibility that the Christian words and phrases which were familiar to the audience had been made known through preaching in the vernacular, before becoming part of the poetic stock. I am by no means arguing that *Beowulf* is a much earlier poem than recent editors have assumed, but I think there is no conclusive reason to accept as Wrenn does a *terminus a quo* of about A.D. 730.[4] In

---

[1] Wrenn, *OE Literature*, p. 61.

[2] Bede's account of Aldhelm's writings is in *HE* v, 18; Plummer I, 320.

[3] Bede, *HE* IV, 24; Plummer I, 259, 4–6: 'Et quidem et alii post illum in gente Anglorum religiosa poemata facere temtabant, sed nullus eum æquiparare potuit.' 'Others among the English after him endeavoured indeed to compose religious poems, but none could equal him.'

[4] Wrenn, *Beowulf*, p. 34.

considering material which might have a bearing upon the poem I have pushed the gate somewhat wider to include Aldhelm's lifetime, looking back to the latter half of the seventh century.

The search for a *terminus ad quem* for the date of composition is similarly hampered by lack of precise evidence. Two sorts of indication may give us a working hypothesis: one is the nature of the subject matter, the other is the quality of the metre. The opening lines of *Beowulf* give promise of a poem in praise of the Danes (though in fact their part proves less heroic than expected) and, as Whitelock reasonably pointed out,[1] a theme like this could hardly appeal to an English audience of the latter half of the ninth century when the Danes had become the national enemy. The high technical quality of the verse and the use of half-lines which require archaic disyllabic forms to make them metrically regular together suggest an early date of composition, but no precise boundaries can be set round the 'early' period. Professor Girvan points to instances of the archaic forms in *Guthlac* A, a poem which is usually dated *c.* 730,[2] and Whitelock adds instances in glosses and charters to support the belief that intervocalic-*h* was still preserved at the turn of the century. It could no doubt persist as a poetic archaism for a generation or two after this, perhaps even longer in view of the conservative nature of the verse technique. Sisam doubts the value of such forms for dating whole poems, since 'Archaic forms may be used as proper to the kind of poetry, or for metrical convenience, or in old-established formulas, or in verses remembered from an earlier poem on the same subject'.[3] The most we can say is that the presence of a large proportion of such forms would invite a presupposition that the poem was composed before the middle of the eighth century. All linguistic tests are hampered by the lack of Old English manuscripts contemporary with the works themselves and the very small

[1] Whitelock, *Audience*, pp. 24–5, cp. also Wrenn, *Beowulf*, p. 41.

[2] R. Girvan, *Beowulf and the Seventh Century* (London, 1935), pp. 16–18, cited by Whitelock, *Audience*, p. 27, among evidence of her own. The absence of Guthlac's name from Bede's *HE* (731) suggests that no *Vita Guthlaci* was available to him. See further on the dating of the poem B. Colgrave, *Felix's Life of St. Guthlac*, pp. 18–20.

[3] Sisam, *Structure*, p. 68, n. 2. I share his scepticism about the value of the isolated form *wundini* (1382) as evidence of date.

number of datable pieces, and it is difficult to see how more precision could be reached in this direction.

Wrenn also uses the evidence of literary history to indicate an end date for the possible composition of *Beowulf*. He states that 'we can be sure that *Beowulf* was well known to Cynewulf and his group'.[1] He shares Schaar's opinion on this point, but more recent scholarly statements are inclined to question or disagree with Schaar's findings. For example, Miss Rosemary Woolf says that

In the poetry of Cynewulf there occur many phrases or half-lines which recall *Beowulf*, but they are unobtrusive, and would perhaps be quite unnoticeable if a larger body of poetry survived. They are obviously used as part of a common poetic stock rather than with direct reference to a precise and previous usage.[2]

I concur with her opinion; the evidence of 'literary history' proves deceptive.[3]

All in all, linguistic and stylistic evidence prove to be very uncertain guides to the date of *Beowulf* and any *terminus ad quem* must be arbitrary: one might suggest A.D. 793, the year of the portents, when the dragons in the sky foreboded the heathen sack of the church at Lindisfarne,[4] the beginning of the era of pillage and destruction which in two generations had brought English cultural life virtually to an end. The Danish attack upon Lindisfarne occurred in the reign of Offa (757–96), whose ancestor and namesake is celebrated in the poem. This *terminus* gives us a broad band of roughly one hundred and fifty years within which *Beowulf* was almost certainly composed.

The nature of the Christian culture possessed by the poet is to be investigated. Once it is granted that he was writing about an earlier, pagan age, no *negative* inferences on this matter can be drawn from the poem. The positive inference I have drawn from his literacy is that he had probably passed through a

---

[1] Wrenn, *Beowulf*, p. 35. He adheres to this view in *OE Literature*, p. 122.

[2] R. Woolf, 'Saints Lives', in *Continuations*, p. 51. Cp. S. B. Greenfield, *Hist. of OE Literature* (London, 1966), p. 144. For Schaar's views see page 9, n. 1 above, and Schaar, *Critical Studies in the Cynewulf Group*, Lund Studies in English, 17 (1949).

[3] These resemblances could as easily be held to indicate the contemporaneity of *Beowulf* and the Cynewulfian poems, if no other factor were taken into account.

[4] *Anglo-Saxon Chronicle*, *Anno* 793; ed. C. Plummer (Oxford, 1892), i, 56.

religious school,[1] though the standard of scholarship he had reached is not ascertainable. This I take to be the chief reason why students of *Beowulf* of an older generation, such as Klaeber, who revealed the Christian elements in the poet's diction, did not pursue the implications of their researches, except in the most general terms. In a period so remote and poorly documented, the study of an author who cannot be placed within a hundred years has obvious scope for an unconscionable deal of error; but the period we are concerned with has a characteristic and narrow range of intellectual activity which makes such a study less unreasonable. Throughout that century and a half, a handful of authoritative books and certain well-known parts of the Scriptures with their glosses provided the staple of Christian education. We can in consequence infer that the fundamental tenets of doctrine, the most often-quoted texts and the most familiar symbolism of those staple works would ring in the head of any thinking Christian man. Many of these things would be constantly brought to his mind in the cycle of the Church's worship; the monk would repeat them in his daily religious exercises, the layman would hear them in sermons and saints' lives and catechism, and would be reminded of them in pictures and sculptures and poetry. Two factors make for a substantial uniformity of outlook throughout the period: the reverence for authority and the passion for orthodoxy.

Linguistic evidence proves as disappointing a signpost to the poet's locality as to his date. The predominantly Late West Saxon language of the sole manuscript includes an admixture of supposedly earlier and dialectal forms. These variants may be vestiges of earlier copies in a succession of manuscripts, but they do not provide enough data to enable scholars to trace the textual history in its earlier stages[2] or to determine the original dialect. Wrenn states: 'Indeed, we can scarcely ever be sure which forms go back to an Anglian original and which are

[1] Instruction in reading and writing was rarely given to boys not destined for the religious life, and would in any case have to be conducted by religious teachers, as there were no others. For more information about schools and teaching, see Chapter 2, below.

[2] See Sisam, *Structure*, p. 69, and his *Studies*, p. 94. He shows reason to think that an LWS exemplar was used by the scribes of *Beowulf* who copied the extant MS, but he is not prepared to speculate about earlier predecessors.

merely local scribal practice or due to the fact that Classical Anglo-Saxon as a *koiné* had some West-Midland admixture added to its Late West Saxon basis.'[1] His ascription of the poem to the Anglian area of England, shared by most scholars, is based principally on general considerations drawn from cultural history. For the purposes of this study, I can only echo the words of Whitelock: 'It may be as well, therefore, to leave the question of original provenance just as open as that of exact date, even though this will put us to the trouble of looking for evidence of conditions in all the kingdoms of the Heptarchy.'[2]

---

[1] Wrenn, *Beowulf*, p. 17. His deduction *from linguistic evidence* that the original dialect was Anglian depends ultimately on two forms only: (1) *hylaces* 1530 and (2) *wundini* 1382. In neither instance is the evidence watertight.

[2] Whitelock, *Audience*, p. 33.

2 Doctrine and Symbolism in the Teaching and Practice of the Christian Faith, A.D. 650–800

For many years there has been a school of *Beowulf* criticism,[1] now chiefly represented by Dr Kenneth Sisam,[2] which regards the Christian thought and expression in the poem as 'vague' and 'elementary'. Another school, more theologically-minded, attributes this vagueness to the influence of a Celtic type of Christianity less governed by dogma than the Roman.[3] Since I believe that *Beowulf* reflects the common beliefs of the England of its time, I devote this chapter to an examination of some historical and literary evidence selected to show the general nature of the Christian teaching promulgated from the beginning of our period by both streams of missionary activity and perpetuated in the religious schools.

It is first to be noted that the words 'elementary' and 'Christian' are sometimes used ambiguously in discussion; the former as applying both to an early stage in the individual's religious training and also to a supposed stage in the conversion of a region marked by the dissemination of a few unglossed pieces of biblical history; the latter as descriptive of a theoretical religious belief valid at all times, and also as descriptive of the beliefs propagated among the Anglo-Saxons. I shall endeavour to distinguish the two relevant applications of the word 'elementary', and I shall entirely restrict my use of the words 'Christian' and 'Christianity' to the second, the purely historical, application.

Our information about teaching methods is almost entirely derived from non-Celtic sources. It is therefore necessary for

---

[1] For an influential statement of this view, see H. M. Chadwick, *The Heroic Age* (Cambridge, 1912), especially pp. 47–56.

[2] Sisam, *Structure*, pp. 72–9.

[3] See especially C. Donahue, *Traditio*, 1965, pp. 55–116.

my purpose to try to establish, before these sources are discussed, that the religious outlook of the teachers trained in Irish centres was substantially the same as that of teachers trained after the continental fashion. For convenience, I shall use the word 'Celtic' to designate the religious centres, writers and compositions which take their origin from missions sent from Ireland or Iona or its daughter houses, and the word 'Gregorian' to designate the centres etc. arising from the continental missions initiated by Gregory I. (The word 'Roman' has too wide an application, and might be judged appropriate for the 'Celtic' branch as well as the continental church.) It may sometimes be convenient also to employ the word 'insular' as used by Dr Charles Donahue[1] to cover the English and Irish churches in their common features in contradistinction from the continental church.

As one studies the historical progress of the conversion of the English, one must be impressed by the interpenetration of the two missionary movements and by the remarkable extent to which both relied upon a common heritage of Latin works for the perpetuation of their religious beliefs. The divergences between the two branches of the Church were largely of temperament, not of doctrine, and their disagreements were mostly about organization. My own reading bears out Kenney's description of the shared thought-world of the churchmen of Ireland, England and the main continent of Europe during our period:

Fundamentally, the Church in Ireland was one with the Church in the remainder of Western Europe. The mental processes and the *Weltanschauung* of the ecclesiastic who looked out from Armagh or Clonmacnois or Innisfallen were not essentially different from those of him whose centre of vision was Canterbury or Reims or Cologne.[2]

The primary source of information on ecclesiastical matters during and following the Conversion is of course the Englishman Bede, who received his education entirely in a Gregorian monastery. By the time he wrote, the Celtic and Gregorian

[1] ibid., pp. 63–4.
[2] Kenney, *Sources*, p. 156.

23

parties in England had composed their differences, and it would be alien to Bede's purposes as a Christian historian to revive or to magnify any earlier sources of disagreement. However, his account of the dealings of the two churches is remarkably fair-minded, and his praise of Celtic saints is clear proof that the Celtic way of life of the previous century was not held in disparagement at Jarrow. On the other hand, his promotion of unity would not have extended to the glossing over of heretical tendencies in any group and he speaks plainly and strongly against 'the poison of the Pelagian heresy'.[1] The absence from his pages of other doctrinal controversy seems to indicate that there was nothing of the kind to record.

Indeed, the substantial harmony which was achieved at the Synod of Whitby could not have come into being if the Celtic interpretation of the gospel message had differed in any important particular from that of the continental church. And, as Godfrey points out, 'At the conference at Whitby in 663, no complaint was made by the Roman party that the Scottish Church was unsound in belief'.[2] The best evidence of unity of outlook, since the reporting of conferences may be coloured by the attitude of the witness, is perhaps not the Synod itself, but the testimony of the lives of churchmen who lived through that time of integration, men such as Cuthbert and Aldhelm who received their religious formation under Celtic teachers and afterwards worked closely with others trained in the Gregorian manner. Cuthbert's education was under Eata, a pupil of Aidan and supporter of Colman, yet twenty years after the Synod of Whitby[3] both master and pupil held northern bishoprics with the approval of Archbishop Theodore, whose training was in the Orthodox church of the East, and whose appointment was made in Rome itself.[4] Aldhelm deserves particular attention, as a man trained by an Irish scholar (Mailduib, founder of the

---

[1] The unfounded accusation of heresy brought against Bede himself in regard to the *De Temporibus* must have made him more than usually sensitive to the need for orthodoxy. See Godfrey, *AS Church*, p. 465. On the Pelagian heresy, see Bede, *HE* II, 19; Plummer I, 123. The quoted phrase is reported by Bede in a papal letter which in another respect he censors (see Kenney, *Sources*, p. 222). On Pelagianism see p. 28 f. below, and Chapter 5.

[2] Godfrey, *AS Church*, p. 56.   [3] ibid., p. 123.
[4] ibid., p. 128.

minster at Malmesbury), who afterwards continued his education at the school founded by the Gregorian mission and enlarged by Theodore and Hadrian at Canterbury. Aldhelm's own journeying extended as far as Rome, and though he spent the latter part of his life in the South-western region of England which became his diocese in 705, his influence as a correspondent extended to Northumbria, Essex and Wales; his fame as a scholar brought him letters from Irish admirers at home and abroad as well as English scholars.

Aldhelm's letters afford striking evidence of very extensive scholarly interchange between England and Ireland in the second half of the seventh century. His letter to the English student Eahfrith who had just returned from study in Ireland is open to more than a suspicion of sarcastic exaggeration when he describes the seaway as thick with boatloads of scholars going in both directions, like so many bees bringing honey to make the honeycomb;[1] nevertheless, if movement of scholars between the two countries was happening on anything like the scale Aldhelm describes, it would evidently be idle to regard Celtic influence in Anglo-Saxon literature (if such could be discerned) as an indication that compositions so influenced originated in a region converted by Celtic missionaries. The effects of this interchange on both nations are incalculable. It was by no means a one-way traffic, as the same letter testifies, in a memorable description of the crowds of Irish students at Canterbury. The tone of Aldhelm's letter is more than usually difficult to catch, because he has chosen to write in a parody of his own Hisperic style. Laistner conveniently summarizes Ehwald's opinion of the point of the letter as expressed in the notes to his edition; the rare words and turgid diction

are meant to demonstrate to the recipient that all the conceits and stylistic mannerisms of Irish scholarship can be acquired in England, and that there is no need to cross the sea to learn them. The letter should not, therefore, be interpreted as a depreciation of Irish scholars; for although Aldhelm reserves his highest praise for Theodore and Hadrian, he assuredly had not acquired his own high-

[1] *MGH AA*, xv, 490, 11–12. Cited by Godfrey, *AS Church*, p. 205, also by Laistner, *Thought*, p. 154, and by M. Deanesly, *The Pre-Conquest Church in England*, p. 133. See also for evidence of the scholarly traffic, Bede, *HE* iii, 27; Plummer, i, 192.

flown style from them. The letter is designed to show that the English
pupils have outgrown their pupilage and can rival their Irish
masters in their own speciality.[1]

Though Ehwald and Laistner are undoubtedly right in this
explanation of the purpose of the letter and its curious style,
there remains some uncertainty about Aldhelm's opinion of
Irish students. The crowd of Irishmen who baited Theodore at
Canterbury are described in no complimentary terms: *turma
supercilii tyfo turgens* 'a crowd swollen with the wind of arrogance',[2] for example, suggests that Aldhelm neither liked their
manners nor respected their scholarship, and this is borne out by
his comment that Theodore put them to rout with points of
grammar and chronography. There is a hint here of a difference
of emphasis in learning which is borne out by other scraps of evidence; I will adduce these later in discussing the methods used by
Christian teachers. Thus, in the period of the first recorded
English poetry, the evidence of Aldhelm's letters bears out that
of his life, which witnesses to much scholarly intercourse through
travel and correspondence between Celtic and Gregorian
centres of learning, and Irish influence far more widespread
than the existence of some Celtic foundations in Northumbria
and the isolated 'Celtic' communities at Malmesbury, Bosham
in Sussex, and *Cnobheresburg* in East Anglia (founded by Irish
monks) would seem to indicate.

The British churchmen of Wales, on the other hand, appear
to have remained aloof and hostile to the English even after the
Conversion. Another well-known letter written by Aldhelm was
addressed to King Geraint of Wales, upbraiding him and his
people for their adherence to the Celtic Easter and the unorthodox tonsure. It paints a picture of uncompromising hostility
on the part of the British priests, who so abhor the church of
their English neighbours across the Severn, *ut nec in ecclesia
nobiscum orationum officia celebrare nec ad mensam ciborum fercula pro
caritatis gratia pariter percipere dignentur* 'that they disdain to
celebrate the office of prayer in church with us or to break
bread at table together for charity's sake'.[3] Across this barrier

---

[1] Laistner, *Thought*, p. 154.
[2] *MGH AA*, xv, 493, 9. (Deanesly in her brief summary of the passage, op. cit.,
p. 133, omits this phrase.) [3] ibid., 484, 9–10.

of national and religious pride it seems unlikely that scholarly interchange was possible. Godfrey says:

So far as the Christianisation of the English ... was concerned, the Church of Wales (and of Cornwall) represented what is virtually a dead-end. To this extent, after the heroisms of the sixth century have been considered, this Church passes out of the main stream of the history of religion and culture in England.[1]

As I have found nothing to connect *Beowulf* with the Welsh church, I leave the matter there.

I come now to Donahue's contention that in the North of England in the late seventh and the eighth century there existed a 'mode' of Christianity shared by the Irish and 'distinct from that of the Western Iron Age';[2] he gives to this mode the name 'insular'. This insular type of Christianity was, he maintains, monastic, rural, and theologically unsophisticated. The nub of his argument is that the heathen hero Beowulf is accommodated in a religious poem in a fashion unthinkable in the Augustinian tradition, but quite natural in the freer theological atmosphere of Irish Christianity as spread from Iona, in which, as he thinks, the good men of the ancestral stories were placed by poets in the *tempus legis naturæ* 'the time of the Law of nature' which preceded 'the Law of the letter', 'the Law of the prophets', and 'the Law of Christ' in Irish tradition.[3] The whole question of natural law is discussed in relation to the religion of the characters in *Beowulf* below, in Chapter 5. Here I confine attention to the evidence offered by Donahue of doctrinal differences between the insular and the continental churches.

It must first be noted that Donahue's material is drawn from three different centuries. His two pieces of evidence for the supposed doctrinal laxness of the insular church are: first, Wilfrid's reference to the *simplicitas rustica* of the Celtic party in his speech to the Synod at Whitby; and second, the appearance and survival of Pelagianism in Ireland. The first point carries little weight; Wilfrid did not, according to Bede, use this patronizing phrase of Colman and his adherents, with whom he was disputing the Easter question, but of Columba and his disciples

---

[1] Godfrey, *AS Church*, pp. 43–4.   [2] Donahue, *Traditio*, 1965, p. 63.
[3] ibid., p. 74.

in the previous century, whose holiness had been offered by Colman as a witness for the Celtic cause. Wilfrid countered this by intimating that miracle-working was no sure proof of sanctity, and then, with a show of fairness, was prepared to accept that Columba and his monks were true servants of God, suggesting however that 'they loved him in primitive simplicity'.[1] He may have intended to imply that Colman shared this quality, but the debating point is hardly evidence of a general characteristic persisting into the eighth century.

The Pelagian question is more important. The emergence of Pelagius himself—if we may trust Jerome, he was an Irishman[2] —testifies, I should have thought, to some vigorous theological thinking in the early Irish church.[3] Donahue takes the continued copying of his heretical commentary on St Paul in Ireland as a sign that Irish scholars were 'unaware of doctrinal issues'.[4] This inference might be acceptable if Pelagius had been copied in Irish monasteries exclusively, but according to Kenney this is far from being the case: he says, 'Later investigations do not support the contention ... that the Irish Pelagian matter was a legacy handed down within the shores of the Western isle from the days of the heresiarch, or that the unadulterated texts were exclusively Irish, the contaminated continental.'[5]

The resurgence of Pelagianism in Ireland in the middle of the seventh century might be pertinent to the study of *Beowulf*.[6] Laistner suggests that Bede's warnings against Pelagianism 'are so numerous and fierce that one must suppose that Pelagianism

[1] Bede, *HE* III, 25; Plummer, I, 187.

[2] Jerome says that he had *progeniem Scoticae gentis*, in his *Commentary on Jeremias* quoted by Kenney, *Sources*, pp. 161–2. Other sources describe Pelagius as a Briton.

[3] Pelagius wrote his heretical commentary before 410 A.D. in Rome. Pelagianism in Britain occasioned the visits of Germanus of Auxerre in 429 and c. 447, which prompts Donahue to comment that 'British Christianity in the fifth century was still sufficiently unsophisticated to be involved in the Pelagian controversy'. But since this was a period of collapse in the British church, it is difficult to see what relevance this business could have to the freshly-rooted Saxon church of two centuries later (cp. Deanesly, *Pre-Conquest Church*, p. 24).

[4] Donahue, *Traditio*, 1965, p. 66.   [5] Kenney, *Sources*, p. 662.

[6] C. C. Batchelor, 'The Style of the *Béowulf*: a Study of the Composition of the Poem', *Speculum* 12 (1937), pp. 330–42. Batchelor seems to be the progenitor of Donahue's attitude: he refers to 'the practical, easy-going Celtic Christianity' (p. 332) and says of the poet, 'His religion might be patterned ... after Pelagius rather than after Augustine' (p. 333). The question is further discussed in Chapter 5 below in its relation to the religious beliefs of the characters in *Beowulf*.

was a living question to him, either because there had been a recrudescence of it in Britain in Bede's own time or because it had never been completely eradicated there'.[1] Laistner's great knowledge of Bede's work adds weight to this conjecture and I would not wish to dissent from what he says. But Pelagianism can certainly not have been an issue between the Celtic and Gregorian parties at Whitby, or Bede would have recorded the matter; and if it threatened the peace of the Church in Bede's day, it must have been a very slight movement since it aroused no official notice. Quite possibly Pelagian thinking lingered in remote areas in both England and Ireland, but it would surely have attracted attention if publicly promulgated at a king's court such as Donahue supposes to have been the milieu of *Beowulf*. He goes so far as to suggest that the theologically unsophisticated mode of Christianity he describes influenced the court of Aldfrith the Learned, king of Northumbria (685–705), whom he regards as a likely royal patron for the *Beowulf* poet. Aldfrith had indeed studied in his youth under Irish teachers. But if he learned unorthodox Celtic practices during his exile, he must have rejected them in his maturity, because it was in his kingdom in 688 or 689 that Adamnan, abbot of Iona, 'observed the rites of the Church canonically performed'[2] and was persuaded by argument to change his own customs to the English use. In such an atmosphere of ecclesiastical debate, it cannot be supposed that doctrinal questions were lightly regarded.

It seems to me clear that Donahue's attempt to harmonize the strange theology he finds in *Beowulf* with actual conditions at a king's court about 700 is misconceived. The 'rustic simplicity' of sixth-century Celtic religious life bears little relation to the conditions in centres of learning after the Synod of Whitby, though the phrase could perhaps apply in some remote areas. I conclude that any theory of an integrally Christian *Beowulf* poem must come to terms with its doctrine in relation to orthodox belief, and this I attempt to do in Chapter 5.

To revert, then, to the nature of the Christian education available to the *Beowulf* poet: it could have been English or Irish, and might have been acquired at a famous school or from

---

[1] Laistner, *Thought*, p. 160.   [2] Bede, *HE* v, 15; Plummer I, 315.

an isolated teacher. I begin by looking at what is known about
the books used in English and Irish centres of learning, in the
confidence that travelling teachers received their training on
the lines laid down in the schools, though they might themselves have small access to books. Our information concerns
monastic libraries and the works of scholars who studied in
them, but since in this early period the pastoral care of the
people chiefly depended on the minsters,[1] it is inherently improbable that the topics of sermons or catechetical instruction
to the laity were different from those delivered to intending
monks. No sermons in the vernacular survive from this period,
but the tenth-century and later collections show close dependence upon the homiletic writings of the Fathers, and this lack
of originality must have obtained from the first, because of the
paramount need to preserve the catholic faith.

Learning flourished in Ireland long before there were any
schools in England, but as no Irish monastic library catalogues
have survived, the scope of studies there must be inferred from
indirect and fragmentary evidence, some of it a century earlier
than the beginning of the period under discussion; we have,
however, the letter of Aldhelm to Eahfrith, already quoted
above, as evidence that the Irish schools still prospered in his
day, and in the same letter a useful list of subjects studied there,
which will be examined below. What Kenney has to say of the
Irish monastic schools in general could equally well be applied
to the English Celtic foundations:

The chief subject of study in the monastic schools of early Christian
Ireland was the Bible. With the exception of such instruction as was
of practical necessity for carrying on the services of the Church, all
other studies, including that of the Fathers of the Church, were an-
cillary to the reading, comprehension, and exposition of the Scriptures. The predominance thereof is witnessed to by the whole literary
remains of the early Irish Church. The monastic traditions as set
down by a later age in almost innumerable Lives of Saints tell the
same story: the important element in an ecclesiastic's education was
the reading of the Scriptures and—it may be remarked—in especial
the reading of the Psalms.[2]

---

[1] Deanesly, *Pre-Conquest Church*, Chapter 9, passim, pp. 191–210.
[2] Kenney, *Sources*, p. 624.

Kenney also remarks on the dependence of Irish writers on older authorities:

It might seem that a sharp division should be made between the personal compositions of the Irish teachers and the copies which they used of patristic and other foreign writings. But actually the works of Irish origin are so largely extracted from or based on the others that the line of division is not very clear.[1]

And what applies to biblical commentary is also true of hagiography, a consideration of some importance to the student of OE poetry, in which saints' Lives have a significant part. Kenney says of the Irish writers:

Also the literary tradition weighed heavily on the hagiographer. The Bible, especially the Pentateuch and the Gospels; John Cassian's Institutes, describing the life of the monks of Egypt; the Latin Life of St. Anthony; the Life of St. Martin by Sulpicius Severus; some of the writings of Jerome and of Gregory the Great—these seem to have been authorities which the monastic writer felt obliged to use for both phraseology and subject-matter. It may well be that many other continental *vitæ sanctorum* were known in the Irish monasteries. Indeed, contemporary Irish and continental *acta* are compositions of the same class, with much less distinction between them than is at times alleged.[2]

The same close dependence on foreign authorities is observable in Anglo-Saxon religious compositions. It is most instructive to compare this list of the Irish hagiographers' sources with the list of books used by Felix, the Anglian biographer of St Guthlac who wrote *c.* 730–40, as compiled by Colgrave in his edition of the Life. His list begins with the Bible—especially the Psalter—and follows with Bede, Aldhelm, Sulpicius Severus on St Martin, Jerome on St Paul, the Latin version of Athanasius on St Anthony, Gregory the Great on St Benedict. It will be observed that Cassian's is the only name on Kenney's list not also to be found on Colgrave's. It is not known where Felix went to school, but quite obviously the religious books he studied there were to a large extent the same as those an Irish religious writer could be expected to study a century or more earlier in an Irish monastery. The religious houses in

[1] ibid., pp. 659–60.   [2] ibid., p. 297.

Northern England which were founded by monks from Iona presumably kept the same emphasis in their educational work. Very little is known about the extent of the scholarship of Columba, the founder of the community on Iona; the one work attributed to him by modern scholars, the hymn *Altus Prosator*, gives some valuable pointers to the nature of the teaching disseminated by the Ionan missionaries in England, and it will be examined rather fully below.[1] One might perhaps deduce that Columba and his younger contemporary Columban could have received a good classical grounding in their Irish schools from the evidence of Columban's wide reading in pagan and Christian poets, but the picture is confused by the fact that Columban spent many years on the continent where other libraries were open to him.[2]

One other general observation about these early Irish schools is of interest. Laistner says:

The preoccupation of Irish scholars with Biblical exegesis ... has very recently been placed beyond doubt and shown to have been intense and widespread. Many Biblical commentaries were composed by them during the seventh and eighth centuries, but most of them survive in only a single manuscript and most are anonymous ... Above all, many stress the literal interpretations of the Bible, a fact which to a great extent explains their ultimate disappearance, because by the ninth century the predominant trend in exegesis was to follow Gregory and Bede and to lay the chief emphasis on the allegorical and moral sense of Scripture.[3]

I have quoted this statement at length because, correcting as it does the over-simplified view that all exegesis in the period was allegorical, it also tends to over-stress the significance of this Irish work, especially since Laistner's discussion of Aldhelm's letter to Eahfrith does not mention the sentence in which Aldhelm describes the kinds of learning brought from Ireland by the swarms of returning students. They have gathered from the flowery fields of Scripture a burden of honey, he says,

non solum artes grammaticas atque geometricas bisternasque omissas fisicae machinas, quin immo allegoricae potiora ac tropologicae disputationis bipertita bis oracula aethralibus opacorum

---

[1] See pp. 42 ff.   [2] Kenney, *Sources*, pp. 190–1.   [3] Laistner, *Thought*, p. 146.

mellita in aenigmatibus problematum siticulose sumentes carpunt et in alveariis sofiae iugi meditatione letotenus servanda condentes abdunt ...[1]

not only the principles of grammar and geometry and the remaining six skills of natural philosophy, but, much more than these, the more important matter of the word of God, divided and divided again (in four planes of meaning) in allegorical and tropological disputation, honey-sweet in the celestial riddles of dark questions; thirstily they drink them in and bear them away to their hives, laying them up as a store in meditation on the height of wisdom, to be preserved until death ...

The extraordinarily inflated style of this passage suggests sarcasm to a modern reader, and in view of Aldhelm's praise of Theodore's factual knowledge in the same letter[2] one might suppose that Aldhelm thought the Irish made too much of allegorical and tropological debate in their schools. Whether this is so or not, Aldhelm certainly advocated the fourfold method of interpreting the Scriptures, and Laistner's mention of the ninth century as the period when allegorical exegesis gained the ascendancy should not be taken to mean that the great scholars of the seventh and eighth centuries did not use it in their teaching. Aldhelm's prose treatise *De virginitate* uses in its opening exhortation to the nuns for whom it was written the same image of the bee gathering honey as in the letter quoted above, and explains more fully what kinds of sweet nourishment can be got from biblical, historical, chronographical, grammatical and poetical studies, particularly emphasizing the importance of the patristic commentaries and their fourfold method of elucidation.[3]

Aldhelm thus takes for granted that allegorical exegesis will be used in extracting the core of spiritual meaning from the gospels; he also refers in the same sentence to the symbolic significance of the plagues of Egypt and the dividing of the Red

---

[1] *MGH AA*, xv, 490, 17–491, 3. I quote Ehwald's note on these lines: Bisternae omissae (= *reliquae*) fisicae artis machinae *intelligendae esse videntur* (cf. *epist. ad Acirc.* p. 71, 23) *arithmetica, musica, astronomia, astrologia, mechanica, medicina* allegoricae *autem* ac tropologicae disputationis bipertitae bis oracula *interpretor regulas declarandi scripturam sacram secundum historiam, allegoriam, tropologiam, anagogen.* cf. *prosa de virg.* c. iv, p. 232, 20.

[2] ibid., pp. 493, 8–9.   [3] ibid., pp. 232, 18–21.

Sea. My impression from the letter to Eahfrith as a whole is that Aldhelm recognized the value of the allegorical method in revealing the truths of the Scriptures, but thought allegorical debate no substitute for a knowledge of grammar! To some minds, then as now, allegory was no doubt uncongenial, and perhaps Archbishop Theodore had something in common with Laistner, who finds Gregory's *Moralia in Job* 'exceedingly far-fetched and tiresome'.[1] Deanesly, discussing some biblical commentaries believed to be the work of Archbishop Theodore, says: 'Gregory the Great had followed the Alexandrian school of interpretation and it was to be widely followed by the Carolingian teachers; Theodore and Bede show more critical, historical interest in the text.'[2] I have come across a delightful reminiscence of Theodore's teaching methods in an anonymous writer of scriptural *Quæstiones*, who says apropos St Paul's *Nocte et die in profundo maris fui* 'A night and a day I was in the depth of the sea' (2 Cor. 11: 25) that Archbishop Theodore 'of blessed memory' did not accept that St Paul had stayed alive under the sea, but thought the Apostle might have referred to a very deep pit, as deep as the sea.[3] Theodore's attempt to find a rational explanation accords strikingly well with Deanesly's account of his exegetical methods and perhaps partially explains his brushes with the Irish students at Canterbury. This commonsense attitude ran counter to the spirit of the age; the writer of the *Quæstiones* prefers to think of St Paul's immersion as a miracle from which one can draw a mystical lesson.[4] I have included this small digression on St Paul in the sea with a double purpose: Beowulf also spent part of a day under the water (1495–6), a feat which may have seemed less fantastic than miraculous to people like this unknown cleric, and apt to demonstrate the Creator's power to sustain those who trust in him.

My general point is that though literal and rational exegesis

<hr />

[1] Laistner, *Thought*, p. 105.   [2] Deanesly, *Pre-Conquest Church*, p. 125.

[3] The *Quæstiones* are printed by Migne among the works formerly attributed to Bede, *PL* 93, 456–7, *Quæstio* III.

[4] ibid., 157: *significat justos de cunctis periculis eruendos a Domino* 'it signifies that the righteous are to be rescued from all perils by the Lord'. The writer compares Peter's walking on the water and concludes by allegorizing: *nec omnino posse sæculi fluctibus immergi, qui præsens semper auctoris sui complectuntur auxilium* 'none of those who grasp the ever-present help of their Creator can be drowned in the waves of this world'.

might sometimes be found in this period, allegoresis provided a valuable means of extracting spiritual and moral nourishment from unpromising texts which few teachers were willing to forgo. Though Deanesly couples Bede with Theodore as showing more 'critical, historical interest in the text', Bede's own homilies, as we shall see below, make full use of moral and allegorical explanations of the scriptural texts.

I return now from this short *excursus* upon literal and allegorical exposition of texts to the point at which Laistner's somewhat one-sided remarks caused me to digress, the preoccupation of Irish scholars with biblical exegesis. I have one more quotation from Kenney upon this subject and an observation to add to it: 'With the probable exceptions of the Gospels and the Pauline Epistles the Psalter was studied in the Irish monastic schools more than any other book of the Old or New Testament.'[1] This fact occasions no surprise. From the early days of the Church the Psalms had formed part of the divine office and the earliest monastic observances in the West make the Psalter a central part of the monk's daily life. The attribution of tropological and mystical meaning to these sacred poems obviously gave them a more personal and a more edifying value, which may go far to account for the general predominance of the Alexandrian tradition of interpretation.

The salient features of the Irish monastic schools which set the tradition of learning for the English Celtic houses are now seen to be: a preoccupation with scriptural exegesis, for which they chiefly used the commentaries of the great Latin Fathers, an interest in Virgil and some lesser Latin poets, and an appetite for saints' Lives, particularly those of the Egyptian hermits, St Martin, and the saints commemorated in the writings of Gregory the Great. Though all the evidence comes from the latter part of the sixth century (with the exception of Aldhelm's comments upon Irish education), there is no reason to think that substantial changes took place during the ensuing hundred years; Aldhelm in his life and writings shows the harmonious marriage of this tradition with the tradition represented at Canterbury (in spite of some hints on his part that the Irish schools had an unjustifiably high reputation).

[1] Kenney, *Sources*, p. 664.

When we turn to the Gregorian schools in England, the evidence is again largely piecemeal. Some things may be inferred from Gregory's attitude to education, since he took a personal interest in the mission to Kent and himself chose the man to lead it. Gregory was opposed to the study of profane works by men devoted to the religious life. It is likely that the school set up by Augustine at Canterbury had a curriculum limited to the needs of a churchman: grammar, computation, scriptural study based on the usual commentaries, and some music for the singing of the offices.[1] The books which Augustine's mission carried with it were likely to be the bare necessities for their task: biblical and patristic texts, perhaps a monastic rule, and (according to King Alfred)[2] a copy of Gregory's *Cura Pastoralis*. However, by the time that Aldhelm studied there, the school at Canterbury had been enlarged and stocked with books by men of broader sympathies and great learning. Deanesly's opinion is that under Hadrian the library at Canterbury

would have had the works of the great Latin theologians, especially those of Augustine and Gregory, Jerome's Latin Scriptures and the commentators on them, and a number of the 'passions' of the martyrs and possibly some saints' lives; works on the monastic life, like those of Cassian, the Rule of the Master, the Rule of St. Basil and, without straining probability, other more modern rules, including St. Benedict's. They would most certainly have the works of that great doctor, Isidore of Seville, the church history of Eusebius, and perhaps some of the works of Cassiodorus.[3]

The first part of this list is strikingly similar to Kenney's summaries of the reading of the Irish exegetes and hagiographers quoted above. (The works on monastic organization would not have been prevalent in Ireland, which had its own traditional systems.)

In the last quarter of the seventh century the libraries of Benedict Biscop's foundations at Wearmouth and Jarrow were stocked with an excellent collection of Latin religious, historical, and encyclopædic works, a few Greek religious works, some

[1] See P. F. Jones, 'The Gregorian Mission and English Education'.
[2] Alfred, *Metrical Preface to the Pastoral Care*, ASPR VI, 110, 1–5.
[3] M. Deanesly, *Augustine of Canterbury* (London, 1964), p. 100.

classical and several Christian Latin poets;[1] for at the turn of
the century, Bede who spent all his life in the region 'certainly
had access to all the learned books in use in western Europe'.[2]
The kind of schooling Bede received at Jarrow may be inferred
from his works. Laistner says of some early compositions:

They prove his thorough training in the subjects of the *trivium*, wide
reading in the grammatical treatises composed in the later Roman
Empire, and his own enviable gift of clear exposition. One other
feature is noteworthy. Whereas in Aldhelm, notwithstanding his
insistence that secular literature should only be a means to an end,
the artist and admirer of great poetry particularly of Virgil, over-
masters the ecclesiastic; in Bede the religious teacher predominates.
His poetic illustrations in the tract on metrics are taken almost entirely from Christian poets. Similarly in his second essay pagan
learning supplies the rules, the illustrative citations are all derived
from the Bible.[3]

The aim of this education is never lost from sight; its objects are
the fuller understanding of the Scriptures, the worthy performance of the divine office, and the rejection of earthly for
heavenly joys.

In the second decade of the century Hexham, under Acca,
the friend of Bede, became a centre of learning; unfortunately,
details of its rich library have not survived; in the middle of the
century York began its rise to international fame under Egbert
and later under his pupils Albert and Alcuin. Alcuin's summary
of its contents in his Verses on the Saints at York is well-known.[4]
It contains a long list of Latin and Greek Fathers, the latter, as
Laistner says, 'no doubt in Latin dress; for neither Alcuin nor
any of his contemporaries would have understood them in the
original'.[5] Laistner would add to the list Isidore of Seville, and
'a good collection of books on the liberal arts'. Virgil, Statius,

[1] There was another Gregorian school in East Anglia, set up by Felix the Bur-
gundian about 630, but nothing is known of its library.
[2] The quotation is from Deanesly, op. cit., p. 99. For the details of Bede's
reading, see Ogilvy, *Anglo-Latin Writers*, passim; also the studies by Laistner (see
bibliography).
[3] Laistner, *Thought*, pp. 157–8. In view of the *Beowulf* poet's possible knowledge
of Virgil, it may be of interest that Laistner ascribes Aldhelm's love of the pagan
poet to his training under Mailduib (ibid., p. 156).
[4] *Alcuini Carmina, MGH Poet.*, pp. 169–206. For the library catalogue, see pp.
203–4. [5] Laistner, *Thought*, p. 229.

and Lucan appear with a much longer list of Christian Latin poets. The name of Pliny bears witness to a study of natural history; Aldhelm and Bede also used his work.[1] The study of the created world was pursued for its witness to the wonderful powers of the Creator. The historians listed are men with a strong religious bias: Orosius, Cassiodorus, Gildas, Gregory of Tours, and, for the better understanding of the Old Testament, Josephus. The curriculum at the school seems to have been wider than at Bede's Jarrow, though Godfrey's phrase 'wide and liberal instruction available at the York school' overstates the situation. Alcuin, like his predecessors in English education, regarded as the purpose of his work the saving of souls.[2]

I think certain conclusions may be drawn from the information available about Christian education during the period under discussion. There is no real evidence for heterodox teaching by Celtic missionaries or in the Celtic houses. There is widespread and continued intercourse between the different branches of the Church. The aims of education do not change, and the basic books used in teaching are substantially the same throughout. A very significant fact, in its testimony to the fundamental similarity of outlook towards their Faith and the prevailing delight in moralizing allegory, is the popularity of Gregory's *Moralia in Job* in Ireland as well as in England. An abridgment of the work made in the first half of the seventh century by an Irish monk, Laid-cend, gained international repute.[3] Laistner says that all Gregory's works 'enjoyed unrivalled popularity and exerted a profound influence throughout the Middle Ages', mentioning particularly the dozen or more such chrestomathies compiled from the *Moralia* and other works.[4] From the beginning of the period, biblical commentaries by the Latin Fathers were regarded as indispensable and both Irish and English writers leaned heavily on staple foreign authors in the writing of commentaries or saints' Lives. From Aldhelm to Alcuin the most influential writers used the traditional allegorical methods of expounding the Scriptures, though a more literal type of exegesis was also in occasional use. However early in the period we are inclined to place the com-

---

[1] Ogilvy, op. cit., p. 73. [2] Godfrey, *AS Church*, p. 466.
[3] Kenney, *Sources*, pp. 278–9. [4] Laistner, *Thought*, pp. 107–8.

position of *Beowulf*, the literate author I have postulated could not have been sheltered from these pervasive influences. The view of God, man, and the world which emerges from such education, and its relation to the corpus of OE poetry, forms a large part of the substance of this study. Before I turn to the content of the doctrines which make up the Faith during those times, I must give some attention to the ways in which the monastic learning I have been speaking of was spread among the laity. I have already made reference to the pastoral work of the minsters and the evidence of the homiletic tradition.[1] I now consider what else is known about the conversion and teaching of the laity, for whom, after all, the vernacular poems were presumably written.

Several opinions on this subject in its relation to *Beowulf* have been published. Whitelock states:

The missionaries to the Anglo-Saxons were not exceptional in this respect. They preached first of the major doctrines; they spoke of the Redemption of the world by Christ's Passion; the detailed stories of the Old Testament could be left till later, special emphasis being laid on such events as were held to foreshadow those of the New. When Benedict Biscop brought back from Rome pictures to adorn the churches of Wearmouth and Jarrow, with the express intent of influencing people who could not read, among those first chosen were pictures from the gospels and the Apocalypse; on a later visit he brought back a series to illustrate the connexion of the Old and New Testament. Any set of persons that is well-informed on the Old Testament can be assumed to be cognizant of the Christian faith as a whole.[2]

As this statement has failed to convince Sisam,[3] it perhaps needs amplifying and substantiating. The decoration of the churches at Wearmouth and Jarrow is of great interest and will go some way to indicate what were regarded as the essentials of the Faith and the symbolic means employed in their propagation. The decorative programme round the walls of St Peter's, which Whitelock mentions first, told of the Incarnation and depicted episodes from the life of Christ, with portraits of the apostles, and concluded with pictures of the end of the

---

[1] See above, p. 30. [2] Whitelock, *Audience*, pp. 6–7.
[3] Sisam, *Structure*, pp. 75–6.

39

world.[1] This sequence clearly speaks of Redemption and Judgment, and assumes in the spectators some knowledge of the Fall of man. (One would be interested to know whether the apocalyptic scenes included the Ancient Dragon.) The pictures which decorated St Paul's at Jarrow were chosen for their symbolic relationship, and certainly required an appropriate typological homily to explain them to the spectators. Bede gives as an example two pairs of pictures which illustrate the saving power of the Crucifixion: Isaac carrying the wood for sacrifice, next to the Lord carrying his cross; Moses raising the brazen serpent, beside the Son of Man raised on the cross.[2] These pictures indicate one important way in which the symbolic meaning found by the exegetical commentators in the Scriptures was made familiar to the unlettered Christian. The typological relationship of these two pairs of pictures is of course in the Bible itself and not derived completely from allegorical commentaries, but the significance of the biblical verses is not apparent without some explanation such as the exegetes give; it is also evident that Benedict Biscop would not have chosen these pictures if the prophetic symbolism of the Old Testament events had not been regarded as a fundamentally important element of the Faith.

The great stone crosses of this period are another means through which laymen could contemplate important religious truths. On the Ruthwell Cross, for example, the figure of Christ treading upon the beasts seems to ask for an exposition of the prophetic meaning and beast-symbolism of Psalm 90:13; the scene of St Paul and St Antony breaking bread not only implies knowledge of Jerome's *Vita S. Pauli* but provides material for sermons on God as the provider of man's needs and on the Bread of Life.

The lines of vernacular poetry carved on this cross are a reminder that from a very early date English poetry brought religious doctrine to those who could not read. Sisam points to the sequence of Cædmon's poems as an indication that Christian teachers may have begun their instruction by speaking of the creation of the world, and then working through the Old and New Testaments.[3] As evidence for a theory of 'partial conver-

---

[1] Bede, *Historia Abbatum*, Plummer, 1, 369. The two churches were built in 674 and 681.   [2] ibid., p. 373.   [3] Sisam, *Structure*, p. 76.

sion' of the *Beowulf* poet and his audience, Cædmon's canon proves nothing, since Bede would naturally place the subjects in their chronological order in his list; but the list is interesting in itself, as offering a fairly complete education in the doctrines of man's creation, fall, redemption, and coming judgment. It is a reasonable inference that the men who taught Cædmon wished to have memorable English versions of these doctrines for use in teaching the laity, and therefore that they chose these subjects as the fundamentals of their instruction.[1]

It is to be noted that the Last Judgment appears both in the church pictures described above and in the list of Cædmon's poems. The need to bear the saving seal of God in that terrifying day[2] would have been part of the Anglo-Saxon missionaries' teaching from the first. Bishop Daniel, quoted by Sisam as a witness for a particular kind of missionary approach, writes very strongly of *sordes et reatus gentilitatis* 'the vileness and guilt of heathenism'[3] from which the missionary hoped to rescue those he taught. It is inconceivable that in such a climate of thought the distinction between heathen and Christian was disregarded by anyone who knew anything at all about the Faith. It is equally inconceivable that men were taught about the Judgment without being offered baptism and without being given the doctrine of the Cross which is the source of the sacrament. One must therefore explain the absence from *Beowulf* of certain kinds of dogma by other hypotheses than that the Christianity of the poet and his audience was 'elementary', either in the sense that they were only partially converted, or in the sense that the Christianity current at the time disregarded the matters of redemption and the sacraments.

Professor Whallon's conjecture that the *Beowulf* poet 'may have been acquainted with stories from the opening chapters of Genesis but ignorant of the opening chapters of Luke' has been shown to be highly improbable. He argues that 'The age in which the men of the epic lived was to the poet neither censurable nor hopeless, nor even heathen; it was his own age, and

---

[1] For more positive evidence of this, see pp. 55 ff., below.   [2] See Apoc. 9: 4.

[3] *MGH Ep. Mer.* 1, 273. This is in the letter from which Sisam quotes, op. cit. p. 76. His inference about teaching methods is dubious since Daniel's letter is not concerned with the introduction of the Faith, but with arguments to be used with the obdurate heathen.

Beowulf and Hrothgar were to him Christians of his own kind.'[1] There are two objections to this statement: one is the unlikelihood that an intelligent man with a great knowledge of legendary history would not know that his sixth-century *dramatis personæ* were heathen;[2] the other is that the characters in the poem do not behave like Christians in their worship or their funeral customs, as one would expect them to do if the poet were treating them anachronistically to make them acceptable to a Christian audience.[3] The religion actually imputed to the men in the poem is discussed below in Chapter 5. Strangely, since he conceives the poet to have been an uneducated *scop*, Whallon suggests that Beowulf's dragon may owe something to the sixth-century hymn *Altus Prosator* 'Great Progenitor', attributed to Columba.[4] The hymn has indeed great interest for the student of *Beowulf*, but as it represents a kind of epitome of the Faith, there is no particular reason to regard it as a source for the poem. What Whallon supposes to be the 'novel' reinterpretation of giants and dragons and 'the perception that the monsters of the moor are allied to the man who slays his kinsman'[5] were already parts of traditional Christian lore.

I propose to examine the contents of this hymn in some detail, for three reaons. First, it is very striking testimony to the catholicity of the Faith, since it was composed by an Irishman contemporary with Gregory the Great and then was appropriated to himself by the great Carolingian scholar Hrabanus Maurus, a pupil of Alcuin at Tours and later Archbishop of Mainz. Its history during our period is not known, but its 'Celtic' modes of thought were so much admired on the continent after two hundred years that it was incorporated into a longer hymn composed by Hrabanus, *Æterne rerum Conditor* 'Eternal Creator'; in this form it has had a long history of use

[1] W. Whallon, 'The Christianity of *Beowulf*', p. 86.

[2] As Sisam says, 'moderately informed Anglo-Saxons would know from traders, missionaries and other travellers across the North Sea, that the Danes, Geats, and Swedes had been in earlier times and were still heathen (op. cit., pp. 72–3).

[3] One might contrast Beowulf in this respect with the hero of the Latin *Waltharius*, who is treated anachronistically as a Christian, as, for example, in praying over his slain enemies (lines 1157–67). The poem is edited by K. Strecker (Berlin, 1907).

[4] Whallon, op. cit., p. 91. R. H. Hodgkin had drawn attention to the 'dragon' stanza in the hymn, in his *History of the Anglo-Saxons* (Oxford, 2nd ed.), 1939, I, 257. [5] Whallon, ibid., p. 93.

in the worship of the Roman church. It was given the title *De Fide Catholica*. Second, it contains several matters pertinent to *Beowulf*, apart from the above-mentioned 'dragon' stanza. Third, it illustrates, better than any example already discussed in this chapter, the way in which doctrine and symbol in the Scriptures were elaborated and interlinked by the Fathers and made the very substance of the Faith.

The *Altus Prosator* is preserved in the Irish *Liber Hymnorum*, a collection of both Irish and Latin hymns extant in seven MSS, the earliest going back to the ninth century.[1] Two eleventh-century MSS contain a preface in Irish which says that Columba sent the hymn as a gift to Gregory the Great. Modern scholars accept the ascription.[2] The legend also says that Gregory found the hymn somewhat wanting in praise of the Trinity; whether the story is true or not, Hrabanus Maurus obviously thought likewise, and remedied the defect with stanzas of his own. In four of the extant MSS, the hymn is ascribed to Prosper of Aquitaine, which witnesses to its orthodoxy of doctrine as well as to its circulation on the continent.[3]

The theme of this alphabetical hymn is the history of the created universe, from the creation and fall of the angels to the imminent terrors of the end of the world. Kenney comments:

Curiously, there are only two slight references to the Redemption ... but in general the theology is that of the early middle ages, in a setting of medieval lore of the supernatural world, here ultimately derived, in the main, from the *Celestial Hierarchy* of Psuedo-Dionysius and the Jewish *apocryphon* known as the *Book of Henoch* ... There are reminiscences of the Bible, the *apocrypha*, and the *Hisperica Famina*.[4]

In his adaptation of the *Altus Prosator*, Hrabanus took over the opening stanzas, which treat of the co-eternal Trinity, the orders of angels, and the pride, vainglory, and envy of Lucifer which brought about the fall of the rebellious angels from heaven. The fourth stanza describes Lucifer's fearful transformation; he who was the seductive serpent becomes the terrible Ancient Dragon who was cast headlong into the infernal regions, dragging a third part of the stars with him. The description is

[1] *The Irish Liber Hymnorum*, ed. and tr. for the Henry Bradshaw Society by J. Bernard and R. Atkinson.   [2] Laistner, *Thought*, p. 142.
[3] *Liber Hymnorum*, p. 142.   [4] Kenney, *Sources*, p. 264.

43

taken from the Apocalypse 12: 9, which identifies the Dragon
with 'the Ancient Serpent who is called the Devil and Satan':

> Draco magnus deterrimus terribilis et antiquus
> qui fuit serpens lubricus sapientior omnibus
> bestiis et animantibus terræ feracioribus ... (20–5).[1]

The Dragon, great, loathsome and ancient, who was once the
slippery Serpent, more subtle than all the beasts and fiercer animals
of the earth.

The fall of the angels is followed by the creation of the earth:
this stanza may be compared with the Creation Song in *Beowulf*
(90–8): the general content is the same, but the Irishman shows
a typical interest in the small creatures, the birds and the fish,
and the domestic creatures, fire and cattle, whereas the English
poet sweeps his gaze across the whole earth and the firmament:

> Excelsus mundi machinam præuidens et armoniam
> cælum et terram fecerat mare et aquas condidit
> herbarum quoque germina uirgultorum arbuscula
> solem lunam ac sidera ignem ac necessaria
> aues pisces et peccora bestias et animalia
> hominem demum regere protoplastum præsagmine. (26–31)

The Most High, foreseeing the structure and order of the world,
made heaven and earth. He formed the sea and the waters, the
growing plants, the young trees in the woods, the sun, moon and
stars, fire and needful things, birds, fish and cattle, beasts and other
living creatures, and then at last the first-created man, to name them
in prophecy and to rule.

This difference of approach to the natural world is very marked
in Celtic and Gregorian compositions generally; one observes
it especially in saints' Lives. The absence of incidental detail
from natural description in *Beowulf* is one sign of its Englishness.
Hrabanus may have felt that description of the wind and rain,
the clouds and the sea, were not fitting for this solemn theme;

---

[1] The traditional nature of the description of the devil is further attested by the
use of *draco* in this sense in 'Ambrosian' hymns. A curious hymn, sung, according
to a marginal note, at daily choir services (in Ireland) is included in the *Liber
Hymnorum*, p. 137, under the title *Lamentatio S. Ambrosii*. It includes two lines about
the Dragon: *cor meum antiqui draconis infelix domicilium* 'my heart, wretched abode of
the Ancient Dragon' (v. 3, 1. 3), and *deus deterrimum draconem de pectore meo eice* 'O
God, cast out of my breast the loathsome Dragon' (v. 4, 1. 4).

at all events, he passed over Columba's stanzas I and K, the former of which describes these things. More probably, he found their language distasteful, for the vocabulary of the sea is noticeably Hisperic, and the tone of the latter verse would hardly commend it to imperial Gaul.[1] In actual fact, the stanza upon the wind and the rain, congenial as it undoubtedly was to the Irish temperament, is not a personal observation, but a reminiscence of Jeremiah 10: 10–13, which praises the immense powers of the Creator; its thought thus leads into the theme of the next stanza, the weakness of the great ones of the earth in face of the power of God.

This stanza K (lines 56–61 of the hymn) seems to me to have various points of interest for the student of *Beowulf*. It runs as follows:

> Kaduca ac tirannica mundique momentania
> regum presenti gloria nutu dei depossita
> ecce gigantes gemere sub aquis magno ulcere
> comprobantur incendio aduri ac suplicio
> Cocitique Carubdibus strangulati turgentibus
> Scillis obtecti fluctibus eliduntur et scropibus.

The frail, despotic and momentary glory of the kings of this present world is laid low by the will of God. Behold, the giants are said to groan under the waters in great pain; burned with fire and torment, and choked by the rising whirlpools of Cocytus, overhung with Scyllas, they are crushed by the waves and rocks.

On a first reading, the mention of 'giants beneath the waters' and the identification of the Virgilian underworld (Cocytus) with Hell bring to mind the underwater contest in *Beowulf*. On reflection, one perceives that the prophecy of the overthrow of the *mundi regum præsenti gloria* could cast a new light upon Hrothgar and Beowulf as *woroldcyningas* (1684, 3180) symbolically related to the *giganta cyn* (1690) whose retribution from the Lord *þurh wæteres wylm* (1693) was depicted on the giant sword-hilt Beowulf brought into Heorot.

The design on the giant sword-hilt was discussed many years ago by Crawford in a short note;[2] he adduced the biblical

---

[1] Similar phrases for hell's torments appear later in the hymn, so the political overtones were probably the decisive factor. There is no question of Hrabanus's rejecting the stanza for its (Gregorian) doctrinal content.

[2] S. J. Crawford, 'Grendel's descent from Cain', *MLR* 23 (1928), 207 f.

source of Columba's line, viz. *Ecce gigantes gemunt sub aquis* (Job 26: 5), to elucidate the purpose of this strange feature of the story, but one needs also more of the patristic complex of thought to understand the implications of this. Columba's stanza K takes for granted a relationship between the kings of the world and the groaning giants which is made explicit in a marginal note found in the ninth-century Milan MS of the hymn:

Sicut gigantes sub diluvio gemere propter crudelem fortitudinem quam habuerant, sic reges huius seculi pro iniustitia sua ac superbia et oppressionibus pauperum proicientur in infernum.[1]

Like the giants groaning beneath the flood because of the cruel strength they had possessed, so the kings of this world will be cast into hell for their injustice and pride and oppressions of the poor.

In patristic commentary, the *gigantes sub aquis* of Job had been identified with the giants of Genesis drowned in the Flood (Gen. 6: 4–7) who are allusively mentioned also in Wisdom 14: 6, as the *superbi gigantes* who perished when the chosen souls were saved in the Ark. Gregory also links them with Proverbs 26: 16 and Isaiah 26: 14, which enables him to treat all these biblical giants as symbols of those who are damned through the sin of pride.[2] It seems likely from the stanza quoted above that Columba regarded them in the same way. The *Altus Prosator* thus shows another means by which the allegorical interpretations of the exegetes were made available to clerics who were not themselves scholars, but who had sufficient Latin to follow the church services and homilies upon the Scriptures.

The *Altus Prosator* resembles *Beowulf* in one or two other respects. The power rather than the love of God dominates the thought of the composition, and this divine power is manifested in the creation of heaven and earth, the terrible subjugation of the adversaries, and in the promise of eternal reward or retribution in the Day of Judgment. The life of Christ upon earth is not mentioned. It is plain that some of the points used by those who have thought that the *Beowulf* poet was not a whole-hearted Christian would also be applicable to Columba, on the evidence

---

[1] *Liber Hymnorum*, I, 75; ed. note II, 161.
[2] Gregory, *Moralia, PL* 76, 24 f. The passage is discussed by M. P. Hamilton, 'The Religious Principle in *Beowulf*', 315.

of the doctrine rehearsed in the hymn. And it is to be re-membered that, 'primitive simplicity' notwithstanding, most of the hymn was incorporated into a Carolingian hymn 'on the Catholic Faith'. The alterations made by Hrabanus Maurus are not insignificant: they may indeed reinforce the general belief that *Beowulf* belongs to the earlier rather than the later part of the broad period I have marked off for study. This impression will perhaps be deepened by some consideration of the attitude of Aldhelm to God and the created world.

Aldhelm's work, like the *Altus Prosator*, has roots in both Irish and Gregorian modes of thought and expression. Before turning to some of his compositions, it will be useful to recapitulate our findings upon the nature of the Christian teachings propagated in England during his lifetime. The evidence of Columba's hymn has strongly supported the witness of historical records and the lives of individual churchmen to substantial agreement between the insular and the Gregorian teachers upon the doctrines con-cerning man's history and destiny. The teaching in both kinds of schools centred upon fallen man's need of redemption and on the eternal reward or punishment which awaited each soul. Nothing less than an exchange of the world's satisfactions for a life devoted to serving God could merit that reward, as the refrain of the *Altus Prosator* reminds the hearer:

> Quis potest deo placere nouissimo in tempore
> uariatis insignibus ueritatis ordinibus
> exceptis contemptoribus mundi præsentis istius.[1]

Who can find favour with God in this last Age, of whatever rank in the orders of truth, except those who despise this present world.

The life devoted to God's service was rendered hard and painful because of the unremitting assaults made upon mankind by the Ancient Enemy, the rebel against God, whose pride, envy and malice had caused his own hideous change into bestial form, and who constantly sought to prevent men from enjoying the heavenly kingdom from which he himself was exiled. In elabor-ating this basic doctrine both types of school made great use of

[1] *Liber Hymnorum*, I, 88. The hymn is also included in *The Oxford Book of Medieval Latin Verse*, ed. S. Gaselee (Oxford, 1928), pp. 25–34. Gaselee relegates these lines to the notes, but remarks that they are found 'in some good MSS' (p. 210).

traditional symbols and a rather loose and variable network of allegorical significations, the most widely-used master of this mode of teaching being Gregory the Great and his most popular work the *Moralia in Job*. The Old Testament atmosphere so frequently commented upon in Old English poetry owes its origin to the important place assigned to the history of the Israelites as prefiguration of the life of Christ and the Church. Certain parts of the Old Testament histories were, by reason of their use in moral teaching, living symbolic stories rather than remote historical events or simply prophecies. Probably the most fruitful of these symbolic stories is that of the wanderings of the Israelites in search of their Promised Land, understood as a figure of God's chosen people, making their pilgrimage through life towards the Kingdom.[1] This allegory was likely to be more generally known and more frequently explained than other Old Testament figures, because of the symbolic part it played in the rite of baptism, a sacrament seen as the freeing of the soul from bondage (to the Devil, figured by Pharaoh) by its passing through the waters (of the font, figured by the Red Sea) into the peregrinate life of the Christian upon earth.[2] Some critics have supposed that this symbolism was in the mind of the *Beowulf* poet as he described his hero's immersion in the giants' mere. It may well have been; but the relevant question is whether he made use of the symbolism of baptism in developing his story of Beowulf. I think that he did not; but the question must be deferred to a later chapter, since it is bound up with the whole conception of the hero and the purpose of the poem. At this stage, I use this well-known example as illustration of the general point I wish to make, that for the Anglo-Saxon Christian certain Old Testament stories were very familiar guides to the conduct of his spiritual life, as well as parables through which he could apprehend the processes of the invisible world. If one accepts, as I do, the view of Tolkien and others that Hrothgar is modelled largely on the Old Testament

---

[1] This salient feature of OE poetry was recognized by Ehrismann in 1909 in his important article 'Religionsgeschichtliche Beiträge zum Germanischen Frühchristentum'.

[2] See J. Daniélou, *Bible et Liturgie*, Chapter 5, passim, pp. 119–32. The importance of this symbolism in the structure of the OE *Exodus* was indicated by J. E. Cross and S. I. Tucker in a joint paper 'Allegorical tradition and the OE *Exodus*'.

patriarchs and kings,[1] it must not be forgotten that the lives of those ancient heroes were known to him not merely as great men of the past, but as moral exemplars, and also as symbolic persons who embodied some truth about God's dealings with mankind. The use of Old Testament heroes as examples to inspire the author is clearly illustrated by the metrical prologue to Aldhelm's *Ænigmata*.[2] The whole work is of interest in its conspectus of a Christian's view of the created world and its Maker.

It is sometimes not recognized that the riddles composed by churchmen of that age, both in Latin and English, were more than *jeux d'esprit*. They flourished, I suppose, because of the belief that mundane objects, whether in the natural world or in art, could disclose to the enquiring mind some part of God's nature and purposes. The belief arose from that famous sentence of St Paul's which in its English translation has given us the proverbial 'through a glass darkly', though textual variations in the Latin Bible have obscured the connection. The verse is frequently quoted by the Fathers in variants of the words *Nunc per speculum cernimus et in ænigmate*.[3] Bede, for example, adapts the words for use in a homily, *non per speculum et in ænigmate sicut nunc, sed facie ad faciem videbitur*.[4] The ambiguity of the word *ænigma*—it covered modern English 'figure' and 'allegory' as well as 'riddle'—made the Pauline phrase a warrant to look for spiritual meaning in every created thing.[5] It is in the light of this doctrine that one should approach Aldhelm's *Ænigmata*.

Aldhelm himself in his prefatory letter refers to the Bible as

---

[1] Tolkien, *Monsters*, p. 270.

[2] *MGH, AA* xv, 97–9. Citations below are to page and line of this edition. Ehwald gives the title as *Enigmata*. I have used the commoner spelling.

[3] 1 Cor. 13: 12; cp. Augustine, *De doctrina christiana*, ed. W. M. Green, p. 25, 8; p. 39, 15.

[4] Bede, *Homelia* I, 9, 200, *CCSL* 72, p. 65; cp. also *Hom.* II, 13, 169: *Videmus nunc per speculum et in enigmate tunc autem facie ad faciem.* (Medieval religious writers frequently quote loosely, so that it is difficult to tell which version of the Bible they were using. Where there are no indications to the contrary, my own scriptural quotations are taken from the Vulgate, except in the case of Psalms, which I quote from the *Psalterium Romanum*. Translations of biblical texts are those of the Douai-Rheims version of the Vulgate where these are appropriate. The variant scriptural texts incorporated in other writings I have translated literally.)

[5] For Augustine's discussion of the meaning of *ænigma* and its relation to scriptural interpretations, see his *De Trinitate*, 9, 15; *PL* 42, 1068–9.

authority for attributing speech to irrational creatures: quoting the well-known allegory of the trees who chose the bramble as their king (Jud. 9: 8–15) and other examples from Scripture.[1] It is clear from this that he took these compositions very seriously; though they are apparently metrical exercises, their purpose is 'the glorification of God and the spreading of his Kingdom'.[2] It is significant of the times that a mundane literary exercise is dedicated to the service of God.

In the opening verses of the prologue to the *Ænigmata*[3] we find the interest in Old Testament heroes of which I have been speaking. To Aldhelm, Moses, David and Job are an inspiration to harder endeavour in his work. The psalmist one might have expected, but Moses as a singer is a little strange to the modern mind; it needs to be recalled that one of the canticles included with the Psalms in a monk's service book was *The Song of Moses*.[4] There are indeed two canticles composed by Moses: the one to which Aldhelm here refers is an exultant hymn of victory which rejoices in the death of the enemy as unashamedly as the Old English *Battle of Brunanburh*.[5] There is, however, an important difference: a monk who rejoiced with Moses at the drowning of Pharaoh and his host saw Pharaoh as a figure of the Devil; it was a victory for God and his host in the continuing spiritual war. Aldhelm asks for strength for his task from the God who strengthened 'warlike Job', and refreshment from him who brought water from the rock in the wilderness.[6] The extraordinary epithet *belliger* describing Job shows plainly that the author saw Job through the eyes of Gregory, as a man in active combat with the Devil, not as the proverbial patient sufferer of later times. Aldhelm also shares with Gregory a fierce hatred of the Ancient Enemy, who appears, as in the Book of Job,

---

[1] *Epistola ad Acircium*, p. 76, 16–18.
[2] The phrase is from J. H. Pitman's Introduction to his edition, *The Riddles of Aldhelm*, Yale Studies in English, 67 (1925), p. iv.
[3] *Ænigmata*, pp. 98 f., 17, 30, 34.
[4] cp. M. C. Morrell, *A Manual of OE Biblical Materials* p. 47. These OT Canticles appear in the earliest mss of the Divine Office (ibid., p. 48). The Canticle to which Aldhelm refers is *Cantemus domino*, Exod. 15: 1–19.   [5] *ASPR* VI, 16–20.
[6] *Ænigmata*, pp. 98 f., 28–34. The imagery of spiritual battle, armour and weapons was by no means peculiar to Aldhelm at this period. See for example a letter written to him by Æthilwald, *MGH Ep.* III, 243, lines 14, 22, 32 for battle and armour images; and *A Prayer*, p. 245, for the darts of the Enemy (*hostium spicula*).

under the name of *Vehemoth* (Behemoth); God's terrible punishment of the rebel is recalled in the lines:

> Horrida nam multans torsisti membra VehemotH
> Ex alta quondam rueret dum luridus arcE.[1]

In retribution once thou didst rack the dread limbs of the terrible
Behemoth, at that time when he fell headlong from high heaven.

In identifying this mighty beast with the Apocalyptic dragon,
Aldhelm was following an old tradition which Gregory per-
petutates in characteristic language in his comment in the
Moralia: *Quem sub Behemoth nomine nisi antiquum hostem insinuat?*[2]

The God who is praised in Aldhelm's opening lines is awe-
inspiring and terrible in the immensity of his power. He is addressed as *Arbiter* and *Genitor*.[3] Nothing in this prologue derives
from the New Testament except a veiled reference to the Son
who was begotten before Lucifer was created.

In the riddles themselves the life of Christ and the Church
provide a very small proportion of the subject-matter; the
stories of Eden and the Flood are more prominent. Thus the
Rood-tree is contrasted with the fatal Apple-tree in *Melarius*,
the Serpent of Eden is recalled by the language of *Basilicus*, the
fig-leaves of Genesis appear in *Ficulnea*; the Flood appears in
both *Corbus* and *Columba*.[4] The two last-named are treated as
moral examples of disobedient and virtuous behaviour rather
than as creatures of the natural world; the same emphasis on
symbolic meaning is seen in *Aquila*, the Eagle who rises renewed
from the waters.[5] The riddle *Palma*, the palm of victory, bears
out what has been said of *belliger Job* in its martial language;
the martyrs are said to earn their reward *dum vincunt prœlia
mundi* 'when they win the battles of the world'.[6]

I have selected from the *Ænigmata* those riddles which bear
out the conclusions I have already drawn from the *Altus
Prosator*. The God who is depicted by Aldhelm, as by Columba,
is a God of retribution, who transformed Lucifer, expelled

[1] ibid., p. 97, 4–5.   [2] On Job 40: 10; *PL* 76, 644.
[3] *MGH AA* xv, 99, 1 and 35. In the Preface to the metrical *De virginitate* we find
Regnator Mundi (4) and even *Tonans* 'Thunderer'.
[4] *Melarius*, p. 132; *Basilicus*, p. 138; *Ficulnea*, p. 132; *Corbus*, p. 126; *Columba*, p.
126. On *Basilicus*, see Augustine's comment on Ps. 90: 13; *Enarr. in. Ps.*, *CCSL* 39,
II, 1276, 28.   [5] *Aquila*, p. 123.   [6] *Palma*, p. 139.

mankind from Eden, and drowned the evil world. He is also a
God of war who strengthens his chosen people, whether in actual
battles like those of the Israelites or in spiritual battles with the
Devil like those of Job, and he gives them the reward of victory.
The examples I have noted show how scriptural and exegetical
symbolism colour Aldhelm's view of the natural world.

In the *De virginitate*,[1] in both prose and metrical versions,
Aldhelm recounts the lives of saints and martyrs largely in the
vein of symbolic combat implied in his phrase *prælia mundi*. Some
of his saintly heroes confront the Enemy in beast or dragon
form, and these are more fully discussed below in Chapter 4.

It might well be objected that the theme of the *Altus Prosator*
and the *Ænigmata* governs the attitude to God and mankind
found in them; since both works praise the Creator, the spirit
of Genesis is appropriate and the almost complete silence about
the other Persons of the Trinity can be attributed simply to the
nature of the subject. I do not deny this. It is my contention
that the subject of *Beowulf* has a similarly restricting nature. The
theme of the *Ænigmata* might be restated as 'the power of the
Creator made visible in the Creation'; all men of every age can
read in this book, Christian and non-Christian alike; and, according to St Paul, all men can recognize their Creator in it:

Invisibilia enim ipsius, a creatura mundi, per ea quæ facta sunt,
intellecta, conspiciuntur; sempiterna quoque ejus virtus, et divini-
tas: ita ut sint inexcusabiles, quia, cum cognovissent Deum, non sicut
Deum glorificaverunt, aut gratias egerunt ...[2]

For the invisible things of him from the creation of the world are clearly
seen, being understood by the things that are made: his eternal power
also and divinity, so that they are inexcusable. Because that, when
they knew God, they have not glorified him as God, or given thanks.

It is for this reason peculiarly appropriate that the *scop* in
Heorot should sing to the heathen Danes of the Creator and his
handiwork, shortly before they are rebuked for their worship
of idols; the noble spirits of that ancient time recognize and give
thanks to God because they see him in his creatures. I do not
doubt that the *Beowulf* poet knew his Epistle to the Romans
and modelled his pagan heroes accordingly.[3]

[1] *MGH AA* xv, prose, 228–323; verse, 350–471.   [2] Rom. 1: 20–1.
[3] The religion of the Danes in the poem is fully discussed in Chapter 5 below.

Nonetheless, it could be argued that a religious poet of a later generation than Aldhelm would probably have gone out of his way to praise Christ or the Trinity in a prologue or epilogue, if the subject of the poem did not call for mention of Christianity. I gain the impression from my reading that in the Anglo-Latin writers from Bede onwards there is a better understanding of the love of God than is manifest in Aldhelm, when due allowance has been made for the partial view we obtain from the surviving works. One finds, for example, in Bede's Latin Homilies[1] a great deal of Old Testament material as prophecy and *figura* of the events he is expounding, but Christ, the Blessed Virgin Mary and the apostles are in the centre of Bede's thoughts. Looking to the end of the period under discussion, one observes that Alcuin's poem on the Saints of York opens in a temper far removed from the opening of Aldhelm's *Ænigmata*:

> Christe, deus, summi virtus, sapientia patris,
> Vita, salus, hominum factor, renovator, amator ...[2]

O divine Christ, power of the Most High, wisdom of the Father, life, salvation, creator, redeemer and lover of men.

One cannot go further on the scanty evidence still extant than to hazard the opinion that *Beowulf* is more in keeping with the spirit of Aldhelm than that of Alcuin; it would be quite unreasonable to assert that *Beowulf* could *not* have been composed in Alcuin's time on such grounds as this.

In respect of the other features of religious doctrine and symbolism I have been illustrating from Aldhelm, there is no sign of a large change. The belligerent saint is prominent in Bede's writings[3] and is even more highly favoured by Alcuin, as the

---

[1] Bede, *Homeliæ*, CCSL 72, passim.

[2] Alcuin, *Versus de Patribus Regibus et Sanctis Euboricensis Ecclesiæ*, MGH Poet., p. 169, 1–2.

[3] See, for example, *Vitæ abbatum*, Plummer, 1, 364–5, of Benedict Biscop: *despexit militiam cum corruptibili donativo terrestrem, ut vero Regi militans, regnum in superna civitate mereretur habere perpetuum* 'he despised the life of an earthly soldier with its corruptible reward, so that, as a soldier serving the true King, he might deserve to have perpetual dominion in the heavenly city' and ibid., 1, 371, of Eosterwine.

It is of particular interest *apropos* the heathen Beowulf that the unbaptized Alban is said to be *accinctus armis militiæ spiritalis* 'girt with the arms of spiritual warfare' (*HE*, Plummer 1, 19).

following rather striking example will demonstrate. In the poem on the Saints of York, Alcuin follows Bede rather closely for much of the time, but when Bede, using St Paul's words about the soldier of God, describes Cuthbert in his spiritual armour quenching 'all the fiery darts of the wicked one' as he drives the demons from Farne,[1] Alcuin, in language reminiscent of Aldhelm, calls Cuthbert *intrepidus Christi bellator opimus* 'dauntless and noble warrior of Christ' and recounts his solitary life thus:

> Hic heremita sacer non parvo tempore vixit;
> Sæpius angelicis felix affatibus usus,
> Toxica mortiferi vincebat tela draconis.[2]

Here the holy hermit lived for a long time; often the blessed man, familiar with angelic voices, was victorious against the poisoned shafts of the death-bringing Dragon.

The last line presents, one may think, a very poor image; the Devil as enemy with lethal darts does not combine happily with the Devil as dragon. But it presents excellent evidence both of the persistence of the battle metaphor and of the commonplace nature of the dragon-symbol here needlessly introduced. The line also shows rather well that the spiritual meaning could hold together quite absurdly diverse images in such conventional religious writing, and that no precise physical detail of the Dragon was insisted upon.[3]

These three English scholars of different generations, when writing in the hagiographic tradition, used the same primary sources and to some extent the same conventional language; there is a basic similarity which differences of style and temperament tend to disguise. Moses and Job appear in Alcuin as in Aldhelm as moral examples in the holy war, the only difference is that Alcuin is more explicit in stating the two parts of the paradox which Aldhelm's poetic language implies, the paradox of the patient victor,[4] and the contrast of weapons and

---

[1] Bede, *Vita S. Cuthberti*, ed. B. Colgrave, *Two Lives of St. Cuthbert* (Cambridge, 1940), p. 214. He uses the phrase *miles Christi* in this passage, and quotes Eph. 6: 16–17. (Bede's metrical *Vita* does not use the image.)

[2] *MGH Poet.*, p. 184, ll. 658 and 663 f.

[3] Sisam, *Structure*, p. 25 n., objects that 'our Dragon has no likeness to the Dragon of the Apocalypse'. E. G. Stanley, '*Beowulf*', in *Continuations*, p. 107, similarly emphasizes the physical difference.

[4] Alcuin, *De Clade Lindisfarnensis Monasterii*, ed. cit., 234, 159.

prayers as a source of strength in the fight.[1] The reward of victory still has an important place in the later poems.[2]

The perpetuation of these attitudes to the spiritual life allows my interpretation of *Beowulf* as an allegory of the fight against the Devil and his subjects to hold good no matter what date within the defined period one wishes to accept for the composition. The works I have used in trying to elucidate the poem were all known to Aldhelm, with the major exception of Bede's compositions; but Bede was largely a compiler of material already available to the previous generation of scholars and it is certainly not necessary to my argument that the *Beowulf* poet should have read Bede's books. The presumption is that all the works I adduce were used in teaching the Faith until the destruction of the monastic libraries by the Danish invaders.

In most of this chapter my inferences about the content of doctrine and the attitudes of those who propagated it have been made from various and somewhat fragmentary evidence, most of it indirect. I have left to the end the one substantial piece of direct evidence, the content of the fundamental teaching advocated by Augustine of Hippo. His two books of instruction provided the basis of Christian education for the whole of western Europe for several centuries. I shall treat them very briefly here, because they are rather better-known to modern readers than the compositions I have been examining so far, and also because much of Augustine's teaching falls outside the scope of this study, and that which seems relevant is used in later chapters.

A convenient summary of the history and influence of the two books now to be considered is given by Professor J. P. Christopher in the introduction to his translation of *De catechizandis rudibus*. He observes:

Since Augustine composed this treatise on such sound principles of pedagogy and psychology, it is not surprising to find that upon it are based almost all subsequent works on catechetics. The monastic schools, which, beginning with the sixth century, gradually supplanted the pagan rhetorical schools, were greatly influenced by the educational principles of St. Augustine, as set forth particularly in

---

[1] ibid., 233, 159.
[2] ibid., 235, 221 f. Alcuin contrasts the rewards of earthly and heavenly battle.

De doctrina christiana and *De catechizandis rudibus*. Cassiodorus (*ca.* 490—*ca.* 583) in his important work *Institutiones divinarum et saecularium lectionum*, in which he makes monastic education to consist in a thorough training in rhetoric coupled with an equally close study of the Scriptures, follows closely these two works. The *Etymologiae* of Isidore of Seville (*ca.* 550–636) which was the encyclopedia of the Middle Ages, was likewise based upon them. In Ireland the influence of Augustine upon monastic education is well-known. In England, Bede and Alcuin, under whom the monastic schools reached their highest development, used *De catechizandis rudibus* and *De doctrina christiana* as textbooks. In Germany, the *De institutione clericorum* of Hrabanus Maurus (*ca.* 784–856), Alcuin's most distinguished pupil, is but these two treatises worked over and adapted.[1]

It will be seen from this that Augustine's teaching was influential in the monastic schools throughout the period under discussion; it is not simply that these books were widely read, but that Augustinian thought and method were incorporated into many other books in general use. As is well known, much of his teaching was popularized by Gregory the Great. Ogilvy goes so far as to say: '[Augustine] is cited by Alcuin as among the authors in York Cathedral Library ... and is widely used by both Alcuin and Bede. In general it would be much safer to assume that the English knew any given work of Augustine than that they did not.'[2] Ogilvy's generalization applies to the Gregorian schools especially; it is very difficult to estimate the direct influence of Augustine upon the Celtic scholars because so little precise information has survived and so much Augustinian thought was incorporated in other authors' works.

The manual *De catechizandis rudibus* is designed to help the teacher to prepare candidates for baptism. Like the other works I have quoted, it gives importance to the Old Testament; a large part of the instruction is a *narratio* which summarizes Old Testament history in a way designed to show how events recorded there came to a focus at the advent of Christ, and *in figura facta sunt nostri*.[3] Though preparation for baptism among

---

[1] J. P. Christopher, *St. Augustine, The First Catechetical Instruction* (Ancient Christian Writers, 2) (Westminster, Md., 1946), p. 8.

[2] Ogilvy, *Anglo-Latin Writers*, p. 14.

[3] cp. 1 Cor. 10: 6, 'Now these things were done in a figure of us.'

the Anglo-Saxons was no doubt often much less elaborate than Augustine's method requires, the book suggests a presentation of doctrine which would soon make the Christian tyro familiar with the allegorical significance of certain events in sacred history; there is therefore no reason to think that the symbolism of the pictures and sculptures described earlier in this chapter would be a sealed mystery to the majority of Christians who saw them, or that reference to Old Testament events would have occult meaning for the scholar and none for the layman. Augustine's catechetical manual is enlightening in another respect: he suggests in his model form of instruction that the teacher should begin with an exhortation to think of the fleeting nature of this world's wealth and success.[1] It is quite apparent that the attitude expressed in Columba's words *Quis potest deo placere ... exceptis contemptoribus mundi*[2] was not an ideal for dedicated ascetics only, and its appearance in so much Old English poetry does not imply that such poetry was designed for a monastic audience.

De doctrina christiana is a more advanced textbook which has as its principal aim to teach men to read the Scriptures with understanding of their spiritual meaning. It treats more fully and with many illustrations the topics I have just referred to in the catechetical manual. The student of Old English poetry will read with particular interest the section upon the pilgrimage of life and the need to exchange temporal for spiritual values, joined here with the thought already discussed above, that through the visible creatures one apprehends the invisible spiritual world:

sic in huius mortalitatis vita peregrinantes a domino, si redire in patriam volumus ubi beati esse possimus, utendum est hoc mundo, non fruendum, ut *invisibilia dei per ea quae facta sunt intellecta* conspiciantur, hoc est, ut de corporalibus temporalibusque rebus aeterna et spiritalia capiamus.[3]

Thus in this mortal life, wandering away from the Lord, if we wish to return to our own land where we can be happy, the world must be used, not enjoyed, so that *the invisible things of God being understood*

---

[1] *De catechizandis rudibus*, ed. G. Krüger (Tübingen, 1934).
[2] Quoted above, p. 47.
[3] Augustine, *De doctrina christiana*, 10, 17–21, cp. Rom. 1: 20.

by the things that are made may be seen; that is, so that we may apprehend through corporal and temporal things those which are eternal and spiritual.

This thought is also linked by Augustine with the *in ænigmate* passage of I Corinthians 13: 12.[1]

Of the other works of Augustine the most widely-read were probably the *De civitate Dei* and the *Enarrationes in Psalmos*; Aldhelm and Bede quote from both of these,[2] and it is fair to assume that the gist of their doctrine was part of the climate of thought in which the *Beowulf* poet composed. Aldhelm also knew the *De libero arbitrio* and some of the sermons, epistles and minor tracts.[3] Where it has seemed to me that a thought from any one of these works could throw light upon the philosophy of the *Beowulf* poet, I have quoted or referred to them, in the confidence that they represent influential current views of the period, without implying that the poet knew these works at first hand, though he well may have done.

I am disposed to think that the poet did know Gregory's *Moralia in Job*, though so popular a book must have provided material for many teachers whose sermons remained unwritten, so we cannot discount the possibility of oral influence. I am confident that he knew several Lives of Saints; I believe one can discern the influence of the *Vita S. Antonii*, available to Aldhelm in the Latin translation of Evagrius,[4] and certainly read wherever monastic life flourished. He may also have known the *Hexameron* of Ambrose.[5] I have used the works named here in various parts of my argument; of other authors I find no identifiable traces and where reference is made to them it is as a guide to the *Weltanschauung* of the age. I have permitted as contributory illustration, on matters not essential to my theory, books which could have been known in England at the

[1] op. cit., p. 39, 13–18.   [2] Ogilvy, *Anglo-Latin Writers*, pp. 14 and 16.

[3] ibid., p. 18. Aldhelm apparently does not quote from the *De Trinitate*, but this could be because his surviving works do not touch on its subject-matter. Both Bede and Acca knew it (Ogilvy, p. 19) and on the strength of probability I have used it in discussion of the Augustinian doctrine circulating in England when *Beowulf* was composed.

[4] Ogilvy, ibid., p. 12, and M. L. W. Laistner, 'Bede as a Classical and a Patristic Scholar', p. 84.

[5] Ogilvy, ibid., p. 6. It was well-known to Bede, who used it extensively in his own work.

time, but of which there is no record, since modern knowledge of the books then available is very far from complete.

The points I hope to have established in this chapter are as follows. First, that an orthodox Christian writer of the period specified, whether of Celtic or Gregorian education, given a subject in which Christ had no necessary part, would tend to produce a work in which the references to God and his world had the harsh and warlike temper which has troubled and confused modern readers of *Beowulf*. Second, that the theme of God's war with his adversaries, with its rewards and its terrifying retribution to the defeated enemy host, was at the heart of current doctrine, and was expressed in conventional symbolic language which included the Dragon as the ancient enemy of mankind. Third, that the Scriptures, and in particular salient events in Old Testament stories interpreted in terms of this cosmic war, were probably taught to candidates for baptism and certainly to young men in the schools as moral and spiritual guides for their own lives, again largely through the medium of traditional symbols. In conclusion, that the whole aim of education at that time was to teach men to look into the Scriptures and in the created world for the *invisibilia Dei* and to reject as delusive the temporal satisfactions of this life, in the hope of eternal reward.

3 The Marriage of Traditions in Beowulf: *Secular Symbolism and Religious Allegory*

My attention has so far been given to the Christian climate of thought revealed in writings made in religious centres in early Anglo-Saxon England. It is now time to consider what kinds of poetic expression and what theories of the nature of poetry could have been at the disposal of the maker of *Beowulf*, and how far these were compatible with the attitudes inculcated in the Latin learning of the schools.

It must be admitted from the start that all statements made about native Germanic poetry anterior to *Beowulf* are inferential. The 'Germanic heroic epic' is an academic construct, since there are no direct, and, what is more important, no uncontaminated sources of information about pagan oral poetry. Of early evidence, there is the brief mention by Tacitus of the *carmina antiqua* which served as oral historical records among the *Germani*, and the battle-songs of 'Hercules' which they chanted before fighting.[1] The custom of preserving in verse the memory of the gods and kings and their great battles is reasonably presumed to have continued right up to the period when written annals and lettered poetry took their place—save that the pagan gods were replaced by the Lord of Hosts. The long memories of the poets could perpetuate the names of kings and heroes for three or four hundred years, as is proved by the two surviving fragments of early secular heroic verse, *The Fight at Finnsburh* and *Waldere*, and the two scopic songs *Widsith* and *Deor*, which, though not themselves heroic lays, include the names of ancient legendary heroes. All these short pieces now survive in late tenth-century manuscripts, but are thought to have been composed by the eighth century, *Widsith* and *Finnsburh*

---

[1] Tacitus, *Germania*, c. 3; quoted by Wrenn, *OE Literature*, pp. 74–5.

perhaps being older than *Beowulf*.[1] These poems are characterized by formulaic diction, a basically similar metrical form,
a highly allusive style and a narrow range of subject-matter.
Only the fragments of *Waldere* by their style give reason to
think that in its entirety this was a poem of some length. But in
this longer poem there are references to the Christian God,[2]
which suggests that *Waldere*, like *Beowulf*, is of mixed ancestry.
We therefore have no evidence at all that the unlettered Anglo-
Saxon poets composed songs of epic length and complexity. The
one surviving secular piece from Germany, the *Hildebrandslied*,[3]
is a short self-contained lay which does nothing to contradict
the impression given by the English corpus that longer poems
were first made upon Latin models, or at least by educated men
familiar with Latin poetry

This impression is strengthened by the results of modern
studies of living oral poetry and the techniques used by oral
poets today. One might quote on this point Professor F. P.
Magoun, who certainly cannot be accused of bias in favour of a
literary *Beowulf*, since the article quoted is an attempt to explain away the fact that *Beowulf* presents an abnormal structure
for an oral composition:

Seldom if ever does a folk-singer, composing extemporaneously
without benefit of writing materials, compose a cyclic poem, that is,
sing in a single session or series of sessions a story which he or she feels
is a unit dealing with several consecutive events in a character's life.
... In view of a general lack of cyclic composition in oral singing the
apparent cyclic character of the Beowulf material in Brit. Mus. MS
Cotton Vitellius A. XV is *a priori* immediately suspect ...[4]

Magoun's explanation of the curious form of 'the Beowulf
material' is that it was put together from separate lays with

[1] For a convenient summary of their contents and scholarly opinion on the
dating, see Wrenn, op. cit., pp. 76–83 and pp. 85–90.

[2] Wrenn, op. cit., p. 87, says 'Its definitely Christian references to God ... would
seem, perhaps, to point to a clerical maker'.

[3] Edited by E. von Steinmeyer, *Die kleineren althochdeutschen Sprachdenkmäler* (Leipzig, 1916).

[4] F. P. Magoun, '*Béowulf B*: a Folk-Poem on Béowulf's Death', in *Early English
and Norse Studies presented to H. Smith*, ed. A. Brown and P. Foote, pp. 128–9. His
observation that one finds no cyclic poem in Old Icelandic (p. 129) is also pertinent.

transition verses 'by some anthologizing scribe'. It will be evident, however, that if one begins with the hypothesis of a lettered poet working with inherited verse-material about Beowulf, there is no abnormality to be explained.

The studies mentioned by Magoun have added further evidence to conclusions earlier drawn from the Homeric poems and other ancient compositions. These indicate that at a certain stage of cultural development, illiterate societies produce, and preserve in oral form, public poetry which acts as a stabilizing factor in the political and social life of the group. It incorporates religious myths, dynastic history, and customs and moral values admired by the society. (Later, when the ruling classes have become literate, oral poetry becomes the prerogative of folk entertainers and the songs become more romantic in type.) It has often been observed that some parts of the Old Testament have the mythic and social qualities I have mentioned. To find something similar today, one must turn to the emergent countries, where warrior societies built upon the clan system still produce such poetry. Recent research into living poetry among the tribes of the Congo by Dr Jan Vansina[1] reveals some very interesting resemblances to the remnants of Germanic tribal poetry, and may help us to realize that primitive poetry of this sort is far from plain or simple in its modes of expression, though simple enough in its message. It seems to me that some of Vansina's informed generalizations about the nature of oral poetry correct some current opinions derived from vestigial folk-singing among more developed nations. In the first place, Vansina finds no marked difference between written and oral literature except for a greater frequency of repetition in oral compositions. He comments on the formal structures inherent in a given literary category, and the conventions of style, which include allusions, stock phrases and many kinds of rhetorical device. He particularly notes: 'Dans les cultures illettrées, une des figures de style les plus appréciées est l'expression symbolique.'[2] His comments on 'symbolic statements' and 'poetic allusion', in primitive societies generally, may incline us to believe that the obscurities, veiled allusions and dramatic ironies found in *Beowulf* by modern critics are natural to poetry

[1] Jan Vansina, *De la tradition orale.*   [2] ibid., p. 63.

dependent on such an oral tradition as has been described, and should certainly not be dismissed as figments of over-subtle modern criticism.

Voiler sa pensée est dans beaucoup de cultures et pour beaucoup d'auteurs un artifice de style très apprécié. Déjà le symbolisme n'est au fond qu'une technique pour exprimer par circonlocutions une pensée qu'on ne veut pas traduire directement. Mais en dehors des cas de symbolisme que tous les participants à la culture peuvent comprendre il existe une série d'artifices, les allusions poétiques, qui restent incompréhensibles pour tous ceux qui ne connaissent pas à l'avance une partie ou la totalité des faits dont le témoignage rend compte.[1]

Vansina gives illustrations from Rwanda poetry, which he says are by no means exceptional.

Dans presque toutes les cultures on pourrait citer des exemples analogues. Il résulte de l'emploi des allusions poétiques, que pour les comprendre il faut disposer de traditions historiques parallèles au poème qui en sont un commentaire explicatif.[2]

The familiar sound of all these statements to students of Germanic heroic poetry needs no underlining. Vansina also discusses stock phrases and stereotyped motifs in the African oral texts, and again the similarity with Germanic poetry is striking. His explanation of the use of these devices is germane to my general argument about the nature of *Beowulf*: 'Les lieux-communs à proprement parler apparaissent dans des textes qui traduisent des idéaux culturels acceptés par tous les tenants de la culture.'[3] The complex stereotypes form the motifs of episodes; one thinks of the washing ashore of an infant in a boat as probably such a motif in *Beowulf*. Vansina explains the inclusion of such motifs:

Il semble bien que ces clichés complexes ne soient que des procédés purement littéraires pour expliquer un fait historique connu, pour colorer le récit ou pour rendre compte d'un événement désagréable du passé sans choquer les valeurs et les idéaux culturels du moment.[4]

Vansina's study brings out very clearly that an initiated illiterate audience can accept and enjoy in poetry much that is

[1] ibid., p. 64.
[2] ibid., p. 65.
[3] ibid.
[4] ibid., p. 67.

obscure and allusive or symbolic in expression. If one supposes that the Anglo-Saxon nobility enjoyed similar qualities in the secular poetry recited to them, not only is the style of *Beowulf* what one would expect, but the obscurity and ambiguity of some other Old English poems such as *The Seafarer* and *Exodus* becomes less remarkable in works composed for laymen. Altogether, the apparent ease with which biblical and exegetical symbolism was absorbed by the Anglo-Saxons is much more understandable if the secular poetic tradition contained the elements Vansina mentions.[1] My purpose in this chapter is to demonstrate the fundamental way in which the change of cultural ideals at the Conversion altered the function of heroic poetry, and at the same time inevitably changed the meaning of traditional secular symbols. In gaining a spiritual dimension, such poetry became potentially, almost necessarily, allegorical.[2]

In the learned tradition, Virgil's *Æneid* was the great model for a heroic poet. The *Æneid*, though vastly more sophisticated, fulfils the secular functions I have been speaking of. It upholds the ruler by celebrating his predecessors and by showing that the gods destined him to reign. It presents in its ancient heroes a pattern of moral conduct. In many respects it would seem to be a fitting model for a Christian epic poet. But it has, inescapably, a pagan religious foundation, which early Christian scholars naturally found repellent, though they could not bring themselves to reject the *Æneid* from the educational curriculum. Instead, they followed the lead of the pagan commentators Servius and Macrobius in discovering symbolic meaning in the more superstitious passages of the epic, so that the *Æneid* came to be read in the Christian schools as a historical epic with allegorical elements.[3]

It would scarcely be an exaggeration to say that every literate

---

[1] Apart from *Beowulf* itself, the remains of Germanic secular poetry are too short to provide a clear general picture, but the allusive style is very marked in *Deor* and *Widsith*.

[2] I use the word 'allegorical' here in a very broad sense, which could be defined as 'saying one thing in order to mean something beyond that one thing' (cp. Angus Fletcher, *Allegory: the Theory of a Symbolic Mode*, p. 4). For further definition of the kinds of allegory and symbolism in *Beowulf*, see below, pp. 68 ff.

[3] cp. D. P. A. Comparetti, *The Study of Vergil in the Middle Ages*, trans. E. F. M. Beneke (London, 1895), especially pp. 57 and 59. For details of the symbolic meanings found in *Æneid* VI, see P. Courcelle, 'Les Pères devant les Enfers Virgiliens', *Archives d'Histoire Doctrinale et Littéraire du Moyen Age*.

poet in Europe from the fourth century onwards was influenced by Virgil, yet though Christian epic poems in Latin appeared, there were no secular epics by Christian authors at that time. The reason is not far to seek. Christendom as a realm on earth to be upheld and defended was a concept not yet formed, and the heroes whose memories were perpetuated in Christian poetry were either the Old Testament *figuræ* of Christ, or the Lord and his apostles, or those famous later disciples who renounced wordly honours and fought their battles with the invisible hosts of the Enemy. A secular Christian epic would have been a contradiction in terms in a cultural environment dominated by the monastic ideal, but the way was still open for the advancement of God's kingdom through allegory. In England and the Germanic countries generally, there was the further obstacle that the ancestral heroes were pagan; again, allegorical treatment would permit the celebration of their nobility and valour, because it could be believed that the good men of the past also fought the Enemy. In fact, since there could not be a legitimate marriage between the politico-social heroic poetry of the secular tradition and the epic saint's Life which celebrates a hero of the invisible Kingdom, the product of such a strange union must, like *Beowulf*, laud a hero who inhabits two worlds, and is not quite at ease in either.

Sulpicius Severus, author of the influential *Vita S. Martini*, plainly states the contrast between the aims of secular and religious writers, the one celebrating great men, the other, the saints. He speaks of the examples of great men whose memory is preserved in literature, but he regards the reading of such secular work as profitless:

quippe qui humanam vitam præsentibus tantum actibus æstimantes spes suas fabulis, animas sepulchris dederint ... unde facturus mihi operæ pretium videor, si vitam sanctissimi viri, exemplo aliis mox futuram, perscripsero: quo utique ad veram sapientiam et cælestem militiam divinamque virtutem legentes incitabuntur. in quo ita nostri quoque rationem commodi ducimus, ut non inanem ab hominibus memoriam, sed æternum a Deo præmium expectemus ...[1]

for, in truth, those who evaluate life by present actions have given their hope to fables and their souls to tombs ... hence it seems to me

[1] Sulpicius Severus, *Vita S. Martini*, ed. C. Halm, 110 f.

that I shall make a work of some worth, if I write the life of a very holy man which will be an example for others in the future: through which readers will be inspired towards true wisdom and heavenly warfare and divine virtue. In this we are also thinking of our own advantage, as thus we may look for, not worthless remembrance by men, but eternal reward from God.

The above passage may have influenced the writer of a discourse on Psalm 52: 1–4 once attributed to Bede: the work begins with a short statement of his purpose in writing:

Cum plures clericos in schola constitutos agnoscerem, ad hoc quam maxime vacare, ut litterarum sæcularium notitiam caperent, quæ auditores suos studiosissime docent carnalia appetere, pro obtinendi mundi gloria contendere ... tractavi et ego litteras legere, quibus aliquos ad sacræ fidei normam, ad timoris amorisque divini curam, ad spiritalis vitæ puritatem, ad humilitatis et charitatis devotionem, ad pænitentiam malefactorum, emendationemque morum incitarem.[1]

When I marked many clerics established in places of learning giving so much time to the acquisition of knowledge of secular compositions, which studiously teach their hearers to desire carnal things and to strive for worldly glory ... I decided that I myself would collect those literary works through which I might encourage some people towards the pattern of the holy faith, towards concern for the love and fear of God, towards the purity of spiritual life, towards devotion to humility and charity, towards penance for wrongdoers and amendment of their ways.

This purpose is served by a discourse made up of a string of biblical parables, similitudes and exempla taken from the common stock, their inclusion justified by the doctrine that God is to be seen in his creation:

Cum enim a Deo ita creata sint visibilia, ut omnes intelligentes et requirentes Deum in his facile possint instrui ad invisibilia agnoscenda, Dei *interrogare* est quem libet subiliter probare per eadem visibilia utrum eum diligat et timeat obediendo præceptis ejus, an propriæ voluptati deserviat consentiendo diabolicis illusionibus.[2]

For since the visible things were created by God such that *any understanding or seeking God* can easily be taught in these to recognise the

---

[1] *PL* 93, 1103. [2] *PL* 93, 1109; cp. Ps. 52: 3 and p. 52, above.

invisible, to *inquire* (of God) is to test someone subtly through those same visible things, to discover whether he loves and fears him by obeying his commandments, or whether he serves his own pleasure by accepting diabolical illusions.

The *Beowulf* poet quite probably knew the *Vita S. Martini,* which Colgrave groups with the *Vita S. Pauli,* the *Vita S. Antonii* and Gregory's *Dialogi* as works 'which had much influence on all writers of saints' lives of the seventh, eighth and later centuries'.[1] And I do not doubt that he also knew material like that assembled in the Ps.–Bede discourse. It will now, I think, be plain that *Beowulf,* if the religious element were removed, would fall into Sulpicius's category of secular works which offer the examples of great men for emulation and celebrate worldly glory. Beowulf himself earns and receives that *inanem ab hominibus memoriam* which Sulpicius contrasts with the *æternum præmium* which those who follow the example of the saints may hope to gain. Without the religious element, the poem would most surely teach its audience *pro obtinendi mundi gloria contendere* but with its 'Christian colouring' it seems to me to lead them *ad veram sapientiam et cælestem militiam divinamque virtutem.* How is this done? Obviously not by an added and extraneous condemnation of everything that the narrative has extolled, but instead by the more subtle use of the ambiguities and ironies which the two scales of values generate when the audience is brought to look *through* the one at the other. I believe that Beowulf is shown being tested as Ps.–Bede describes, through a 'diabolical illusion': the treasure hoard. The poet achieves this effect by exploiting the plurality of meanings which inheres in symbols and the essential irony of the *visibilia,* that 'what appears is so unlike what is'.[2] No sceptical reader need think that a use of symbols in the manner I have described would be alien to the mind of an Anglo-Saxon author. It seems to me quite congruent with the treatment of persons, objects and events in commentaries upon the Bible, remembering the arbitrary and occasionally antithetical meanings which may be attached to a single symbolic word or event.

[1] B. Colgrave, *Felix's Life of Saint Guthlac,* p. 16.
[2] The phrase is from Christopher Fry. *A Phoenix too Frequent* (Oxford, 1946), p. 31.

At this point, some theoretical discussion is required to explain the nature of the symbolism we are concerned with and its relation to the allegory I have postulated. Vansina's use of the word symbol needed no explanation: it implied simply the substitution of a veiled term for a literal one.[1] Some of the substitutions he quotes are quite trivial, others would deserve the name of symbolism on almost any definition: for example, the rumbling of a storm as sign of the coming of a king in war (the king being the tribal rainmaker), or the loss of a tribal drum signifying the break-up of a kingdom.[2] The latter example brings to mind Mrs Winifred Nowottny's statement on symbolism in her book *The Language Poets Use*:

It is as though ... the poet were trying to leap out of the medium of language altogether and to make his meaning speak through objects instead of through words. Even though he does not tell us what the object X stands for, or even that it does stand for anything, he makes us believe that it means, to him at least, something beyond itself.[3]

This statement will serve very well as a point of departure. It will be recalled that my explanation of the purpose of Aldhelm's riddles in Chapter 2 involved this 'speaking through objects', and my examples of the symbols used in religious teaching could be so described. There is, I need hardly say, a profound difference between Aldhelm's speaking universe and a drum which speaks of a tribal kingdom, in respect of their philosophical implications, but as literary devices they can be classified together. Because of this, a social and political poem which uses symbolism of the latter sort can be enlarged to include religious symbolism without much violence to its surface literary integrity. This, I believe, is what happened in the making of *Beowulf*.

Augustine's literary theory in *De doctrina christiana* makes no fundamental distinction between secular and sacred symbols; he divides them into *signa naturalia* (such as smoke signifying fire) and *signa data* (which include all kinds of communication through sound or gesture, picture or object).[4] Among his illustrative examples are the dragon-standards of the army which

---

[1] See p. 63
[2] One is reminded of the loss of *meodosetla* signifying the end of tribal independence in *Beowulf* (5).   [3] W. Nowottny, *The Language Poets Use*, p. 175.
[4] Augustine, *De doctrina christiana*, ed. W. M. Green, p. 34.

per oculos insinuant voluntatem ducum 'indicate to the eye the generals' intent', the perfumed ointment poured over Christ's feet, and the woman touching the hem of his garment.[1] These, which nowadays would probably be called symbolic objects or symbolic gestures, he uses to illustrate the various ways in which meaning can be conveyed, before he introduces the reader to the obscurities and ambiguities of Scripture. Augustine also warns his readers that similitudes in the Bible may sometimes have contrary meanings, one good, the other bad, as in the example of the lion, which signifies Christ in the Apocalypse 5: 5, and the Devil in 1 Peter 5: 8.[2] He moves on from figures to tropes, with a special mention of *allegoria, ænigma* and *parabola,* and a special paragraph on *hironia.*[3] It is evident from this classification and also from his explanation of *allegoria* in *De Trinitate,*[4] that 'allegory' for him was a general term for a literary device *aliud ex alio significare,* which included in its sub-classes both irony and enigma, the latter being an obscure allegory. A student brought up on *De doctrina christiana* would therefore have a very different conception of allegory from the modern student, who tends to think primarily in terms of personification allegory and the clothing of an abstract theme in a fictional dress.[5] Bede agrees with Augustine in regarding *allegoria* as a class of tropes including irony and enigma. He also rather unsuccessfully tries to find a theoretical category into which to fit the famous 'four senses' found in Scripture; his difficulty, of course, is that these multiplex tropes do not identify themselves by any formal sign

[1] Augustine, ibid., p. 35.

[2] ibid., p. 100. Had he not been writing for beginners in biblical study, he might have included also St Peter's ambivalent symbols which mean one thing to the faithful and something quite other to the unbeliever, viz., the corner-stone which is the foundation of a spiritual edifice to the Christian and a stumbling-block to the unbeliever (1 Pet. 2: 7–9), and the Flood-waters which prophesy baptism and salvation to the former and destruction to the latter (1 Pet. 3: 20–2); cp. Jean Daniélou, *Bible et Liturgie* pp. 89–104.

[3] Augustine, op. cit., p. 103.

[4] Augustine, *De Trinitate, PL* 42, 1068, on the text 1 Cor. 13: 12. Here he compares *in ænigmate* with *in allegoria* (Gal. 4: 24), explaining that translators who did not wish to use the Greek word have employed the circumlocution *which signify one thing by another.*

[5] Personification allegory was of course also known to the Anglo-Saxons from Virgil's use of it and from Prudentius's *Psychomachia.* The last part of Aldhelm's verse *De virginitate* is written in this mode; see *MGH AA* xv, pp. 452–71.

and completely resist rhetorical classification.[1] (He puts them, quite wrongly, under *asteismus*; Augustine is content to include them under *ænigma*.)

In view of the attitudes to literary composition revealed here, one would not expect an allegorical work composed in Bede's time or thereabouts either to identify itself by formal signs or to preserve consistent levels of meaning. Allegory to these scholars was not a literary form, but, in the convenient phrase adopted by Angus Fletcher, 'a symbolic mode' of thinking and writing.[2] It is quite clear from the works I have just quoted that there was no theoretical separation of symbol and allegory; an allegorical work was simply one in which there was a great deal of hidden or obscure meaning conveyed in parable, enigma, proverb or almost any kind of metaphorical or ironic statement. When allegory is conceived in this way, the distinction between allegorical interpretation (of Scripture or of pagan writers) and allegorical creation (in new compositions) dissolves away. Fletcher, though in another context, makes a penetrating statement on this point:

The modern question as to how we relate the interpretative and the creative activities could not arise before a break-up of the medieval world-view. Modern empirical science, on the other hand, depends in part on the disjunction of creative (imaginative and synthetic) and interpretative (empirical and analytic) mind, a major intellectual shift which might explain the modern distaste for allegory.[3]

[1] Bede, *De schematibus et tropis sacræ scripturæ, PL* 90, 184–6. His definition is as follows:

Allegoria est tropus quo aliud significatur quam dicitur.

Allegory is a trope in which something other is signified than what is said.

Among the kinds, he brings in the four senses thus:

Item allegoria verbi, sive operis, aliquando historicam rem, aliquando typicam, aliquando tropologicam, id est moralem rationem, aliquando anagogen, hoc est sensum ad superiora ducentem, figurate denuntiant.

In like manner they intimate in a figure allegory of word or deed, sometimes a historical matter, sometimes a prefiguration, sometimes a tropological matter (that is, a moral concern), sometimes an anagogical relation (that is the sense guiding us to things above).

[2] Fletcher, op. cit., pp. 2–3, takes very much Augustine's general view based on the linguistic process involved in making an allegory: 'In the simplest terms, allegory says one thing and means another. It destroys the normal expectation we have about language, that our words "mean what they say" ... In this sense we see how allegory is properly considered a mode: it is a fundamental process of encoding our speech. For the very reason that it is a radical linguistic procedure it can appear in all sorts of different works ...'   [3] Fletcher, op. cit., p. 135.

A great deal of modern argument about the possible existence of allegorical meaning in Old English secular compositions has developed simply from confusion of terms and failure to accept allegory as a literary mode rather than a form.

Much confusion has been caused by the existence of the 'four senses' or 'planes of meaning' in scriptural interpretation. The first point to be noted is that though the great exegetes recognized the coexistence of different kinds of meaning in scriptural passages, they were not always sure how to differentiate these kinds, and in practice they might find two, three or four planes of meaning in some verses, and only literal meaning in others. For example, Augustine in the *De utilitate credendi* distinguishes four senses which he calls historical, ætiological, analogical and allegorical, covering respectively the actual Old Testament event, its cause, its agreement with the doctrine of the New Testament, and its figurative meaning. (His example is Abraham's two wives signifying the two covenants.)[1] As to the existence of these senses in a given text, he suggests the proper direction of scholarly enquiry in a series of rhetorical questions in the tract *De vera religione*:

an aliae significent gesta visibilia, aliae motus animorum, aliae legem aeternitatis, an aliquae inveniantur in quibus haec omnia vestiganda sint?[2]

Do some [scriptural stories] signify visible events, others the motions of the mind, others the law of eternity, or are some found in which all these are to be discovered?

Gregory, explaining his own method in the dedicatory letter to the *Moralia*,[3] has a slightly different system; he distinguishes historical, typological, and moral-allegorical kinds of interpretation, which may be applicable severally or in conjunction.

[1] Augustine, *De utilitate credendi*, ed. J. Zycha, I, 70.

[2] Augustine, *De vera religione*, ed. W. M. Green, pp. 7 f.

[3] Gregory, *Moralia*, PL 75, 513:

Sciendum vero est, quod quædam historica expositione transcurrimus, et per allegoriam quædam typica investigatione perscrutamur; quædam per sola allegoricæ moralitatis instrumenta discutimus; non nulla autem per cuncta simul sollicitus exquirentes, tripliciter indagamus.

It is to be recognized that we hasten over some things in a historical exposition and we scrutinize some by the use of allegory in search of typological significance; some we discuss only as instruments of moral allegory; on the other hand, some we explore in three ways, carefully looking for all these senses together.

Bede in his commentaries compiles from the work of his predecessors; in his homilies, which are based on New Testament texts, he recognizes historical, moral, and spiritual or mystical meaning.[1]

In one homily, Bede makes an unusually clear distinction between the different ways in which a story can be understood. He uses the changing of the water into wine at the Marriage at Cana as an allegory of the transformation of the meaning of the Old Testament stories by the significance of the life of Christ. The six vessels are six Old Testament stories from which the Jews drew, and any man can draw, moral lessons: this is the water. From the same six vessels the Christian can draw a more precious spiritual nourishment: this is the wine.[2] The spiritual meaning comes from the typological relationship between the acts of Noah, Isaac and the other *figuræ* in the stories and the acts of Christ himself:[3] the kind of prophetic symbolism already mentioned above as the subject of pictures brought by Benedict Biscop from Rome to Jarrow. There are of course two kinds of symbolism involved in Bede's homily. Each of the Old Testament stories is symbolic in its own right, and it teaches a moral lesson, as the religious pictures might. But each in conjunction with a New Testament story reveals typological symbolism and teaches a spiritual lesson.

Beowulf, I suggest, is a symbolic history from which one can draw the refreshing water of moral lessons; some critics have been tempted to suppose that one might also draw wine, by treating Beowulf as *figura* or 'type' of Christ like Noah or Isaac. They are, I believe, mistaken. Beowulf and Hrothgar are quite

---

[1] Bede, *Homeliæ*, *CCSL* 72, passim.

[2] ibid., *Liber Primus, Homelia* 14, pp. 95–104. There is further complexity in the homily in that each of the O.T. stories represents one of the Ages of the World. The homilies also include a good deal of incidental symbolism. One example contrasts dove and raven, which could conceivably shed light upon the raven who wakes the men of Heorot:

Habent autem oscula et corvi, sed laniant, quod columba omnino non facit: significantes eos *qui loquuntur pacem cum proximo suo, mali autem sunt in cordibus eorum.* Ravens too have kisses, but they tear with them, which the dove never does, signifying those *who speak peace with their neighbour but evil thoughts are in their hearts.* (*Hom.* 1, 15, p. 107). One remembers the hints of hidden hostility in lines 1164 and 1015 ff. of the poem.

[3] For a clear explanation of the theory of *figura*, see E. Auerbach, *Mimesis*, trans. W. R. Trask (Princeton, 1953), pp. 73–5.

probably modelled on Old Testament characters, and are, like them, moral examples. But this resemblance does not make them a part of prophetic sacred history. Typological interpretation in the strict sense has no certain place outside of the inspired Scriptures.[1] It might, I suppose, be legitimately extended to poems in which Christ himself is the hero, such as the Old English *Phoenix,* or to a paraphrase of part of the Old Testament in which the *figura* occurred in the source. It could only be extended to the acts of a man living in the Christian era by someone who had an incomplete grasp of the theory of typological interpretation. There is, I believe, an intended relationship between Beowulf and the warrior-Christ, but it is not a direct and simple one.[2]

It is true that no line was drawn at that period, as in modern times, between the mythical and legendary parts of the Old Testament narrative and later history properly so called, as witness, for example, the *Chronica*[3] of Sulpicius Severus, whose views on the purpose of literature have been quoted above. His compact history of the world includes Cain's murder of Abel, the miscegenation which spawned the giants, and the Flood, just as the 'historical' poem of *Beowulf* does, and proceeds through such events—to take a few at random—as the burning of Rome under Nero, the finding of the Cross by Helena, and several notable synods of the Church, down to doctrinal controversies in his own day. This work was not intended to be a church history; it is a Christian's view of the history of mankind; and though there is no separation of biblical history and later events there is a line of demarcation between the era of prophecy which led up to the Incarnation and the Christian era which followed. Typology in the patristic sense of the word belongs only to the era of prophecy. There is in the holy men of

[1] Auerbach, op. cit., sees 'figural thinking' in Dante's view of the universal Roman monarchy as the earthly anticipation of the Kingdom of God. 'An event taken as a figure preserves its literal and historical meaning' (p. 196). As I have said elsewhere (*Neophil.* 1964, p. 67) an Augustinian view of history perhaps underlies the symbolic treatment of events in *Beowulf.* But it is difficult to believe that an Anglo-Saxon poet saw the wars of the Swedes and Geats as part of the divine plan of salvation, or that he disregarded the fact that Beowulf lived after the Incarnation, from which the *figuræ Christi* take their meaning.

[2] For further discussion of this matter, see pp. 241 ff., below.

[3] Sulpicius Severus, *Opera,* ed. cit., pp. 1–105.

the world before Christ a partial revelation of the pattern of perfection; after the life of Christ the witness of holy men is *imitation* of Christ; the word 'type' in its narrow exegetical sense can no longer apply.

Christian literature is naturally full of reminiscences of New Testament incidents and sayings. To recognize these is not the same thing as to discover *figuræ Christi* in the heroes of the works concerned. I quote in support of this contention that great student of medieval symbolism, Rosemond Tuve, who has discussed this question in relation to Guyon in *The Faerie Queene*. She speaks of Spenser's use of allegorical images to indicate

that we are to read them with this reach into ultimate questions. We recognise them as instruments for the discussion of just such matters —but able to speak in the present of the timeless, and locally of the universal. I do not mean that images repeat the story they told in the past. It does not turn Guyon into a 'Christ-figure' when in Canto vii. 9 Spenser directs us to see the parallel with Christ's three temptations. Rather, this indicates the amplitude of the issue and states a doctrine about the relation between all human temptations and Christ's.[1]

This quotation seems to me to point to the right way to read Beowulf's descent into the world of his demonic adversaries, which recalls Christ's descent into hell in rather the same way as Guyon's temptations recall the temptations of Christ. It indicates the allegorical amplitude of the issue, but it does not turn Beowulf into a 'type' of Christ.

If we put aside typological significance as inappropriate to *Beowulf*, we are left with the other kinds of allegorical meaning, the moral and the spiritual. One might distinguish these as appertaining to right conduct upon earth, and that conduct viewed in the perspective of eternal life and man's relationship with God. I think that the *Beowulf* poet is intermittently writing on both these planes.

[1] Rosemond Tuve, *Allegorical Imagery*, pp. 32–3. Professor Tuve makes a clear distinction between a moralization and an allegory in discussing late medieval and Renaissance texts. I do not think such a distinction is valid for Old English poetry, and I have not used 'allegory' in Tuve's more precise sense, following her own principle: 'It is as well to repeat periodically that we do not seek to define allegory as if it were some changeless essence, and then in turn use the definition to admit or shut out poems from the category. We seek something quite limited and historical —what was involved in reading allegorically to certain writers at a given time, and for reasons we can trace.' (ibid., p. 33).

It should by now be evident that when I speak of *Beowulf* as an allegory of the life of man I mean something rather different from what C. S. Lewis had in mind when he said of Fulgentius's *Expositio Virgilianae continentiae*, 'The whole story of the *Æneid* is interpreted as an allegory of the life of man'.[1] Fulgentius's interpretation of the *Æneid* calls for a far greater degree of abstraction than I find in *Beowulf*, and all the incidents are treated as images in the progress of a life. Whether Fulgentius was available to the *Beowulf* poet remains uncertain. There is no positive evidence that the *Mitologiae* and the *Virgilianae continentia* were known in England before the ninth or tenth century.[2] An instance in Bede of the Fulgentian method, namely, his allegorizing of the fabled nature of Cerberus, merely demonstrates a similar approach to the pagan myths, since Bede does not follow Fulgentius in his interpretation of the monster's three heads.[3] One might deduce that Bede would have found the work of Fulgentius congenial in some respects; his lack of reference to the mythographer's books is therefore significant. Aldhelm, who uses allegorical beasts as symbols of the vices,[4] would undoubtedly have been interested in Fulgentius had he known his compositions, but he betrays no acquaintance with them. On the whole, it seems unlikely that Fulgentius had direct influence on the Anglo-Saxon poets; those who were able to read the *Æneid* probably found latent symbolic significance in particular objects or actions rather than a continuous didactic underthought. Æneas's descent into the underworld had received particular attention from religious writers;[5] this could have provided a model for the allegorical treatment of Beowulf's descent into the hellish depths of the mere. It must, however, be

---

[1] C. S. Lewis, *The Allegory of Love: a study in medieval tradition*, pp. 84 f.

[2] Alcuin's catalogue of authors in the library at York includes the name Fulgentius, but it is by no means certain that the mythographer was intended. For discussion of the extant works ascribed to Fulgentius and argument against identifying the mythographer and the Bishop of Ruspe, see M. L. W. Laistner, 'Fulgentius in the Carolingian Age', in *The Intellectual Heritage of the early Middle Ages*, ed. C. G. Starr (New York, 1957), pp. 202–15.

[3] Fulgentius had related the three heads to three kinds of contention in the world (*Opera*, ed. R. Helm, Leipzig, 1898, pp. 20 and 98 f.); Bede interprets the Dog of Hell as *Avaritia*, and its three heads as the three kinds of concupiscence in 1 Jo. 2: 16. (*Ep. Ecg.*, Plummer 1, 422 f.).

[4] cp. pp. 76 and 135, below.

[5] See P. Courcelle, op. cit., for the patristic treatment of the scene.

said that the supposed Virgilian reminiscences in this part of *Beowulf* are rather dubious.

A minor but interesting question which pertains to the Beowulf poet's conception of allegory is whether or not he employs personification allegory in his poem. Virgil provides a model for the occasional appearance of abstractions in living form, notably in the vices which cluster round the portals of Hades.[1] There is nothing quite of this kind in *Beowulf*, but as Professor Bloomfield has pointed out, the names Unferth and Hygd could suggest that these characters were invented to fill the role the names connote.[2] It seems to me rather more in keeping with the poet's general practice to suppose that the characters had a traditional part to play and the names were perhaps modified to underline the nature of that part. Personified vices in beast form, on the other hand, such as appear in the battle with the vices at the end of Aldhelm's *De virginitate*,[3] might well have guided the poet to awareness of the allegorical potential of Beowulf's monster-fights.

I have now, I hope, shown that *allegoria* in Bede's time was not a category of formal structure, but a mode of figurative writing which might inhere only intermittently in a given work, and that it involved moral and spiritual symbols and figurative passages. The allegory in *Beowulf*, as I believe, is intermittent and concerns only one aspect of man's life, the contest with the Enemy. Though the poet quite probably knew the *Æneid* with its accompanying symbolic commentaries, there are no signs that he was influenced by it except in the most general way; for the kind of subject he was interested in, the saint's Life, the Bible as read by the commentators, and perhaps the *psychomachia* type of allegory, would provide him with sufficient models for the religious aspect of his composition.

In a rather different respect, the way in which the *Æneid* was read may have offered the *Beowulf* poet a pattern. It provided

---

[1] *Æneid* VI, 273–89.

[2] M. W. Bloomfield, '*Beowulf* and Christian Allegory, An Interpretation', *Traditio* 7 (1949–51), 410–15. He suggests that Unferth = *Discordia*, as in Prudentius's *Psychomachia*. As Prudentius is thinking in terms of schism and heresy within the Church, the connection is not very likely.

[3] Aldhelm, *De virginitate*, *MGH AA* xv, 452–471, lines 2446–2914; see also p. 135, below.

an authoritative warrant for the composition of a historical epic with moral and philosophical symbolism and with divine intervention. Whether or not *Beowulf* can be called an epic depends entirely on whether one sets up a theoretical category distinguished by certain formal requirements. It is of course much shorter and more restricted in its range than the classical epic, but I suppose that by the standard of the time it would have been included in the epic genre. Its shortness would hardly have been a bar, since Homer's reputation was perpetuated in Western Europe through the *Ilias Latina,* a first-century Latin abridgment of the *Iliad* in 1070 lines.[1] According to the definitions given by Isidore of Seville, which Bede used in his own brief literary treatise, *Beowulf* would belong to the *heroica species* of the *genus commune* (i.e. that in which both poet and characters speak). Our poet performs his function well according to Isidore's definition of the poet's task:

Officium autem poetæ in eo est ut ea, quæ vere gesta sunt, in alias species obliquis figurationibus cum decore aliquo conversa transducat.[2]

A poet's function lies in this, that he presents things which have actually taken place transformed into other images through oblique and figurative modes of expression, adding beauty.

I now turn more particularly to the means by which the poet transforms the *gesta* in *Beowulf* and gives the historical narrative a new significance.[3] It will be useful to return to Rosemond Tuve's criticism of the *Faerie Queene.* She speaks of Spenser's employment of classical symbols, such as the golden apples, which

evoke all those sad stretches of human history when men's concupiscence, for power of all kinds, had brought all the great typical 'ensaumples of mind intemperate' to their various eternities of frustrated desire. He uses what he calls 'the present fate' of these long-dead persons to tell the powerful who have *not* yet left their mortal state for that other, 'how to use their present state'; this is evidence that he wishes us to read allegorically of the relations between a virtue Temperance and what can happen to a soul, and not

---

[1] E. Curtius, *European Literature and the Latin Middle Ages,* p. 49.

[2] Isidore, *Etymologiae,* ed. W. M. Lindsay; *De Poetis,* Book 8b, 7.

[3] I do not of course imply that he was working with raw historical material; no doubt a good deal of transformation had been effected by the oral poets who transmitted the matter.

merely morally of a character Guyon and his confrontation of covetous desires.[1]

One cannot press the analogy with the *Faerie Queene* very far, but some of Tuve's observations appear to me also appropriate to *Beowulf*. The poem is undoubtedly addressed to the powerful and is designed to warn them of the dangers attendant upon power; I believe that the hero's 'confrontation of covetous desires' when he fights for the buried hoard is to be read as an image of the soul's struggle and not merely morally of a character Beowulf. Tuve reminds us that the images carry their history with them, to deepen the conviction 'that all things though fully present to the senses are meaningful beyond what sense reports'.[2] The dusty gold of Mammon's cave has a long line of predecessors, among which I do not think it wrong to place the rust-eaten treasures for which Beowulf fought. The modern reader is unhappily ill-equipped with material in which to trace the history of the images used by the *Beowulf* poet, but some of the associations of dragon and treasure in classical and Christian writings can be recovered so as to deepen their meaning for us.

Tuve also recognizes that a poet writing in this mode must sometimes guide his readers by 'outright conceptual statement.' She cites 'Here is the fountaine of the worldes good' (*F.Q.* 7, 38).[3] The equivalent in *Beowulf* is the blunt observation,

> Sinc eaðe mæg,
> gold on grund(e),   gumcynnes gehwone
> oferhigian,   hyde se ðe wille.   (2764–6)

The audience has been prepared for this by the didactic matter in Hrothgar's admonition, which by reaching 'into the area ... of man's metaphysical situation'[4] requires the hearer to think of Beowulf's subsequent life in terms of the *bellum intestinum*. Thus Beowulf's dragon-fight can be read as an image of the interior struggle of the king with the Enemy. The symbolic significance of Beowulf's great contests will require a separate chapter: in what remains of this, I shall examine the purely

---

[1] Tuve, op. cit., pp. 32 f. See my observations above, p. 74, n. 1, on her use of the word 'allegory'.
[2] Tuve, ibid., p. 32.   [3] ibid.   [4] ibid., p. 17.

secular symbols which the poet makes the instruments of his purpose.

It is rather obvious that the rhythmic, alliterative, and syntactic frames within which an Anglo-Saxon poet has to work inhibit precise utterance; the compound word is more useful to him than the corresponding phrase, and inevitably less specific; a range of interchangeable words is required by the metre, so that fine distinctions are worn away; and the traditional vocabulary is relatively small. All these handicaps notwithstanding, a satisfying communication is apparently achieved; and this can only be through the lighting-up of part of the spectrum of associations shared by poet and audience. As Vansina's observations showed, traditional oral poetry is one means by which a people preserves its social stability and its cultural ideals. The associations of the stylized diction are familiar and predictable, and necessarily so. This was presumably true of the oral poetry of the heathen Anglo-Saxons. But upon their conversion to Christianity, they did not discard their inherited poetry. A very strange state of affairs is thus brought about when the traditional diction serves both the old and the new ideals. It is not simply that the vocabulary has to be enlarged and adapted; more curious and interesting is that it has to accommodate the paradoxes of Christianity: that man's home is *elpeodigra eard*,[1] that the strong are weak and the rich poor, that the tangible sword snaps and the helmet splits, but the invisible shield of faith endures. The trappings of life remain as before and the poets retain the words for them, but their significance as symbols becomes ambivalent. In general, symbols of magnificence and grandeur will take on connotations of pride and mutability, and symbols of military prowess connotations of strife and vainglory. In addition, the old vocabulary is analogically stretched to provide a language for the invisible and eternal world. Words like *woroldcyning*, *wuldorfull*, *dream* and *dom* take on two aspects, changing as the poet shortens or lengthens his focus. *Beowulf* as a poem about the departed world has its own particular ambivalence.

---

[1] cp. *The Seafarer* (38) where the paradox is exploited by the poet. See also the discussion of the phrase by P. L. Henry in *The Early English and Celtic Lyric* (Belfast, 1966), pp. 195 ff., following up a suggestion by Professor C. L. Wrenn.

The Marriage of Traditions

There are, I suggest, a number of objects, persons and actions in the narrative to which the term symbol (in Nowottny's sense) can be applied, because they are given prominence in a manner not actually called for by the movement of the plot: such objects as Scyld's funeral boat, Grendel's hand, Hrethel's sword, such persons as Heremod and Hama, such actions as the arming of Beowulf.[1] For convenience in discussing them, it will be useful to class these symbols according as they have primarily religious, mythic,[2] social, or contextual significance. The categories are not, of course, exclusive: the second may impinge on the first, and the fourth embraces the others. The first three are probably inherited by the poet with his source material, the last comes as near as this public poetry allows to revealing the personal concerns of the poet. His interests are indicated by the selection and disposition of the material to hand; the relative importance accorded to the life of Sigemund and the funeral of Hnæf, for example, can be taken as evidence of particular preoccupations of the author, since neither is demanded by the action. I take for granted that once the Creator is introduced into the narrative, a perspective is opened through the whole history of the created world; the natural elements may speak of their Maker and the historical events speak of his purposes.

The poem opens with praise of the might of the Danes *in geardagum*, represented through the symbolic person of Scyld.[3] It is remarkable that the mysterious and exciting life of this royal hero is so slightly treated in comparison with his obsequies. The episode of the child in the boat, which as an ancient mythic, or social, symbolic motif may have recorded in a veiled form a profound change in the Danish way of life, is used by the poet chiefly to illustrate the power of God in effecting reversals of fortune and bringing comfort to the afflicted. The reversal of fortune is pointed by the contrast of the two boats, but of the

---

[1] Of the objects and persons mentioned, Grendel's greedy and grasping hand and Hrethel's symbol of prowess require no special comment; for Heremod, cp. pp. 184 ff., for Hama, p. 91, for Beowulf's weapons and armour, pp. 86 f.; Scyld's funeral boat is treated here.

[2] I use the word *mythic* here in the sense 'pertaining to an anonymous story telling of origins and destinies'; cp. R. Wellek and A. Warren, *Theory of Literature*, 3rd ed. (Peregrine Books, 1963), p. 191. Under this definition both Scyld and Cain are mythic symbolic persons.

[3] *In geardagum* (1) is to be noted, as clearly placing the story in remote time.

two only the funeral ship is fully described, so that Scyld's mysterious origins and subsequent prosperity are quite over-shadowed by the scene of his death. The *heiti* for God, *Liffrea* (*auctor vitæ*),[1] places emphasis on the fact that the provision of an heir for Scyld and the continuation of the royal line were signs of God's care for the unhappy nation; the second name, *wuldres Wealdend* (17),[2] may have the double aspect I have spoken of, praising the Lord who dispensed earthly glory to Scyld as well as the Lord who rules in Glory in his heavenly Kingdom. The effect of the two phrases in conjunction is like that of the prayer *Deus, et temporalis vitæ auctor et æternæ, miserere.* ...[3] In birth and in death, man lies in God's hand: this is the affirmation made by the poet as he surveys the pagan king's prosperous career and magnificent parting from life. By this simple means he opens the perspective of eternity, and the brilliant foreground picture of Scyld's costly foreign spoils shades from a symbol of magnificent power into a symbol of transience.

The funeral ship is one of the most memorable secular symbols of the poem: *isig and utfus* (33), it gathers into itself the human feelings which accompany death. Both epithets have figurative meaning, icy coldness evoking misery, the readiness for a journey figuring the parting from life; nevertheless it would

---

[1] For Latin equivalents to the OE names for God, see F. Klaeber 'Die Christlichen Elemente im *Beowulf*'. He draws upon the liturgy and Latin hymnaries and the earlier work of J. W. Rankin, 'A Study of the Kennings in Anglo-Saxon poetry'.

[2] Rankin, op. cit. notes the parallel development of Latin *gloria* in Christian use.

[3] The prayer quoted is among *Orationes tempore belli* in *The Gelasian Sacramentary* (ed. H. A. Wilson, London, 1893, pp. 275 f.). It reads:

Deus, et temporalis vitae auctor et aeternae, miserere supplicium in tua protectione fidentium, ut per virtute brachii tui omnibus qui nobis adversantur revictis, nec in terrenis nec a caelestibus possimus excludi.

O God, author of life both temporal and eternal, have mercy upon the suffering of the faithful within thy protection, that we, having conquered through the strength of thine arm all who oppose us, may not be hindered in things earthly nor from things heavenly.

It is not possible to establish whether this particular prayer was in use where the *Beowulf* poet was educated, but rather similar prayers also occur in *The Gregorian Sacramentary* revised by Alcuin (ed. H. A. Wilson, London, 1915). In both prayer-books the enemy attacks are attributed to the sins of the nation. (e.g. *Gelasian*, p. 273, *Gregorian*, pp. 198 f.) For the circulation of these two prayer-books, see Deansely, *Pre-Conquest Church*, pp. 156–9. My point is that such prayers represent a current attitude towards God's giving or withholding success in war which is relevant to the whole of *Beowulf*.

be wrong, I think, to empty them of literal meaning;[1] the boat shining with ice and straining at the mooring-ropes is beautiful, as the treasure is brilliant, because the poet is keenly aware of the beauty of the created world and the works of men's hands. It is the great strength of *Beowulf* as a poem that it does not become abstract. What more does the poet achieve with the boat-symbol? Some of its potency depends perhaps on its universal significance; it is not simply a reminiscence of an ancient custom (which a Christian poet could hardly wish to revive for its own sake), but as Cope says,

The boat is a universal symbol connected with both birth and death —cradle and coffin are alike special cases of a boat. We are reminded of such diverse examples as the boat-crib of Moses and the ship-burials of Germanic peoples right back to the Bronze Age.[2]

As universal symbols framing a life, Scyld's two boats form a brilliant contrast between the destitution of the child and the wealth of the old man. But even here there are ironic undertones. The use of litotes (43–4) sets up in the mind two opposed possibilities; the words assert what the syntax denies, that Scyld in death was no better furnished than the destitute child. The reader of The Book of Job who remembers the words, *Nudus egressus sum de utero matris meæ, et nudus revertar illuc* 'Naked came I out of my mother's womb, and naked shall I return thither' (Job 1: 21) will be well aware that the treasure passed into the sea's keeping; though Scyld remained *on Frean wære* (27). This latter phrase seems deliberately chosen to stress God's continuous governance of mankind without introducing the issue of salvation.[3]

Other ships appear in the course of the narrative, the return of a treasure-laden keel serving as a sign of victory and the victor's reward in the stories of Sigemund and Hengest as well as

[1] E. G. Stanley, in 'OE poetic diction and the interpretation of *The Wanderer, The Seafarer*, and *The Penitent's Prayer*', *Angl.* 73 (1955) 441, suggests that *isig* (*Beow.* 33) is the equivalent of *winterceald*, figuratively evocative of sorrow. However, there seems no good reason also to reject the literal 'icy', since the season of Scyld's death is not otherwise mentioned, and the beginning of spring with its breaking-up of the ice would fit the circumstances.

[2] Gilbert Cope, *Symbolism in the Bible and the Church*, p. 36.

[3] The word *wær* is used of God's covenant with Abraham in the OE *Genesis* (2204); apart from its general sense of 'protection' here it may therefore have associations suggesting a pre-Christian man's relationship with God.

the story of Heorot. The faint memory of the loading of Scyld's treasure-ship may intrude its shadow in these other scenes; it is very striking that the piling of the treasure round the dead man is much more fully treated than Scyld's death, and of actual funeral rites there is nothing at all. The ships in the poem are not described objectively; like Scyld's cold and deathly funeral ship, the others reflect some of the emotions of the seamen. Beowulf's ship beginning the adventure presses on eagerly, and Hengest's ship is the prisoner of winter.[1] Of itself, Scyld's funeral ship could hardly act as *memento mori* in the way I have suggested, but the dark shadow is soon reinforced by other scenes in which the splendour of gold is accompanied by the thought of death.

The second great symbol of the poem is the royal hall which Scyld's descendant Hrothgar caused to be built. The narrative moves with great economy through the king's ancestry and his early successes in war, so that the building of Heorot becomes the dominant feature of the king's life-story. Hrothgar conceives the idea of having his men build the largest hall in the world, where he will hold court and dispense his bounty (67–73). The huge project needs the labours of craftsmen from many nations, and when it is finished it is a towering landmark (81 f.). He names it *Heorot*, and lives liberally and in convivial splendour within, at the centre of his great court. Heorot is a monument to Hrothgar's power, success and wealth. He is a good and generous ruler, and as a social symbol Heorot reflects nothing but the greatness of the king. Its name 'Hart' appears to connote royalty,[2] the descriptive terms *horngeap* (82) and *hornreced* (704), whatever their literal meanings, help to build an image of the majestic beast with wide-curving antlers, *hornum trum* (cp. 1369). That the name Heorot has some symbolic significance we cannot doubt, for no other hall is given a name. I am inclined to relate that significance to the associations given to the beast by the

---

[1] Wind and weather likewise mirror the feelings of men, as for example in the struggle with the sea (545–8) followed by the peace and brightness of morning (569–72); when Beowulf voyages, the wind is with him (217, 1907–9).

[2] Wrenn calls attention to the bronze stag found in the Sutton Hoo deposit, apparently designed to be carried as a standard (*Beowulf*, p. 314). The use of *hornas* in *Finnsburh* (7) shows that a derived sense 'gable' had developed, but the name 'Heorot' would surely recall the older meaning of *horn*. The epithet *banfag* (780) also brings the stag to mind.

Latin fabulists and later woven into the Bestiaries, because these associations consort remarkably well with what I take to be the *Beowulf* poet's view of splendid palaces. Some years ago, C. S. Lewis offered the suggestion that a fable by Phædrus perhaps had something to do with Beowulf's dragon.[1] The evidence concerning the dragon is discussed in Chapter 4. I do not wish to anticipate that argument here, because the connection is at best unproven, but if the one fabled beast is acceptable, so perhaps is the other. In any case, the moral meaning which Phædrus and later fabulists found in the hart is one which any hunter of a reflective turn of mind might independently reach when he came upon a stag caught in a thicket. The animal's stance suggests pride in his spreading antlers, and when he is trapped by them, the moralist would find it hard to resist the thought that his pride was his undoing.[2] Is it too far-fetched to suppose that Heorot's towering gables drew Grendel to its doors and so brought death among the Danes?

It is convenient here to mention in passing that the hart as a Christian religious symbol deriving from Psalm 41:2, *Sicut cervus desiderat ad fontes aquarum ita desiderat anima mea ad te Deus* 'As the hart panteth after the fountains of waters, so my soul panteth after thee, O God', seems to me to be unrelated to Heorot. The hard-pressed hart of line 1369 is more problematical. An Anglo-Saxon educated as I have described could not fail to know this symbol for the thirsting soul, but it is not drawn into the allegory of Beowulf.[3]

What I am suggesting is that the symbolism of the name Heorot could reinforce the moral attitude conveyed by the poet's juxtaposition of its building and its coming ruin (74–85). It was regal and magnificent, and as durable as good craftsmen could make it (cp. 770–82) but the poet reminds his hearers that within the lifetime of the builders it was maliciously destroyed by fire (cp. 781 f.). Thus the social symbol summing up the

[1] C. S. Lewis, *The Discarded Image*, p. 152.

[2] See *The Fables of Phaedrus*, ed. C. H. Nall (London, 1895), pp. 7 f., *Cervus ad Fontem*.

[3] As Augustine's examples showed, a biblical scholar had no difficulty in accepting contrary meanings for the same symbol in different contexts. D. W. Robertson finds in the hunted hart a symbol of the faithful soul which will not enter the waters of cupidity; for discussion of Robertson's argument, see pp. 120 f., below.

magnificence of a line of great kings is altered by a single stroke into a symbol of *þeos læne gesceaft* in which nothing endures. It may also, as I have suggested elsewhere, act as an eschatological symbol, bringing to mind a subject zealously treated by Anglo-Saxon poets, namely the destruction of the cities of earth and the engulfing of the wealth of kings by the devouring fire which was expected to bring the world to an end in some not distant time.[1]

Contextually, Heorot acts as an image of the Danish court, first in its splendour, then in its uselessness during Grendel's persecution of the Danes. At the conclusion of the Grendel story, the hall bears the marks of Grendel's ferocious strength (997–1000). The cracks and breaks are partly masked by gold hangings which are brought out for the feast of celebration. On the surface, the court at Heorot is brilliant and splendid, but half-hidden enmities are hinted (1017–19) and as the company assembles for the feast, the author, in a rather longer moral statement than he usually permits himself, speaks of death:

> No þæt yðe byð
> to befleonne, fremme se þe wille,
> ac gesecan sceal sawlberendra,
> nyde genydde, niþða bearna,
> grundbuendra gearwe stowe,
> þær his lichoma legerbedde fæst
> swefeþ æfter symle. (1002–8)

By his brilliant placing of two quite commonplace images, escaping from death and sleeping after the feast of life,[2] the poet makes his hearers aware that just as Grendel vainly ran away from death over the wastes, and now after his monstrous feasting lies asleep in death, so the Danes, sitting now at the table, rejoicing that the shadow has been lifted from Heorot with the defeat of Grendel, have not escaped death after all, because the feud is not over (cp. 1251–5). And the Grendel feud has its echo in the bloody thoughts of Hrothulf which at a later time end Hrothgar's renewed hopes of a settled time of peace

---

[1] cp. The Judgment scene in *Christ* II, especially 811–14 (*ASPR* III, 25), also *Phoenix* 500–8 (ibid., p. 108).

[2] A variant of the same image is used of the sea-beasts cheated of their supper and put to sleep by the sword in lines 562–7. (The *Andreas* poet also uses it of the dead cannibals (1002 f.), perhaps in imitation of *Beowulf*.)

ahead. The cracks in the fabric of Heorot are an image of the treacherous hatreds which are already—to judge by the setting and tone of Wealhtheow's speech (1162–91)—making rifts in the concord of the kinsmen.

The other royal halls which appear in the poem have no recognizable identity. The Geatish royal hall is burnt down by the dragon without any preliminary description of it or prophecy of its destruction. These facts make the emphasis on Hrothgar's hall more striking and justify my inclusion of it among the symbols of the poem. The furnishings of the hall consist of ornamental hangings, a high seat, benches, beds and pillows, and drinking-cups. Some of these may be inferred to have symbolic significance, since the poet does not describe them as objects interesting in themselves and there is no detailed account of feasting or ceremonial. For example, the passing of the cup honours the king's guests, and with this piece of social ritual the poet succeeds in giving an impression of civilized conviviality.

Deeper meaning seems possible in two particular objects belonging to social life, namely the *gifstol* of line 168, and the *fæted wæge* of line 2282, which was brought from the dragon's hoard. I postpone discussion of the *gifstol* to Chapter 4, because the interpretation of the word has bearing upon the poet's conception of Grendel. The gilded cup could have come into the story simply as the cause of contention between the dragon and the Geats, but the symbolism of the cup in religious writing seems to indicate an allegorical significance; I believe it to be a reminder of Adam's *poculum mortis* and, as such, a symbol of cupidity. My reasons for looking upon it in this way are bound up with exegetical interpretation of the war with the Serpent-Dragon, which is treated apropos of Beowulf's contest in Chapter 7.

Swords and armour have an important place in the poem. Their costly materials and fine workmanship are often praised by the poet, and he records, without adverse comment, that Beowulf's mail-coat was Weland's work and that three of the swords were forged by the giants; he also describes the boar-images which surmounted the warriors' helmets as protective talismans. One may guess that these three elements were more prominent in his source-material, since they smack of heathen superstition and magic, if not of pagan worship. They add an exciting air of antiquity to the story and there is no sign that the poet himself believed in their magical power. His obvious veneration for great craftsmanship is a very different matter, enhancing the stature of the heroes and magnifying the perilous adventures in which even these stout accoutrements failed those who bore them.

The poet's attitude to the boar-figures which adorned his warriors' helmets has some interest for his handling of a remnant of pagan superstition in the poem. Beowulf's own helmet, rather fully described in the careful preparations for his dive into the mere, had boar-figures round its crown:

> swa hine fyrndagum
> worhte wæpna smið, wundrum teode,
> besette swinlicum, þæt hine syðþan no
> brond ne beadomecas bitan ne meahton. (1451-4)

The ancient smiths believed in the protective power of the boar, but if one looks rather closely at the poem, one observes that nowhere in the action does the wearing of such a helmet affect the course of events. There is instead a mute denial of the power of the boar in the scene of Hnæf's funeral, where the slain men's gold-adorned helmets lie on the pyre:

> Æt þæm ade wæs eþgesyne
> swatfah syrce, swyn ealgylden,
> eofer irenheard, æþeling manig
> wundum awyrded; sume on wæle crungon. (1110-13)

Shields are surprisingly unimportant in *Beowulf*, until one remembers that Beowulf prefers to wrestle, and there are otherwise very few of the conventional cut-and-thrust combats of battle in the poem. The one memorable shield is the huge device which protected both Beowulf and Wiglaf from the dragon's fire (2675-7). Its function was to give cover to Beowulf until he was near enough to strike at the dragon, and this it did, but, like his sword, it failed him at the last (2570-2). I have already published[1] the opinion that the great shield represents the strongest human defence a man can make, and that its

---

[1] In 'The Christian Perspective in *Beowulf*', *Brodeur Studies*, p. 85.

meaning in the allegory is that without spiritual defences (*scutum fidei*)[1] no man can successfully oppose the Dragon. The development of this religious aspect of the poem is treated in Chapters 6 and 7 below.

The sword is a potent symbol of varying significance in *Beowulf*. In the society depicted, a good sword is a sign of the prowess of the wearer; such are Unferth's Hrunting, lent to Beowulf in recognition that the Geat was the better man, and the sword of Hrethel presented to the hero on his triumphant return from Heorot. Probably also traditional is the use of a sword as signal of a re-kindling feud: such are the sword which roused Hengest, the sword which incited Ingeld's man to kill his father's slayer, and the sword *Eanmundes laf* which Wiglaf bore. This last example is contextually used to very subtle effect, drawing together the scattered incidents which had marked the progress of the Geatish feud with the Swedes during Beowulf's lifetime, and representing—in something the same fashion as the cracks in the walls of Heorot—at the moment when the dragon is felled, the imminent strife with the Swedes which will make an end of the tribe.

The swords which Beowulf possesses all fail him, and my observations on the iron shield in the allegory would apply also to the sword. In a quite different category is the sword which Beowulf found in the underwater hall. With this giant-made sword he beheaded his giant adversaries, and in so doing destroyed the sword, save for the curiously-patterned hilt which he took back to Heorot. I regard this as an important element in the allegory. As a symbol of the prowess of the giants, its wasting away in the corrosive blood of the slain Grendel kin has an obvious significance, but the enduring hilt brought back to the world of men has a much more complex story to tell. The ramifications of this story of the feud of the giants with God will be explored in my next chapter.

The giant sword is not said to have had magical power, nor is magical immunity offered as a reason for Hrunting's failure to bite on the giantess's hide.[2] The audience is left to think that

---

[1] cp. Eph. 6: 16.
[2] The swords of Eofor and Wiglaf are also described as *eotenisc* (2616, 2979), so the word obviously carried no necessary connotation of magical properties—for

the extraordinary weight of the ancient weapon gave Beowulf's blow the necessary force. The description of its melting blade merits special notice: the poet has focused attention upon it by his simile of the melting of icicles in the spring. The simile, beautiful and apt as it is for the change that comes over the hard iron, is remarkable in another respect. The presence of God in this dark infernal place *under gynne grund* (1551) is gradually manifested, first by the line,

> rodera Rædend   hit on ryht gesced,   (1555)

then by the appearance of light as bright as day,

> efne swa of hefene   hadre scineð
> rodores candel.[1]   (1571 f.)

Then, with the simile I have mentioned, thought of the Father's control over all times and seasons turns the mind away from the curious wonder of the melting blade to the annual miracle of melting ice, and the giant sword and the power of the giant race become small in the comparison.

Beowulf carries the hilt of the wonderful sword to Heorot, together with Grendel's head, and in presenting these trophies to Hrothgar he ascribes his escape from the monster to God's protection (1658) and his sight of the giant weapon to God's favour (1661–2). The hilt is described: it is decorated with serpentine patterning and runic letters. Thus an aura of mysterious and malevolent antiquity is created about it, and at its centre is the engraved picture of God's retribution on the giants in the days of Noah. I pass over for the present the meaning of this backward extension of the feud with the giants into Old Testament times, to show the complex of symbolic meaning given to the giant sword, which is for the Danes a symbol of victorious revenge in the feud, for Beowulf a symbol of God's protective care for those who fight in his battles, and for the

---

Eofor at least fought in ordinary human wars. Grendel had put a spell upon swords (804), but he uses no magical arts against Beowulf, so he is hardly more of a magician than the ancient princes who wove a spell about the hoard (3051 ff. and 3069 ff.). That Anglo-Saxons of the period believed in the power of incantations may be inferred from the Act of the synod of *Clofesho* (747) which commands the bishop to travel about his diocese forbidding pagan observances, including incantations. (cited by Whitelock, *Audience*, p. 79.)

[1] The significance of the light in the allegory is further discussed in Chapter 8.

audience a symbol of the enduring cosmic war in which Beowulf's contests are brief incidents.

Weapons and armour, being costly and valued possessions, also appear in the poem as a species of wealth. Like the *beagas* which are prized as much for the status they confer upon the wearer as for their intrinsic value, the splendid accoutrements are symbols of social relationships in the society depicted. They signal the munificence of the royal giver as much as the worth and deserts of the great warrior who receives them. The poet openly approves the ancestral custom of dispensing rich gifts from the throne,[1] and considerable attention is given to the princely gifts which were conferred on Beowulf in recognition of his triumphs.[2] To a Christian poet, riches were the means through which a man could exercise the virtue of charitable giving and therefore were not invariably evil, but as the cupidity of man was potent for harm, great treasures were a source of danger. The evil which treasure could beget was both moral and spiritual, as causing violent quarrels for possession, and as contaminating the soul of the possessor. The *Beowulf* poet treats all these aspects of treasure while not losing sight of its social importance, principally by emphasizing the brevity of a man's possession of costly objects, and by making them the focal point in stories of bloodshed and death. The spiritual danger inherent in accumulated wealth is a major theme in the latter part of the poem.

Standing out among the regal gifts described in the tale of Heorot is the *healsbeah* (1195) which Queen Wealhtheow gave to Beowulf. Like the sword *Eanmundes laf* (2611) in the later story of the Geats, it acts as a linking symbol in a series of historical incidents. The necklace stands as a symbol for treasure as plunder, in the way that Eanmund's sword stands as a symbol of fraternal strife.

The necklace given to Beowulf reflects nothing but glory on the hero; in the social sphere it speaks of his pre-eminent achievements, in the moral sphere it shows him untouched by personal vanity or covetousness, since he does not try to keep it for himself. Hygelac later received it, and wore it on the plundering

---

[1] See, for example, line 80 f. and cp. 20 f.

[2] The whole passage from line 1020 to 1055 describes the rewards given to Beowulf and his men.

expedition which cost him his life. His premature death set in train the events which led to the death of Eanmund and the resurgence of Swedish power and enmity which Beowulf's own reign could only temporarily hold back. At the level of historical narrative therefore, the necklace serves as a useful means of uniting the histories of the Danes and the Geats. At the moral level it points the contrast between Beowulf and Hygelac. It is also made to act as a symbol of the vanity of human life. Between the queen's presentation (1192–6) and the applause of the company (1214) are sandwiched two stories of robbery and death[1] which dim the brightness of the jewel in just the way that the prophecy of consuming flame casts the shadow of death over gold-adorned Heorot (80–5).

The first of these interposed stories remains very obscure, since the incident of the necklace does not occur in any of the legends concerning Hama which survive in later German and Norse epic and saga.[2] The allusion is made still more obscure by the vagueness of the two phrases *to þære byrhtan byrig* (1199) and *geceas ecne ræd* (1201). The identity of the *burg* is quite unknown, and the meaning of the latter phrase is doubtful. In the present state of knowledge, one can only conjecture what the poet intended by the reference to Hama. Comparison with the structurally rather similar treatment of Sigemund and Heremod (874–915) suggests that some contrast between Hama and Hygelac is intended; the line

>   syþðan he for wlenco   wean ahsode   (1206)

---

[1] It is likely that some of the poet's audience would sympathize with the plundering. Guthlac's early life was spent in such enterprises, and his biographer Felix shows no disapproval (since he gave back a third part of his booty), *Vita Guthlaci*, ed. cit., p. 80. The author of *Guthlac* A, on the other hand, describes how the saint's evil angel incites him to join a raiding band,

>   swa doð wræcmæcgas
>   þa þe ne bimurnað   monnes feore
>   þæs þe him to honda   huþe gelædeð
>   butan hy þy reafe   rædan motan.   (129–32)

It was presumably one of the tasks of the early Anglo-Saxon church to dissuade young princes from taking up a life of pillage.

[2] For a general survey of the references to Hama in early literature, see R. W. Chambers, *Widsith* (Cambridge, 1912), pp. 52–7. The sources seem to be agreed that Hama lived by plunder and that he acquired treasure; in *Widsith* he rules with Wudga over a people (129–30), which may suggest, as Chambers thinks (p. 223), that 'the bright city' of *Beowulf* (1199) was his own stronghold.

implies an adverse judgment on the king's action, which would support any interpretation of Hama as an admirable person in spite of his carrying off the Brosings' (Brísings'?) necklace. The unpleasant word *searoniðas* (1200) alienates sympathy from the wronged Eormenric, and the phrase *geceas ecne ræd* seems to imply that he made a good end.[1] Whatever the lost details of the story, the effect of the two interposed incidents is undoubtedly to remind the hearers that man's possession of wealth is short-lived in the perspective of eternal reward. I think it can be seen that the poet deliberately created this effect, because he has separated the matter of the robbing of Hygelac's corpse on the battlefield from Beowulf's reminiscent account of his revenge on the despoiler (2503 f.). In the more natural later position, the incident would have enhanced Beowulf's reputation as an ideal retainer and winner of treasure rather better than in its present place: one cannot avoid the conclusion that the notes of tragic irony in the happy scene at Heorot were integral to the poet's theme, and that praise of Beowulf was only one element in that theme.

I come now to the last of the great secular symbols of the poem, and the most controversial in significance: the burial mound with its hidden treasure-hoard. There are only two such monuments in the poem, the one inhabited by the dragon, and the other raised over Beowulf's ashes as his memorial. This fact is in itself worth remarking. The other heroes whose death is recorded have no memorial; for Hnæf and his kinsmen there is no compensatory ritual of remembrance, only the ugly bursting of their bodies in the flame, and their epitaph: *wæs hira blæd scacen* (1124). Beowulf's *blæd* would be remembered as long as the mound remained on *Hronesness* (cp. 2800–8), and in a secular society that is the most that a man could ask or deserve. The poet's interest in funerals does not involve him in repetitions; each is different in conception and effect. Scyld's passing speaks of the mystery of the unknown otherworld, Hnæf's pyre is a frightening image of physical destruction, Beowulf's funeral fire is blotted out by the great beacon of earth which is his grave and his glory.

The feature common to all three funeral descriptions is the placing of treasure with the dead, and the Christian poet does

[1] The phrase is discussed with similar phrases in Chapter 5, pp. 167 ff., below.

not censure the practice. He speaks through the treasure itself. Scyld's vast wealth goes into unknown hands (50–2), Hnæf's treasure is swallowed up in the devouring fire (1122–4). Only of Beowulf's hard-won gold does the poet say in his own voice,

> forleton eorla gestreon   eorðan healdan,
> gold on greote,   þær hit nu gen lifað
> eldum swa unnyt   swa h(it ær)or wæs.   (3166–8)

This is a kind of epitaph upon the treasure; consigned to earth, it is seen at the last to be intrinsically worthless, though a man should give his life for it.

The burial of a treasure within the new-made tomb which the dragon afterwards made his lair is an incident which belongs to a different imaginary world from the rest of the poem. The other funeral-treasures belong to the heroic world as it was remembered; the Sutton Hoo burial might have been within living memory when *Beowulf* was composed,[1] and other less elaborately furnished graves were possibly known to the poet and those he wrote for; *gold on greote* was no imaginary thing. Though the Sutton Hoo deposit appears to have been a cenotaph, it is presumed that the grave goods were intended for the use of their royal owner in the next world. The burial of the treasure which became the dragon's hoard is, in contrast, a motiveless gesture, irrational in a different way from the second burial of the same treasure, since among the pagan Geats such an action could be thought to honour their king.

My justification for taking this view of the burial of the dragon's hoard lies in the nature of the character who commits it to the grave. He does not exist as a quasi-historical person like the other characters in the poem. His nearest kin is the nameless old man who grieves for his hanged son (2444 ff.). The nameless father can be absorbed into the narrative, because he exists only in a simile. He is a literary device and pretends to be nothing more. But the man who buries the treasure inhabits the same world as the exile and the wise man in *The Wanderer*.[2] They are faceless speakers invented by the poets to give utterance to some universal human feeling. Each is a *persona* of the poet, given no

---

[1] For a convenient survey of articles on the Sutton Hoo Ship-Burial, see the Supplement by C. L. Wrenn to R. W. Chambers, *Beowulf: An Introduction*, 3rd edition.   [2] See p. 2, above.

more individuality than his condition requires—in this they differ sharply from dramatic characters who speak in soliloquy, or the central figures in dramatic monologues. The uncomfortable truth about the man who buries the hoard is that he too is a literary device, but he needs to be more than this, because the story of the rifled hoard begins with him. He has to be believed in, like Scyld or Sigemund, as a remote historical person, but the poet has here allowed his theme to take charge of the narrative, and the beautiful elegy almost blinds one to the unreality of the whole episode.

The ritual action has no other celebrants, and no social or religious significance. Professor Smithers has interestingly argued that this scene is the garbling of a pagan story in which the last owner of the treasure was himself transformed into a dragon —as happened to several Norsemen in similar circumstances, according to the sagas.[1] But one has to admit that the *Beowulf* poet has altogether erased any possible former connection between man and dragon, and the critical problem remains. The burial of the treasure of a lost tribe is the improbable excuse for the lament *Heald þu nu hruse* ... (2247–66). Man must return the treasure to earth because no other has claim upon it. It is an image signifying that the worth of gold-plated sword and goblet, helmet and armour derives from their use by men. When the heroes are dead, their treasures begin to decay. Inert, tarnished and crumbling, the buried treasure becomes for the poet a focal symbol for the transience of the material world. A critic may carp, but the bold device succeeds. Before Beowulf sets out to win the hoard, the poet has planted doubt as to whether it is worth the winning. In the outcome, his victory does not ameliorate the lot of anyone concerned, and the second burial of the treasure symbolically re-enacts the tragedy of the lost race.

The hoard, as I see it, is from the outset conceived as a symbol of transience. Another element in the conception is indicated by the epithet *hæðen* (2216, 2276). The word is elsewhere applied to Grendel and to the idolatrous Danes; the use of it for the treasure might be an oblique condemnation of the pagan custom of burying grave goods, but it undoubtedly gives a general atmosphere of evil to the hoard.

[1] G. V. Smithers, *The Making of Beowulf*, p. 11; see also p. 103, below.

I come now to the most curious aspect of the treasure-hoard as symbol, the curse upon it. The oddity about the curse is that the poet makes no good use of it, and it becomes a literary blemish. Without it, there is a satisfying moral sequence; with it, there is a conflict of causes which obscures the circumstances of Beowulf's end. I have shown that this hoard was from the first mention associated with death; the imagined owner, with a sentimental attachment to his possessions which the Anglo-Saxon audience might find understandable, made a grave for the treasure of his dead tribe. The consequence of his act was the appearance of the dragon, and ultimately Beowulf's death and the ruin of the Geatish people stem from the burial of the hoard. The curse, as it is reported, sealed up the gold in the tomb until God should grant the power to touch it to some man of his choosing (3051–7). It looks as though the poet was working with intractable material, since his faith required an affirmation of God's power to break the ancient spell, but his moral and his religious theme are considerably weakened by the existence of the spell, and even more by the proviso that God could prevent its dire effect. One may wonder why he kept the curse in the story at all. Two reasons suggest themselves: the first, that the heathen *þeodnas mære*, by invoking evil powers to protect their hoard (3069 f.), were thought to have called the dragon into being; the second, more prosaic, possibility is that the curse was a well-known feature of the given story which the poet felt obliged to include. Having brought it in, he could make no effective use of it, since if Beowulf was estranged from God it needed no curse to consign him to hell-bonds, and if on the other hand he remained uncorrupted by the gold, he retained his Lord's favour and would be divinely protected from the curse. An operative curse belongs to a poem of a different kind, in which the characters are unwitting victims of fate, and such a conception could not be harmonized with the doctrine of God's watchful care for mankind expressly affirmed more than once in *Beowulf*.

The inconsistency between the *þeodnas mære* who sang the incantation and the lone survivor who buried the hoard is a very clear sign that in this part of the poem the author's thoughts were dominated by his theme, to the detriment of the

95

narrative. Uppermost is the doctrine that the burial of the hoard was itself a wrong action. The lone survivor's imagined gesture and the curse upon despoilers each sprang from men's desire to store up possessions even when they have no use for them. This is the characteristic desire of the dragon of European fable, as will be shown in the next chapter. Every pile of gold is potentially dangerous to mankind, as readers of St Antony's Life were reminded, for when the saint found gold in his path he passed by as though going over fire, knowing it for another temptation of the Enemy.[1]

I think it is fair to conclude from the transformation of the secular materials I have described that the poet was very much aware of the ambivalence of his symbols, which reflect the paradox of earthly life as it was then understood. The two great symbols, Heorot and the treasure, embody the magnificence and the wealth which are a hero's reward. But in the longer perspective they can be seen to be the images of man's pride and cupidity, the two fundamental sins which tie the carnal man to earth. To their possessors they seem to be durable; to the Christian audience they are presented as brilliant and destructible, costly and without worth.

[1] Athanasius, *Vita S. Antonii*, PG 26, 862.

4 *The Nature of the Adversaries*

(i) *The Giants*

The creatures who haunt Heorot are portrayed as cannibal giants who frequent the fens, moors and wastelands, places shunned by men. They inhabit a strange hall at the bottom of a lake, to which they carry off their human prey. Though bestial in habit, they are understood to be human beings who hate their own kind.[1] Grendel is mortal. His soul leaves his body when Beowulf has wounded him:

> siððan dreama leas
> in fenfreoðo   feorh alegde
> hæþene sawle;   þær him hel onfeng.   (850–2)

His dam is despatched with a sword-stroke that breaks her neck, after a fight in which she uses a knife in human fashion. As he hunts alone across the dark marshes, Grendel behaves as might be expected of a *þyrs* (426) according to the gnomic verse:

> þyrs sceal on fenne gewunian
> ana innan lande.[2]

The collection of gnomic verses from which these lines are taken is typically strung together in a loose chain of associated ideas; the author moves from bad weather to the thief who goes about in the dark, from him to the *þyrs*, and on to the woman with a secret lover. These are evidently all creatures of the night, and nothing suggests that the *þyrs* is more alien to the normal

---

[1] Though Grandel uses teeth and claws like a beast, he and his mother are credited with human emotions in the fighting.

[2] *Maxims* II, 42 f., *ASPR* VI, 56. Whitelock (*Audience*, p. 75) approves Dickins's translation, 'a *þyrs* shall inhabit the fens, alone in the depths of the country'. The last phrase is not as precise as the rendering suggests, but if any weight is placed on *ana innan lande*, a suspicion is roused that the Grendel kin are not entirely typical of the species. If, as the Danish setting implies, the original monsters were of a foreign kind, some discrepancy is not surprising.

world than the others. His habits are no further described, and the only other information we have, outside of *Beowulf*, is that a dozen or more English place-names include *þyrs* as an element, several times in combination with words meaning mere, pit, or valley, three times as part of the name of a cave.[1] The name Grendel also occurs in place-names, but there appears to be no way of determining whether it has any relation to the character of the poem, or whether it is a common noun.[2] In many respects Grendel and his dam seem to be English ogres, though they belong to a Danish story. It is hardly strange that the adversaries should have taken on characteristics familiar to the Anglo-Saxon poets during the oral circulation of the tale.

In the last few years there has been a resurgence of interest in the marvels described in the other works bound in the *Beowulf* codex,[3] and since Professor Whitelock brought to the notice of *Beowulf* scholars the curious matter of the probable English origin of the *Liber Monstrorum*,[4] with its unexpected reference to the prodigious King Higlacus of the *Getæ* who was killed by the Franks, there have been several attempts to decide how this piece of evidence changes our view of *Beowulf*. Whitelock points to the 'very odd coincidence, if it is nothing more',[5] that the *Liber Monstrorum* uses the *Letter of Alexander to Aristotle* and *The Marvels of the East*, the two books of monstrosities which accompany *Beowulf* in the tenth-century codex. However, the one solid conclusion to be drawn from the English origin of the *Liber Monstrorum* is that the eighth-century Anglo-Saxons knew the story of the death of Hygelac apart from *Beowulf*; this is a confirmation of what might have been surmised from the allusive handling of the story in the poem. There are no signs that either author knew the other's work.[6] It does not seem to me

---

[1] For an account of the place-names and their distribution, see Whitelock, *Audience*, pp. 72 f. [2] ibid., p. 66.

[3] It was first suggested by W. W. Lawrence in *Beowulf and Epic Tradition* that 'the *Wonders of the East* and the *Letter of Alexander to Aristotle* describe marvels fitly to be grouped with Grendel and his dam, with the dragon and water-monsters of *Beowulf*.'

[4] Whitelock, *Audience*, p. 46; see also Jane A. Leake, *The Geats of Beowulf*, pp. 123 f. and pp. 132 f. [5] Whitelock, *Audience*, p. 51.

[6] Leake states (ibid., p. 124) 'Thus the *Beowulf* poet utilizes the essence of the brief notice of Hygelac in the *Liber Monstrorum*, so the likelihood that he either read the

very likely that King Hygelac would have been extracted from *Beowulf* without mention of the giant Beowulf himself, quite apart from the monsters, though Whitelock offers some possible reasons for the monster-compiler's interest in Hygelac and neglect of Grendel and the dragon. I quote these reasons because they incidentally bring out the point I would wish to make, that the monsters in *Beowulf* are not in the least like the monsters in *The Marvels of the East* or any other of the Mediterranean sources mentioned:[1]

The mere fact that they were of popular, and not learned, origin, might be enough to disqualify Grendel and the dragon, and in any case the poet had given his dragon only the commonplace dragonesque characteristics, and had refrained from any precise description of Grendel's physical appearance. It would have been difficult to convey an impression of him in a few Latin sentences, and both he and the dragon might have looked tame beside some of the other monsters the author describes.[2]

The more one reads literature of the *Mirabilia* type, the more one is aware that these works have the fascination of the grotesque, like the two-headed calf at the fair; they depend upon their fantastic physical details for their appeal. In complete contrast, the adversaries in *Beowulf* are never fully visualized. There is only one point in which the learned and the native monster-descriptions coincide, and that is in the ugly light which shines from Grendel's eyes (726 f.). It is a striking feature, but

book on monsters or himself knew the local Frisian legend repeated there is very great'. This is a distortion: the *essence* of the 'monster' legend is that Hygelac was abnormally big (too big for a horse to carry), and in *Beowulf* there is only one possible reference to his size, and that very dubious, since the word *heah* (1926) may with equal probability refer to the hall.

[1] Sisam, who has made a special study of the *Beowulf* Codex, recognizes the difference between the two sorts of monster: 'Beowulf fights against monsters that lived in the imagination of the Anglo-Saxons; sea-monsters that attacked ships and swimmers; man-eating giants; a fiery dragon. There are none of the exotic monsters that a reader of Latin would meet with occasionally in Virgil, or abundantly in such texts as the *Epistola Alexandri*, the Latin *Wonders of the East*, and the *Liber Monstrorum*, of which the last two seem to be compilations made in England in early Anglo-Saxon times.' (*Structure*, p. 6.) The contrary argument offered by Leake, op. cit., pp. 132 f. disregards this difference.

[2] Whitelock, *Audience*, pp. 53.

not, I think, enough to establish a connection, when one remembers that in dark surroundings the eyes alone will catch a gleam of light and stand out as if disembodied. The eyes of Glámr the undead shepherd in *Grettissaga* strike unnatural fear into Grettir:

Nú í því, er Glámr fell, rak skýit frá tunglinu en Glámr hvesti augun upp ì móti. Ok svá hefir Grettir sagt sjálfr, at þá eina sýn hafi hann sét svá, at honum brygði við.[1]

Since this episode is the closest analogue we have to the scene of the wrestling in Heorot, in which it is said of Grendel,

> him of eagum stod
> ligge gelicost   leoht unfæger,   (726 f.)

it is a fair inference that the adversary's gleaming eyes were a traditional feature of the story, which each author has fitted to the surroundings, the eyes of the *draugr* reflecting the moonlight, the eyes of the giant glinting red in the glow of the fire so that they seem to emit flame. We have no means of knowing at what stage in the transmission of the story the detail of the frightening eyes appeared; it is quite conceivable that it had become a commonplace of horrifying tales.[2]

Mrs Nora Chadwick makes a fair case for the origin of the story of the monster-fights in 'a hereditary feud between a heroic member of a ruling Scandinavian dynasty and a closely knit group of supernatural foes, located to the east of the Baltic.'[3] The saga incidents she assembles support the observations made by Whitelock concerning the theme of the deliverance of the Danish royal hall; the historical details about the Geatish deliverer of Hrolf's hall are enough to establish an original identity between part of *Hrólfs Saga Kraka* and Beowulf's cleansing of Heorot, though the type of haunting is not at all similar. Mrs Chadwick toys with the idea that the differences have to do with the *Beowulf* poet's interest in the *Mirabilia* monsters, even throwing out the suggestion that the 'epic of Alexan-

---

[1] Text quoted from Chambers, *Beowulf: An Introduction*, p. 155.

[2] I have here assumed that *Grettissaga* and *Beowulf* are partially based on the same folk-tale; see also pp. 102 f., below.

[3] Nora K. Chadwick, 'The Monsters and Beowulf', in *The Anglo-Saxons*, ed. P. Clemoes, p. 193.

der's eastern campaign against monsters' was the immediate stimulus to the writing of *Beowulf*.[1] It will be evident from what I have already said that I find this idea quite unacceptable. If the stimulus to write *Beowulf* had been an interest in monsters *qua* monsters, the poem would surely have turned out very differently. There is, in fact, one place in the poem which obviously invites the author to display his monster-lore, and the chance is not taken. The *untydras* who are the progeny of Cain are merely named:

> eotenas ond ylfe   ond orcneas.   (112)

What could have been done with this passage is clearly shown by the twelfth-century German *Genesis und Exodus*, quoted by Emerson, in which a great many monsters from Isidore of Seville's *Etymologiæ* make an ill-assorted posterity for Cain.[2]

Professor James Carney discusses the short list of Cain's progeny in *Beowulf* at some length, in an attempt to prove that the *Beowulf* poet used an Irish source for this passage. His argument has two main planks: one, that the spellings *cames* (altered to *caines* 107) and *camp* (an obvious error for *cam* 1261) show an attribution of the monstrous progeny to Ham (Cham) instead of Cain, as in some Irish documents; two, that the list of only four kinds of progeny is paralleled by a similar list of four in the Irish *Sex Ætates Mundi*[3] (preserved in manuscripts of the eleventh

---

[1] ibid., p. 200.

[2] O. F. Emerson, 'Legends of Cain, especially in Old and Middle English', p. 833; cp. J. Carney, *Studies in Irish Literature and History*, pp. 103 ff.

[3] The Irish short list of the progeny is explained by Carney (pp. 103–5) as from Isidore, *Etym.*, *De Portentis*, XI, 3, 7, being instances of monstrosity, in respect of huge bodies (*gigantes*) or pygmy bodies (*nani*) or misshapen bodies, the Irish version B of *Sex Ætates* having giants, leprechauns and *goborchind*, which he translates 'horseheads'. The English *eotenas* and *ylfe* fit the first two categories, the third has no semantic connection as *orcneas* is usually explained. Carney points to the common element *-orchin-*, *-orcn-*, suggesting that the *Beowulf* poet used a source in Irish, not Latin (p. 105). This supposed connection seems very dubious indeed, in view of the probable etymology of *orcneas*: *orc* (Latin *Orcus*, used by Anglo-Latin writers for hell) and **ne* 'corpse', giving 'corpse animated by a spirit from hell' (see Wrenn, *Beowulf*, p. 280, s.v. *orcnē*). It remains a possibility that at an earlier stage the substitution of *orcneas* for some word suggesting physical abnormality came about through the agency of an Anglo-Irish writer who knew the list with *goborchind* but, not understanding its meaning, related it to *Orcus*. The point is a minor one for the interpretation of *Beowulf*, since Grendel is an *eoten*, a name presumably synonymous with *þyrs*, and the other kinds of Cain's progeny do not appear in the story.

century and later). This work also shows an interesting double account of the monstrous race, one giving the progenitor as Cain, the other claiming that nothing remained of his seed after the Flood, and that Ham was Cain's heir. Carney's argument seems to me to prove no more than that there were two traditions, and remembering Aldhelm's description of the boat-loads of travelling students upon the Irish sea,[1] can one say which way tradition passed? As to the substitution of Ham for Cain, it is quite obviously wrong for *Beowulf*, since the killing of Abel[2] is part of the story, and the spellings of the name therefore only indicate that at some time in its transmission the manuscript was copied by a man who believed the Ham version of the origin of monsters.

The rest of Carney's book is largely concerned with demonstrating similarities between the Irish tale *Táin Bó Fraích* and *Beowulf*.[3] There are a number of interesting resemblances among the Irish stories he quotes (including a version of *The Hand and the Child*),[4] but the author fails to take account of the international character of motifs[5] in oral story-telling as well as basic plots. His conclusion is:

The only theory which will include all the evidence, Irish, Anglo-Saxon, and Icelandic, is to regard *Beowulf* as a complex consisting of a story-pattern borrowed from Ireland and a historical background deriving from Anglo-Saxon oral tradition. This complex was borrowed and introduced into the Icelandic area, being fitted, in the process, with a new historical background.[6]

This theory is obviously incompatible with Mrs Chadwick's Scandinavian theory and certainly does not explain why the *English* poet should have associated the monster-story with the Geats and Danes, if he got the tale from Ireland. Carney's conclusion is unconvincing, but he does seem to me to establish that the underwater dwelling of the monsters, a hall at the bottom of a lake, is more Irish than Scandinavian[7] (though

---

[1] See p. 25, above.   [2] cp. lines 108, 1262 f.

[3] For comment on Carney's general theory, see Wrenn's Supplement to Chambers, *Beowulf: An Introduction*, p. 547.

[4] cp. Chambers's views on the resemblances of this folk-tale to *Beowulf*, ibid., pp. 478–83.

[5] On the *lieux-communs*, see Vansina, *De la tradition orale*, p. 65, and see p. 63, above.   [6] Carney, op. cit., p. 99.   [7] ibid., pp. 97–9.

again one must add the reservation that since we know practically nothing about Anglo-Saxon water-monsters apart from *Beowulf*, it cannot be said that the lake-dwellers are distinctively Irish).

The pre-literary history of *Beowulf* comes within my purview here only in its relation to the monsters and their dwelling. The evidence is too widely scattered and uncertain in its implications to allow of any fixed conclusion such as Carney gives, but I think it is possible to suggest a working hypothesis which reconciles some of the conflicting theories about the origin of the monster-story. It is reasonable to suppose that the story of the haunting of Heorot took shape in Denmark or Sweden, perhaps with some such antecedents as Mrs Chadwick suggests.[1] The nature of the monsters in the story as it came to England is unknown. It may be presumed that this story became contaminated with English or Irish tales circulating in England, so that the underwater contest became an element in the cleansing of the hall (perhaps in place of an episode involving a waterfall), the monsters themselves took on the nature of the Anglo-Saxon *eoten* or *þyrs*, and other episodes, such as the earlier fight with the sea-monsters, were added. Whether or not the dragon-fight was part of the story from the first remains in doubt; certainly there are dragons in the Norse analogues, but they are different in important respects.[2] It would seem that there are three main reasons for thinking that the *Beowulf* poet refashioned the dragon episode in a rather thorough way. First, there is Magoun's statement that oral poetry is not normally cyclic, which militates against the existence of an oral version of the same scope as the present poem, passing from Beowulf's childhood to his old age.[3] Second, there are the marks of rearrangement of the hoard-material discussed at the end of my previous chapter.[4] Third, there is the fact that in none of the analogues is the hero mortally

---

[1] I can find no indication in the poem itself that the author was familiar with any Latin historian or geographer. Learned influence such as Leake postulates (op. cit., passim.) is unlikely to have shaped new legends in the short period since the Conversion brought literacy to England.

[2] The chief Scandinavian analogues are treated by Chambers, op. cit., pp. 458–60, 476–7, 498–502, Chadwick, op. cit., pp. 178–93, and G. V. Smithers, *The Making of Beowulf*, passim. The differences are surveyed in *Part 2* of the present chapter.

[3] Quoted above, p. 61.   [4] See pp. 93 ff., above.

wounded in the fight. If the general supposition is correct, we may expect more bookish elements in the latter part of the poem, in other words, a more literary dragon.

I have so far been considering the giant monsters as the *Beowulf* poet inherited them. The connection with Cain may have been his own addition to the story, or it may have come in during oral circulation of the story after the Conversion. My interest is in the way he uses and develops this relationship of the haunted hall story with the progenitor of the evil race. I have argued that the conception of Grendel and his dam in the poem is that of monstrous creatures of flesh and blood, but there are of course other elements in their nature which must be examined.

In respect of their physical being, there is one striking oddity. The second giant, who came to Heorot to avenge her dead son, and is plainly stated to have caused less terror because she was a woman (1382–4), is also referred to by masculine pronouns.[1] There has been much speculation about the implications of this, particularly as concerning possible variants in the poet's sources, imperfectly worked together. I do not pursue these arguments, because there is nothing to go upon: all the analogues are too remote to give any definite idea of what version of the story the poet had to work with. Indeed, Dobbie has somewhat deflated the whole controversy by pointing to other places in *Beowulf* where a feminine noun relates to a masculine pronoun.[2] Reduced to a carelessness about grammar, the inconsistency still implies an extraordinary lack of interest in the sex of the ogre.

One argument only must be specially mentioned, because it relates to the poet's basic conception of these assailants. I quote from Wrenn's note:

Perhaps *qua* mother she is thought of as f., but *qua* demon as of either sex. For the Germanic demons seem—like some others—to have been ambisexual: and the Gothic Scriptures render the Greek

---

[1] The lines are 1260, 1392, 1394, 1497. The phrase *felasinnigne secg* (1379) put in the mouth of Beowulf is metrically irregular and suspect. Dobbie notes, 'It is probable that something is wrong with the text here, but Heyne's omission of *fela-* is not the best solution of the difficulty, since the scribe was always more likely to omit than add to his copy' (*Beowulf*, p. 193).

[2] Dobbie, *Beowulf*, p. 189, n. to 1260.

neut.-pl. *daimonia* sometimes by f. *unhulþons*, sometimes by m. *unhulþans*. Milton shows a similar tradition in his demonology, where "Spirits, when they please, can either Sex assume, or both" (*Paradise Lost*, i, 423-4).[1]

This way out of the difficulty seems to me to be jumping out of the frying-pan into the fire, for if this view is accepted, as it has been by many scholars, there is a new inconsistency in the treatment of a bestial human creature descended from Adam as an evil spirit which puts on a body to suit its own nefarious purposes and changes or discards it at will. There was no doubt a good deal of popular confusion on this matter, owing to the hagiographers' habit of treating demonic contests in decidedly physical terms—a matter to which I shall return. In fact, Felix's *Vita S. Guthlaci* bears witness to such confusion when his Saint Guthlac is made to say to the demonic foes—who are proper demons who vanish like smoke when worsted—*Vae vobis, filii tenebrarum, semen Cain, favilla cineris* 'Woe to you, sons of darkness, seed of Cain, dust of ash'.[2] If *semen Cain* was appropriate, to Felix's way of thinking, why not a similar association in *Beowulf* of *Caines cynn* (cp. 107) with spirits who 'can either Sex assume, or both'? The answer lies plainly enough in the lines I quoted in the first paragraph of this chapter: whereas Guthlac's demons vanished, Beowulf's foe *feorh alegde, hæþene sawle* (851 f.). It is possible to interpret *semen Cain* figuratively, and I think it is also possible to take such expressions applied to Grendel as *feond on helle* (101) figuratively, but the mortal body wounded by Beowulf and the heathen soul sent to hell are parts of the literal narrative which cannot be explained away. And there is no need to do so. Grendel presents human nature utterly depraved, as according to the Scriptures it was before the Flood. The poet has no truck with rabbinical legends that the Devil fathered Cain upon Eve:[3] the plain word *fæderanmæg* (1263) used of Cain's relationship with Abel makes this clear. Nor is there any sign that he followed those ancient Fathers who

[1] Wrenn, *Beowulf*, p. 209, n. to 1260.

[2] *Felix's Life of S. Guthlac*, ed. B. Colgrave, p. 107; cp. also p. 100. Whitelock draws attention to the former passage, *Audience*, p. 80.

[3] For a summary of patristic theories on the matter, see *Dictionnaire de Théologie Catholique*, iv, 1, pp. 339–83, under *Démon d'Apres les Pères*; cp. also Emerson, op. cit., pp. 831–929.

interpreted the famous passage: *videntes filii Dei filias hominum quod essent pulchræ acceperunt sibi uxores ex omnibus, quas elegerant* 'the sons of God seeing the daughters of men, that they were fair, took to themselves wives of all which they chose' (Gen. 6: 2) as referring to the fallen angels. Augustine, and Bede after him, had a better understanding of the immaterial essence of the heavenly intelligences and therefore preferred the tradition which regarded the sons of God as the offspring of Seth.[1] If Grendel is a fleshly creature, as the whole story of the fight indicates, he cannot literally be a devil. An educated Christian would know this very well, because the same kind of difficulty arises in interpreting biblical passages which ascribe devilish parentage to human beings, and the question had been thrashed out in the great Manichæan controversy, the orthodox conclusion being that such passages are figurative. I use the same argument to resolve the apparent contradiction in *Beowulf* as Bede uses in expounding the two verses in which St John appears to say that Cain, and human sinners generally, are fathered by the Devil. The first of these passages is in St John's gospel, where Jesus addresses the scribes and pharisees with the words, *Vos ex patre diabolo estis, et desideria patris vestri vultis facere* 'You are of your father the Devil, and the desires of your father you will do'. (Jo. 8: 44). This verse is recalled by Bede when he explains the meaning of the lines in the Epistle which call Cain a son of the Devil:[2] the whole passage is important to our understanding of the relationship between Grendel, descendant of Cain, and Unferth the fratricide, and all the other men in *Beowulf* who kill or meditate murder out of hatred and envy. Bede begins his commentary on these verses with a firm repudiation of the idea that the Devil physically fathers or creates any man.[3] He then explains how the first-created angel sinned through pride and was turned into the Devil, and how Adam *quando consentit diabolo, ex diabolo natus est, et tales omnes genuit qualis erat* 'when he consented with the Devil, was born of the Devil, and engendered all men in a like state'. By this spiritual birth, mankind was doomed to death; but

---

[1] Bede knows the 'fallen angels' theory, but rejects it: *In Pent. Comm.*, *PL* 91, 210 f. Alcuin also follows the same tradition, *Interr.* 90, *PL* 100, 526. The OE *Genesis* poem (1245–52) agrees with Bede.

[2] 1 Jo. 3: 8–12.   [3] Bede, *In Ep. 1 Jo.*, *PL* 93, 101.

those who are 'born of God' are given new life. These 'sons of God' are distinguished by brotherly love:

Exponit quomodo ex maligno erat Cain, quia videlicet et ipse maligna habebat opera. Ergo ubi est invidia, amor fraternus esse non potest ... Hinc itaque discernuntur homines. Nemo attendat linguas, sed facta ... Tentationibus probantur homines.[1]

He [John] explains how Cain was *of the Evil One* because manifestly he himself was characterized by evil deeds. For where envy is, brotherly love cannot exist ... Hence, therefore, men are to be distinguished. Let no one give heed to what a man says, but to what he does ... Men are proved by temptations.

With this doctrine in mind, one sees that Grendel's relationship with Cain is not used in *Beowulf* simply as an explanation of his monstrous shape. His devilish motives and behaviour are also those of his human progenitor. This is most evident in his first appearance, when his murderous spite is roused against the Danes both because they are happy and because they are praising the Creator in his works (86–98).

I return, then, to the point with which I began, that the Grendel kin are physical creatures, in fact, misshapen and denatured human beings, such as existed, according to the scriptural story, before the Flood. That they behave more like beasts of prey than men is in accordance with ancient traditions about the giants begotten by the sons of Cain. The earliest History of the Church has this to say about the outcast race:

As nomads, they passed their lives in deserts, like wild and fierce beasts, destroying, by an excess of voluntary wickedness, the natural reason of man, and the seeds of thought and of culture implanted in the human soul. They gave themselves wholly over to all kinds of profanity, now seducing one another, now eating human flesh, and now daring to wage war with God and to undertake those battles of the giants celebrated by all; now planning to fortify earth against heaven, and in the madness of ungoverned pride to prepare an attack

---

[1] ibid., 102. There is a curious resemblance between Bede's words, *Hinc itaque discernuntur homines. Nemo attendat linguas, sed facta,* and the words of the coast-warden to Beowulf:

> Æghwæþres sceal
> scearp scyldwiga   gescad witan,
> worda ond worca,   se þe wel þenceð.   (287–9)

upon the very God of all. On account of these things, when they conducted themselves thus, the all-seeing God sent down upon them floods and conflagrations as upon a wild forest spread over the whole earth.[1]

It is perhaps unlikely that the *Beowulf* poet had read this passage from Eusebius, for with the decline of Greek studies the *Ecclesiastical History* was read in the Latin version of Rufinus, which very much shortens the early chapters of the work and fails to include this piece. But it was very probably read by the students of Theodore and Hadrian, including Aldhelm,[2] and it seems to me the kind of subject which would catch the imagination and become part of orally circulating ideas about antediluvian man. Ambrose transmits the general thought of this transformation of Cain's progeny into the state of savage beasts, but without the interesting detail of their eating human flesh; he says of Cain's banishment:

Repulit enim eum a facie sua, et a parentibus abdicatum separatæ habitationis quodam religavit exsilio; eo quod ab humana mansuetudine transisset ad sævitiam bestiarum.[3]

For he drove him from before his face and bound him, disowned by his parents, in a kind of exile, in a habitation apart, with the result that he passed from human gentleness to the savagery of beasts.

Grendel as a savage outcast inhabiting the wastes and living according to his bestial appetites fits very well into this ecclesiastical tradition, and as far as one can tell also fits into the popular tradition that the fens were the home of ogres. I now turn to two other aspects of the poet's treatment of him which are indicated by the two words *healþegn* (142) and *helrunan* (163).

The former word belongs entirely to the literal level of the story. It is contained in the passage (129–93) which describes Grendel's assaults upon Heorot and his virtual reign over the

---

[1] Eusebius, *Ecclesiastical History*, trans. A. C. McGiffert, pp. 19 f. The Greek text is printed in *PG* 20, 62.

[2] Bede describes the education in Latin and Greek introduced to England by Theodore and Hadrian, and its widespread effects: 'pupils of theirs were still to be found who knew Latin and Greek as well as they knew their mother-tongue' (*HE*, IV, 2; Plummer I, 205).

[3] Quoted by Emerson, op. cit., p. 886, from *De Cain et Abel*, II, 10.

Danish court. The affair is handled ironically in terms of a human feud, as if an outlaw, forbidden to participate in the normal life of the king's hall, were to show his hate and his contempt for laws and lives by ambushing and slaying one after another of the king's men, remorselessly and with impunity. It is in this context that one comes upon the lines

> Heorot eardode,
> sincfage sel   sweartum nihtum;
> no he þone gifstol   gretan moste
> maþðum for metode,   ne his myne wisse.
> þæt wæs wræc micel   wine Scyldinga
> modes brecða.   (166–71)

The ambiguities of these lines are notorious: I do not think they can be *or should be* resolved by a commentator's attempt to single out the most appropriate simple sense. Grendel has become the *healþegn* he desires to be, but only during the hours of darkness; it is an empty triumph, for there is no king to reward him from the *gifstol*. The Creator's curse is still upon him, and he cannot know the love of a normal human being. The ambiguity of *his myne* is necessary to lift the meaning on to the allegorical plane. The human rejection Grendel experiences, unable to know the love and bounty of a lord, is an image of his eternal rejection from the Throne of Grace. As the hearer grasps these words, the literal sense of *gifstol* obviously comes to him first, then *for Metode* reminds him of the ban upon Cain, and the double application of *his myne* demands a moment's reflection which retrospectively enlarges the *gifstol* into an image of God's throne. As the recitation proceeds, the further ambiguity of the word *þæt* (170) again drives the listener's mind back as well as forward, back past the deserted gift-seat in Heorot to Grendel's occupation of the hall. The *wine Scyldinga* (170) cannot approach his throne while Grendel occupies Heorot, and the mind is set wondering whether this separation is not also *for Metode*.[1] The poet's thoughts obviously move in this direction, for this passage about Hrothgar leads into his diatribe against the idolatry of the Danes.

[1] This aspect of the passage struck Professor A. G. Brodeur, but he did not recognize that the condition of *listening* to the poem naturally carries the mind back to Grendel before Hrothgar is mentioned. See *The Art of Beowulf*, pp. 203 f.

The whole scene I have been describing has the longer perspective; in addition to the language of the human feud there is also intermittently the language of devilry and hell, illustrated by my second example *helrunan* (163). To this may be added from the same passage *wergan gastes* (133), *þæm feonde* (143), *deorc deapscua* (160), *feond manncynnes* (164), and the culminating passage about hell itself (183–6). I think it is rather evident from the mingling of these expressions with words like *healþegn* (142), *æglæca* (159) and *angengea* (165) that the poet found no incompatibility in the simultaneous presentation of Grendel as a giant human enemy and as a devilish enemy; there can be no question here of the kind of inconsistency that might come from incomplete working-over of heathen material. Grendel behaved like a devil in being the implacable enemy of mankind, and, like his forefather Cain, *ex maligno erat*, in a spiritual sense. It seems to me that attempts to find a precise human equivalent for *helrunan* (163) may cause fresh confusion by giving a new and incongruous aspect to the devilish giant. Dobbie, for instance, suggests 'wizards, magicians' (?),[1] and Wrenn, defining the word *s.v. hell-rune* as 'one having knowledge of the secrets of the place of the dead', hence 'necromancer' or 'sorceress', cites Gothic *haliarunæ* 'magæ mulieres' and the Old English glossators' *hellerune* for *pythonissa*.[2] Mrs Chadwick further explores the glosses.[3] In late glosses, *hellerune* is given as an alternative to *hægtesse*, and *hægtesse* glosses words for the Furies. Armed with this, Mrs Chadwick notes that in two glossaries *erinys* and *tisifone* are glossed *wælcyrge/wælcyrre*. By this chain, we arrive at an association of *hellerune* and 'valkyrie', as 'a fierce and vengeful spirit of the underworld'.[4] On the strength of this and some evidence from the Charm against pain caused by *hægtessan* or *ða mihtigan wif*, Mrs Chadwick ventures to suggest that in Grendel's mother we have the English conception of a valkyrie.[5] As I read this evidence, *hellerune* and *hægtesse* mean 'witch': the connection with valkyries is very dubious. The *pythonissa* gloss with which the chain of glosses begins probably derives from the demonically-possessed girl who appears in Aldhelm's little

---

[1] Dobbie, *Beowulf*, n. to 163, p. 125.
[2] Wrenn, *Beowulf*, p. 262.
[3] Chadwick, op. cit., pp. 174–7.
[4] ibid., p. 177.
[5] ibid., p. 177. For the Charm, see *ASPR* VI, 122.

poem on St Paul.[1] The girl made a living for her masters by soothsaying, and St Paul drove the demon out of her. One could therefore make a case for Grendel's mother as a woman possessed by a demon, and Grendel as likewise a human frame animated by a demon; but if this had been the poet's conception, he obviously had a vocabulary which allowed him to say that the demon escaped to hell on Grendel's death, instead of the phrase *alegde hæpene sawle* (851 f.) which he did use.

In the interest aroused by this witch-hunt, it is easy to lose sight of the fact that *helrunan* is not applied to Grendel's mother at all, but appears in a generalization prompted by Grendel's nightly wanderings on the moors. Though the masculine form of the noun is not elsewhere recorded, the context suggests that *helrunan* is masculine here, or, perhaps one should say, not distinctively feminine. The etymological sense of the compound, 'one who knows the secrets of hell' appears to me to fit all the examples discussed above and to be quite appropriate for the Grendel pair, who consort with demons (cp. *wolde ... secan deofla gedræg* 755 f.) and possess hellish qualities themselves (cp. *feond on helle* 101, *hellehæfta* 788, *hellegast* 1274). It is unfortunate that modern English appears to have no equivalent general term. In some passages, it therefore seems, the spiritual kinship with the Devil is emphasized by the use of words normally applied to the devils of hell,[2] in others the physical presence of Grendel is more important—as, for instance, when Beowulf seizes him; then he is called *eoten* (761), *se mæra* (762), *se hearmscapa* (766), and he and Beowulf are ironically coupled in *renweardas* (770).

The doctrine which explains the seeming duality of the nature of Grendel and his dam was indicated by Professor M. P. Hamilton some twenty years ago: 'In the life temporal Grendel is but a cannibalistic monster in the likeness of a man. ... Yet in the mind of the poet, his folklore giants, like those in *Genesis*, seem to have become associated with "the whole company of the damned", the Body of Satan.'[3] She quotes from

---

[1] *Carmina Ecclesiastica* II, *MGH AA* xv, p. 21. For the biblical story, see Acts 16: 16.

[2] Christ's words to the disciples, *ex vobis unus diabolus est* (Jo. 6: 71) gave authority to the idea of a human devil; cp. also OE *Daniel* (750) and *Judith* (61, 112).

[3] Marie P. Hamilton, 'The Religious Principle in *Beowulf*'. She continues, 'One is tempted to surmise that the author of *Beowulf* in the manner of Bede and Augustine envisioned the race of Cain in its timeless as well as its transitory state, and thus

Gregory's *Moralia* to illustrate this doctrine that 'our old enemy is one person with the whole company of the damned', and relates it to the doctrine of the two cities in *De civitate Dei*.[1] The *Beowulf* poet does not treat the theory of the two cities as such; it could not be worked into the scheme any more easily than the Church itself. But I think Hamilton is right to draw attention to the Body of Satan, which appears a great deal in the *Moralia*, especially in allegorical interpretation of the Body of Leviathan. From this and allied sources the poet receives 'the perception' commented upon by Whallon 'that the monsters of the moor are allied to the man who slays his kinsman'.[2]

It thus becomes clear that the men of Heorot who plot or commit murder are also spiritual sons of Cain. Another attribute of Cain's race which seems relevant to our view of the building of the great royal hall is that these men are the builders of cities, for Cain, according to Genesis 4: 17, first built a city. Bede explains the verse thus:

... in civitate quam ædificavit Cain typice intimabatur quod spes tota pravorum in hujus sæculi regno esset ac felicitate figenda, ut pote qui futurorum bonorum aut fidem aut desiderium nullum haberent.[3]

In the city which Cain built is intimated in a figure that the whole hope of the wicked was in the kingdom of this world and in making their own happiness, inasmuch as they had no faith in or desire for benefits to come.

It therefore seems that the poet discloses through the image of Heorot,[4] gold-adorned, damaged, and finally destroyed, the true nature of the *spes tota* of the Danes, *hæþenra hyht*: the spirit of Cain occupies the hall in an allegorical sense as the skulking presence of Grendel haunts it in the historical narrative.

The lair of the monsters has a literature of its own, so puzzling have the commentators found it. A large part of the

by a bold metaphor, conceived of Grendel and his dam as already denizens of hell'. I think this may be partly true, in that an anagogical interpretation of the chief parts of the action is possible, but this is not the same thing as a bold metaphor. (op. cit., p. 332.)

[1] ibid., p. 322.   [2] See p. 42, n. 1, above.
[3] Bede, *Hexaemeron, PL* 91, 72,; cp. *In Pent. Comm. PL* 91, 219.
[4] The imaging of flaws in men by flaws in a building could have been suggested by the exposition of Exod. 20: 25 and 1 Pet. 2: 5; cp. also the symbolism of *Christ* 1–14, *ASPR* iii, 3.

scholarly debate has turned upon the supposed corruption by the *Beowulf* poet, and perhaps his oral predecessors, of a water-fall scene which they either failed to recognize as such, or which they confusingly embellished with features from other dangerous landscapes. One of the great books of *Beowulf* criticism, *Beowulf and Epic Tradition* by W. W. Lawrence, has perpetuated mis-understanding about Grendel's mere for many years, and Lawrence has stoutly defended his point of view in articles on the topography of the lair.[1] Chambers's authoritative book supports Lawrence in finding in *Beowulf* a confused waterfall scene with 'the water falling, the spray rising'.[2] Both these great scholars have an ingrained preference for naturalism in literature: Lawrence is able to read lines 1354–76 of the poem and then assert:

This is a vivid picture of what may be seen in Norway at the present day—a waterfall breaking over beetling cliffs, which seem to over-hang it, into a pool below. The spray rises to the sky in a fine mist; gray trees grow round about.[3]

He comments upon the lines which say that the water could not touch Beowulf in the underwater lair 'on account of the roof of the hall' (1515 f.),

Take this 'hall' as a cave under a waterfall, and the whole scene clears up. The poet of *Beowulf* did not visualize things as clearly as the saga writer. ... Perhaps he had never seen a waterfall; and if he had, it was probably different from the lofty Scandinavian forces.[4]

By his phrase 'the whole scene clears up', Lawrence obviously means 'the scene becomes rational and in accord with scenery in life'. He does not recognize that naturalism is proper to *Grettissaga* but alien to the mode of *Beowulf*. In order to create his Norwegian scene, he has to translate the passage in a highly contextual way, translating *fyrgenstream* 'waterfall', though elsewhere it is used of the ocean,[5] and *yðgeblond* 'spray', though

---

[1] See particularly W. W. Lawrence, "Grendel's Lair'.

[2] Chambers, *Beowulf: An Introduction*, p. 463.

[3] Lawrence, *Beowulf and Epic Tradition*, p. 184.

[4] ibid., p. 185.

[5] Lawrence, of course, is not ignorant of this, and defends his translation in the article cited (n. 1 above), pp. 479 f.; cp. also Kemp Malone, 'Grendel's Abode', especially p. 298.

in later parts of the same scene (1593, 1620) it clearly means 'turmoil of the waves', and *hrofsele* (1515) as 'the roof of the cave'. It is very doubtful whether any of these translations would occur to the student of *Beowulf* who had not read the Icelandic analogues, and it does not appear to me axiomatic that the more rational version of a tale is necessarily the older version. And, however one may 'clear up' the passage under discussion, there remains the fact that the mere has been visited earlier in the poem (841–52), and there were to be found the swirling waves, *atol yða geswing* (848), but no waterfall, and the lair was called *fenfreoðo* (851). What is more difficult to explain away on rational grounds is that the journey to the mere on the cheerful morning of victory is not difficult, and the place apparently not remote or inaccessible; whereas at the start of the perilous adventure the landscape itself has become frightening and inhospitable. This is the most extreme example in the poem of the symbolic treatment of natural and inanimate objects to reflect the feelings imputed to the men in the story. It is quite evident that Professor Malone is right when he says, contrasting *Beowulf* with the sagas in their descriptions of the monsters' lair, 'Parallels to the scene in *Beowulf* belong to the world of the imagination'.[1]

Malone's personal interpretation of Grendel's abode is summed up in his own words:

It is now clear I think that the poet gives us not a confused and distorted description of natural scenery but a consistent and carefully-wrought picture of a hell on earth, an imaginative construction based on traditional Christian ideas about hell.[2]

Though some of the detailed arguments used by Malone are questionable, I believe that his conclusion comes closer to the truth than Lawrence's view. The 'hell on earth' is, I believe, an incidental aspect of the lair; Beowulf does not 'descend into hell' in the literal sense.

At his first appearance, Grendel is a creature of the outer darkness, *se þe in þystrum bad* (87), a darkness directly contrasted through the Creation song with God's world of light. As an outcast, he frequents the wastelands, moors and fens, desolate

---

[1] Malone, op. cit., p. 298.   [2] ibid., p. 306.

country given over to Cain's outlawed progeny, *fifelcynnes eard*
(104). At his second appearance, though it is here in the wrestling that his physical presence dominates the scene, there are
also several hints of the presence of a devil: *under sceadu bregdan*
(707) connoting a dragging into evil ways (cp. *Guthlac* 675:
under scæd scufan) and especially *besyrwan* (713) which suggests
the snares of the Devil rather than the simple snatch which the
giant makes.[1] When he recognizes that Beowulf's strength is
greater than his own, Grendel's only desire is to get out into the
darkness, *secan deofla gedræg* (756);[2] I take this to mean that he
wished to escape into his own territory, which was haunted by
demons who would succour him. None of this is inconsistent
with *helle hæfton* (788) and *on feonda geweald* (808), for those who
are aided by evil powers in life are nonetheless their prisoners in
death.

Grendel's death takes place in *fenfreoðo*, in the lair under the
waters of the turbulent lake; *þær him hel onfeng* (852). Malone
argues from this a literal identity of the *fenfreoðo* with hell.[3] He
has to support his theory the 'Vision' features of the landscape,
i.e. those which *Beowulf* shares with the Blickling Homily version
of the *Visio Pauli*:[4] the downward-flowing water, the grey rock,

---

[1] A. S. Cook, '*Beowulf* 159–163', *MLN* 40 (1925), relates *mistige moras* (162) to
Jer. 13: 16, a passage which includes both *montes caliginosos* and *umbram mortis* (cp.
160). I doubt whether this is more than a general association of ideas, but the connotations of sin and death may well be there. Shaded marshy ground is the haunt
of Behemoth: *Sub umbra dormit ... in locis humentibus* (Job 40: 16), hence allegorically
associated with evil. Gregory explains several scriptural meanings of *sub umbra*, of
which the relevant significance for *Beowulf* (707) might be: *Calorem enim charitatis
fugiens, veritatis solem homo deseruit, et sub umbra se interni frigoris abscondit* 'Fleeing from
the warmth of charity, man left the sun of truth and hid himself in the dark places
of inward cold' (*Moralia*, PL 76, 672).
Interpreting the phrases quoted above, he describes how Satan (Behemoth) sleeps
in those souls *quos a veri solis ardore subtrahendo frigidos facit* 'which he makes cold by
dragging them away from the heat of the sun of truth'. Thus, though all these
phrases in the poem signify a literal dragging away to death in the darkness, in
Grendel's fen-retreat, the exegetical associations also imply the Devil's attack upon
Heorot's inhabitants and his dragging them to damnation. This leads into the
passage on their idolatry (175 ff.).
[2] Klaeber's notes at this point show a despairing attempt to interpret the action
in realistic terms—e.g. on line 756: 'This cannot be literally true, as Grendel is
supposed to live alone with his mother' (*Beowulf*, p. 155); cp. also p. 260 below.
[3] Malone, op. cit., p. 852.
[4] For the resemblances, see the editors' notes to lines 1357 ff., and also Carleton
Brown, '*Beowulf* and the *Blicking Homilies*', *PMLA* 53 (1938), pp. 905–9.

the frosty woods, the dark mists and the abyss. He adds to these a sentence from *Snorra Edda: niðr ok norðr liggr helvegr*,[1] and a reminder that the *fyrgenstream* which Lawrence took to be a waterfall could as easily denote the enormous ocean which was thought to encircle the earth in the old northern cosmography. He concludes that the place in the north where the sea flows down into the infernal regions is 'slightly shifted' by the poet to become localized in the region of Heorot. It is a bold theory, and useful for its attention to the sea and Vision elements in the scenery about the lair, but it will not altogether serve, because the place is not in the least like hell when Beowulf arrives there. The hero explored the place when he was looking for Grendel's corpse (1572–90) and he found nothing other than a hall containing treasure and dead Grendel upon a couch. Here was an opportunity to speak of measureless caverns or dark and fearful abysses, but there is not the least whiff of devilry once the giants are dead. How, then, can one account for the 'Vision' features of the environment?

I believe that the answer is this: the lair is in the terrain occupied by the Enemy. Its symbolic topography is for the poet a part of the real world, a world deformed by the presence of evil as Grendel and the rest of Cain's progeny are physically as well as spiritually deformed by the evil which is in them. A territory occupied by devils will naturally—I use the word deliberately—have some of the attributes of hell. The modern reader's confusion arises from his scepticism about the real presence of devils in the cosmos, and the effects upon physical matter of the evil—and, of course, the good—intelligences which for the early Christian invisibly populated the universe. If we wish to understand *Beowulf*, we must by an effort of the imagination accept this belief. We can then recognize the environs of the lair as a hostile part of earth which looks menacing because it *is* menacing; a place from which the turbulence and darkness will disperse when the evil presences are driven out. It is illuminating to read the Old English *Guthlac* poems alongside *Beowulf*. They belong to the same thought-world; their relation to one another and to the Antonian tradition generally are examined in Chapter 8. For my present point it is sufficient to notice how Croyland

---

[1] *Snorra Edda*, ed. F. Jónsson (Rekjavík, 1931), p. 66.

is treated by the poet of *Guthlac* A as Enemy territory. The island in the fens is peopled by devils, and Guthlac invades and liberates the place, the liberation being signalled by the restoration of serenity and joy to the region. This is the 'historical' narrative of the poem, just as in the 'history' of *Beowulf* Heorot is occupied by Grendel and its environs are dominated by the evil powers, to be freed and cleansed by Beowulf as God's champion.

In the case of *Guthlac*, the reader, alerted by his knowledge of temptation-allegories, is likely to read the contests between Guthlac and his assailants simply as a metaphorical presentation of the inner struggles of the solitary hermit, missing the physical battle altogether, because the *bellum intestinum* is quite clearly dominant. In *Beowulf*, on the other hand, the physical battle is dominant and it is rather easy for the modern reader to miss, or to regard as metaphorical embellishment, the signs of the interior conflict, at least until it is brought into the foreground in Hrothgar's 'sermon'. One of these signs is in the language of temptation used as Grendel approaches Heorot.[1] Beowulf's strength is sustained by his virtue, and his ability to succeed where the Danes have failed is pointed not only by the stories of his prowess but by the evidence of Danish depravity, a depravity aggravated by the devilish assaults. I read the situation of Hrothgar as somewhat similar to that of Job, who is tested in afflictions by which the Devil hopes to capture his soul.[2] Many of the Danes do become subservient to the *gastbona* (175–8) as a result of the devilish persecution, but Hrothgar, like Job, becomes humble, and endures in sorrow, until God gives him deliverance through Beowulf's coming. Beowulf, facing Grendel, opposes his moral and spiritual as well as his bodily strength to the assailant. His faith that God will help him overcome the adversary is magnificently proved. The forces of the Enemy are driven back, but, as in *Guthlac* the repulse of one assault is succeeded by a fresh trial, so Beowulf is now tested by a harder task; he must carry the war into Enemy territory.

On the historical level, therefore, the place in which Beowulf must fight his second great combat is elaborated with symbolic

---

[1] See pp. 114 f., above.
[2] See also p. 177, below, for qualification of this statement.

natural features which express the hostility of the terrain itself to human invasion. Here also one encounters the narrative mode already remarked, in which the inanimate features of the scene are affected by the emotions involved in the action. Hrothgar describes the giants' lair in an atmosphere of the Danish fear of the place; it becomes more frightening and mysterious in the telling. At night uncanny fire is seen there; no man has sounded the bottom of the lake; the very beasts sense the evil of the waters. Even the air above the lake is tormented and stormy (cp. 1365–75). When the troop of men sets out, the difficulty of their task is reflected in the topography, the rocky paths resisting their incursion (1408–11). The carping reader will object that *uncuþ gelad* (1410) is at variance with the fact of the earlier journey to the mere following the track of Grendel's blood (841–9); one could argue that the second blood-trail took a different and more arduous route through unexplored country, but I doubt very much whether the poet or his audience was disturbed by this sort of inconsistency. After the second victorious contest, the turbulent waters are cleansed (1620–2) and the Geats' return is unimpeded (1632–4).

Nevertheless, this explanation in terms of nature symbolism and a particular narrative technique will not answer all the questions which the description of the journey and the features of the uncanny lake rouse in the mind. If I am right in adducing as a parallel the trials of the *vir Dei* portrayed in *Guthlac* A, it is to be expected that the poet will draw attention to the moral-allegorical significance of Beowulf's second trial. I believe that he does so through those features of the lake-scenery which 'belong to the world of the imagination'.

First, it must be remembered that the saint's external fight with the devils mirrors his soul's struggles with temptations. The overthrow of the one represents the mastery of the other. So, Beowulf's victory over Grendel in the moral-allegorical, or tropological, sense can present his repulse of those sins which the giants figure, the sins of the race of Cain, namely, pride and cupidity.[1] It has often been remarked that his second combat

---

[1] The great sins are pride and cupidity, for all others derive from these, and these are the sins of the Devil himself. Satan is also actuated by envy of mankind, and his spiritual son Cain has the same malicious hatred of the good. The giants engendered

proves more difficult, and the third the hardest of all. This is not strange as regards the moral allegory, because at each stage the hero's fame and wealth are greatly increased, so that the temptations to self-admiration and satisfaction in the world's solaces are correspondingly greater in each trial.

When Beowulf sets out to pit his strength against the second giant, he passes through a desolate countryside. The most striking and curious line in the scenic description is

enge anpaðas,   uncuð gelad.   (1410)

An identical line, as is well known, occurs in the Old English poem *Exodus* as part of the description of the wilderness through which Moses led the Israelites. Wrenn refers to the biblical desert journey as 'the ultimate source of this passage' in his note on the lines under discussion,[1] suggesting also that the *Beowulf* poet has the *Exodus* poem in mind. That this is right has support in patristic allegorical interpretations of the desert journey which fit admirably into the allegorical situation in *Beowulf*. It is to be remembered that the Song of Moses, as part of the monastic cycle of psalms, brought this particular piece of the Old Testament with its personal applications particularly to the fore in Anglo-Saxon Christian communities, and that its symbolic use in the liturgy of baptism made it familiar even to the catechumen.[2] The interpretation needed to make plain the allegorical meaning of Beowulf's journey to the mere was adduced by Professor Cross and Miss S. I. Tucker in their joint article on the Old English *Exodus*.[3] The passage comes, not unexpectedly, from the *Moralia*. Gregory, making the usual relation of the Crossing of the Red Sea with baptism, saw the life of the good man as beginning with this victory over the Devil (Pharaoh) and as then proceeding in a series of battles across the desert, *in eremo vitæ præsentis*.[4] The non-Christian Beowulf

by Cain have the same vicious qualities; tropologically, they represent these sins. Bede, *In Pent. Comm.*, PL 91, 224, moralizes the engendering of the giants, 'good thoughts' uniting with 'evil thoughts' to produce 'great sins': *Gigantes qui hic dicuntur indicant magna peccata, etenim magnitudine peccati nati sunt* 'The giants here spoken of indicate the great sins, since they took their origin from the enormity of sin.'

[1] Wrenn, *Beowulf*, p. 210, n. to 1409–11.   [2] See p. 50, above.
[3] See p. 48, n. 2, above; Cross-Tucker, op. cit., p. 126.
[4] Gregory, *Moralia*, PL 76, 301.

does not begin his military service under God with baptism, but with his victory over the devilish Grendel, and he must then proceed to face the Enemy as he crosses the desert of life.

The battles in the desert figure the temptations which the victor now faces:

Jam peccata præterita velut extinctos Ægyptios post terga relinquimus; sed ad huc nocentia vitia, quasi alii hostes obviant, ut ad terram promissionis pergentibus cœptum iter intercludant.[1]

Now we leave our past sins behind like the dead Egyptians, but still the pernicious vices like other enemies come to meet us, to block the road the marchers have taken to the promised land.

Aldhelm similarly uses the death of the Egyptians in the Red Sea as a figure of victory over temptation in his verse *De virginitate*. This first battle in his *psychomachia* is against Greed; the second is against Lust, the third against *Philargiria* 'Avarice'.[2] It is noticeable that the sins of the flesh are absent from *Beowulf* as from *Guthlac*; the hero is shown battling with only those temptations which attack the dedicated and noble warrior. The nature of Beowulf's second temptation is not unlike the first, as the kinship of the second giant to the other indicates. The poet adds a reminder that she too has her dwelling in the *cealde streamas* (1261) because of Cain's sin. I think that the topography of the mere has been slightly elaborated in the same way as the desolate country which leads to it, in order to alert the audience to the hidden significance of Beowulf's entry into the waters.

On this matter I find Professor Robertson's article upon the symbolism of mediæval literary gardens illuminating,[3] though also confused and perhaps erroneous in some of its detail. He recognizes that an evil landscape, 'the evil garden', belonging to a Christian tradition of such symbolic places, will have a good deal of resemblance to traditional visions of hell, because hell is 'simply the evil garden taken anagogically'.[4] Exclusion of God's sunlight causes darkness and cold in the evil landscape, and the editors are clearly right to regard the *hrinde bearwas*

---

[1] *PL* 76, 302.

[2] Aldhelm, *De virginitate*, 2485 f., 2571 f.; *MGH AA* xv, 454, 457.

[3] 'The Doctrine of Charity in Mediaeval Literary Gardens: a Topical Approach through Symbolism and Allegory.' [4] ibid., p. 32.

(1363) as evil rather than just wintry.[1] This feature is undoubtedly the most striking point of resemblance with the Blickling Homily vision of hell; however, in this light, it does not identify the Beowulfian lake with hell itself, which is my reason for saying, concerning Malone's theory, that the resemblance is incidental. Robertson comments upon the topography in these words:

Frost and ice are traditional symbols of Satan whom God permits to tempt the human spirit to fall in cupidity. Moreover the chill of cupidity may be considered characteristic of the evil garden as opposed to the warmth of Charity in the good garden. The trees, the rock and the pool all point strongly to the theory that what the poet had in mind was the evil garden of the Scriptures.[2]

This last sentence is probably too positive; Robertson is inclined to go beyond what the poem asks, in speaking, for instance, of 'hiding under the wrong trees';[3] the poet does not *use* the trees in Beowulf's adventure, and my impression is that he employs discrete symbols as pointers rather than imposes a symbolic construct, 'the evil garden', on the existent lake and marshland scene.

In the same article, Robertson reminds his readers that the giants engendered by Cain can figure men, in Bede's words, *terrenis concupiscentiis adhaerentes* 'who cling to earthly desires'.[4] He also sees the pertinence of the inclusion of the Flood story in the poem (1687–93), though he confusingly describes the giant sword as 'a relic of the struggle between the giants and the just in the days before the Flood'.[5] He finds in the sword-hilt a specific reference to the character of the pool and its inhabitants, though he considers that 'the relationship between the stream and the rock is not entirely clear in the poem', when he attempts to connect these features with the evil equivalents of the Rock from which flow the streams of Living Water.[6] As I have already said, such exact allegorical correspondences

[1] ibid., p. 33; see also Klaeber, *Beowulf*, p. 183. [2] ibid.
[3] ibid., p. 34. There is only one oblique mention of hiding under the trees: *no he on helm losaþ ... ne on fyrgenholt* (1393 f.) and this is not part of the action.
[4] ibid., p. 32; the quotation is from *PL* 91, 84 f. I have already noted Gregory's association of the giants with pride (above, p. 46).
[5] ibid., p. 32. The sword-hilt had a design of the Flood and the destruction of the giants upon it. [6] ibid., p. 33.

seem incompatible with the narrative mode of *Beowulf*, but
Robertson is clearly right to single out the *fyrgenstream* (1359)
as a particularly significant feature of the landscape. Its oddity
has struck almost every commentator on the poem, and the
various theories I have been discussing bear witness to its ambiguity: these are very good reasons for regarding it as a symbol
in the allegory rather than a piece of realistic description.

I hazard the opinion, in the light of my earlier comments upon
the desert of life, that the poet has once more remembered the
Moralia while writing of the giants. I have already noted the
symbolic meaning given to *Ecce gigantes gemunt sub aquis* in Job
26: 5, in my discussion of the hymn *Altus Prosator*;[1] a little later
in the Book of Job comes a passage which describes the dwellings
of outcasts: *in desertis habitabant torrentium, et in cavernis terræ, vel
super glaream* (Job 30: 6). 'They dwelt in the desert places of
torrents, and in caves of the earth, or upon the gravel.' Gregory
takes these 'torrents' to be streams swollen by the winter snows,
which enables him to relate them to cupidinous men, *a calore
charitatis* 'away from the warmth of charity'. The phrase *in
cavernis terræ* implies a rocky landscape, and might have suggested that the mountain-streams flowed into subterranean
caverns: cp. *fyrgenstream ... flod under foldan* (1359–61). (The third
part of the verse, *vel super glaream*, belongs to the sandy desert
of a Mediterranean country and will hardly adapt itself to the
marshy terrain envisaged in *Beowulf*, even in so eclectic a
landscape as this; it has no counterpart in the poem.) Gregory's
commentary on the verse is diffuse and largely concerned with
heretics, which may explain why Hamilton, who mentioned
this text in a footnote,[2] did not follow up its implications. The
one piece of his exposition which provides a link with Cain's kin
and cupidity runs as follows:

Eadem de carnalibus dici possunt quæ de hæreticis. ... Sed quia
pravorum mentes ea in hac vita adipisci appetunt, quæ justi dere-

[1] See p. 46 above. A link with this text was first suggested by S. J. Crawford,
'Grendel's Descent from Cain', *MLR* 23 (1928), 207, and was approved by Hamilton,
op. cit., p. 315.
[2] Hamilton, op. cit., p. 322, n. 79. She says: 'cf. the Vulgate version of Job 30.6,
wherein godless outlaws are said to dwell "in the desert places of the torrents and
the caverns of the earth", a fairly accurate description of the site of Grendel's abode,
and as figuratively conceived.'

linquunt, in desertis torrentium habitare referentur. Illa enim quæ sanctis indigna sunt, ipsi percipere pro magno concupiscunt. Cavernæ autem terræ sunt cogitationes pravæ in quibus se ab humanis oculis abscondunt.[1]

The same can be said of carnal men as of heretics. ... But because the minds of the wicked seek to have in this life those things which the righteous forsake, they are said to inhabit the desert places of torrents. For those things which to the saints are vile, they desire to obtain as valuable. Now, the caves of the earth are the wicked thoughts in which they conceal themselves from human eyes.

There seems to me enough here to warrant my suggestion that the ambiguity of *fyrgenstream*, which, in view of the seascape of lines 1421–30, quite possibly referred to an arm of the sea in the poetic source, has allowed the poet to use the word as another signpost to allegorical meaning for those who have ears to hear, i.e. those who know their Book of Job. It is, however, a pointer only: the cold waters of cupidity lie before Beowulf even if one disregards the word *fyrgenstream*, since there remains the general doctrine relating Cain's giants and proud and cupidinous men. It is noteworthy that the giants' dwelling contains a great deal of treasure which Beowulf does not touch; he takes only the trophies of his victory:

> Ne nom he in þæm wicum   Wedergeata leod,
> maðmæhta ma   þeh he monige geseah,
> buton þone hafelan   ond þa hilt somod
> since fage. (1612–15)

The hero of a romance would not behave like this; no rational explanation is offered; but it is exactly what one would expect of an allegorical hero who had just overcome a temptation to cupidity.

There seem to me, therefore, sufficient indications in the poem to warrant the reading of the story of Heorot as an allegory. On the historical level, the cleansing of the region is brought into line with beliefs then current about the physical presence of evil giants upon earth, whose superhuman powers stemmed from

---

[1] Gregory, *Moralia, PL* 76, 152 ... 157 f. In the intervening sections he speaks of the different effects of cupidity upon different men and the need to fix one's gaze upon *veras divitias æterne patriæ* 'the true treasures of the eternal homeland' (153).

their spiritual sonship to the Devil. The hero, deriving his strength from God, was able to drive out the giant from Heorot and to free the neighbouring waters of the evil creatures. The story can simultaneously be interpreted as an allegory of the hero's spiritual battles with the sins which the giants figure, pride and cupidity.[1] In killing the giants, he overcomes the temptations which his increasing fame and wealth bring upon him. The allegory is brought to the surface in the final scene of this part of the story, when Hrothgar, gazing on the sword-hilt, speaks of the temptations of a rich and powerful man. This speech is fully discussed in Chapter 6.

The major critical problem is to set bounds to this allegory. By invoking scriptural and exegetical symbolism, the poet opens a perspective of the whole sacred history of the human race and its relation to the life of the contemporary Christian. It is obviously for this reason that the descent into the infernal waters has been seen by some critics as an allegory of baptism, or of the Harrowing of Hell. These theories are critically reviewed in the course of my final chapters: it is enough to reiterate here that the criterion, in admitting any allegorical significance in the poem, must be its relevance to the structure of the whole.

(ii) *The Dragons*

The dragons in *Beowulf*, like the giants, are physical creatures hostile to mankind. There are two main species. *sædracan* and *eorðdracan*, the former inhabiting the evil lake, the latter living in the earth as guardians of hidden treasure. Only one has an important role in the story, but the others demonstrate by their presence that savage fauna of the serpent kind were believed to infest inaccessible places of the world, from which they sometimes emerged to cause terror and devastation. The sea-creatures wrecked ships and devoured the sailors, the land species destroyed buildings and people with their flaming breath. In the literature which has grown up round the poem, attention

---

[1] Other sins are subsumed in these. Both Grendel and his dam show greed; Grendel envies the men of Heorot and shows anger against them. Within Heorot, Unferth shows the same flaws, and after Beowulf's victory appears to be a changed man.

has naturally focused on Beowulf's greatest adversary; though dragon-fights are not uncommon, this one is in several respects unique, and it has been very variously interpreted.[1] I shall not attempt here to review all the theories which have been advanced about its significance, but I shall bring forward evidence which suggests that as flame-spewer and treasure-guardian Beowulf's dragon belongs to North European oral tradition, possibly developing out of the dragon of Roman popular belief, and that as malicious enemy of man, attacking like a serpent and wounding with its venomous teeth, it owes something to the hagiographers and a great deal to patristic interpretations of the *dracones* of the Bible.

I begin with a reminder that modern habits of classification on zoological principles must be put aside in this investigation. The Old English words *draca* and *wyrm*, like their Norse equivalents *dreki* and *ormr*, are used interchangeably of a variety of creatures of the reptilian kind. The Latin Bible shows a similar vagueness in the use of *draco* and *serpens*, and the commentators frequently treat them as synonymous. Other words such as *natrix*, *regulus*, *anguis*, and *coluber* are employed in Christian Latin poetry as alternatives to *serpens*; all the biblical and early Christian uses are coloured by the curse on the Serpent of Genesis. The serpent-dragon is the natural enemy of man in Christian tradition, and is the particular enemy of the saint. It is not possible to say whether the dragon of Northern Europe was sprung of a different stock from the Mediterranean creatures, because the spread of the Roman dragon-standards— those which Augustine described in his discussion of symbols[2]— must have brought the fear of the dragon as far as Britain and Germany, during the early days of the Empire, whether or not it met and fused with a native belief in the existence of such beasts. The absence from record of a specific word of Germanic

[1] For the earlier theories and the analogues, see Chambers, *Beowulf: An Introduction*, pp. 458–60, 476 f., 498–502; more recent discussions include T. M. Gang, 'Approaches to *Beowulf*', *RES*, NS, 3 (1952), 1 ff.; A Bonjour, 'Monsters Crouching and Critics Rampant: or the *Beowulf* Dragon debated', *PMLA* 68 (1953), 304 ff.; A. E. Du Bois, 'The Dragon in *Beowulf*—Symbol or Image?', *PMLA* 73 (1957), 819 ff.; K. Sisam, 'Beowulf's Fight with the Dragon', *RES*, NS, 9 (1958), 129 ff.; and G. V. Smithers, *The Making of 'Beowulf'* (already cited). For a general survey of dragons in early European literature, see F. Wild, *Drachen im Beowulf und andere Drachen* (discussed below on p. 131.)   [2] See above, pp. 68 f.

origin inclines one to think that the flying creature and its name came from the south together.

For the Roman of the first century A.D., the dragon was both destroyer and treasure-guardian, as in *Beowulf*. Already in Cicero the creature appears to be an image of covetousness; otherwise the orator would not have found in it a useful comparison to drive home to his audience the avarice of the man he was attacking, who, as he says, *patrimonium complexus est quasi thesaurum draco* 'grasped his patrimony like a dragon grasping treasure'.[1] It is possible that Cicero had in mind dragon-images used as custodians of temple treasure, but the Fables of Phædrus, written in the time of Tiberius, show a living belief in the existence of dragons in caves. In the fable *Vulpes et Draco*, the fox

> pervenit ad draconis speluncam intimam, custodiebat
> qui thesauros abditos.[2]

reached the innermost cave of a dragon who guarded hidden treasures.

Both the *Philippica* and the fables were useful school-books which presumably spread, with literacy, through Europe. There is no probability, however, that Phædrus was one of the *Beowulf* poet's direct sources. Indeed the whole classical group of treasure-guardians may be dismissed as immediate models for *Beowulf*'s dragon, because he does not possess the trait which qualifies them for that duty: he is not *pervigil* 'ever-wakeful'.[3] The dragon of Phædrus's fable is an unsleeping watcher over his treasure; the fox is astonished that he should spend his lifetime in this apparently purposeless vigil, and asks,

> quem fructum capis
> hoc ex labore, quodve tantum est praemium,
> ut careas somno et aevum in tenebris exigas?

What profit do you receive from this toil, or what reward is so great that you go without sleep and spend your life in darkness?

[1] Cicero, *Philippica* 13, 5.
[2] *The Fables of Phædrus*, ed. G. H. Nall, pp. 45 f.; Book 4, 20, 3 f. See also p. 84, above.
[3] cp. Ovid, *Metamorphoses*, Book 7, 2, 149. Beowulf's dragon requires no sleeping potion; that he sleeps is taken for granted (cp. 2218, 2287).

The dragon replies that it is his nature to do this and he gains no reward by it:

> nullum, inquit ille, verum hoc a summo mihi
> Iove adtributum est.

None, said he, but this charge was assigned to me by great Jove.

The fox's response to this is that anyone who is like the dragon was born unfortunate:

> dis est iratis natus, qui est similis tibi.[1]

anyone who is like you was born when the gods were wrathful.

The use of the dragon as a moral example thus has a long history, and since the curious natural lore used by the fabulists is not usually invented by them, this passage from Phædrus reinforces the impression one has from Cicero that the avaricious dragon was then a current piece of popular belief, as it obviously became in England some centuries later.

Phædrus's work was not much used by later Latin writers; the mention of his name by Martial and half a line borrowed by Prudentius is all the influence that Professor Robinson Ellis could discover; and only one complete early manuscript survives, in a hand of the late ninth or early tenth century, possibly written in Gaul.[2] There is thus no documentary evidence that he was read or even known in Anglo-Saxon England. The later fabulists who incorporate some of his work do not include the *Vulpes et Draco* story. The survival and spread of the idea of the avaricious dragon, like that of the proud stag whose horns are his undoing,[3] most probably depended, therefore, on popular interest in such matters.

The early natural historians were interested in dragons and a conflation of their opinions is to be found in Isidore of Seville.[4] There are no indications that the *Beowulf* poet drew on this learned source at all. The dragon as Isidore knows it is a very large flying serpent which inhabits a cave—treasure is not mentioned—whence it emerges in flight, causing turbulence

---

[1] Phædrus, ed. cit., p. 46, 9 ff. See p. 141, below, and cp. *Beowulf*, 2275-7.
[2] Robinson Ellis, *On Phædrus' Fables* (Oxford, 1894).   [3] See p. 84, above.
[4] Isidore of Seville, *Etymologiae*, ed. W. M. Lindsay, Lib. xii, 5, 1: *De Serpentibus*.

with its wings. It has only a small mouth and uses its tail as a weapon:

Vim autem non in dentibus, sed in cauda habet, et verbere potius quam rictu nocet. Innoxius autem est a venenis, sed ideo huic ad mortem faciendam venena non esse necessaria, quia si quem ligarit occidit.[1]

Its strength does not lie in its teeth, but in its tail, and it wounds by lashing rather than by using its jaws. Indeed, it is innocent of venom, but it has no need of venom to cause death, because if it has coiled round anyone, it kills him.

It is to be recalled that Beowulf's dragon, apart from breathing flames, inflicted a poisoned wound upon him with its teeth (2691 f.; 2714 f.). It is evidently a quite different sort of beast.

Other Old English secular poems add very little to our knowledge of the species as understood by the Anglo-Saxons. The dragon's flaming breath is referred to in *The Fight at Finnsburh*[2] (as in the *Anglo-Saxon Chronicle*);[3] this characteristic is quite unknown to the learned tradition. In the gnomic verses already quoted above concerning the *þyrs*, the dragon guards treasure, but whether or not he is a flame-spewer is not recorded:

> Draca sceal on hlæwe
> Frod frætwum wlanc.[4]

Here a new element has entered into the picture: the lair in a burial mound. None of the Mediterranean dragons are associated with the dead, but it might be conjectured that dragons of the Phædran kind would be more likely to find gold in barrows than in caves throughout Germanic territory. It might further be conjectured that the dragon took its place beside the *draugr*, the animated corpse which guards the treasure of the dead,[5] as a consequence of the mingling of Roman soldiers and German tribesmen; but such speculation does not directly illuminate *Beowulf*, as it is fairly clear from the brief reference

---

[1] Isidore of Seville, op. cit., XII, 5, 4.
[2] Ne ðis ne dagað eastan,   ne her draca ne fleogeð,
    ne her ðisse healle   hornas ne byrnað.   (*Finnsb.* 3 f.)
[3] sub Anno 793; see p. 19, n. 4, above.   [4] *Maxims* II, *ASPR* VI, 26 f.
[5] See N. Chadwick, 'The Monsters and *Beowulf*', p. 178.

in other Anglo-Saxon compositions and from the allusive way the first dragon in *Beowulf* is mentioned that the poet took over a living belief in the firedrake and the barrow-guardian. Whether or not the Geatish hero Beowulf had already become associated with such a creature is a question that cannot be resolved. The rather exhaustive search for parallels which has gone on all this century has not revealed a dragon-slaying similar in all essential points to this one. In the Norse and German analogues the physical nature of the dragon is different; the course of the fight, involving a second hero at its climax, is also different; and most curious of all is the outcome, which seems to combine a typical treasure-winning contest with a second type of dragon-combat in which the hero dies in ridding the land of the scourge.[1] The natural conclusion is that the *Beowulf* poet considerably modified his source, if he did not completely invent this episode from discrete elements. The modification presumably involved the nature of the dragon itself as well as the course of the fight.

The most considerable difference between the dragon Fáfnir who is slain by Sigurð or Siegfried in the analogues and Beowulf's adversary is that Fáfnir had been a man.[2] The *Beowulf* poet appears to have known a version of this story attached to the name of Sigemund Wælsing and his nephew Fitela;[3] but he gives no hint of the origin of Sigemund's dragon and makes the creature rather a nonentity. Thus there is no evidence anywhere that the Anglo-Saxons knew of the existence of the man-dragon. If the poet did know the story in substantially the form it takes in the *Vǫlsunga Saga*, his suppression of the motif of the curse, which takes its rise from the originally human nature of the treasure-guardian, makes my case even stronger. I believe that the dragon has been modified so as to become a more potent symbol of spiritual evil, as it already was a symbol of moral evil.

I turn now from this brief look at the kinds of secular dragon-material probably available to the poet to the dragons which appear in religious writings. I have already illustrated the way in

[1] For the two types of dragon story, see Chambers, *Beowulf: An Introduction*, p. 96.
[2] See Chambers, ibid., p. 458, and p. 94, above.
[3] See lines 875, 877, and 879, 881.

which *draco* was used by Anglo-Latin writers and their sources as a synonym for the Devil.[1] I have also stated that several saints' Lives current in England in Aldhelm's time included a contest with a dragon.[2] I now wish to consider the way biblical and hagiographical dragon-lore intertwine, and how, as I believe, they impinge upon *Beowulf*. I begin with some general observations, and then examine some significant features of the dragons in the poem.

From his reading of the Bible and its glosses, the *Beowulf* poet would know a good deal about dragons—including fiery serpents—as plagues and dreadful visitations. The reader of the English Bible is likely to have quite separate and distinct ideas of the appearance and attributes of these creatures, relating them to snakes, crocodiles, hippopotamuses and the like, but, as I said at the beginning of the chapter, natural history must be forgotten in following the patristic commentators, who use the verbal similarities to produce a horrifying conflation of all these plagues, as agents of the Devil or as *figuræ* of the Ancient Dragon, the Enemy himself. I have already spoken of Pharaoh, the great dragon of Egypt,[3] who has a political significance in the history, but also, more importantly for the exegetes, a figurative relationship with the Devil; in the same way Nebuchadnosor, King of Babylon, 'devouring' Israel, was treated both as historical scourge and image of the Dragon.[4] In moral-allegorical interpretation, the dragonish visitations can be explained as images of the wounding sins of the people; this is particularly true of the *serpens flatu adurens* 'the serpent burning with his breath' which afflicted the Israelites in their journey across the desert (cp. Deut. 8: 15).[5]

---

[1] See pp. 43 ff., above.
[2] See p. 52, above.
[3] See Ezech. 29: 3, and p. 119, above.
[4] See Jer. 51: 34, *absorbuit me quasi draco*.
[5] The same plague of fiery serpents is described in Num. 21: 6, where the people are cured by Moses's brazen serpent. This symbol of salvation was no doubt the subject of many homilies (see p. 40, above). It appears in Bede's Homily II, 18, *CCSL* 122, 316; and the bites of the fiery serpents are there allegorized as sins:

Recte enim per serpentes peccata quae animam simul et corpus ad interitum trahunt, exprimuntur non solum quia igniti quia uirulenti quia ad perimendum sunt astuti uerum etiam quia per serpentem primi parentes nostri ad peccandum persuasi ac de immortalibus sunt peccando mortales effecti.

Modern scholars who have reviewed the biblical references to dragons in considering their possible relevance to *Beowulf* have quite ignored the patristic underthought which unites them all. Professor A. E. Du Bois listed and discussed the twenty-one dragons in the Authorized Version of the Old Testament in an attempt to show that they 'do not have the same meaning, but vary, chiefly against context'.[1] He then used his findings to bolster a theory that Beowulf's dragon must be interpreted against its context of political upheaval and warfare. What he says may well be true of the original writings, and *in vacuo* it could be true of *Beowulf*, but, in the climate of thought I have been discussing, the activity of the exegetes had 'rubbed off the husk' of the contextual differences in order to reveal the spiritual affinity of these dragons. Professor F. Wild in his very comprehensive and detailed review of classical, post-classical, and scriptural dragons in European literature, which includes an appendix on dragons in religious art, takes no account of the patristic reinterpretation of them, and, what is more surprising, does not mention any of the early hagiographers' dragons.[2] Because of this large gap in his survey, he sees a resemblance between *Beowulf* and classical serpent and dragon contests without recognizing that these had largely been supplanted in Christian education by the heroic contests of the saints.

There is one very remarkable difference between the secular dragon-fights and the dragon-contests of the saints' Lives we are concerned with. The saint needs no weapons, or rather, his spiritual weapons are so powerful that the monster can make no defence against them. The conventional modern picture of St George with a lance seems to be a chivalric modification of the

---

Rightly are the sins which drag soul and body together to death represented by serpents, not only because they are fiery and virulent and because they are cunning in destroying, but especially because through the serpent our first parents were induced to sin, and by sinning were changed from immortal to mortal.

The possible application of this to the allegory in *Beowulf* will be considered in Chapter 7.

[1] Du Bois, 'The Dragon in *Beowulf*', p. 821.

[2] Wild, *Drachen im 'Beowulf'*. His researches show a rather surprising absence of dragons from religious art before the period of the Benedictine revival. I am unable to account for this, but it is matched by a similar sparsity of religious dragons in vernacular poetry. The ninth-century decline in Latin studies perhaps had something to do with it?

older legends, in which the beast miserably capitulates before the sign of the Cross, or at the saints' command.[1] It may well be that *Beowulf* scholars have dismissed these tales as irrelevant precisely because there are no visible weapons and no wounds in the saints' contests. I have no wish to pass over or to minimize the difference. On the contrary, I contend that anyone to whom the saints' Lives were familiar fare would be conscious that Beowulf was less powerful than the saint. As a latter-day Hercules, his strength could not compare with that of the humblest *bellator Christi*; Aldhelm makes the point explicitly,[2] and I believe that the *Beowulf* poet does so by implication. This matter is pursued in Chapter 7; at this point I intend only to suggest that the prevalence of saints' Lives in the poet's putative milieu is important, and the dragons in them should not be disregarded. Perhaps it also needs to be said that I do not propose to look for religious allegory in every secular dragon-fight; I do not find any occult significance in Sigemund's dragon, for example. But Beowulf's case is different, because his earlier adversaries have been expressly called God's enemies and his victories over them have been ascribed to divine aid: these references to the cosmic war bring all the scriptural and hagiographical associations of the Dragon flooding in.

Of the saints listed by Ogilvy[3] as being known in England at the relevant time, five face and overcome dragons; only one of

[1] St Michael fighting the Ancient Dragon with his flaming sword is unique in his kind.

[2] At one point in the verse *De virginitate*, St Julian overthrows the pagan statues in the temple by prayer. Among them is a statue of Hercules, which prompts the comparison:

> Alcides fertur Centauri victor opimus,
> Flammea qui pressit latronis flamina Caci,
> Quamvis fumosis ructaret flabra loquelis:
> Herculis in cripta sed torquet dextera; clava
> Non tamen in templo rigida virtute resultat,
> Qua famulus Christi supplex oramina fudit.
> *MGH, AA* xv, 409, 1343 ff.

The grandson of Alceus is said to be the great victor over the centaur, he who choked the fiery breath of the robber Cacus; although he belched blasts of smoky utterance, yet Hercules' hand strangled him in the cave; nevertheless, his stout club does not spring up in strength in the temple, where the servant of Christ has cast it to the ground through the virtue of his prayers.

[3] Ogilvy, *Anglo-Latin Writers*, pp. 1–4. The five saints who overcome dragons are Julian, Hilarion, Sylvester, Victoria, and Germanus.

these, Germanus, is not included by Aldhelm in his *De virginitate*. The story told of Germanus has a setting in Gaul, whereas all the others belong to Mediterranean countries; since the mastering of the dragon follows the same pattern in the Life of St Germanus[1] as in that of Victoria and others, it is reasonable to think that the incident told of the Gallic saint is influenced by the earlier Lives. The most famous of these dragonstories is that of Hilarion, originally told by Jerome in his *Vita S. Hilarionis*;[2] Aldhelm retells it, emphasizing the dragonish qualities of the adversary.[3] The dragon contests in these and other saints' Lives may be distinguished as having three different kinds of significance, apart from the essential point that the saint overcomes the Enemy in his subject creature: there are monstrous beasts who terrorize a neighbourhood, and are physically slain or made captive;[4] there are dragons who emerge from idols, being demons who were worshipped there, and these run away or vanish;[5] and lastly, there are dragons who are apparitions of the devils of hell or Satan himself, appearing in visions or dreams.[6] The first kind reveal the power of the saint's virtue in face of physical ferocity, the second kind show the saint figuratively freeing the people from the Devil's domination by stamping out a pagan cult, while the third kind are revelations or warnings of the grisly enemies who await the soul as it

---

[1] *ASS, Maii* i, 265, 1.   [2] Jerome, *Vita S. Hilarionis eremitae, PL* 23, 2, 50.

[3] Aldhelm, *De virginitate*, ed. cit., prose, pp. 266 f.; verse, pp. 387 f. He compares the feat with that of Daniel (p. 267, 12), whose story he also includes as a prophetic example (pp. 366 ff., 323–66). The scriptural story of the killing of the dragon by Daniel is in Dan. 14: 22–6. E. G. Stanley, *Continuations and Beginnings*, pp. 107 f., quotes the Daniel story, contrasting Daniel's flesh-and-blood dragon with the Dragon of the Apocalypse, with the comment on the former, 'The dragon in *Beowulf* is more like that: lo, he liveth, he eateth and drinketh, and can be destroyed, by Daniel's trick or by the courage of men like Beowulf and Wiglaf—suitably protected by a flame-proof shield.' Beowulf's dragon (who is not shown eating or drinking) certainly has a physical body, but Aldhelm is unconcerned about the distinction the modern scholar makes.

[4] The dragons overcome by Hilarion, Victoria and Germanus are of this kind, but they also appear to symbolize for the hagiographer the paganism of the people. Sylvester's dragon has rather more in common with Daniel's. For Victoria see Aldhelm, ibid., p. 309 and pp. 449 ff.; for Sylvester, ibid., pp. 257 f. and 375 f.

[5] See, for instance, the Life of Bishop Julian, a missionary to Gaul, in *ASS, Jan.* ii, 765.

[6] The best-known of these are in Gregory's *Dialogi* iv, 40; *PL* 77, 440 f.; another is to be found in his *Hom. XIX in Evang., PL* 76, 1158.

leaves the body. As the dragons in *Beowulf* are nowhere linked with the idolatry of the people, the second kind is irrelevant to this enquiry. *Beowulf*'s great adversary is obviously a creature of the first kind, but its allegorical significance, indicated in Hrothgar's admonitory sermon, gives it something in common with the third sort. The dragons of these saints' Lives owe nothing to Phædrus or to Isidore; as in *Beowulf*, no attempt is made at a complete physical description, but the details which the story requires, such as serpentine movement, blasts of noxious vapour or devouring jaws, emerge in the course of the action. In each instance the monster inhabits a cave and the saintly hero goes to its lair to combat it. The monsters do not fly or breathe flame—the only flame-breather in Aldhelm's works is Cacus, the monster vanquished by Hercules in the *Æneid*[1]—but they kill with their poisonous breath, or with their venomous teeth. It is evident that some of the features I have mentioned can be paralleled in *Beowulf*, and that there are some very large differences.

Like the biblical commentators, Aldhelm confounds the physical varieties of adversary by the synonymous use of *draco*, *gypsas* (= snake), *bestia*, and so on. It is also rather evident that as he composes his narration, Aldhelm's mind runs upon the Ancient Dragon as well as upon these earthly *dracones*; he slips easily into such phrases as *strofa stimulante draconis*[2] 'urged by the artifice of the Dragon', and uses as metaphor for the rage of persecution,

> Interea veteris ructantur fauce draconis
> Atra venena sacras Christi torquentia turmas.[3]

Meanwhile spurts of black venom are spewed from the jaws of the Ancient Dragon, tormenting Christ's holy band.

The distinction between metaphorical and actual dragons thus becomes very fine; the dragon mastered by Sylvester was worshipped by the local people, which makes it akin to the dragon-demons who inhabit idols, but there is nothing in Aldhelm's description of it to single out the demonic beast from the pestiferous monster who devours men and cattle.[4] The demonic

[1] See p. 132, n. 2, above.   [2] Aldhelm, op. cit., p. 412, 1421.
[3] ibid., p. 408, 1308 f.
[4] In the stories of Germanus and Victoria the people are converted from idolworship as a result of the saint's victory, though the beast is not expressly related to the idol-demon.

monsters are not expressly said to be devilish, or to be God's enemies; the reader is left to infer this from the context. It is also to be noted that the saints' conflicts are, in one and the same composition, with hostile men, with monstrous beasts, and with personified vices. I have already referred above to the *psychomachia* element in Aldhelm's work; in the verse *De virginitate*, the *bellator Christi* fights his way past the monstrous sins in turn, until he comes upon *Vana Gloria* and *Superbia*, and when he does not yield to these, he can conquer Lucifer himself. The Devil is described in his transformation as he fell from heaven, and he faces the warrior as *pestiferum natrix ructans de fauce venenum* 'the baleful Serpent belching venom from his jaws', which the man of earth shrinks from wounding.[1]

When one returns to Beowulf's dragon fresh from a reading of Aldhelm, one is not likely to look on him as 'a more genial adversary'[2] or 'a being originally human',[3] but as an *attorsceaða* (cp. 2839) who plagues mankind. One particular piece of evidence has seemed to a few scholars to make a specific link between *Beowulf* and the *De virginitate*, namely the phrase *oreðes ond attres* (2523) accepted by all editors as the right emendation of the manuscript reading *reðes ond hattres*.[4] Cook pointed out that Aldhelm's prose account of Victoria's dragon contest contained the phrase *virus et flatus squamosi draconis* 'venom and breath of the scaly dragon'. The use of the same hendiadys for 'venomous breath' appeared to him to indicate that the *Beowulf* poet knew Aldhelm's work and consciously echoed it.[5] Later scholars have been rather sceptical. Wrenn, for example, says: 'One might as plausibly argue that St. Aldhelm—a notable exponent of his native poetry—had been echoing *Beowulf*.'[6] The evidence is certainly not conclusive; the phrase might have been rather

---

[1] Aldhelm, op. cit., p. 461, 2678 to p. 465, 2761. The quoted line is 2749.

[2] Lawrence, *Beowulf and Epic Tradition*, p. 208.

[3] Smithers, *The Making of 'Beowulf'*, p. 11.

[4] For the emendation, see the edd. notes and the strongly-reasoned defence of it by J. C. Pope, 'The Emendation *oreðes ond attres, Beowulf* 2523', *MLN* 72 (1957), 321–8.

[5] Aldhelm, op. cit., p. 308, 24. A similar hendiadys is used by Boniface, *Ænigmata de Virtutibus, PL* 89, 887. The bitter fruit which Adam ate were *infecta antiqui flatuque et felle draconis viperea* ... 'tainted with the breath and serpentine poison of the Ancient Dragon'. This could be imitation of Aldhelm; it shows a spreading of the idea. [6] Wrenn, *Beowulf*, p. 222, n. to 2523.

common, or derived from a lost source; but the balance seems to me to weigh slightly in favour of the *Beowulf* poet's being influenced by Aldhelm or some other Anglo-Latin writer, principally because the phrase is less apposite in *Beowulf*, since the hero is not suffocated by poisonous breath, but wounded by venomous teeth. As the surviving literature represents such a small proportion of what was composed, and plagiarism was not thought a vice, it is hardly possible to establish direct borrowing from one author to another when both use commonplace ideas. The general resemblances I have indicated between the *De virginitate* and *Beowulf* suggest that they share a climate of thought, and perhaps no more than that.

In Old English religious poetry there are occasional references to the Devil as *draca*; they are far less numerous than in Anglo-Latin compositions. In the *Physiologus* (16),[1] the Dragon is the inveterate enemy of the Panther, who symbolizes Christ; in *Elene* (765)[2] the phrase *in dracan fæðme* is found for 'in hell'; in the late *Solomon and Saturn* (25 f.)[3] the word is used as a variation on *deofol*. In *Christ and Satan* (97 f.)[4] firebreathing dragons guard the doors of hell; the Devil himself is not called *draca*, but when he makes a speech sparks of fire and venom shoot from his mouth, a detail obviously combining the description of flame-breathing Leviathan in Job 41 : 12 with the idea of the venomous Serpent. A few dragon-devils appear in late prose homilies; these are apparitions deriving from Gregory's *Dialogues* or other saints' Lives.[5] They add nothing of moment to this argument.

Having, as I hope, now shown that for the contemporary audience the dragon fought by Beowulf needed no pedigree as Grendel did, I come back to the poem itself, and the attributes and behaviour of the dragons in it. Under this head I class the sea-beasts (*sædracan*, cp. 1425–41) and the two treasure-guarding dragons in the stories.

---

[1] *The Panther, ASPR* iii, 169. [2] *Elene, ASPR* ii, 87.

[3] *Solomon and Saturn, ASPR* vi, 32.

[4] *Christ and Satan, ASPR* i, 138; the fire-breathing passages are on pp. 137, 78 f., and pp. 141, 161 f.

[5] For dragon-visions in Gregory, see *PL* 76, 1158; *PL* 77, 392 f. The Latin and OE Lives of St Margaret include an incident in which the Devil, as a fire-breathing dragon, swallows her. (In B. Assmann, *Ags. Homilien und Heiligenleben*, Kassel, 1889; reprint, Darmstadt, 1964, pp. 171 ff. and 208 ff.) There are no early records of the legend in England.

Professor Carney has pointed out that Irish saints must fight water-monsters, in the unregretted absence of the serpent kind from Ireland.[1] The *wildeor* (1430) of *Beowulf* who haunt the evil waters and harass men who try to sail upon them (cp. 1423–9) have some kinship with the *bestia aquatilis* which attacked Columba's follower as he swam across the River Ness.[2] But for the saint's intervention, the man would have been devoured. As in the dragon-stories I have been discussing, the beast is helpless before the sign of the cross and it scurries off at Columba's command. This is rather clearly a Celtic equivalent of the saintly-deliverance tales recounted by Aldhelm. I surmise that the story of Beowulf's underwater fight has been embellished with other hazards from circulating tales, perhaps of the Columban kind. These have Irish sources, but I do not think it is possible to say in the present state of knowledge that this or that incident in *Beowulf* derives from a particular Irish source. The poem indiscriminately peoples the lake with *wyrmas* and *wildeor*; and *nicras* (1427), *sædracan* (1426) and *sædeor* (1510) appear to be used as general terms for the water monsters. Klaeber and others have tried to distinguish the inland from the ocean creatures,[3] but as Malone pointed out in his discussion of *fyrgenstream*, much of the description of the waters conveys an impression of the sea. Perhaps all the elements could be

[1] Carney, op. cit., 97 ff. and 122 ff.

[2] *Adomnan's Life of Columba*, ed. A. O. and M. O. Anderson (London, 1961), pp. 386 f. Carney finds in this the 'ultimate derivation' of the underwater fight in *Beowulf*, the Irish *Táin Bó Fraích* being the intermediary; the argument is unconvincing.

[3] For example, Klaeber in his note on 1428 f. (p. 185) says:
ða on undernmæl oft bewitigað ...; i.e. water-monsters 'such as' (of the same kind as those which) ... These *nicras* do not ply in the sea (*seglrad*).

Malone reviews the linguistic evidence for 'sea' or 'lake' in 'Grendel and his Abode', *Spitzer Studies*, especially pp. 302–4, in support of his theory that the monsters are in the ocean (cp. pp. 115 f., above). Belief in the existence of man-eating water-monsters is attested by the story of Columba cited above, and of sea-beasts by the Ps-Bede discussion about St Paul's sojourn in the sea (quoted above, p. 34); the latter writer concludes:

Unde et inter miracula divina ascribunt quod homo tanto tempore sub undis retentus, neque a circumpositis præfocari aquis, neque a belluis maris devorari potuerit. (*PL* 93, 457)

Thence they include also among divine miracles that a man preserved for such a long time under the waves could not be choked by the waters around him or devoured by the sea-beasts.

conceived as belonging to some vast loch on which fishing-boats ply (hence *seglrad* 1429), surrounded by marshy ground with occasional outcrops of rock; but I am convinced rather that the *Beowulf* poet thought only of hostile waters and inhospitable land. The harassed boats are as likely to have come from recollections of Psalm 103 as from sailors' stories; the rather unexpectedly crowded waters (1425 ff.) bring to mind, as perhaps they were meant to do, the psalmist's words,

> Hoc mare magnum et spatiosum illic reptilia quorum
> non est numerus, animalia pusilla et magna.
> illic naves pertransibunt draco iste quem formasti
> ad inludendum ei.   (Ps. 103, 25 f.)

So is this great sea which stretcheth wide; there are creeping things without number, creatures little and great. There the ships shall go. This sea-dragon which thou hast formed to play therein.

This verse was naturally associated with

> tu confirmasti in virtute tua mare
> tu contribulasti capita draconum super aquas.
>   (Ps. 73: 13)

Thou by thy strength didst make the sea firm: thou didst crush the heads of the dragons upon the waters.

The commentators found in these texts a reference to overcoming the Devil in the sea of life, as well as reference to the Saviour of mankind descending into the depths of hell.[1]

Beowulf's descent into the infested waters is made more dangerous by the presence of these creatures, and if the recollection of the Psalms is intentional, there is here another image, like the crossing of the desert, of the perils of the soul's journey, since the Psalms make that 'reach into ultimate questions' of which Professor Tuve speaks.[2]

Before examining Beowulf's greatest adversary, I must say something of the dragon slain by Sigemund (cp. 874–97). The

---

[1] See Augustine, *Enarr. in Psalmos*, *CCSL* 40, in Ps. 103, 1524–30; and *CCSL* 39, 1014, *in Ps.* 73, especially *Intelligimus dracones omnia daemonia sub diabolo militantia* 'We understand by dragons all the demonic host serving under the Devil.' (1014, 15). Tropologically, both passages are interpreted as overcoming temptations in the stormy seas of life.

[2] See p. 74, above.

first deduction one will make from the way in which this tale is narrated is that the slaying of giants (cp. 883 f.) and treasure-guarding dragons (887, cp. 892–9) was a familiar occurrence in contemporary story-telling: the beast's nature and appearance are taken for granted. Rather strangely, in view of Beowulf's own discomfiture, the other hero meets no difficulty in thrusting his sword right through the dragon. The treasure is won at a single stroke and the creature conveniently melts in its own heat—a circumstance which excites no comment from the poet. The mention of heat (897) suggests that he thought in terms of a firedrake, but Sigemund is not said to be harassed by flaming breath; moreover, Beowulf's indisputably hot dragon did not melt away, so there is no simple correlation between flaming insides and melting. It seems rather obvious that the poet was not particularly interested in the details of Sigemund's fight.

If he knew a story substantially like that told of Sigurð in the *Volsunga Saga*,[1] his selection of material for the summary account he gives is peculiar, and indicative of a desire to avoid the darker features of Sigemund's life. There is nothing about Fitela's incestuous birth[2] or the origin of Fáfnir, or, most strangely of all, the curse upon the dragon's hoard. The poem presents a singularly unclouded life of heroic bravery, loyal companionship between uncle and nephew and the splendid rewards of valour. It may be, as some have suggested, that the story was so well known that the dark side of the picture is to be filled in by the poet's audience, since the allusive manner assumes some degree of knowledge in the hearers, but even so, one would have expected some hint of irony if that were the case. The only shadow I find has been already mentioned above[3]—the loading of the treasure ship might recall the loading of Scyld's death-ship and so emphasize the transience of Sigemund's possession of the gold. I surmise that the poet kept his account short because any dwelling upon Sigemund's fight would surely diminish Beowulf's own reputation, since Sigemund needed no aid and emerged unscathed. In allegory, such

[1] *Volsunga Saga* is edited by M. Olsen (Copenhagen, 1906–8).
[2] Whitelock, *Audience*, p. 57, suggests that *eam his nefan* (881) is a deliberate and ironic use of understatement, but the general tone of approbation in the passage makes it difficult to accept this.　　　　[3] Above, pp. 82 f.

a contrast could have been intended, but there are no signs of allegory in the episode and no hint that Sigemund was divinely favoured. A wish not to compare the two heroes too closely might explain why the matter of the curse, which seems to have a proper place in both stories, is passed over. Another reason might be the man-dragon element in the curse, which conflicts with the presentation of dragons in *Beowulf* as of the serpent kind. I conclude that the Sigemund lay raises Beowulf to the ranks of the great heroes by implication, but that further comparison between them is not to be pressed.[1] Sigemund's dragon enlarges our knowledge of the kind very little; it is almost a nonentity in the fight.

Beowulf's final adversary is introduced into the poem in words remarkably like those which introduce Grendel[2] in the Heorot affair. A time of prosperity is interrupted by the intrusion of the enemy who gains the mastery of the region during the night-time. The men of Heorot lived

> eadiglice, oððæt an ongan
> fyrene fre(m)man feond on helle   (100 f.)

and similarly Beowulf's people were prosperous

> oððæt an ongan
> deorcum nihtum draca rics(i)an   (2210 f.)

The parallelism between the two incursions is continued in the manner in which the two aged kings react to the calamity with grief rather than with anger (cp. 170 f. with 2327 f.). In their affliction, they are brought, like Job, to contemplate their relationship with God (I pursue this point in Chapter 5).

---

[1] Klaeber, *Beowulf*, p. 158, says that in reciting the adventures of Sigemund, the poet is 'raising Beowulf, as it were, to the rank of pre-eminent Germanic heroes.' Bonjour approves this statement, but perceives that the comparison is not altogether to Beowulf's advantage. 'The contrast between Sigemund and Beowulf ... is that while the former survived the Dragon fight, the latter did not. That those who knew should not remain under the impression of the contrast (however light the touch) needed the introduction of a second parallel, that with Heremod' ('The Digressions in *Beowulf*', p. 48).

[2] A very slight incidental link between the two kinds of adversary is Grendel's *glof*,

> sio wæs orðoncum eall gegyrwed
> deofles cræftum ond dracan fellum.   (2087 f.)

This seems to imply that giants and dragons frequented the same regions.

The dragon's nature is most explicitly revealed in the descriptive passage which accompanies his taking possession of the hoard:

> Hordwynne fond
> eald uhtsceaða opene standan,
> se ðe byrnende biorgas seceð,
> nacod niðdraca, nihtes fleogeð
> fyre befangen; hyne foldbuend
> (swiðe ondræ)da(ð). He gesecean sceall
> (ho)r(d on h)rusan, þær he hæðen gold
> wara ð wintrum frod, ne byð him wihte ðy sel.
>
> (2270–7)

The last three lines are in accord with the dragon-description in the Cotton gnomic verses (26 f.) already quoted above. The moralizing half-line at the end, however, recalls the wretched miser of Phædrus's fable.[1] Thus the great adversary is compounded of cupidity and malice (cp. *niðdraca* 273); he terrifies the people of the region and he hoards treasure which he cannot use.

When the dragon's wrath is aroused by theft from his hoard, his reactions are described thus:

> þa se wyrm onwoc, wroht wæs geniwad;
> stonc ða æfter stane, stearcheort onfand
> feondes fotlast. (2287–9)

There are three points of interest here. First is the use of the word *feond* for the thief, coupled with a phrase which would ordinarily mean 'strife was renewed' (2287 b);[2] this suggests to me that a feud exists between mankind and the dragon, such as existed earlier with the Grendel kin. Second is the neutral quality of the word *stearcheort* (2288), compared with the glossaries' 'stout-hearted'; I suggest that in a context of cruelty 'stony-hearted'[3] would be more appropriate (cp. *Juliana*, 636). Third is a minor but rather tantalizing point: the meaning of

---

[1] See p. 127, above.

[2] Klaeber, *Beowulf*, p. 210, n. to 2287, suggests a contextual reading: 'Probably not "strife was renewed", but (lit.) "strife arose which previously did not exist".'

[3] If the reminiscences of Leviathan which I find elsewhere are accepted, this word might also be an incidental link; cp. Job 41: 15, *Cor eius indurabitur tanquam lapis* 'his heart shall be as hard as a stone'. Gregory takes the verse figuratively.

stonc (2288). The editors have been much exercised about this, and have on the whole rejected the idea that it could mean 'snuffed (the scent)' in spite of the partial parallel of the German *Ortnit* (570) quoted by Klaeber,[1] and the naturalness of the action in following a trail. It is just possible that this dragonish habit was learned by the poet from the *Moralia*. On Job 30: 29, *Frater fui draconum* 'I was the brother of dragons', Gregory relates the dragons to wicked men, adding,

De quibus et per prophetam dicitur: *Traxerunt ventum quasi dracones* (*Jerem.* XIV, 6). Perversi enim quique ventum quasi dracones trahunt, cum malitiosa superbia inflantur.[2]

About these it is also said by the prophet, *They snuffed up the wind like dragons.* For the perverse as it were snuff up the wind like dragons when they are becoming puffed up with wicked pride.

Can it be that this passage suggested the snuffing of the thief's scent?

As this last point illustrates, subhuman and diabolical qualities combine in Beowulf's dragon: he follows the footprints (2300 ff.), he rejoices at the thought of fighting, he is impatient and vindictive. He is occasionally described in neutral words appropriate to any savage fighter, e.g. *gearo guðfreca* (2414); coupled with Beowulf, he is called *aglæca* (2592). One human-sounding phrase used about him has a special significance: I refer to *him seo wen geleah* (2323), applied to his false confidence in the strength of his defences. The phrase appears to be an Englishing of *spes ejus frustrabitur eum* 'his hope shall fail him,' used of Leviathan in Job 40: 28. The phrase sounds ordinary enough, and without other indications the echo of Job might be dismissed as coincidental. It is not, however, a common phrase in Old English, and the other instances of its use reinforce the impression that it has diabolical associations: one is applied, as in Job, to the defeat of Satan and his forces (*Genesis* 49); a second refers to the Mermedonians' vain hope of devouring the men of God (*Andreas* 1076)—and they are conceived throughout the poem as subjects of the Devil, or, putting it in patristic

---

[1] Klaeber, *Beowulf*, p. 210, n. to 2288. Wrenn, *Beowulf*, p. 289, *s.v. stincan*, gives 'move quickly', but admits the possibility of 'an otherwise unknown sense of *to take up the scent* or *sniff*, as earlier editors thought'.

[2] Gregory, *Moralia*, PL 76, 183.

terms, as part of the Body of Leviathan; the third example of the phrase is in the description of the Flood (*Genesis* 1446), where the defection of the raven and the phrase *se feonde* show that the poet was thinking about the Devil when the phrase came into his head.

The large feature of his flaming breath,[1] the cryptic statement that he will 'strew gold beneath him like mire',[2] and various small points in description and behaviour, link Beowulf's dragon with Leviathan. None is conclusive in itself: it is only in the context of the spiritual war that they take on significance, in telling the hearers that the dragon, like the giants, has a diabolical nature. Anyone to whom Aldhelm's phrase *bellator Job* made sense would, I think, pick up the hint of *him seo wen geleah*, which immediately follows the verse containing the watchword of the spiritual warrior: *Memento belli* 'Remember the battle' (Job 40: 27). The covert allusion to Leviathan, the flame-breathing shape of the Enemy, signals that the great struggle foreshadowed in Hrothgar's sermon is about to begin. When the surges of flame envelop Beowulf's royal hall, the hero suffers great disturbance of mind and spirit. Gregory describes this effect of the flames and smoke spewed by Leviathan.[3] Beowulf feels God's anger upon him, and for the first time the outcome of the spiritual battle is in doubt. But to pursue the allegory here would take me beyond the bounds of this chapter. The poet has made a preparation for his hearers, and his readers, in what Hrothgar has to tell of the moral and spiritual dangers which beset an aged king, and it would be wrong to approach Beowulf's final trial without passing along the path the poet has laid.

I therefore leave the adversaries, now, I hope, revealed in their complex nature: in the history they are physical plagues, like the *igniti serpentes* of the Israelites' desert journey or the devouring beasts mastered by the saints, actuated by malice, spawned in those parts of the universe which lie under God's

---

[1] cp. Job 41: 12. Gregory's moralizing of the passage (*PL* 76, 712–18) is used in interpreting Beowulf's spiritual battle with the dragon on p. 243, below. For his complete identification of Leviathan with the Ancient Dragon of the Apocalypse, see ibid., 646.

[2] *Sternet sibi aurum quasi lutum* (Job 41: 21).

[3] Gregory, ibid., 712–14.

ban. As physical beings, the giants are descendants of the out-cast Cain, the dragons descendants of the cursed Serpent. The shape imagination gave them was naturally that of the hostile and man-slaying creatures believed to infest the treacherous places of the countryside and the gloomy depths of great waters. The habits of the great dragon were compounded of the hostility of the serpent kind to man and the traditional (perhaps Roman) association of the creature with hoarded treasure. In the allegory of the individual man, the monsters are the embodiment of evil forces which beset a man, tempting and testing him, proving or destroying him. The evil powers have made incursions not only in Heorot or Geatland, but in every man's private kingdom, and in fighting them, as the poet gives his audience to under-stand, the hero must also fight an inner battle. In this realm, Beowulf's dragon is compounded of Leviathan and Mammon, the powers which govern the proud and the cupidinous.

In the history of one man's battles, the poet also creates an image of the battle of mankind *sub specie æternitatis*. When one reflects on the story in this way, Heorot recalls Babylon; the giants in the waters, the proud of the earth cast down into the depths of hell; the dragon's gold, the glory of the world with its *calix aureus Babylon*;[1] the great dragon enlarges into the Ancient Enemy himself, whose poison has infected human kind, and who is *auctor mortis* as God is *auctor vitæ*. This enlarging of the sig-nificance of the story is done chiefly through Hrothgar's sermon, as I hope to show in Chapter 6. But before this exposition can proceed, another important question must be examined. How

---

[1] The relevance of the dragon's cup to the allegory is indicated by Gregory's comment on Leviathan's gold (Job 41: 21),

Rursum auri nomine, nitor gloriæ temporalis exprimitur, sicut per Prophetam dicitur: *Calix aureus Babylon* (Jer. 51: 7). Quid enim Babylonis nomine, nisi hujus mundi gloria designatur? Quæ calix aureus dicitur, quia dum pulchra esse tem-poralia ostentat, stultas mentes in sua concupiscentia debriat, ut speciosa temporalia appetant et invisibilia pulchra contemnant. Hoc aureo calice prima sponte sua Eva debriata est. ...(*PL* 76, 733)

Again, by the word *gold* is signified the splendour of temporal glory, as is said by the prophet: *Babylon, a golden cup*. For what could be denoted by the name of Babylon, if not the glory of this world? This is said to be a golden cup because when temporal things appear to be beautiful, foolish minds become drunk with desire for them, so that they covet the outwardly splendid temporal things and spurn the beautiful things which are invisible. From this golden cup Eve of her own free will was the first to become drunk.

can there be a Christian allegory without a Christian hero? I have said a good deal about saints contending with demons and overcoming noxious monsters: the reader may well object that Beowulf is no saint, but a noble man living in a pagan world. What relevance can the saints' Lives have to such a man? In what fashion can Beowulf be a Christian's hero? To answer this, I now turn to the poet's conception of the beliefs of the men in the story and the springs of their behaviour.

5   God and Man in the Poem

In my opening chapter, I stated my general belief about the *Beowulf* poet's presentation of the religious faith of his characters, which may be summed up in the phrase: a Christian conception of the godliness of unregenerate man. I also said that salvation was outside the scheme of the poem, and that no unequivocal answer could be given to the question, 'Was Beowulf saved or damned?' because it was a question not asked or answered in the composition itself. I must now expatiate upon these ideas and offer some attempts at explanation of the few but obtrusive passages which may appear to be at variance with this view.

I begin with the text itself. There are some very singular features in the religion imputed to the characters and some apparent inconsistencies in the poet's own attitude towards them. These are well known, but it will be convenient to assemble them here for discussion.

The first curious feature is that there are no priests and no specific religious rites, either Christian or heathen, at the courts of Hrothgar, Hygelac, or Beowulf. This can hardly reflect the real-life situation either of the historical Danes and Geats or of the Anglo-Saxon courts known to the poet.[1] It is in marked contrast with classical epic practice, in which prayers and libations to the gods accompany every great undertaking. When Beowulf set off for Denmark his friends *hæl sceawedon* (204), but what they actually did, and whether some rite was involved, the poet does not reveal.[2] The disposal of the dead involves no religious ceremonial, though certain ancient customs—such as riding round the grave—are mentioned. Even when the Danes pray

---

[1] Bede accepts the presence of the *pontifex* Coifi at Edwin's court without comment, *HE* II, 13; Plummer I, 111 ff.

[2] Sisam suggests a translation 'took the omens' for *hæl sceawedon* (204), and remarks 'There is no adverse comment from the poet and perhaps the meaning in this context is simply that they observed the natural signs of wind and sea'. (*Structure*, p. 73.)

to idols in their fear of Grendel, no pagan god is named and the nature of their sacrifices remains mysterious (175–8).

The second strange feature is a combination of circumstances: both Danes and Geats speak of God and acknowledge his governance of the world, yet they offer no prayers to God in direct address, and the poem also says in a notoriously confusing fashion, that they did not know God:

> Metod hie ne cuþon,
> dæda demend,   ne wiston hie drihten god,
> ne hie huru heofena   helm herian ne cuþon
> wuldres waldend.   (180–3)

In spite of this passage, Hrothgar speaks at length to Beowulf about God's gifts to man and the need to shun the evil of pride, showing a good understanding of the doctrine and language of temptation (1700–81). This long speech, rightly regarded as a homily, has more specific relevance to the action than is usually conceded; because of its importance and complexity I have treated it separately in Chapter 6. Hrothgar is credited with sound knowledge of God's law and the Devil's attempts to alienate man from God. Beowulf, too, expressly speaks of God's part in mortal affairs, and at one point fears that he has angered the eternal Lord (2329–31).

On another level of theological improbability are Beowulf's direct mention of hell and judgment in two of his speeches, one concerning Unferth's guilt as a fratricide (587–9), the other in his account to Hrothgar of Grendel's death and present wait for God's judgment upon him (974–9).

In his own voice, the poet several times speaks of God's rule over the world in all ages. He makes no reference to the Trinity: his own phrases about divine subjects are not markedly different from those put in the mouths of the characters. He imputes sin, in an allusive form of words, to Grendel (137) and to Heremod (915); he also describes Grendel as *hæþen* (852, 986). This word is otherwise employed only twice, in reference to the buried gold and in the context just mentioned of the Danes' idol-worship (179). He says very little concerning the after-life; apart from the plain statement that hell received Grendel (852), the expressions he uses are notably vague and sometimes ambiguous. Nowhere does he speak of heaven outright, or of its joy.

It will be seen that the matters I have put first present no great problem; granted that a Christian poet wished to create an impression of a pre-Christian world, he would understandably not wish to revive memories of the displaced deities, or forms of worship now decently forgotten, or, worse, still lurking in the half-light of memory among the Anglo-Saxon people.[1] The conflict of fundamental conceptions about the Danish religion which I mentioned next will require a special discussion. If this one specific statement about pagan worship is for the moment put aside, the other religious references can, I think, be reasonably accommodated in a theory that the poet has used his patristic learning (or that of his teachers) about the nature of man to create an imagined world upon which the revelation of God in Christ has not impinged. For information about the beliefs of good men ignorant of the scriptural law of God he would naturally turn to the Book of Job, in which a just man who was neither Jew nor Christian[2] showed unmistakable faith in his Creator and defeated the Devil's attacks upon that faith. He would, of course, be influenced by Gregory's view of Job's life and interpretation of Job's words. Gregory frequently

---

[1] C. Donahue, 'Beowulf, Ireland and the Natural Good', *Traditio*, 1949–51, notices a similar reticence over the names of pagan gods on the part of Irish saga-writers. (p. 27, n. 42)

[2] Augustine in the *De civitate Dei*, 18, 47, used the piety of Job as proof that men of Gentile nations could belong to the celestial city. (cited by Donahue, loc. cit., p. 266, n. 20).

Populus enim re uera, qui proprie Dei populus diceretur, nullus alius fuit; homines autem quosdam non terrena, sed caelesti societate ad ueros Israelitas supernae ciues patriae pertinentes etiam in aliis gentibus fuisse negare non possunt; quia si negant, facillime conuincuntur de sancto et mirabili uiro Iob, qui nec indigena nec proselytus, id est aduena populus Israel fuit, sed ex gente Idumaea genus ducens, ibi ortus, ibidem mortuus est. (*CCSL*, 48, 645)

For in truth there was no other people which was specially called the people of God; but they cannot deny that there have been certain men even of other nations who belong, not by earthly but by heavenly fellowship, to the true Israelites, citizens of the heavenly homeland; since, if they deny this, they are very easily confounded by the instance of the holy and admirable man Job, who was neither a native nor a proselyte (that is, one who came to join the people of Israel), but being born of Idumaean stock, lived and died in that same place. Augustine was referring to men born before Christ, which is an important consideration when salvation is in question, but the pertinent point here is that Job knew of God and right conduct without benefit of Scripture.

uses other Old Testament texts to elucidate Job's speeches, often quoting the Psalms for this purpose. Here, I suggest, lies the explanation of Beowulf's anachronistic knowledge of hell and judgment and Hrothgar's knowledge of temptation: they are modelled upon Job in this respect,[1] and we shall also find illumination of the attitudes imputed to them in the network of patristic thinking which formed a web round the Psalms.

In this chapter I present first some statements from the Bible, and from Augustine and Gregory, about man's natural knowledge of God and his law, in substantiation of the general theory I have propounded. I then take in turn the elements I have referred to as being out of harmony with the Augustinian view, including particular discussion of some phrases of uncertain meaning, such as *ece ræd* (1201), *Godes leoht geceas* (2469), and *soðfæstra dom* (2820). In the course of the chapter, I review some of the critical arguments which have been put forward to explain these difficult passages, and add some conjectures of my own.

At the outset, I must refer to what has already been said above in Chapter 2 about St Paul's doctrine that all men of every age can recognize their Creator in his works.[2] In the verses there quoted from the Epistle to the Romans, the Apostle states that men are without excuse when they worship images and neither glorify nor give thanks to the God who made them. This verse may well have suggested to the *Beowulf* poet that blessing and thanksgiving were the two kinds of religious activity to be expected of noble men in pre-Christian times. Hrothgar and Wealhtheow, Hygelac and Beowulf and the Geatish warriors are all said to give thanks when events turn out well for them.[3]

Augustine takes up St Paul's doctrine and explains it to the catechumen in *De catechizandis rudibus*. He describes the creation of the visible and invisible worlds, and then speaks of man:

---

[1] The concepts of judgment and hell occur in a number of Job's speeches, as Gregory interprets them; apart from the explicit mention of *infernus* in Job 17: 13, 16 and 26: 6, the *terra tenebrosa* (10: 21 f.) is so understood; he finds mention of judgment in many places in the book, including 21: 30, 36: 6, 40: 5. I return to some significant points in these passages on p. 164 below.

[2] See p. 52, above. The verses quoted are Rom. 1: 20 f.; cp. also p. 64, above.

[3] Klaeber, *Angl.* 1912, 127, cites a number of prayers and hymns on the theme *Gratias agamus Domino*, but these are not as important for the non-Christian characters of *Beowulf* as the Pauline passage quoted above.

149

fecit et hominem ad imaginem suam; ut quemadmodum ipse per omnipotentiam suam præsest universæ creature, sic homo per intelligentiam suam, qua etiam creatorem suum, cognoscit et colit, præesset omnibus terrenis animalibus.[1]

And he made man in his own image, in order that as he himself in his omnipotence rules the whole creation, so man by means of his understanding, through which he knows and worships his Creator, might rule all the living things of earth.

This reiteration of the doctrine in an influential book of instruction would ensure that it was generally known. The *Beowulf* poet most probably learnt at school, therefore, the axiom that all men can recognize the existence of God and glorify him. He would also have been taught that there is a universal moral law recognized by man's inborn conscience. Again St Paul is the author of the doctrine; the basic text is as follows:

Cum enim gentes, qui legem non habent, naturaliter ea quæ legis sunt faciunt, ejusmodi legem non habentes, ipsi sibi sunt lex; qui ostendunt opus legis scriptum in cordibus suis, testimonium reddente illis conscientia ipsorum et inter se invicem cogitationibus accusantibus aut etiam defendentibus. (Rom. 2: 14–16)

For when the gentiles, who have not the law, do by nature those things that are of the law, these having not the law, are a law to themselves, who shew the work of the law written in their hearts, their conscience bearing witness to them, and their thoughts between themselves accusing, or also defending one another.

This passage makes explicit the deduction which readers of the Book of Genesis are impelled to make on consideration of the story of Cain. Whereas Adam and Eve are said to disobey a commandment, Cain in murdering his brother did not contravene a prohibition of murder, yet sin is imputed to him, and his own consciousness of guilt is implied by his lying answer to the question, *Ubi est Abel frater tuus?* 'Where is thy brother Abel?'[2] Cain's anger and chagrin when God showed favour to Abel and not to him were passions which ousted his natural love for his brother. His transgression was twofold: he was resentful towards God and towards his brother. The eternal law is epitomized in the proper relationships which Cain rejects—love towards

[1] Augustine, *De catechizandis rudibus*, ed. cit., p. 35, 5. [2] cp. Gen. 4: 7–9.

God and his brother man.[1] The story of Cain has particular significance in *Beowulf* as providing a paradigm for the evil characters in the story, who do not show the work of the law 'written in their hearts'. The noble characters, Hrothgar and Beowulf, demonstrate a trust in God (which may at times be dimmed) and a concern for their fellow-men, which accord with this view of the law of nature.

Gregory and Bede are alike quite sure that men know when they do right or wrong, and that all are guilty who fail to keep the law of God. Gregory insists that man's rational nature makes it impossible for him to be ignorant of what he is doing, *naturæ enim lege compellitur seu pravum sive rectum sit quod operatur* 'For he is bound by the law of nature to know whether what he is doing is wrong or right'.[2] Bede is even more specific about the guilt of every sinner, since all have received the law of nature as sons of Adam:

Omnes enim qui peccant prævaricationis rei sunt, hoc est, non solum illi qui datam sibi scriptæ legis scientiam contemnunt, sed et illi qui innocentiam legis naturalis quam in protoplasto omnes accepimus sive infirmitate, sive negligentia, sive etiam ignorantia, corrumpunt.[3]

All who sin are charged with wrongdoing: that is to say, not only those who disregard the knowledge of the written law given to them, but also those who mar the innocence of the natural law which we have all received in the first man, whether through weakness, or through negligence, or even through ignorance.

These quotations from authorities who represent the sort of thinking the *Beowulf* poet probably absorbed at school make clear that such expressions as *wæs to fæst on þam* (137) of Grendel's sins of violence and murder, or *hine fyren onwod* (915), of

---

[1] The justice of Job (29: 14) is discussed by Gregory under the heading *Justi sollicite attendunt, quid Deo, quid proximo debeant*. 'The righteous solicitously consider what they ought to render to God and what to their neighbour' (*PL* 76, 119 f.).

[2] ibid., 427.

[3] Bede is commenting on *Omnis qui facit peccatum, et iniquitatem facit* 'Whosoever committeth sin, committeth also iniquity' (*In 1 Ep. Joan.* 3: 4; *PL* 93, 100). There appears to be an element of contradiction in the thought that one can break the natural law in ignorance; this may have some bearing on Beowulf's sense of guilt (2329 ff.). This biblical chapter has already been cited as the source of the doctrine of Cain as a spiritual son of the Devil. I refer to both matters again on p. 174, below.

Heremod's change into a cruel and murderous tyrant, or Beowulf's denunciation of Unferth for killing his brothers (587– 589) would not have seemed out of place in a world untouched by the gospel of Christ. There are, in fact some signs here that he has chosen his examples of wrongdoing to illustrate what happens when men reject the natural law.

The universal law of human nature according to Augustine's theory requires men to direct themselves towards God and away from worldly possessions and pleasures: 'Iubet igitur æterna lex avertere amorem a temporalibus et eum mundatum ad æterna convertere.'[1] 'Thus the eternal law commands us to turn our love away from temporal things and to direct it, purified, to things eternal.' It is a tenet of his doctrine that the human mind can never entirely lose the memory of God:

Sic itaque condita est mens humana, ut nunquam sui non meminerit. ... Non tamen in his tantis infirmitatis et erroris malis amittere potuit naturalem memoriam, intellectum, et amorem sui; propter quod merito dici potuit ... *Quanquam in imagine ambulat homo, tamen vane conturbatur. Thesaurizat, et nescit cui congregabit ea* (Ps. 38: 7).[2]

The human mind was so created that it can never fail to remember itself. ... Even in the great evils of weakness and error it cannot lose the natural memory, understanding, and love of itself: because of this it could justly be said. ... *Surely man walks in an image, yet he is vainly disquieted. He stores up treasures, and does not know for whom he will gather them.*

This verse from Psalm 38 is much used in patristic discussions of the nature of man; Gregory demonstrates his familiarity with it by using it without indication that he is quoting, in a passage in the *Moralia* about the vanity of life on earth compared with *bona æternæ patriæ*.[3] The complex of doctrine which surrounds this scriptural verse explains a good deal of the outlook of *Beowulf*, and I shall return to it *apropos* of Hrothgar's admonition. I mention it here because it applies to Gentile as well as Jew, and the exegesis of it could support the Book of Job in giving the poet his attitude to Hrothgar and Beowulf, who, though ignorant of the Bible, can speak of God and know sin. A further

---

[1] Augustine, *De libero arbitrio*, CSEL, 74, p. 32.
[2] Augustine, *De Trinitate*, PL 42, 1049 f. [3] Gregory, *Moralia*, PL 76, 276.

paragraph from the *De Trinitate* will conclude my evidence on this point: Augustine here uses two verses from the Psalms to show that nations sunk in error cannot so forget God as not to think of an eternal world and make righteous moral judgments in the light of natural law. In the chapter which precedes that from which I have already quoted, he reconciles Psalm 9: 18, *omnes gentes quæ obliviscuntur Deum* 'all the nations that forget God', with Psalm 21: 28, *commemorabuntur et convertentur ad Dominum universi fines* 'all the ends of the earth shall remember, and shall be converted to the Lord', by observing,

Non igitur sic erant oblitæ istæ gentes Deum, ut ejus nec commemoratæ recordarentur. Obliviscendo autem Deum, tanquam obliviscendo vitam suam, conversæ fuerant in mortem, hoc est, in infernum. ...
Nam hinc est quod etiam impii cogitant æternitatem, et multa recte reprehendunt recteque laudant in hominum moribus.[1]

Thus these nations had not so far forgotten God that they did not remember him when they had been reminded. For by forgetting God, as if forgetting their own life, they had been turned into death, that is, into hell. ...
Hence it is that even the impious think of eternity, and rightly censure and rightly praise many things in human conduct.

I do not pretend that the whole doctrine of man's nature given in Augustine's treatise has relevance for the world of *Beowulf*: the fundamental doctrine of the *electi* is not treated in the poem.[2] But it is, after all, a poem, not a theological tract, and I have quoted these patristic arguments not as sources but as indications that the *Beowulf* poet was doing nothing novel or inconsistent with Christian teaching in portraying pagans who think about God and the moral law.

I have written so far as if *lex æterna* and *lex naturæ* were one and the same thing; they are in fact God's law considered under

---

[1] Augustine, *De Trinitate, PL* 42, 1049, 1052. If the poet knew this passage, it could have supplied him with the thought, *Sinc eaðe mæg ... gumcynnes gehwone oferhigian* (2764 ff.); cp. Augustine, ibid., 1050: *Thesauri enim mentum possunt plerumque subvertere.* 'Treasures can very often overthrow the mind'. But the idea is commonplace.

[2] M. P. Hamilton, 'The Religious Principle in Beowulf', assumes that Beowulf belongs to the *electi* (pp. 330 f.) but her conclusion is not founded upon any specific statement in the poem, since she admits the ambiguity of *soðfæstra dom* (2820).

different aspects, the one being contrasted with *lex temporalis*, human law which governs affairs in the world,[1] and the other with *lex scripta*, the Mosaic and Christian law to be found in the Bible. The *lex natura* is not abrogated, but supplemented, first by the Mosaic and then then by the Christian commandments. St Paul distinguishes periods of time during which mankind was governed by these different aspects of God's law: before Moses there was no written law for God's people, so there are three stages in the development of the law—natural, Mosaic, Christian.[2] One might add that for the Gentile nations ignorant of the law of Moses, the stages are effectively reduced to two, the time of natural law and the time of Christian law, the latter dating from their conversion to the Faith. It would seem a matter of common sense to refer to these as the Old and the New Law, and if Beowulf was afraid he had sinned, knowing nothing of the scriptural law, it would evidently be *ofer ealde riht* (cp. 2330) 'against the Old Law', that he thought he might have acted. The lines in which the phrase occurs have puzzled modern readers, including myself, for many years, largely because they are followed later in the poem by words which appear to say that Beowulf's soul joined the just in heaven (2819–20). The question of Beowulf's salvation is, I believe, a separate issue; I do not see any way of interpreting *ealde riht* as Christian moral law, so it is impossible to suppose that Beowulf met death as a Christian. I shall come to this matter shortly, but first I wish to suggest that the phrase *ofer ealde riht* is vague, perhaps purposely so, and critics are probably wrong to try to attach a precise theological meaning to it. The context shows that it means 'God's law as the men of old understood it' which would mean, according to the passages I have quoted, the law *scripta in cordibus suis*, which requires men to serve God above all else and to love their fellow-men. Augustine's arguments about the nature of man's being and his need to turn towards his Creator, constantly denied by his perverse desire to cling to *temporalia*, consort well with the philosophical guidance Hrothgar offered to Beowulf, and provide a useful clue to the kind of guilt Beowulf thought he might have incurred.

[1] See Augustine, *De libero arbitrio*, CSEL 74, pp. 32 f.
[2] See Ep. Gal., 3: 16–26.

The contents of the 'Old Law' as Beowulf understood them have been related by Donahue to 'the traditional precepts of Germanic morality', on the grounds that Beowulf before his death declared that the Lord could not accuse him of 'treachery, false oaths, and the slaughter of kinsmen'.[1] This argument can hardly be altogether right, because Beowulf's troubled mind, when he supposed he had angered God, cannot have been perturbed by thoughts of these sins about which his conscience was clear. The unease that he felt seems more probably the realization that he had become content to enjoy the *temporalia* that were his in abundance, and, as Hrothgar had foretold, had neglected the service of his Lord. The poet does not explicitly say this, but the hero's gloom and the completely different atmophere of his last struggle, in which God has no part, keep the audience unsure what his state will be in the hour of death. His motives and the allegorical meaning of the fight are outside the theme of this chapter, but I suggest that a Christian poet would not introduce the thought of God's anger without having a cause of that anger in mind. However, it must not be forgotten that the form of words is *wende se wisa þæt he Wealdende ... bitre gebulge* (2329–31); the poet never plainly says that the supposition was right. He may also have wished to remind his hearers that Beowulf, who knew nothing of God's purposes as revealed in the Scriptures, would find God's ways even more mysterious than they themselves did. Augustine describes a state of mind rather like this in his discourse upon Psalm 2, a psalm which admonishes the kings of the earth. He comments as follows upon the phrase 'lest at any time the Lord be angry' (Ps. 2: 12):

Nequando autem *irascatur Dominus*, cum dubitatione positum est; non secundem uisionem prophetae, cui certum est, sed secondum eos ipsos qui monentur; quia cum dubitatione solent cogitare iram Dei, quibus non aperte reuelatur.[2]

Lest at any time the Lord be angry is put as if there were doubt, not in the vision of the prophet, for whom there is certainty, but in those who are being admonished; because those who have not had the full revelation of God are wont to ponder uncertainly upon his anger.

[1] Donahue, *Traditio*, 1949–51, p. 275.
[2] Augustine, *Enarr. in Ps.*, *CCSL* 38, p. 6; cp. Ecclus. 10: 14 f.

One might apply this to the *Beowulf* poet; the uncertainty about the sudden wrath of God is not in the mind of the author, but is part of the mind of his ancient king.

The sense of sin, not fully understood, but grievous to the man who wishes to serve God, is also found in the Psalms:

> delicta quis intelligit
> ab occultis meis munda me Domine. (Ps. 18: 13)

Who can understand sins? from my secret ones cleanse me, O Lord.

On this, Augustine speaks of the darkness of sin, which darkens the eyes of the sinner: *si uidentur tenebrae, intelleguntur delicta* 'if darkness is visible, sins are understandable'.[1] A Pseudo-Bede commentary which carries a good deal of Augustinian doctrine puts the matter more bluntly: '*Munda me ab occultis*', *id est, a pravis cogitationibus et cupiditatibus, quæ latenter in me sunt.*[2] '*From my secret ones cleanse me,* that is, from the wicked thoughts and desires which are hidden within me.' The next two verses of the same psalm speak of the author's desire to be freed from the domination of sin, and especially *a delicto magno*, which Augustine identifies with *superbia*:

Quaeritis quam magnum sit hoc delictum, quod deiecit angelum, quod ex angelo fecit diabolum, eique in aeternum interclusit regnum caelorum? Magnum hoc delictum est, et caput atque causa omnium delictorum. Scriptum est enim: *Initium peccati omnis superbia.* Et ne quasi leue aliquid contemnas: *Initium*, inquit, *superbiae hominis apostatare a Deo.*

Do you ask how great is this sin, which cast down an angel, which made a devil out of an angel, and barred him from the kingdom of heaven for eternity? This sin is great, and it is the head and cause of all sins. For it is written: *The beginning of all sin is pride.* And lest you should regard it at all lightly, it is said: *The beginning of man's pride is turning away from God.*

Drawing together, therefore, the evidence of the quotations I have brought forward on the general question of the knowledge of God, and of the law of God—and sin as a breach of that law—imputed to the central characters in *Beowulf*, it will be seen that an author educated in the Augustinian-Gregorian tradition

---

[1] Augustine, op. cit., pp. 111 f.
[2] Ps. Bede, *In Psalmorum Librum Exegesis*, PL 93, 584.

would expect his non-Christian men to know in their hearts of the existence of the Creator and to recognize his greatness in his works; to know from the operation of conscience when they were breaking the eternal law of love and brotherhood, and therefore to have a primitive sense of sin; and to err, if they erred, first through pride, which is a turning away from God towards the self and its terrestrial satisfactions.[1]

It is now to be considered whether the poem's references to God, sin and retribution, and the after-life, can be accommodated to this doctrine of God and man. In looking afresh at the text in this light, I shall not attempt to resume all the theories which have been published on this aspect of the poem, but I shall incorporate or discuss a number of scholarly opinions with reference to passages which remain doubtful in meaning.[2]

Two kinds of religious passage are to be distinguished: the first kind comprising the thoughts and utterances imputed to the characters in the poem, the second, observations in the poet's own voice which state or imply his attitude towards the matter he is recounting. I begin with the former group.

Hrothgar is the first of the characters to be developed as a person. His scheme for the building of a great hall includes the thought of himself as royal provider of bounty, liberally sharing all his possessions *swylc him God sealde* (72). This indication that Hrothgar believes in God's control over all that happens to him is borne out in several speeches. When he hears of Beowulf's coming, he says

> hine halig god
> for arstafum   us onsende.   (381 f.)

The epithet 'holy' with its Old Testament associations no doubt seemed fully appropriate in the mouth of a pre-Christian king; *for arstafum* is one of a number of phrases in the poem which may have secular or religious overtones.[3] The secular use of the word is found in Hrothgar's speech of welcome to Beowulf,

> For gewyrhtum þu,   wine min Beowulf
> ond for arstafum   usic sohtest.   (457 f.)

[1] Augustine, ibid., p. 112.
[2] For a general survey of the evidence and some current theories, see Brodeur, *Art*, pp. 182–219.
[3] See also the coast warden's blessing on Beowulf (316 f.).

God and Man in the Poem

Tolkien describes the language of *Beowulf* as 're-paganized':

The language of *Beowulf* is in fact partly 're-paganized' by the author with a special purpose, rather than christianized (by him or later) without consistent purpose. Throughout the poem the language becomes more intelligible, if we assume that the diction of poetry was already christianized and familiar with Old and New Testament themes and motives.[1]

This is an attractive theory, which has been further developed by Donahue,[2] but I am not very confident that it holds in the conditions of recitation before a Christian audience; I cannot quite conceive how the ordinary associations of the words could be curtaned off in order to make the characters appear ignorant of what the Church taught, all for the purpose of creating verisimilitude to a world which never existed. All that the 're-paganization' amounts to, I suggest, is a general avoidance of purely ecclesiastical words and the choice of indefinite rather than precise words for religious concepts, so as to give an effect of intuitive rather than inculcated knowledge. The translation of this vocabulary into modern English presents some difficulty, because the modern equivalents often have no relevant secular connotation. In the present instance, 'grace' for *arstafas* seems to me wrong, because it lacks the connotations of princely favour which the secular use shows to have been still living in the word;[3] the best modern translation I can find is 'gracious kindness'.

Hrothgar shows continuing faith in God's benevolent power, and ascribes Beowulf's victory over Grendel to *Drihtnes miht* (940). In praising Beowulf he says that the hero's mother was blessed by *Ealdmetod* (945) a unique and curious word which may have been suggested by Daniel's vision of the Judge who is called *antiquus dierum* (Dan 7: 9 and 7: 22); it has an appropriately antique sound in Hrothgar's mouth.[4] This speech ends

---

[1] Tolkien, *Monsters*, Appendix (b), p. 286.

[2] Donahue, *Traditio*, 1965, pp. 55–116, especially pp. 80 ff.

[3] The same considerations apply to *ar* (1272), *hyldo* (670, 2293), *est* (as I interpret it, 3075). For the adaptation of native vocabulary to Christian use, see A. Keiser, *The Influence of Christianity on the Vocabulary of OE Poetry*.

[4] Neither Rankin (*JEGP* 1909, 417 f., 420) nor Klaeber (*Angl.* 1912, 124) offers an explanation of *Ealdmetod* (945) or *scir Metod* (979). I believe that Brodeur (*Art*, B. 191) is right to translate the former 'the Ancient of Days', recalling Daniel's

with a blessing on Beowulf which again recognizes that the hero's success has been due to divine favour (955 f.). When sorrow comes again, Hrothgar's thoughts turn to God as the Almighty Ruler who directs his life (1313 ff.), and he thanks God that his champion proves ready for the new challenge (1397 f.). Beowulf's second victory draws from the king a long speech about God's gifts to men and the deterioration that comes with age.[1] Once more he thanks God for the death of his enemy (1778 ff.). He makes a final speech to Beowulf before they part, in which he praises the hero's wise words as sent by the Lord (1841 f.). In sum, Hrothgar's thoughts and speeches show faith in God as an almighty and benevolent Lord who is the source of men's strength and wisdom.

Queen Wealhtheow, like Hrothgar, gives thanks to God for Beowulf's aid to them (625). Of the other Danes, only one man speaks of God: the captain who guards the shore takes leave of Beowulf with a blessing on his enterprise, in the words,

> Mæl is me to feran; fæder alwalda
> mid arstafum eowic gehealde
> siða gesunde. (316–18)

Klaeber points out that the concept of God as Father occurs in both Germanic and classical paganism,[2] but it is hardly necessary to look beyond the Bible for this usage; the tone of the poem is very much in accord with the fighting spirit of Psalm 88, in which the psalmist puts into the mouth of God these words concerning the warrior David:

> ipse inuocabit me, pater meus es tu,
> Deus meus et susceptor salutis meae. (Ps. 88: 27)

he shall cry out to me: Thou art my father, my God, and the support of my salvation.

vision; the epithet *scir* might have suggested by the phrase *vestimentum ejus candidum quasi nix* 'his garment was brilliant white like snow' (Dan. 7: 9). The Judgment scene appears in the *Moralia* (*PL* 76, 640), drawn out of Job 40: 5 by Gregory, who stresses the brilliance of light surrounding the Judge; he compares the brightness of Christ's garments at the Transfiguration, *candida sicut nix* (Matt. 17: 2), with the glory of God *amictus lumine sicut vestimento* 'clothed in light as a garment' (cp. Ps. 103: 2); the light being the glorified saints. It seems likely that the passage in Gregory invited the recollection of Daniel's vision and the choice of these terms for God.

[1] I postpone further elaboration of this statement to Chapter 6, below.

[2] Klaeber, *Angl.* 1912, 125.

It seems very probable that the *Beowulf* poet imagined the pre-Christian world of his heroes as being rather like the world of David; the verse I have quoted with its *pater* and *susceptor salutis* might very well have been in the poet's mind as he composed lines 316 ff.[1] In all respects, therefore, the God of the Danes is like the God of ancient Israel. It is natural enough that the poet should use the Old Testament to supply him with suitable religious language for his pre-Christian wise men, since any authentic pagan phrases known to him would smack of error or blasphemy. Hrothgar is presented as a man to whom adversity has taught something of the true nature of human life; any purely pagan expressions put in his mouth would blur this picture in the interests of historical likelihood, a much less important aspect of story-telling in those days.

The religion of the Geats is even more lightly sketched in. Beowulf's little band thank God for their safe journey (227 f.), and on their return Hygelac gives thanks that his nephew has come back unscathed (1997 f.). Wiglaf speaks as a man with faith in God, first when he calls God as witness of his desire to die beside his lord (2650 f.), and after Beowulf's death, when he tells the deserters that God allowed Beowulf to avenge himself upon the dragon without their aid. His statement does not accord with the narrative of the dragon-slaying:

> hwæðre him god uðe
> sigora waldend,   þæt he hine sylfne gewræc
> ana mid ecge,   þa him wæs elnes þearf.   (2874–6)

Here occurs one of those inconsistencies which arise through the habit of composing individual scenes each with their appropriate emotions and moral attitudes. It is fitting that Wiglaf should give the credit of the dragon-slaying to his king, emphasizing Beowulf's greatness beside the cowards' corporate

---

[1] If the poet knew Augustine's *Enarr. in Psalmos* well, he could hardly fail to think of this psalm as he wrote of Beowulf's fights in the water, because Augustine relates the verse, *Tu humiliasti sicut uulneratum superbum* 'Thou hast humbled the proud one, as one that is slain'. (Ps. 88: 11) with *superbus draco in mari ... est draco de quo dicitus Draco hic quem finxisti ad illudendum ei, cuius caput contundit super aquam* 'the proud dragon in the sea ... is the dragon about whom it is said, *This sea-dragon which thou hast formed to play therein,* whose head he broke upon the water'. (*CCSL* 39, 1227); cp. p. 138, above.

panic, and this leads to the exaggeration of *ana mid ecge* (2876), in contradiction with

> Feond gefyldan   (ferh ellen wræc),
> ond hi hyne þa begen   abroten hæfdon,
> sibæðelingas   (2706–8)

In the latter passage the narrator's mind is on the loyalty of Wiglaf in the moment of crisis (cp. 2708 f.), and the event takes on a different aspect. It would therefore be unsafe to use Wiglaf's words to the deserters as proof that the poet regarded Beowulf's dragon-slaying as an unqualified God-given victory for the hero; on the contrary, before Wiglaf enters the fray, the poet hints at defeat for Beowulf (2573–5 and 2583 f.), and it is evident from the course of the fight that Beowulf was mortally wounded before the dragon was weakened by Wiglaf's sword-stroke, and could not have finished off the monster alone (cp. 2688–705). On this occasion, Beowulf does not ascribe the death of the foe to God's aid, so Wiglaf's words of lines 2874 f. stand unsupported. The expression *sigora Waldend* is probably a commonplace; many variants of the phrase are found in Old English poetry,[1] and already in *Genesis* (1036) the synonymous *sigora Drihten* is mechanically used, without reference to a particular victory. The implication of Wiglaf's words, *him God uðe ... þæt he hine sylfne gewræc*, that God approves blood-revenge, was no doubt in keeping with many Anglo-Saxons' views on the matter,[2] and could certainly be regarded as part of primitive moral law, since it even has scriptural support in the Old Testament: 'Propinquus occisi homicidam interficiet; statim ut apprehenderit eum interficiet' (Num. 35: 19). 'The kinsman of him that was slain shall kill the murderer: as soon as he apprehendeth him, he shall kill him'.

Beowulf's own utterances concerning God have been subjected to detailed examination, especially since Tolkien gave currency to the idea that Beowulf and Hrothgar were differentiated by the poet in respect of their religious philosophy.[3] This opinion has, I think, been demolished by Professor A. G.

---

[1] cp. Rankin, *JEGP*, 1909, 420 f., and Klaeber, *Angl.*, 1912, 115.
[2] See Whitelock, *Audience*, pp. 13–14.
[3] Tolkien, *Monsters*, pp. 285 f.

Brodeur in his analysis of Tolkien's argument, from which I quote:

Beowulf three times 'refers to God ... as the arbiter of critical events' (lines 440b–441; 685b–687; 967–979)—as often as Hrothgar. The hero acknowledges God's help, or gives thanks to God, *not* twice, but three times, twice in single speech.

Brodeur then quotes the three passages referred to (1657 f., 1661 f., 2794–8). He continues,

In the three passages just quoted Beowulf expresses a gratitude to God and recognition of His protection and goodness, fully as deep and strong as any of the pious expressions of Hrothgar. The second, moreover, contains an explicit recognition of God's special favour to the friendless—a sentiment which no pagan would have been moved to utter in praise of Fate. The third passage, in its threefold designation of God as Lord of All, King of Glory, and Eternal Lord, is fully as Christian as anything spoken by Hrothgar.[1]

Brodeur demonstrates that Beowulf and Hrothgar are not differentiated in this respect. His own conclusion is that the poet 'wisely admitted' the paganism of the Danes (168 ff.): 'Thereafter he was free to let them speak in those terms of gratitude and reverence for God which, by the standard of his own time and country, good men use.'[2] I take up the matter of the inconsistency of lines 171 ff. later in this chapter: here I would observe that the designations of God which Brodeur mentions have more in common with the Psalms[3] than with the New Testament, and there is a restriction on the terms of reverence used by Hrothgar and Beowulf which indicates that they are not altogether on a par with good men of his own time and country.

The contexts of Beowulf's pious speeches are interesting: the hero resigns himself to accepting God's judgment on the outcome of the fight before he wrestles with Grendel (440 f. and 685 ff.), and when he looks back on the course of the fight, he ascribes his inability to slay Grendel outright to God's will (967 ff.). Nevertheless, he supposes that Grendel cannot live long in his wounded state and concludes:

[1] Brodeur, *Art*, p. 192. [2] ibid., p. 207.
[3] cp. Rankin, *JEGP*, 1909, p. 375. It is worth noting that the adjective *witig* (*sapiens*) applied to God by Beowulf (685) and Hrothgar (1841) occurs in Job 9: 4 (Rankin, ibid., p. 378). For Gregory's comment, see *PL* 75, 860.

Ðær abidan sceal
maga mane fah   miclan domes
hu him scir metod   scrifan wille.   (977–9)

To most critics it seems that Beowulf is here speaking of the Last
Judgment;[1] Brodeur does not even mention alternative possibilities, saying simply 'in lines 977b–979 he couples his mention
of the Last Judgment with the term *scir Metod*'.[2] Others, for
various reasons, deny that *dom* need have this meaning in the
passage. Blackburn sets aside the natural sense of the words,
because the speech is put in the mouth of Beowulf; he says 'the
doom that Grendel must abide seems therefore to be death'.[3]
Donahue elaborates Blackburn's argument, suggesting that
Grendel will wait in pain for the divine decision that he is to
die,[4] because he cannot reconcile the precise theological awareness he attributes to the poet and the audience with the theological discrepancy that a man living under natural law knows
of the Judgment Day. I have already suggested early in this
chapter that the poet probably took his ideas of what a naturally
good man would believe from Gregory's interpretations of the
speeches of Job. If this is accepted, there is no need for the kind
of special pleading offered by Blackburn and Donahue. Even if
my suggestion should be wrong, the idea of Judgment appears
to be a necessary corollary of Beowulf's belief in an eternal Lord
of retribution, and it is no extraordinary license that the hero
should be credited with imagining a great assembly in which the
King will pronounce his decrees. I think it most improbable that
the putative audience would think Beowulf's knowledge strange.

That Grendel is said by Beowulf to be awaiting the sentence
of the Judge has been a stumbling-block to some readers, because it seems to conflict with the poet's own statement *þær him
hel onfeng* (852); it is also observed that no wait for Judgment is
mentioned in Beowulf's own case, when his soul goes to seek

---

[1] The parallel phrases in *Christ* (1204) and *Judgment Day II* (15) show that in later
poetry the phrase certainly referred to the Day of Judgment. See also the further
phrases in Keiser, op. cit., pp. 122 f. and Klaeber, *Angl.* 1912, pp. 263 ff., and in
W. H. Deering's general study, *The Anglo-Saxon Poets on The Judgment Day* (Halle,
1890). There seems to be no good reason to deny that this is the meaning in
Beowulf, 978.   [2] Brodeur, *Art*, p. 192.
[3] F. A. Blackburn, 'The Christian Coloring in the *Beowulf*', p. 209.
[4] Donahue, *Traditio*, 1965, pp. 94 ff.

soðfæstra dom. I do not think there is a real problem here; if there is inconsistency of thought it is shared by other Christians of the period. Anglo-Saxon religious writers are all extremely vague concerning the whereabouts of the soul when it has parted from the body;[1] they all believe in the Resurrection when souls and bodies will be united, and in the subsequent assembly for the Judgment. There was, however, a conflict of scriptural authorities about the judging of all the souls, because of the plain words of Psalm 1: 5, *Ideo non resurgunt impii in iudicio, neque peccatores in consilio iustorum* 'Therefore the wicked shall not rise again in judgment, nor sinners in the council of the just'. This statement seems plain enough, and it convicts Beowulf of ignorance in respect of Grendel's appearance before *scir Metod*. Nevertheless, Beowulf is no more wrong than Job, whose words, *in diem perditionis servatur malus, et ad diem furoris ducetur* 'the wicked man is reserved to the day of destruction, and he shall be brought to the day of wrath' (Job 21: 30), indicate that the wicked who are to be condemned will be led to judgment on the Day of Wrath. Gregory certainly interprets this verse as a reference to the state of the impious man on Judgment Day;[2] he therefore has to reconcile these and other conflicting texts, and does so as follows:

Reproborum alii judicantur, alii non judicatus. Duæ quippe sunt partes, electorum scilicet, atque reproborum, sed bini ordines eisdem singulis partibus continentur. Alii namque judicantur et pereunt, alii non judicantur et pereunt. Alii judicantur et regnant, alii non judicantur et regnant.[3]

Among the reprobate some are judged, some are not judged. There are of course two groups, of the chosen and the reprobate, but two ranks are contained within these separate groups. For some are

---

[1] See on this point Milton McC. Gatch, 'Eschatology in the Anonymous OE Homilies', especially p. 123, 'The mind of the early medieval theologian was not plagued as ours is with the *bête noire* of consistency. Tradition and orthodoxy tended to outweigh consistency and structure, especially in works so synthetic as the Anglo-Saxon homiletic collections.' Gatch finds 'no indication', in the Blickling Homilies, of what the condition of the soul is during the period of its separation from the body. (p. 124). The unrepentant sinner is 'doomed by his present conduct to damnation, and it is at least implied that his torments begin at death' (p. 125).

[2] *PL* 75, 1116.

[3] This is part of his interpretation of Job 36: 6, *Sed non salvat impios, et judicium pauperibus tribuit* 'But he saveth not the wicked, and he giveth judgment to the poor.' *PL* 76, 378. For other patristic opinions on this matter, see Carleton F. Brown, 'Cynewulf and Alcuin', *PMLA* 18 (1903), pp. 308–34.

judged and perish, others are not judged and yet perish. Some are judged and reign, others are not judged and yet reign.

I suppose, therefore, that the poet, knowing both possible fates of the evildoer, has put into Beowulf's mouth a view similar to that attributed to Job. For his own part, he has no doubt of Grendel's immediate damnation. Beowulf's other reference to damnation, when he speaks of Unferth's future punishment for brother-murder (588 f.), should be taken as a forecast; in both cases Beowulf's understanding of the law of God leads him to think that the malefactor will be condemned by the Judge.

The departure of Beowulf's own soul into a nebulous other world is discussed more fully below;[1] it will now be clear that his immediate journey to *soðfæstra dom* after death is in keeping with Grendel's immediate journey *in feonda geweald* (808), and indeed with the other vague expressions about the after-life used by the poet. It is also in keeping with the description of the death of Japheth in the Old English *Genesis* A, of whom it is said:

> He wæs selfa til,
> heold a rice,   eðel dreamas,
> blæd mid bearnum,   oðþæt breosta hord,
> gast ellorfus   gangan sceolde
> to godes dome.[2]   (*Gen.* 1606–10)

This passage implies that Japheth went into the presence of God on his death. The gnomic verses also indicate a belief in an immediate journey of the just soul into the presence of God:

> Meotod ana wat
> hywder seo sawul sceal   syððan hweorfan,
> and ealle þa gastas   þe for gode hweorfað
> æfter deaðdæge   domes bidað
> on fæder fæðme.[3]   (*Maxims* II, 57–61)

It would appear, then, that in the absence of a developed doctrine of the place of Purgatory, the just were thought to wait for the General Resurrection in heaven, the unjust being in hell.

Turning now to the remaining religious utterances of Beowulf, I note particularly his dependence upon God in his second contest. He says himself that the issue was in the balance until

---

[1] See p. 178, below.   [2] *ASPR* I, p. 49.

[3] *ASPR* VI, p. 57; cp. also *Durham*, 20, *ASPR* VI, p. 27. Both these references are given by Klaeber, *Angl.* 1912, p. 263, n. 3.

God intervened (1657 f.) and that God granted him sight of the ancient sword with which he triumphed (1661 f.). Since the hero placed the issue of the first combat in God's hand, it is remarkable that no similar speeches are made about the last contest. There is, if one compares the preparations for combat, a progression away from the simple confidence that God would judge the outcome, expressed before the Grendel fight, through a concern for his men, his possessions, and his fame (1490 f.) before the second contest, to a tone of fatalism (2525 ff.) and a boast that he will win the gold (2532 ff.) in the speech which precedes the dragon-fight. The implications of this are more fully treated in Chapter 7; the relevant point, in considering his religious beliefs, is the apparent equation of *wyrd* and *metod* in line 2526 f. In place of *witig God, halig Dryhten* as arbiter, Beowulf here assigns the issue to the decree of *wyrd, metod manna gehwæs.* Brodeur has discussed this passage rather fully,[1] pointing out that *Metod* is one of the commoner terms for God in Old English Christian poetry, and that in an earlier speech the word is put in Beowulf's mouth in two places; the former (967) would allow a translation 'fate', but the latter, in the phrase *scir Metod* (979), clearly would not, which makes 'fate' unlikely in line 967. Brodeur rightly accuses Tolkien of overstating the case[2] when he says, 'We have in Beowulf's language little differentiation of God and Fate'.[3] Nevertheless this one fatalistic speech is not to be disregarded altogether. Tolkien also wrote an illuminating footnote on *wyrd* and *metod* in which he quoted the Old Saxon *Hêliand*:

There remains always the main mass of the workings of Providence (Metod) which are inscrutable, and for practical purposes dealt with as 'fate' or 'luck'. ... In Old Saxon *metod* is similarly used, leaning also to the side of the inscrutable (and even hostile) aspects of the world's working. Gabriel in the *Hêliand* says of John the Baptist that he will not touch wine: *so habed im* uurdgiscapu, metod *gimarcod endi maht godes* (128); it is said of Anna when her husband died: *that sie thiu mikla maht* metodes *todelda uured* uurdigiscapu (511).[4]

The instance put in the mouth of Gabriel is instructive; it suggests that no inference about Beowulf's heathenism can be drawn from his speaking of *wyrd* and *metod* in the same breath.

[1] Brodeur, *Art*, p. 193. [2] ibid., p. 191.
[3] Tolkien, *Monsters*, p. 285. [4] ibid., p. 294, n. 35.

But it would probably be reasonable to infer that Beowulf is thinking of the darker and inscrutable workings of Providence when he makes the speech under discussion.[1] There is certainly a change from the splendid confidence in God's watch over him when he waited for Grendel's coming.

Beowulf makes three speeches near to the time of his death. He does not commend his soul to God, but his mind turns to the coming judgment of his deeds (2471 ff.), which he contemplates calmly, as one who has obeyed his Lord's laws.[2] He does not speak of his soul; the word is never used by him, though it occurs in Hrothgar's sermon and several times in the narrative. In his dying speech, he gives thanks to God for the treasure which he is bequeathing to his people. He makes no other spiritual preparation for his journey.

One incidental reference to God comes in Beowulf's account of his perilous test of endurance in the sea as a youth. When he had shaken off the grip of the sea-monsters and killed all the hostile creatures that assailed him:

> Leoht eastan com
> beorht beacen godes;   brimu swaþredon,
> þæt ic sænæssas   geseon mihte
> windige weallas.   Wyrd oft nereð
> unfægne eorl,   þonne his ellen deah.   (569–73)

I cannot agree with Tolkien that this mention of *beorht beacen Godes* is 'casual and formal';[3] this triumph is an earnest of Beowulf's capability in the great underwater struggle still before him, and as in the more significant combat the victory over the evil creatures is signalled by light and calming of the waters, so in the preliminary trial the boy is aware of the Creator's presence as the sun rises and brings the hope of landfall.

Another and more controversial phrase concerning God comes in Beowulf's long reminiscent speech before he goes out

---

[1] It is notable that he uses the same sort of language in relation to the death of his kinsmen (2814 f.). In 1960 I adduced a passage from the Alfredian Boethius to show how the working-out of Providence was called *wyrd* in Alfred's time (*MÆ* 29 (1960), 86); the article was with the editor from 1958, so it takes no account of Brodeur's very similar comments in *Art* (1959), p. 196.

[2] The change of mood from the perturbation of line 2331 f. is remarkable; the meaning of the change is discussed in Chapter 7.

[3] Tolkien, *Monsters*, p. 285.

to meet the dragon. The speech is so long and deals with so
many different incidents that it is easy to forget that the old king
and not the poet kimself is acting as narrator: it seems possible
that the poet did not altogether sustain the fiction himself in
writing the line in question; of King Hrethel it is said,

> gumdream ofgeaf, godes leoht geceas.   (2469)

The latter phrase is of uncertain meaning, and its implications
for Beowulf's belief about the after-life have been much debated.[1] Klaeber has adduced a number of parallels to support
his view that *Godes leoht* is *'umschriebung für himmel'*.[2] The most
important of the parallels is in *Guthlac* B, in a passage lamenting
the saint's death. Guthlac's servant says his Lord has

                        to godes dome,
       werigra wraþu,   worulddreamum of,
       winemæga wyn,   in wuldres þrym,
       gewiten, winiga hleo,   wica neosan
       eardes on upweg.   Nu se eorðan dæl,
       banhus abrocen   burgum in innan
       wunað wælræste,   ond se wuldres dæl
       of licfæte   in leoht godes
       sigorlean sohte ...   (*Guthlac* B, 1362–70)

It will be noted that Guthlac's soul has *worulddreamum of ...
gewiten*, to seek its reward *in leoht Godes*. Here the two phrases
cannot mean anything other than that he has left earthly life
for heavenly life. Later uses of the word *leoht* establish that it
became conventional in expressions for death.[3] Whitelock[4] and
Wrenn[5] assume that already in *Beowulf* the phrase *Godes leoht* is
conventionally used, with weakened connotation. This explanation does not satisfy Donahue because it conflicts with his
general theory that the poem was written for men who were
theologically alert: he argues for a translation 'he opted decisively
for God's light' for line 2469b.[6] His explanation is that Beowulf
is expressing admiration for his grandfather's moral heroism in
not taking vengeance on the unfortunate fratricide Hæðcyn. The

---

[1] See the evidence presented by Klaeber, *Angl.* 1912, 455 f.
[2] ibid., p. 455.   [3] See Klaeber, *Beowulf*, p. cx, and especially n. 3.
[4] Whitelock, *Audience*, p. 11.
[5] Wrenn, *Beowulf*, p. 221, n. to 2469, says 'Probably a Christian euphemism for
"he died"?'   [6] Donahue, *Traditio*, 1965, p. 102.

divine light is understood to be the merciful code of conduct written in Hrethel's heart. This argument is quite unacceptable: the poem does not imply that Hrethel had a choice (cp. 2464 f.), the 'merciful code' and Beowulf's admiration are nowhere even hinted. Nevertheless, though Donahue's argument is unsubstantiated by the text, he does draw attention to different connotations of the word *leoht,* and in accordance with my general principle that ambiguous phrases in the poem should not be resolved into simple meanings, I suggest that *Godes leoht geceas*—like the phrase *beorht beacen Godes* discussed above—is not entirely 'casual and formal'.

Hrethel was overwhelmed with grief and shame, and subsequently died. The old father whose state is compared with his reacted to his son's death by withdrawing *on sealman* (2460), and the phrase used of Hrethel *gumdream ofgeaf* (2469) could imply a similar withdrawal from human society before he died.[1] Imagery of light is frequently used in the early Church in describing men who have turned towards God.[2] I suggest therefore that Donahue is not altogether wrong in thinking that Hrethel's grief turned his thoughts to spiritual things. If this hint is deliberate, as I suppose, the conclusion of Hrethel's story would be very similar to the conclusion of the brief account of Hama, who *geceas ecne ræd* (1201); the stories of the two men would then both have bearing on the major theme stated in Hrothgar's sermon: that men may lose sight of God in prosperity and find him in adversity. As for the propriety of such a thought in a speech by Beowulf, it is in keeping with the natural understanding the poet imputes to Hrothgar, who urges Beowulf himself to turn his mind away from mundane preoccupations and choose *ece rædas* (1760).[3] I suggest, therefore, that Beowulf's words about his grandfather imply that Hrethel withdrew from court and subsequently entered God's other world without reluctance. As elsewhere in the poem, the nature of that life beyond the grave is not specified. Other aspects of Beowulf's

---

[1] cp. the rather similar expressions for Cain's exile (1264b) and Heremod's exile or death (1714 f.). Heremod's case is discussed in Chapter 6, pp. 189 ff., below.

[2] A basic text is Eph. 5: 8: *Eratis enim aliquando tenebræ, nunc autem lux in Domino* 'For you were heretofore darkness, but now light in the Lord'.

[3] The meaning of this phrase and of the related *geceas ecne ræd* is examined more closely in Chapter 6.

religious beliefs are treated in the chapter I have devoted to the hero.

I come now to those religious passages in the poem which are spoken by the poet himself as narrator or commentator. The majority of these may be shortly summed up as affirmations of faith that God governs the lives of men in all ages: these have the subsidiary effect of reminding the audience that the events described took place in remote time. It would be tedious to resume them, and unnecessary, since all those which gave a new aspect to the episode in which they occur are more conveniently discussed in the context which they illumine.[1] Yet a few general observations are in place, and special attention must be given to the so-called 'Christian Excursus' (175 ff.) and its implications for the theory of a natural religion which I have put forward in the earlier part of this chapter. Something must also be said concerning the controversial debate about the salvation of the hero, to which I have already alluded.[2]

The most unexpected and violent of all the Christian comments upon the action is the denunciation of the Danes' idol-worship (175–88). Their idolatry is not in itself difficult to accept within the scheme of the poem, since the Israelites in similar fashion turned from the One God to the worship of a golden image,[3] and the religious beliefs of the characters in *Beowulf* are, as we have seen, conceived as similar to the religion of ancient Israel. The inconsistency which presents the real problem is the explicit statement:

> metod hie ne cupon,
> dæda demend,   ne wiston hie drihten god.   (180 f.)

It is true that Hrothgar himself is not explicitly included in this statement, since he is not named among the idolaters; nevertheless, the *scop*'s song of Creation (90 ff.) and the words of the coast warden to Beowulf (316 ff.) combine to give an impression that the Danes generally reverenced their Creator; the flat denial that they knew God therefore comes as a much greater shock than the statement that they turned to idols.

Most *Beowulf* critics have made some attempt to resolve the

---

[1] A clear summary of these religious passages is provided by Blackburn, op. cit., pp. 210–15.   [2] See pp. 12 f., above.   [3] Exod. 32: 1–6.

inconsistency, either by explanation or by excising the offending lines. Only those, like Sisam, who regard the poet as a rather muddled Christian, can accept the situation with a shrug. Sisam does not wish to alter the text; he simply disregards the fundamental inconsistency and finds the Danes' resort to idol-worship quite acceptable:

I see nothing in the passage (175 ff.) to establish the view that any part of it has been added to a text essentially the same as that which has come down to us. There is inconsistency in making Hrothgar's people turn to idols; but the poem has many inconsistencies, and probably the audience did not notice them. As I understand the poet, he is emphasizing here the desperate state of the Danes before Beowulf came to deliver them: they had tried in vain every remedy they could think of.[1]

So far one could agree, but the lines which state that this worship was their hope, because as heathens they did not know God, seem to contradict the idea that the idol-worship was a final desperate remedy. Perhaps the author was carried away by his horror of idolatry, forgetting for the time being the fictional world he created. Taken so, the lines would be a blemish, and would certainly decrease our admiration for the author's management of his theme. What other possibilities are there?

Tolkien relies on two different lines of argument. He surmises that the passage from lines 181–8 has been altered from an original which said that they *forsook* God under tribulation and incurred the danger of hell-fire.[2] A reasonable solution—but, as Brodeur objects—a 'questionable procedure'.[3] Tolkien's alternative suggestion is this:

If it is original, the poet must have intended a distinction between the wise Hrothgar, who certainly knew of and often thanked God, and a certain party of the pagan Danes—heathen priests for instance, and those that had recourse to them under the temptation of calamity—specially deluded by the *gast bona*, the destroyer of souls.[4]

Again this seems an agreeable way out, but it involves what Tolkien calls 'the loss of knowledge and praise',[5] a forgetting of

[1] Sisam, *Structure*, p. 73, n. 1. [2] Tolkien, *Monsters*, p. 288.
[3] Brodeur, *Art*, p. 197. [4] Tolkien, op. cit., p. 287.
[5] ibid., p. 288.

God rather than an ignorance of God, which lines 180 ff. will hardly support. Brodeur will have none of Tolkien's solution:

But this is open to serious objection: it is incredible that the poet could have thought of the Danish society of Heorot as divided into a thoroughly pagan priesthood and a laity which, normally worshipers of the true God, could relapse into paganism.[1]

I cannot agree that this is the real objection; I can imagine the deluded priests dwelling in dark groves away from Heorot, to be secretly visited by the superstitious in time of trouble; but it is still necessary to explain how the superstitious, within earshot of Hrothgar, *Metod ne cupon*. It is also necessary to reconcile their ignorance with the general Christian belief in natural knowledge of the Creator.

In his own argument, Brodeur embraces the inconsistency as 'wholly genuine and most deliberate'.[2] He includes lines 164–71 in his evidence that the poet intended to show that Hrothgar was pagan like the other Danes, and to defend them as best he could on grounds of inherited ignorance. He concludes that after saying 'once for all' that the Danes were punished for their idolatry, the poet was free to let them speak in 'terms of gratitude and reverence for God', and then most curiously adds 'In spite of the lines with which the Christian Excursus concludes, we can hardly imagine that the poet or his public seriously thought of Hrothgar as doomed to damnation.'[3] This argument seems to me to present worse inconsistencies than the poem itself; it quite fails to explain how Hrothgar could be pagan and yet speak in terms of reverence for God; worse, it implies that God is punishing the Danes for a 'natural misfortune'[4] which the poet is ready to overlook, namely, their paganism.

If lines 180 ff. mean, as Tolkien states, that some of the community at Heorot 'did not know (*ne cupon*), nor even know of (*ne wiston*), the one God, nor know how to worship him,[5] there is a complete contradiction of St Paul's doctrine of natural knowledge of the Creator, which accounts so well for the religion of the characters in the rest of the poem. Are we then faced with

---

[1] Brodeur, *Art*, p. 197.   [2] ibid., p. 207. See also p. 162, above.
[3] ibid., p. 215.   [4] ibid., p. 204.   [5] Tolkien, *Monsters*, p. 287.

the alternatives of excising the offending lines as inept interpolation or of accepting them with a shrug as no more inconsistent than other passages in the poem?

I made a suggestion in 1962[1] which I should like to restate
here, that if *ne wiston hie drihten God* were taken as a veiled
reference to Christ, and *hie ... herian ne cupon* as an allusion to the
worship of the Church, the curiously repetitive appearance of
the lines would be explained and a way opened to fit them into
the general situation of the Danes. The verb *cunnan* can mean
'to know' in the sense 'to be familiar with the nature of (a person)' as in the lines,

> ic minne can
> glædne Hroþulf, þæt he þa geogoðe wile
> arum healdan ...   (1180-2)

It has already been observed above[2] that none of the men in the
poem addresses God as a person in the normal manner of Christians praying. It seems to me that they 'know of' Metod, but
they do not 'know' him as revealed in Christ, who is completely
unknown to them. The oblique mode of their thanksgiving bears
out that *herian ne cupon*; they had not been taught to worship.
It is not easy to find examples of *drihten God* pointing exclusively
to God the Son, largely because the doctrine of the Trinity was
so important to Anglo-Saxon religious poets that separation of

---

[1] Goldsmith, *Brodeur Studies*, p. 79. The verbs *cunnan* and *gecnawan* could be used
in the sense 'to know' (a person). In the better-known gospel verse about knowing
God, Christ says to his disciples: *Si cognovissetis me et Patrem meum utique cognovissetis; et amodo cognoscitis eum, et vidistis eum.* 'If you had known me, you would
without doubt have known my Father also: and from henceforth you know him,
and you have seen him.' (Joan 14: 7.) The West-Saxon version has: 'Gif ge
cuðon me, witodlice ge cuðon minne fæder; and heonan-forð ge hyne gecnawaþ
and ge hine gesawon.' (Corpus MS, publ. by W. W. Skeat, *The Gospel of St. John
in Anglo-Saxon and Northumbrian Versions*, Cambridge, 1878, p. 132.)

The 'inconsistency', therefore, lies in the Bible itself: St Paul in the passage
concerning natural knowledge of God (Rom. 1: 21) uses the phrase *cum cognovissent
Deum*; St John says *omnis qui peccat non vidit eum, nec cognovit eum.* Bede embraces
both; cp. p. 174, below. For the kind of 'knowing' which the non-Christian could
have, cp. the commentary of C. H. Dodd on this chapter: 'for the Hebrew, however, to know God is neither (primarily) an intellectual exercise nor an ineffable
mystical experience. It means rather to acknowledge God in His ways with man,
to recognize his claims upon man, to understand His Law with the intention of
obeying it' (*The Johannine Epistles*, London, 1946, p. 30).

[2] See p. 147, above.

the Persons is not common. The only unequivocal instance I can adduce is in *Panther* (55):[1]

> Swa is drihten god,   dreama rædend
> eallum eaðmede   oþrum gesceaftum
> duguða gehwylcre,   butan dracan anum
> attres ordfruman.   þæt is se ealda feond
> þone he gesælde   in susla grund ...
>   ond þy þriddan dæge
> of digle aras,   þæs þe he deað fore us
> þreo niht þolade ...   (*Panther* 55–63)

I find some support for my supposition in verses from the First Epistle of St John (3: 2–6), in the chapter from which I have already twice quoted, once upon the Devil's relationship to Cain (3: 12), and once upon the doctrine of natural law. As we have seen, Bede's strong statement about the universality of natural law was made in comment upon this chapter, so obviously he saw no contradiction between the belief in a natural recognition of God and St John's statement that sinners have not seen or known him. Here perhaps is the answer to the strange inconsistency in the poem: the idolaters among the Danes, having no hope in God, are among the sinners, of whom it is said *et omnis qui peccat, non vidit eum, nec cognovit eum*[2]—or, in other words, *Metod hie ne cupon*. It seems not unlikely that this chapter from St John was in the *Beowulf* poet's mind, because of the verses about Cain and homicide (3: 12–15) It provides one more link between the evildoers in Heorot and the kin of Cain who haunt the hall if we can suppose that in writing of *hæþenra hyht* the poet was thinking of the verses quoted above and the *filii diaboli*.

I suggest, therefore, that the disputed lines (180–3) mean 'They did not know God, the Judge of deeds (as a Person, because they had no hope in him, being sinners), they did not know of the Lord (Christ); indeed, they did not know how to worship the Lord of heaven, the Ruler of glory.' It may well be objected that the biblical knowledge required to understand

---

[1] *The Panther*, *ASPR* III, pp. 170 f. Other more doubtful examples are *Andreas* (1281); Psalms 67: 4 and 108: 25 in the Paris Psalter, *ASPR* v, pp. 23 and 93.

[2] I Ep. Joan. 3: 6; these 'sons of the Devil' are contrasted here with those who have hope in God (v. 3).

the passage as I have interpreted it would be outside the range of laymen. This is probably true. But untutored laymen would not be disturbed by the inconsistency; as Sisam says,[1] they would probably not notice it at all. The point is really of no importance to the narrative. However, it probably did not seem a particularly abstruse matter to a clerical poet, and as we have seen elsewhere, he uses a number of veiled expressions which could only have been appreciated by an intelligent and informed Christian audience. My particular concern is to vindicate the poet from the charge of ignorance or ineptitude in his handling of Christian doctrine, and this I believe the suggested interpretation will do. If it should be asked why the poet did not name Christ in line 181, supposing my surmise to be right, I can only point to the extraordinary absence of the name of Christ from the whole poem; the omission must be deliberate, and the only reason I can suggest has already been stated above—that the poet wished to avoid open discussion of the salvation of the righteous heathen. He obviously feels no reticence about the damnation of the unrighteous heathen, and I cannot find in this passage the 'tinge of pity' which Brodeur detects.[2]

The phrase *herian ne cupon* may seem to be denied by the reported performance in Heorot of a song which is somewhat similar in content to Cædmon's famous Hymn of Creation. If the two are compared, however, it is noticeable that the repeated praise of God by name which is an important feature of the Hymn is absent from the *Beowulf* passage; Cædmon sings of the Creator, the Dane primarily of the Creation. The distinction is very slight, but perhaps significant when one considers with it the absence from the poem of corporate or private prayer to God. Even Beowulf, whose thanksgiving and praise in his dying speech (2794–8) come very close to a Christian prayer, does not use the vocative form of address or the second person pronoun for God.[3] The whole assemblage of near-Christian attitudes is explicable if the poet's theory was that Hrothgar and Beowulf honoured their Creator in their natural wisdom, but because of their

---

[1] Sisam, *Structure*, p. 73; cp. p. 171, above.　　　[2] Brodeur, *Art*, p. 216.

[3] In other poems, persons living under the Old Dispensation use the second person form of address to God: cp. the prayers of *Abraham* (*Gen.* 2165 ff.) and Judith (*Jud.* 83 ff.).

ignorance of Christ could not progress to a personal relationship in prayer. In the case of the Danes, the custom (*þeaw*) of making vows to idols might have grown out of the panic caused by Grendel's repeated attacks and been continued during the twelve years of his oppression. Hrothgar is neither involved nor exculpated, and I think Brodeur is mistaken in arguing that a Danish society divided in its religious observances is incredible: he enlarges the significance of *þeaw* unduly.[1] The mistake many modern readers make is to try to create a logical real-life situation out of a poem which only treats limited aspects of an imagined world. There is an ambivalence in the poet's attitude to Heorot which will inevitably produce contradictions if each distinct point is pushed further in the direction to which it tends. The liberal king and the happy community are also the impotent king and the divided, sinful, and scared *heorðwerod;* the men subjected to the *gastbona* are ruled by a man who has learnt in a long trial of grief and humiliation to fear the Lord and to mistrust the seeming security offered by abundance, stout walls and a strong bodyguard. Hrothgar's patient endurance and hope that one day God will change his lot present one kind of response to adversity, the idolaters' vows and prayers to their images present another kind of response to the trial.[2] Some men emerge from adversity spirtually strong, others take the road to despair and damnation. This thought lies behind the seemingly gratuitous lines 183–8. One phrase in these lines, *þurh sliðne nið*, is ambiguous, in respect of the malice or malicious acts involved, and in respect of the agent or agents. Again the commentators have attempted to narrow its application, or to treat it as a vague adverbial phrase of manner.[3] Brodeur recognizes that 'the poet's comment is a generalization from the situation in which the Danes find themselves in consequence of Grendel's persecution', he therefore translates 'through cruel persecution'.[4] This is not wrong, but it is unduly limiting, for the malicious attacks of Grendel are only one of the cruel means which the Devil's ill-will finds to harass men and drive them into despair: 'through cruel malice' should stand.

This brings me to the often misunderstood matter of God's

---

[1] Brodeur, *Art*, p. 197.   [2] cp. Tolkien's final comments, *Monsters*, p. 289.
[3] See Klaeber's note, *Beowulf*, p. 136.   [4] Brodeur, *Art*, p. 208.

role in the ravaging of Heorot. Augustine's authoritative view of persecution, punishment and humiliation as part of the workings of Providence provides the doctrinal background needed to interpret the monster-attacks in *Beowulf*.[1] Though the creatures' malicious desire to harm men is their own, the power to work their evil designs is given them by Providence. Augustine, while recognizing the *occulta dispensatio prouidentiae Dei*, distinguishes three reasons why Providence should permit the evildoer to have his way—to punish, to test or to martyr. I do not think the categories are exclusive: the martyr is tested before he comes to his martyrdom, and even the just man who is tested is also a sinner who may merit punishment. Certainly it is difficult to fit Hrothgar,[2] Beowulf and their peoples simply into one category. The peoples appear to be punished like the people of Israel, the Danes perhaps for their idolatry, the Geats for no specified reason. Hrothgar is undoubtedly like Job in many respects, but in view of the idolatry of his people it is perhaps better to think of him as a leader like Aaron, who must be censured for permitting the idol-worship, who must suffer with his people, but who is, like Aaron, forgiven his weakness, when the time of tribulation is over.[3] In the case of Beowulf, the reason for the dragon's devastations must be inferred from the hint of God's anger, but the element of *probatio* 'testing' is also important in the combat itself, as I try to demonstrate in Chapter 7.

I come finally to the vexed question of *hæðenra hyht*, a subject to which Professor E. G. Stanley has devoted an essay.[4] For much of the way his thoughts on the poem run parallel with mine, but there is a very important difference of emphasis which

---

[1] Augustine, *Ennar. in Ps.*, *CCSL* 38, p. 178.

[2] The poet's final comment on Hrothgar is somewhat obscure:

> þæt wæs an cyning
> aghwæs orleahtre   oþ þæt hine yldo benam
> mægenes wynnum,   se þe oft manegum scod.   (1885–7)

The word *orleahtre* means 'without blemish'; *leahter* can mean a physical defect but is more often used of moral or spiritual faults. In the context, the poet may be excusing his failure to protect his people on grounds of physical weakness; but in view of Hrothgar's earlier speech relating the downfall of a proud king to his own misfortunes (cp. 1769 ff.), it is also possible to see in the lines quoted above an allusion to moral or spiritual weakness in old age which allowed Grendel into Heorot.

[3] For Aaron's lapse and restoration to God's favour, see Exod. 32: 1–6, 32: 35, and 40: 12–16.

[4] E. G. Stanley '*Hæthenra Hyht* in *Beowulf*' in *Brodeur Studies*.

leads him, I believe, to a mistaken conclusion. We could agree upon his preliminary general statement that the poet 'deals in ambiguities based on a twofold system of values, the one secular and the other monastic, which existed side by side in Anglo-Saxon times',[1] save that his choice of the word 'monastic' and his subsequent use of the phrase 'standards of asceticism' rather obscures the fact that Christian teaching among the Anglo-Saxons was then largely carried out by monks: there was no 'secular Christianity' for laymen. His concluding words are that Beowulf's life 'being without faith, is in the strictest sense of the words, without hope', and that 'we reread the poem with sadness and compassion of an ideal that avails nothing'.[2] This seems to me a much too simplified view, which herds Beowulf with Ingeld and pays no heed to the positive worth of the hero's virtues, or to his faith in God, which seems to go to the limits attainable by reason alone. It is surely not only a modern audience that would 'demand poetical justice for Beowulf, if not in this world, then in the next'?[3] If the poet had believed as strongly as Alcuin, *Non vult rex celestis cum paganis et perditis nominetenus regibus communionem habere*[4] 'The King of heaven has no wish to have communion even in name with these pagan and damned kings', he could not have written this poem at all. The doubts which he leaves with his audience could be honestly held, and there are no grounds for suspecting insincerity in his praise of the hero.

The *soðfæstra dom* which awaits Beowulf's departed soul is most probably the weighing of his merits in the scales of divine justice. The word *soðfæste* can be used of Christian saints,[5] but it is also used to translate the Latin word *justi* in the Psalms. It is among these just men of the pre-Christian era that Beowulf might be supposed to belong; but owing to the ambiguity of *dom*, and the uncertain logical relationship of the genitive *soðfæstra* to *dom*, the sense of the phrase as a whole remains obscure.[6] There are no analogous phrases in Old English, and it is by no means certain that the poet is thinking of that *judicium*

---

[1] ibid., p. 136.   [2] ibid., p. 151.   [3] ibid., p. 151.
[4] Alcuin's letter to Hygbald, quoted by Stanley, op. cit., p. 149. (cp. *MGH Ep. Kar.* II, 183).   [5] As, for example, in *Guthlac*, 762 ff.
[6] Donahue, *Traditio*, 1965, p. 110, calls it 'a deeply serious pun'.

or *consilium justorum*[1] referred to by the psalmist and identified by Augustine with the great assembly at the Judgment, though the phrase could bear this meaning, with the implication that Beowulf's soul went to be judged by, or among, the saints. As Tolkien has pointed out, *dom* in secular use is *'judgement, assessment, and in one branch just esteem, merited renown'*. He contrasts its use in the Christian period with that of *lof*: 'In the Christian period the one, *lof*, flowed rather into the ideas of heaven and the heavenly choirs; the other, *dom*, into the ideas of the judgement of God, the particular and general judgements of the dead.'[2] Stanley is able to reconcile the phrase under discussion with the possibility that Beowulf is damned, quoting Hamilton's words:[3]

Our English poet, whose genius lay rather in indirection, understatement, and the power of suggestion, merely asserts that the soul of Beowulf departed from his breast to seek *soðfæstra dom*. 'The glory of the saints', are we to suppose? Or, perhaps, 'the judgement meted out to the righteous?' Or merely 'whatever reward awaits just men in Beowulf's situation'?[4]

Among these critics, only Stanley can accept that Beowulf is consigned to the fires of hell, and surely it would make nonsense of the whole poem if Beowulf's last state were no better than that of Unferth or Heremod, or Grendel himself? I think that Brodeur's non-committal translation of *soðfæstra dom*, 'the judgement of the righteous', is acceptable.[5] I suppose that the poet numbered his hero among the *justi*, but to put him in this company is not necessarily to put him with the saints in heaven, for the *justi* of the Old Testament, such as Job—though there were one or two miraculous exceptions—became the Devil's prisoners after death, until the day when Christ himself descended to release them. If Beowulf, like Job, had lived on earth before that day, his soul could have been set free with those of the patriarchs, but we do not know for certain whether or not the poet believed that his hero lived before Christ. Some fairly simple

[1] Wrenn, *Beowulf*, p. 288, *s.v. soð-fæst*, equates *soð-fæstra dom* with 'Latin Patristic *justorum judicium*', but makes no further comment on this in his notes. Klaeber, *Angl.* 1912, p. 453, translates the phrase 'die den gerehten bestimmte herrlichkeit', and in his edition glosses *soð-fæst* 'true, righteous', and *dom* 'glory'.

[2] Tolkien, *Monsters*, p. 281.

[3] Stanley, '*Hæthenra Hyht* in *Beowulf*', *Brodeur Studies*, p. 151.

[4] Hamilton, op. cit., p. 328.   [5] Brodeur, *Art*, p. 218.

computation from the genealogical tables of the royal houses could have shown him that Beowulf lived long after the Incarnation, but there is no knowing whether he was chronologically-minded, or whether the question occurred to him at all.

For a heathen hero who lived after the resurrection of Christ, what hope was there? Augustine himself saw only the stark alternatives of heaven or the abyss of fire, but there appears in Gregory the germ of an idea which by the thirteenth century had blossomed into the doctrine of Limbo. He needed to find an explanation of Job's words: *Si sustinero, infernus domus mea est et in tenebris stravi lectulum meum* 'If I wait, hell is my house and I have made my bed in darkness' (Job 17: 13). Exegesis was made still more difficult by another sentence three verses later: *In profondissimum infernum descendent omnia mea* 'All that I have shall go down into the deepest pit' (Job 17: 16). Gregory concluded from the mention of a bed that there must exist a place of peace in the upper regions of hell where the just soul could live without torment, deprived only of the light of God's presence (hence *in tenebris*); by a remarkable piece of special pleading he decided that even this upper region, viewed from heaven, would appear *profondissimum*. Gregory, like Augustine, saw Job as a type of the pre-Christian just man, excluded from heaven because of Adam's sin and forced to wait in the infernal regions for his liberation:

Tunc vero homo suum lectulum in tenebris stravit, quando lucem justitia persuasori callido consentiendo, deseruit. Et quia in ipsis quoque inferni locis justorum anima sine tormento tenebantur, ut et pro originali culpa adhuc illuc descenderent, et tamen ex propriis actibus supplicium non haberent, quasi in tenebris lectulum stravisse est in inferno sibi requiem præparasse.[1]

Then indeed man made his bed in the darkness, when he left the light of righteousness by consenting to the sly persuader. And since in all these infernal regions the souls of the just were held without torment, as they had descended there up till then through original sin and yet had no torment through acts of their own, to have made a bed as if in darkness is to have prepared one's rest in the pit.

As there are several indications that the *Beowulf* poet knew some of the doctrine of the *Moralia* rather well, it seems to me not unlikely that he thought of his hero in the company of other just

---

[1] Gregory, *Moralia, PL* 75, 1038 and 1040.

but unbaptized souls in this place, awaiting God's mercy at the General Judgment. That this is mere conjecture I admit, but a solution on these lines provides a poetically fitting end to the story without involving the poet in heretical belief.

There are very few pronouncements on the subject of the salvation of the heathen among early Christian writings, simply because the preaching of baptism and the suppression of pagan cults were vital to the existence and growth of the Church, whereas the problematical fate of the dead heathen was an academic and a possibly dangerous question to explore. The question remains academic in relation to *Beowulf,* since the hero is simply left to the mercy of the Judge, but an interesting side-issue has been raised by Donahue, who has argued that Celtic attitudes to the heroes of the past, being more liberal than the Augustinian, probably gave the *Beowulf* poet models and a climate of thought in which the celebration of a heathen king seemed a proper subject for a Christian poet.[1]

Donahue clearly indicates the weakness of Hamilton's attempt to find the Augustinian doctrine of the two cities in *Beowulf.*[2] We agree that Augustine's historical vision of the past, present and future struggle between the forces of good and evil and his emphasis upon Cain as the progenitor of the reprobate race account for some features of *Beowulf,* but, as Donahue says,

a difficulty arises when we are asked to believe that the poet identified his good people as citizens of the Celestial City. This is the crucial point, and here, in my opinion, the case for an Augustinian interpretation breaks down. The distinguishing mark of the members of the Celestial City is that they are pilgrims in this world. Their hope and their destiny are in the world to come. But nowhere does any good man in *Beowulf* express any hope for the world to come, and it is noteworthy that the poet carefully avoids saying explicitly that Beowulf, or any of the other just men in the poem, went to heaven. The good characters in *Beowulf* in short, seem to belong neither to the City of the elect nor to that of the reprobate. They belong rather to what we might call a 'third city', a city which without supernatural hope fights a brave and losing fight against the forces of evil.[3]

[1] Donahue, *Traditio,* 1949–51, pp. 264 ff.; cp. also his later article, *Traditio,* 1965, passim.
[2] *Traditio,* 1949–51, pp. 265 ff.   [3] ibid.

This is well put, and up to this point I completely concur with Donahue. He also writes a long and suggestive footnote on Dante and Riphaeus (cp. *Paradiso* 20: 118–24) and on Dante's treatment of Limbo,[1] but thinks it improbable that the author of *Beowulf* could have developed similar ideas without the benefit of the whole tradition of medieval humanist thinking. However, as my quotation from the *Moralia* shows, Job could have provided the required model. The compromise between theological doctrine and historical reality that we find in *Beowulf* could have been suggested to the poet by Celtic compositions, as Donahue thinks, and I by no means discount the possibility.[2] However, the kind of poem I believe *Beowulf* to be is not inconsistent with Gregorian thinking and could have arisen quite independently of such inspiration. Hrothgar and Beowulf now seem, in Donahue's words, 'lonely figures' in Anglo-Saxon England, but it must not be forgotten that only a fraction of the poetry composed at that period is known to us.

[1] ibid., p. 266.

[2] In the work just cited, pp. 266 ff., he brings forward some interesting examples of 'natural goodness' in Celtic writings; two of these are from Adamnan's Life of St Columba (ibid., pp. 266 ff.) and might easily have been known to the *Beowulf* poet. In the hagiographical examples he cites, the good heathen is later baptized by the saint. He has, however, two examples of noble monotheists among the Irish kings, Cormac and Morand (pp. 272 f.), neither of whom was baptized; the fate of their souls is not recorded, but of Cormac Donahue says, 'His burial outside the pagan cemetery with his face towards the east was doubtless considered an augury that he would be numbered with the saved on the last day. But Irish *pietas* contented itself with a hint rather than a definite statement regarding the eternal destiny of the citizens of the third city' (p. 274).

6   Hrothgar's Admonition to Beowulf

When Beowulf returns victorious from his second great contest, bearing the head of Grendel and the hilt of the giant sword, he presents his trophies to the Danish king. With the golden hilt in his hand and his eyes upon its curious design, Hrothgar makes a long moralizing speech addressed to Beowulf (1700–84), which has seemed to many readers of the poem inappropriate in its length and moral advice, if not completely irrelevant. A large part of the speech can fittingly be called a sermon, since it is a tissue of patristic doctrines and familiar homiletic themes. The objections to its style and content which have led several scholars to regard it as an interpolation in the poem are of two kinds: it is thought to be too Christian in its language and out-look, and also to be dramatically out of place because 'Beowulf scarcely needed a discourse on pride and greed of this nature'.[1] When I began my study of *Beowulf*, it seemed to me that both the engraving of the antediluvian war upon the sword-hilt and the central thought of the admonition—that the Devil is always seeking an opening for a fresh assault in his war upon mankind—must have something to do with one another, and that Hrothgar's warning that power and prosperity could make a man spiritually vulnerable must have some relevance to Beowulf's later life. Further reading of Christian authors known in the period convinced me that this approach made the structure of the latter part of the poem more understandable; in fact, that the sermon was written as a key to the interpretation of the story.

As I have already noted above, Professor Smithers has made incidental reference to the importance of Hrothgar's speech in his essay, 'The Meaning of *The Seafarer* and *The Wanderer*'.[2] In discussing the similarity between the *schema* of Hrothgar's ser-mon and that of *The Rhyming Poem*,[3] he says: 'This scheme is

---

[1] cp. Wrenn, *Beowulf*, p. 70.   [2] See p. 4 and n. 2, above.
[3] *The Rhyming Poem*, ASPR III, 166 ff.

simply a way of presenting (i) the senescence and decay of man and the world, (ii) the death that awaits every human being, and (iii) his heavenly home. What is characteristic in it is the elaborated contrast of youth and age.'[1] Later in the article, he relates this *schema* to the structure of *Beowulf*:

> That he (Hrothgar) aims his speech at Beowulf is also significant: he explicitly states for us, in general terms referring to a hypothetical example, the contrast which is built into *Beowulf* as a whole in the representation of Beowulf's career in the two appropriate stages, *viz.*, his prime and his old age. The passage is thus entirely appropriate as a hinge on which the two halves of the poems are set; and the entrenched view that it is an interpolation must now be abandoned.

> The main point to be made about Hrothgar's 'harangue' and its congeners is that they use the contrast between man's flourishing and careless youth and his miserable old age to reinforce the eschatological ideas that accompany it.[2]

Though I wholeheartedly agree with Smithers's principal point, that Hrothgar's speech is a hinge on which the two halves of the poem are set, it seems to me that he has obscured an important factor in this hinge-function by omitting from the *schema* the theme of the growth of cupidity with age; on the other hand, 'the senescence of the world' and 'man's heavenly home' are not specifically treated in *Beowulf*—no doubt because the former with its accompanying idea of the weakening of the human race[3] would be incongruous in Beowulf's lifetime, and the latter is beyond the reach of Hrothgar's supposed natural understanding of God and his law. In other respects, the similarity between the two poetic passages is very striking, and rather closer than Smithers's summary suggests. Both Heremod and the unnamed king of the *exemplum* lose the esteem of their followers because of their avarice, Heremod being driven from the throne into exile on account of his tyranny; in *The Rhyming Poem* the royal speaker apparently suffers a similar fate, though the highly compressed and figurative language makes this

---

[1] Smithers, op. cit., p. 8.   [2] ibid., p. 10.

[3] For the theme of man's physical and moral deterioration, see J. E. Cross, 'Some Aspects of Microcosm and Macrocosm in OE Literature, *Brodeur Studies*, 1 ff., especially pp. 5–10. (First published in *CL*, Winter 1962.)

somewhat uncertain. The beginning of his misfortunes is signalled by the phrase *sinc searwade* (37), which one might perhaps
translate 'treasure made mischief', and his unhappiness after
his exile is aggravated by *brondhord* (46), a burning disease which
spreads from his breast to invade his whole being. I concur with
those scholars who believe that this disease is avarice, and have
tried elsewhere[1] to show that the poetic compound refers to the
'rust' or 'corrosion' which damages hoarded treasure, conceived by the poet as a contagion which passes to the covetous
possessor. This interpretation of the latter part of *The Rhyming
Poem* reinforces the theme of the senescence of man referred to
by Smithers, and provides us with an example of the treatment
of an individual as a type of mankind, which may serve to
strengthen the belief that Beowulf is so treated. Both poems apparently use the contrasted youth and age of a king as a figure
for mankind's Golden Age and this Last Age of discord and in-
satiable concupiscence which awaits the final dissolution. There
are, of course, large differences between Beowulf's state and that
of the exiled king; the hero is neither infirm nor wretched;
though he stands alone, it is through his own choice, and when
his men leave him it is out of panic, not out of hate. Nevertheless, we may expect that Beowulf as an old man facing death will
feel the pull of his worldly possessions more strongly than in his
youth, and one purpose of Hrothgar's admonition is to fortify
him against the spiritual disease which afflicted Heremod and
the king of *The Rhyming Poem*.

There is little reason to suspect direct influence from *Beowulf*
upon the author of *The Rhyming Poem*; each writer is drawing
upon familiar homiletic material. Hrothgar's speech incorporates a greater variety of themes, and it is probable that no
single homiletic source will be found; I suppose that the poet
assembled from current ideas about man's life those elements
which had bearing upon Heremod's downfall, Hrothgar's
tribulation, and Beowulf's trial in old age. He also enlarged the
subject by speaking generally of mankind, hinting, as I believe,
that Beowulf, as son of Adam, must re-enact the primal struggle
with the Serpent-Dragon, the consequence of which is death.

[1] In 'Corroding Treasure: a note on The OE *Rhyming Poem*, lines 45–50', *NQ*,
May 1967, pp. 169–71.

This chapter consists of a fresh explication of Hrothgar's admonitory speech. I use as illustration some passages from Ambrose, Augustine and Gregory which may have been among the poet's sources, but I have not attempted to review all the patristic and other parallels which scholars have adduced. Klaeber's analysis of the speech conveniently assembles many of these,[1] and I have made reference where appropriate to some of his findings, but on the whole it has seemed more useful to concentrate upon distinctions between the Beowulfian sermon and similar passages in religious writings, and to seek for an interpretation which will strengthen the links between this speech and the rest of the poem.

I recall at the outset the evidence of the *Altus Prosator* that the drowning of the giants by the Flood was regarded as an image of the overthrow of earthly power and pride.[2] The design of the giant sword-hilt not only closes the episode of the death of the Grendel kin, it also introduces a second account of the overthrow of King Heremod; the *woroldcyningas* (cp. 1684) who ponder upon the destruction of the giants must not ignore its lesson for themselves, and Hrothgar's admonition to Beowulf expatiates most fittingly upon the persistence of the sin of pride amongst mankind.

The opening sentences of Hrothgar's speech exalt Beowulf above the many heroes in the old man's memory. The first words of doubtful meaning occur in the following lines:

> Eal þu hit geþyldum healdest,
> mægen mid modes snyttrum.   (1705 f.)

The commentators gloss *geþyld* 'patience' and the adverbial *geþyldum* as 'steadily', 'in steadfastness'.[3] None of these seems to be exactly what the situation requires, since the experiences of Beowulf as described have not called for patience or steadfastness. Since Hrothgar goes on to speak of the contrasting behaviour of Heremod, whose violence was not governed by reason (cp. 1711–14), it seems probable that line 1705 f. commends

---

[1] Klaeber, *Angl.* 1912, 117 f., 128–33, 474–80.

[2] cp. pp. 45 ff., above, and Gregory, *Moralia, PL* 76, 24 f.

[3] Klaeber translates 'steadily' (*Beowulf*, p. 343); Dobbie (*Beowulf*, p. 203) compares *Gifts of Men*, 79 f. in which *geþyld* is parallel to *fæstgongel ferð*, and quotes Malone's translation 'in steadfastness' (given in *Angl.* 55 (1931), 271).

Beowulf's even-tempered and wise control of his extraordinary strength; I surmise that 'with equanimity' is the contextual sense of *geþyldum*. The parallel phrase *mid modes snyttrum* should be related to line 1726, in which *snyttru* is one of God's gifts to man, and line 1734, in which, *for his unsnyttrum*,[1] the well-endowed man forgets the brevity of mortal life. There is no doubt that *snyttru* means wisdom (in some sense of that word) and *unsnyttru* its opposite: I should like to suggest that Augustine's teaching about the nature of a wise man in the *De libero arbitrio* illuminates all three passages. His argument is that a wise man is one whose reason dominates his lower desires, among which he includes not only the animal characteristics of man, but also the love of praise and glory and power.[2]

Beowulf is wise because his mind controls his physical strength and rules his desire for personal glory (cp. 1703–6), unlike Heremod, who allowed himself to be dominated by violent anger and greed (cp. 1711 ff.). Moreover, this doctrine explains the reference to *snyttru* and *his unsnyttrum* in the *exemplum* which follows, if Augustine's argument is pursued. For the wisdom to which he here refers is the Truth in which the *summum bonum* 'the highest good' is possessed.[3] Thus Augustine reaches his position that it is the eternal law of human nature to turn towards God and away from *inferiora bona*;[4] a man who tries to find satisfaction in temporal possessions which he must soon leave behind is foolish (cp. 1733 f.); he has a perverse will, which is *conversa ad proprium bonum aut ad exterius aut ad inferius* 'turned towards a private good, either outside or below [the unchangeable good]',[5] in other words, he is governed by pride and cupidity. The well-ordered man, in whom reason is dominant, will turn towards the lasting good, not to these temporal satisfactions, for this is the

----

[1] Dobbie, Wrenn and von Schaubert (1963) read *for his unsnyttrum*, following Thorkelin A; the older edd. omit *for*.

[2] Augustine, *De libero arbitrio*, CSEL 74, pp. 19 f. Professor R. E. Kaske also adduces this tract (though not this passage) in his discussion of Hrothgar's speech, in '*Sapientia et Fortitudo* as the Controlling Theme of *Beowulf*'. His footnotes provide further evidence of the currency of the general thought of the sermon, but he does not cite any of the passages I use in the course of this chapter. I cannot accept his contention that different kinds of *sapientia* are revealed in Hrothgar and Beowulf. His general argument is reviewed in Chapter 7, below.

[3] Augustine, op. cit., p. 61.

[4] ibid., p. 73; cp. p. 13, n. 2, above.   [5] ibid., p. 86.

lex æterna written in his heart.[1] Thus there is a discernible Augustinian pattern of thought throughout Hrothgar's speech. Beowulf is first praised in terms that emphasize his wisdom in not being moved by fame or carried away by wrath; he is then asked to think about two unhappy examples of men who lost this wisdom; finally he is urged to remain wise, by continuing to prefer eternal to temporal advantages; and by keeping in mind the brevity of man's possession of the latter. Augustine's argument was based on his beliefs about human nature in general; in the dialogue from which I have quoted, he does not argue from Scripture (though scriptural texts are used to illustrate or to clinch his points); there is therefore no impropriety in imputing such thoughts to the naturally wise Hrothgar.[2] The old king's erring steps to self-satisfaction and pride in possessions had been halted, it may be supposed, by the humiliation of Grendel's reign of terror and the consciousness of his own infirmity.

Hrothgar next forecasts that Beowulf will be a source of comfort and help to his people for a long time (1707 ff.), thus giving an opening for the reintroduction of King Heremod, whose rule brought misery to his subjects. The relevance of Heremod's career is not simply in the obvious antithesis just mentioned; in order to follow the allusive account in Hrothgar's speech it is necessary to put with it the information given earlier in the poem, and to examine some of the cryptic phrases used about him. The story is important because the Danish king, wise in his years, considers that it has a lesson for Beowulf (1722–4); the meaning of that lesson is then made plainer by a general example of the life of a proud ruler (1724 ff.).

Heremod and Beowulf had something in common as young princes: both were endowed by God with prodigious strength (cp. 1716 f.). The Danes had therefore hoped to find in Heremod a powerful protector, such as Hrothgar forecasts that Beowulf will be to the Geats (cp. 909 f.); instead, Heremod proved a

---

[1] cp. p. 152, above.

[2] A large part of this Augustinian thinking was transmitted by Gregory to later generations, and it would certainly not be necessary to assume that the *Beowulf* poet had read *De libero arbitrio* before he composed this speech. The following references in Gregory to *sapientia*, the love of *terrena*, and the cares of the world, are cited by Kaske: *Moralia*, PL 76, 243 f.; 75 f. and 98; 76 ff.

tyrant, because *hine fyren onwod* (915). Though *fyren* has the secular meaning of 'crime' or 'wickedness' it is also the Christian word for 'sin', and the slight personification indicated by *onwod* makes the religious sense more probable here.[1] The sin which took possession of Heremod is not named, but the passage now before us in Hrothgar's admonition shows that he became cruel, violent and close-fisted. In Augustine's terms, he ceased to be governed by reason and became subject to lower desires; thus he became the negation of a true king, the protector turned destroyer and the provider turned niggard.

The consequences to Heremod himself of his inner transformation are somewhat ambiguously described. The earlier account refers to a betrayal:

> He mid eotenum wearð
> on feonda geweald   forð forlacen,
> snude forsended.[2]   (902–4)

In Hrothgar's speech, his fate is twice alluded to in obscure fashion:

> oþ þæt he ana hwearf,
> mære þeoden   mondreamum from ... (1714 f.)
> dreamleas gebad,
> þæt he þæs gewinnes   weorc þrowade,
> leodbealo longsum.   (1720–2)

All that can with certainty be deduced from these three passages is that Heremod's followers rejected him, so that he died lonely and wretched. Such a conclusion is perhaps all that the *exemplum* requires, but the consequences of his evildoing upon the history of the Danes are not to be disregarded, since the poet is also interested in the effects of a king's good or ill conduct upon his people.[3]

The details of Heremod's story as the Anglo-Saxons knew them are lost to us.[4] However, the West-Saxon genealogical

---

[1] All the other recorded uses of *onwadan* have some connection with sin: cp. *Gen.* 1260, 2579 and *Dan.* 17. See also Klaeber, *Angl.* 1912, 128.

[2] I have changed Dobbie's initial capital on *Eotenum* (902) in order not to prejudice the discussion of the meaning of the word.

[3] Thus, the Danes share Hrothgar's humiliation, the premature death of Hygelac in Frisia affects the Swedish wars, and Beowulf's own people suffer because he chooses death rather than diminution of his glory.

[4] The coupling of his name with Sigemund shows an interesting similarity to the late ON poem *Hyndlúljóð*, stanza 2, in which Heremod and Sigemund are rewarded

tradition places Heremod immediately before Scyld,[1] which points to a belief that the circumstances of Heremod's disgrace caused the unhappy interregnum described in the opening section of *Beowulf* (13 ff.). For the rest of Heremod's story the modern reader depends on the allusions in *Beowulf*, unless he is prepared to identify Heremod with the father of Skioldus in Saxo's history of the Danes, whose name is there given as Lotherus;[2] scholars are divided on this question. The chief point of interest for the student of *Beowulf* is that a seventeenth-century Swedish chronicler, Messenius, records of Lotherus that, being driven from his throne because of his tyranny, *in Jutiam profugit*.[3] This reference to flight into the land of the Jutes has seemed to some to tip the balance in favour of a translation 'among the Jutes' for *mid eotenum* (902), but I would agree with Wrenn that the evidence is insufficient to make the identification sure.[4]

In re-examining the matter of the exile of Heremod, I note first that Sigemund, whose name was coupled with that of Heremod in the first account, was celebrated for his exploits against the giants (883 f.). There is no inherent improbability in placing Heremod also in giant territory. The phrase *on feonda geweald* (903), though equally applicable to men and demonic foes, has been used less than a hundred lines earlier of Grendel's capture by the fiends (808). The parallel phrases *forð forlacen, snude forsended* (903 f.) mean something like 'treacherously sent forth, quickly banished', with implications either of exile or of death. The ambiguity of the lines allows two distinct interpretations: the first, that an act of treachery left Heremod a

by Odin; the juxtaposition of the two in *Beowulf* is most plausibly explained as a traditional association going back to heathen times. See also Chambers, *Beowulf: An Introduction*, p. 91, and Klaeber, *Beowulf*, p. 164.

[1] See Klaeber, *Beowulf*, p. 164; cp. also the genealogies printed by him on pp. 254 f. and the *Langfeðgatal*, pp. 260 f.

[2] See Klaeber's discussion of the passage, *Beowulf*, p. 163.

[3] Quoted by Klaeber, *Beowulf*, pp. 163 f.; cp. also Chambers, op. cit., pp. 97 and 261 f.

[4] Of the recent editors, Klaeber, Dobbie and von Schaubert read *Eotenum* as a proper noun. Wrenn reads *eotenum* 'giants', commenting, 'The historical evidence is hardly sufficient to justify 'Jutes' here, though the suggestion is very plausible. Moreover, the Lotherus of Saxo Grammaticus (I, ii) is not very like Heremod; and it is of him only that Messenius says that he fled to the land of the Jutes (in Jutiam profugit)' (*Beowulf*, p. 201).

wretched exile in enemy country, where he died; whether the enemy were giants or Jutes does not much affect his miserable state; there is some propriety in visiting upon the murderous Heremod the punishment of his spiritual father Cain. The second possible interpretation is that *forsended* means 'dispatched' and that *on feonda geweald* here, as in line 808, implies that his soul went to hell.[1]

In support of the latter view, we have the further echo of the description of Grendel's death in *dreamleas* (1720); cp. line 850. When two different and equally pertinent versions of Heremod's fate, the one relating to earthly requital for his evildoing, the other to his dispatch into the power of the fiends, can justly be made out of these lines, is it not reasonable to think that the author had both in his mind as he composed them? In the poem, three heroes are compared for their deeds of valour and their reputations among the people, and in this history the merited decline of Heremod's fame and his banishment by his own followers have a proper place. But the poet also sees actions and events in the long perspective, and Heremod would not appear in Hrothgar's sermon if he were not also an example of a man dominated by sin and in the power of the Devil; his earthly banishment is the shadow of the unending exile which is the lot of those who break the eternal law.

The words with which Hrothgar concludes his observations about Heremod pointedly suggest that a similar downfall could happen to Beowulf—*ic þis gid be þe awræc* (1723 f.)—for as yet the hero has not been tested against the corrupting influence of power and success. Here is a signpost to the nature of Beowulf's final contest with the forces of the Enemy. To make still plainer

---

[1] N. F. Blake, 'The Heremod Digressions in *Beowulf*', *JEGP* 61 (1962), 278–87, has argued that lines 902 ff. mean that Heremod was seduced (by the Devil)—*forlacen* as in *Gen.* 647—and sent to hell, the abode of the giants (*eotenas*). His argument does not convince: he says, 'I think there can be little doubt that the *eotens* belonged to the devilish brood and that they lived in hell, for they are descended from Cain, they are in the company of *orcneas*, and Grendel, an *eoten*, went to hell' (p. 284).

The last clause of this sentence calls attention to the weakness of the argument. Grendel lived in an underwater hall, where Beowulf found his lifeless body after his heathen soul had departed to hell; he did not simply disappear into the infernal regions; the *eotenas* fought by Sigemund and Beowulf inhabited the wastelands of the earth: one cannot infer a meaning 'in hell' for the phrase *mid eotenum*.

the perils which age will bring to Beowulf, the speech is continued with a generalizing passage which describes the spiritual
dangers which beset a fortunate man.

The opening sentence of this part of the sermon has sometimes been misunderstood, largely because of a resemblance to
the Old English *Christ* (660 ff.).[1] Both passages speak of God's
gifts to man, but with a fundamentally different purpose. The
theme in *Christ* is the variety of endowments, leading to the
conclusion:

> Nyle he ængum anum   ealle gesyllan
> gæstes snyttru,   þy læs him gielp sceþþe
> þurh his anes cræft   ofer oþre forð.   (683–5)

The theme in Hrothgar's sermon, on the other hand, is that the
man who is too well-endowed is likely to become proud and
covetous; it is a theoretical consideration of what could befall
one who receives *snyttru, eard ond eorlscipe* (1726 f.).[2] The Creator,
who dispenses talents as well as rank and possessions—*he ah ealra
geweald*—endows a king with authority over a region of earth
and the mental capacity to rule both himself and his subjects.
If the ruler, like Adam, forgets his dependence upon God and
thinks he is self-sufficient, he has become deaf to the inner voice
of wisdom and foolishly acts as if all that had been lent to him
were his by right for ever (cp. 1733 f.). It seems to me significant
that the introductory statement of lines 1725 ff. refers to 'mankind', widening the scope of the sermon to include not only the
ancient kings of the story but all those who are given the
responsibility of rule, from Adam onwards.

In the description of the fortunate man's early life (1728–39),
the difficult phrase *on lufan* (1728) has been very variously
interpreted by the commentators.[3] Either of the common trans-

---

[1] See the detailed parallels pointed out by Klaeber, *Beowulf*, p. cxii, and his comments upon them. A. S. Cook, 'Cynewulf's Part in our Beowulf', *Transactions of the
Connecticut Academy of Arts and Sciences*, 27 (1925), 385 ff., stresses the differences between the parallel passages in *Christ* and *Beowulf*, and gives his opinion that the
Beowulf poet took his doctrine on pride directly from the *Moralia* (see especially
pp. 396 ff.).

[2] Kock, *Angl.* 46 (1922), 87, reads *snyttru* (1726) as instrumental, but the recent
edd. prefer to construe it as accusative, as I have done (Klaeber defends this view in
Angl. 50 (1926), 207).

[3] For a summary of opinions, see Dobbie's note on this line, *Beowulf*, p. 204.

lations 'in delight' or 'in his beloved home' will fit into the
general interpretation I am proposing, but I should like to
suggest that the clause might simply mean, 'Sometimes he
allows the thoughts of a man of noble stock to turn to love', with
reference to marriage and the founding of a family, which would
be the normal accompaniment of the life of royal pleasure and
would be apt if Hrothgar is supposed to be drawing on his own
experiences; it would also be fitting if the poet had in mind
man's paradisal state before the Fall. This interpretation of the
phrase would complete the blessings of the fortunate man, who
then has every good thing this world can offer; he knows no
sickness, no anxiety. The words *inwitsorh* (1736), *gesacu* (1737),
and *ecghete* (1738) recall, whether consciously or not, the afflictions which came upon Hrothgar, thus giving some particularity
to his account of the ruler's life.[1]

The seeming security of his life is the fortunate man's undoing; all the world goes as he wishes; he knows no less happy
state of affairs (1738 f.).[2] From lines 1740 to 1768 the poet draws
on a number of patristic images for temptation and sin, each
of which brings with it a complex of doctrine about the nature
of man and his spiritual trials. In his characteristic manner, the
author does not develop these images fully; just as in reading the
story of Heremod one is conscious that, though the narrative
serves its purpose, it could mean a good deal more to people who
already knew more of the facts, so in reading the sermon one
recognizes that it is designed for an informed audience who will
understand the allusions. The homiletic material used is the
common property of Christian teachers; a good deal of it is to
be found in the *Moralia*, but I have little doubt that both poet
and audience would have been familiar with these ideas and
images from sermons and religious poems they had heard.

The general sequence of thought in the whole sermon,
stripped of its figurative language, is very similar to Gregory's
statement about those whose minds are directed to earthly satisfactions:

---

[1] cp. *inwidsorg* (831), *sacu* (154) *ecghete* (84).
[2] I see no need for Dobbie's interpretation of *þæt wyrse* as 'the worse (part),
i.e. wickedness'; I suppose that it means 'the less good (condition)' i.e. the state of
one who is unhappy (*Beowulf*, p. 205).

Adipisci quippe terrenam gloriam cogitant, multiplicari rebus temporalibus exoptant, ad mortem quotidie cursu rerum labentium tendunt; sed cogitare mortalia mortaliter nesciunt. Carnis vita per momenta deficit, et tamen carnale desiderium crescit.[1]

They think about obtaining earthly glory, they keenly desire to be made richer in temporal things, they move towards death in the daily course of transitory things, but they do not know how to think of mortal things as mortal beings. The life of the flesh fails every instant and still carnal desire grows.

This teaching applies to all men in every age, because it springs out of the biblical doctrine of human nature and its lapse into mortality. It is not surprising that some of the strands the poet has woven in have to do with the making of man; some of the thought which underlies lines 1740 ff. can be found in Ambrose's *Hexameron.*

Ambrose describes man as he was shaped by his Creator *in imagine Dei,* using a text from Isaiah 49: 16, which on the surface refers to the building of Jerusalem, but is to Ambrose an image of the soul:

cui dicit deus: *ecce Hierusalem, pinxi muros tuos,* illa anima a deo pingitur, quæ habet in se virtutum gratiam renitentem splendoremque pietatis.[2]

to whom God says: *Behold, I have adorned your walls, O Jerusalem.* That soul is adorned by God which has in itself the grace of virtues and the shining brightness of piety.

The figure of the walled city of the soul which he employs here is further developed in a subsequent chapter, in which he introduces a watcher on the walls protecting the city from the incursion of the besieging enemy—for it is *obsessa per diabolum.* The lines which have relevance for the *weard, sawele hyrde* of *Beowulf* (1741 f.) read as follows:

... dicit *pinxi muros tuos* ualida se adserens homini murorum dedisse præsidia, ut si peruigil speculator in muris sit, obsidionis possit periculum propulsare.[3]

---

[1] Gregory, *Moralia, PL* 75, 943.
[2] Ambrose, *Exameron, CSEL* 32, p. 233. The Vulgate version is different from Ambrose's Old Latin.　　　　[3] ibid., p. 240.

... he says *I have adorned your walls*, asserting that he has given strong defences to the walls of man, so that if he is an unsleeping watcher upon the walls, he can ward off the danger which besets him.

Ambrose returns to the theme of the look-out later in the chapter, exhorting his reader: *Miles es, hostem diligenter explora, ne tibi nocturnus inrepat ... uulnus uigilanti aspectu exeas*[1] 'You are a soldier, attentively spy out the enemy, lest he steal in upon you by night ... so that you may, by vigilant watching, escape a wound'. The wound he speaks of is of course dealt by the Enemy, but it is not an arrow-wound as in *Beowulf* (1745 f.), though it is a *woh wundorbebod* (cp. 1747), an insidious word in the heart: *Adtende tibi, ne fiat uerbum absconditum in corde tuo inicum: serpit enim sicut uenenum et letalia confert contagia*[2] 'Take heed, lest the wicked word become lodged in your heart, for it spreads like venom, and it carries lethal contagion'. Ambrose continues, *Adtende tibi, ne obliuiscaris deum* 'Take heed, lest you forget God', and gives authority to his exhortation by quoting the words of Moses to the Israelites before they crossed the Jordan, a classic instance of the kind of admonition Hrothgar gives to Beowulf: not to forget God in the days of plenty, and not to say inwardly, *Fortitudo mea, et robur manus meæ, hæc mihi omnia præstiterunt*[3] 'My own might, and the strength of my own hand, have achieved all these things for me'.

Ambrose thus joins together three of the themes woven into Hrothgar's sermon: arrogance in a time of plenty, the need for a vigilant watch against the besieging Enemy, and the venomous wounds which are caused by the Devil's promptings. These are all, it will be noted, thoughts which arise out of Ambrose's meditation upon the making of Adam. And one can follow Ambrose further, for as Hrothgar goes on to speak of death and man's inevitable parting from his treasured possessions, so Ambrose continues with thoughts of the vanity of earthly treasure, and the ruin of the house, the body itself being but ash.[4] These thoughts are commonplace, and the *Beowulf* poet had no need to read Ambrose in order to look at human life in this way, but the particular combination found in the *Hexameron*

---

[1] ibid., p. 242.
[2] ibid., pp. 242 f. It will be recalled that Beowulf died from the spreading venom of the dragon's bite.　　　[3] Deut. 8: 11–18.　　　[4] Ambrose, ibid., p. 243.

suggests not only the outline of Hrothgar's sermon but even the outlook of the whole poem, in which Hrothgar's great hall awaits destruction, Beowulf's hard-won treasure profits no-one, and at the end the mourners circle the ashes of the hero.

If the *Hexameron* is a possible source of some of the thoughts and images of the sermon, it is evident that other material has been incorporated as well. The *oferhygda dæl* (1740) which grows within the mind of the prosperous man is the attitude described by Moses in the passage I have quoted,[1] in which a man forgets God and ascribes his success entirely to his own efforts. Arrogance of this kind deflects the whole purpose of man's being, according to patristic doctrine; the arrogant man inevitably becomes covetous, as Gregory explains, because anything less than God cannot satisfy the human soul.[2] Then the Devil takes a hand in increasing this covetousness.

The appearance of the Enemy in person upon the scene introduces a complex of patristic imagery into the sermon. In the passage quoted from Ambrose,[3] the soul was beset by the Enemy and his legions of temptations, against whom the preacher urged his reader to keep a constant watch. In *Beowulf*, the *weard* (1741) fails to perform his duty as *pervigil speculator*, and the soul is in jeopardy; the Enemy here is called *bana* 'slayer'. The exact identity of the *weard* is uncertain; I defer discussion of this problem until I have considered the image as a whole more fully. The Devil is the *bana* of mankind in two different senses: as the death-bringer who caused the physical death of Adam, and as the slayer of the soul.[4] Each of these senses of *bana* has some relevance to Hrothgar's sermon; though the idea of spiritual wounding leading to the 'death' of the soul is uppermost, the Devil's purpose is to bring the man to *improvisa mors* 'unforeseen death', and this he achieves (cp. 1750 f.).

The problem of *se weard ... sawele hyrde* (1741 f.) is that the image is insufficiently developed. The wide range of meaning of the Old English words *weard* and *hyrde* would allow either a military or a domestic metaphor here. I have already quoted Ambrose's military figure in the *Hexameron*, and this seems to me

---

[1] See p. 195, n. 3.   [2] Gregory, *Moralia*, PL 76, 395.
[3] See p. 194 and n. 3, above.
[4] Augustine, *Enarr. in Ps. 48: 2*, CCSL 38, p. 566.

to consort best with *under helm drepen* (1745). Nevertheless, two biblical passages which are interpreted as parables of the invasion of the soul by the Enemy's forces also deserve consideration; namely, the murder of Isboseth (2 Reg. 4: 5–7), quoted by Klaeber from Gregory's moralization of the story;[1] and the coming of Death the robber while the master of the house is asleep (Luc. 12: 39), the passage which gave rise to the Middle English allegory *Sawles Warde*.[2]

The former story involves an *ostiaria*, a woman door-keeper who was sifting wheat when she fell asleep at her post and gave the murderers their chance to enter. To Gregory this signifies that the faculty which guards the mind by separating virtues from vices can grow negligent and allow the spirits of evil to enter and kill the soul.[3] As Klaeber recognizes, the image of the sleeping guard is rather similar to the Beowulfian passage under discussion (1741 ff.); but it is obviously not the simple source, because in *Beowulf* the assailant does not enter, but lurks nearby with his bow. The other details of the story and its interpretation have no counterpart in *Beowulf*. On the whole it seems unlikely that the poet was thinking specifically of this scriptural passage.

The verse from St Luke's gospel is also different in respect of the mode of attack, but is much more likely to have been in the poet's mind, both because of its greater familiarity and because of the general theme of the chapter in which it appears: the folly of storing up earthly instead of heavenly treasure. In a homily upon this chapter, Gregory explains the verse as follows:

Nesciente enim patrefamilias fur domum perfodit, quia dum a sui custodia spiritus dormit, improvisa mors veniens carnis nostræ habitaculum irrumpit, et eum quem dominum domus invenerit dormientem necat, quia cum ventura damna spiritus minime prævidet, hunc mors ad supplicium nescientem rapit.[4]

While the householder is unaware, the thief breaks into the house, because while the spirit sleeps, neglecting its guard, unforeseen death

---

[1] Gregory, *Moralia*, *PL* 75, 549 f., quoted by Klaeber *Angl.* 1912, p. 132. (The Vulgate gives the alternative title *Lib. 2 Samuelis* for Gregory's *Lib. 2 Regum*.)

[2] For *Sawles Warde*, see the edition by R. M. Wilson (Leeds English Language Texts and Monographs 3, 1938).

[3] Gregory, *Moralia*, *PL* 75, 549.

[4] Luc. 12: 39; cp. Gregory, *Hom. in Evang.*, *PL* 76, 1126. The Gregorian passage is repeated *verbatim* by Bede, *PL* 92, 496.

comes to burst into the little dwelling of our flesh, and kills him whom he finds sleeping, the master of the house, since when the spirit does not look ahead to the penalties to come, death snatches him unawares to torment.

Again, there is some resemblance to Hrothgar's sermon, in the matter of the sleeping guard, but Hrothgar speaks of a wounding of the man's soul, not directly of his death and the seizing of his soul. For this aspect of the situation one might look again to Gregory, who, in another context than those already adduced, uses the image of the military guard in relation to a proud man's invasion by the evil forces; he quotes Proverbs 4: 23, *Omni custodia serva cor tuum* ... 'With all watchfulness keep thy heart ...'

Dicturus enim custodia, *præmisit* omni, *ut videlicet unusquisque hinc inde se diligenter inspiciat, et quandiu in hac vita est, contra spiritales inimicos in acie se positum sciat, ne mercedem quam per has actiones colligit, per alias amittat, ne hinc hosti fores obstruat, et aliunde aditum pandat.*

About to say *watchfulness*, he first puts *all*, evidently so that every person shall thereupon look diligently within himself, and while he is in this life know that he has posted his defence against the hostile spirits, so that he does not lose through other actions the prize which he gains through these, and that he does not shut the door against the enemy here and leave the way open elsewhere.

He relates this to the Pharisee who despised the publican (Luc. 18: 11): *Ecce civitatem cordis sui insidiantibus hostibus per elationem aperuit, quam frustra per jejunium et eleemosynas clausit*[1] 'See how through pride he opened to the waiting enemies the city of his heart, which he vainly shut through fasting and alms.'

---

[1] Gregory, *Moralia, PL* 76, 118 f.; Cook (op. cit., pp. 394 f., n. 12) called attention to Gregory's use of Prov. 4: 26; at the same time he withdrew his earlier statement on *sawle weard* (*Chr.* 1550), 'Wisdom may well be regarded as the keeper of the soul'. His later view is given as follows: 'The original Latin for "the keeper of the soul" is doubtless to be found in Prov. 16.17: *Custos animæ suæ servat viam suam*; cf. Prov. 22.5: *Custos autem animæ suæ longe recedit ab eis.*'

The other passages I have quoted support Cook's later view. Klaeber, *Beowulf*, p. 191, n. to 1741 f., cites Cook's comment, but still adheres to his opinion that 'conscience' or 'intellect', 'reason' is meant in *Beowulf* (1741 f.). The one piece of evidence which appears in favour of Klaeber's interpretation is the reference in *Chr.* (1550 f.), as construed by Dobbie, *ASPR* III, 46; but the arguments offered concerning *Beowulf* (1741 f.) indicate that the older scholars were right to take *lifes wisdom* as accusative object, not as nominative in apposition to *se sawle weard*, in *Chr.* 1550 f.

It will be noted that in Ambrose and Gregory the metaphor of the guarding of the walled city of the soul is not accompanied by any real personification of the faculties of the inner man; the custodian is the man himself, who makes his inspection and sets his watch against the besieging hosts. If *se weard … sawele hyrde* in Hrothgar's speech is similarly interpreted as 'the custodian, the soul's lord' with reference to the negligent man who posts no watch to protect the *civitas cordis sui* from the Enemy's arrows, some of the difficulties of the passage disappear. It is he who is figuratively asleep, *bisgum gebunden*, unready to defend himself (cp. 1746), rather than any abstract quality such as Wisdom or Conscience, creatures who seem altogether alien to the rest of the poem.[1]

A parallel to this figure can be found in the Old English poem *Vainglory*:

> læteð inwitflan
> brecan þone burgweal, þe him bebead meotud
> þæt he þæt wigsteal wergan sceolde. (37–9)[2]

Here, as in *Beowulf* (1745 f.), the author represents the tempted man as a soldier entrusted with the duty of guarding the *civitas cordis sui*; in his somnolent or negligent state he is unable to defend himself, and the arrows of the Enemy penetrate the heart (*on hreþre*), to poison the affections. The Devil's victim continues his carnal life, but he has sustained wounds lethal to his soul.

Klaeber is undoubtedly right to relate the word *bisgum* (1743) to *ærumnæ sæculi*[3] 'worldly cares'; I suggest that *gebunden* here means 'vanquished', 'overcome', though 'surrounded' would also serve. The wealthy man is taken up with the administration of his affairs; he has no time or energy for spiritual matters. The Devil's suggestions (1747) persuade him not to think of man's inescapable destiny, death (*forðgesceaft* 1750), so that he remains unrepentant in his sins, when he ought to be busy about provision for his soul (cp. *ferhðes foreþanc* 1060).

It is of considerable interest when one looks for connection

---

[1] The personifications which occur in this speech, apart from the disputed *weard*, are not aspects of the personality, but invading elements, such as 'sickness', 'sorrow', 'enmity'; the possible exception 'arrogance' is treated in the same way, as something implanted like a disease (1740 f.).

[2] *Vainglory*, ASPR iii, 148.   [3] Klaeber, *Angl.* 1912, 131.

between Hrothgar's *exemplum* and Beowulf's later life that Gregory in his moralizing upon Job equates the death-bringer and his evil suggestions with the gaping jaws of Leviathan. Of Leviathan, he says that to men *semel culpam prævaricationis intulit, et hanc usque ad æternem mortem quotidie pessimis suggestionibus extendit*[1] 'once he has introduced the sin of transgression, he daily enlarges this sin by means of his evil promptings even to eternal death'. The whole chapter is taken up with description of the open mouth of Leviathan which devours men, but which was caught unawares by the hook of Christ's hidden divinity. Another curious passage about Leviathan's mouth explains that the just must be willing to enter it in order to discover the true meaning of the Devil's suggestions, since he seems to promise good:

In medium igitur oris ejus intrare est calliditatis ejus verba penetrare, ut nequaquam pensetur quid resonant, sed quo intendant. Intrare Adam in medium oris ejus noluit, quando intentionem persuasionis illius caute pensare neglexit; divinitatem quippe se per illum accipero credidit, et immortalitatem amisit.[2]

To go into the midst of his mouth is to penetrate the words of his slyness, so that in no wise will it be considered how they sound, but to what they are directed. Adam would not go into the midst of his mouth when he neglected to weigh carefully the intent of his persuasions: indeed, he believed that he would receive divinity through the Devil's agency, and he lost immortality.

I have quoted this paragraph in full because it shows rather well that a man who knew his *Moralia* would see a connection possibly invisible to the ordinary modern reader between promptings to sin, death brought into the world by Adam, and the constant attacks of the Serpent-Dragon—who is also Leviathan —upon the soul of man. In other words, the arrow-attack upon the proud man, transposed into another figure, could be the gaping venomous jaws waiting to snap upon their prey. The central part of Hrothgar's sermon directs the hearer to think of the temptations which Beowulf, the fortunate man, will need to guard against: principally the temptation to forget God and to trust in his own strength. If he allows such arrogant thoughts to grow in him he must expect an attack by the Enemy, who will

[1] Gregory, *Moralia, PL* 76, 682. [2] ibid., 702.

try to persuade him of the worth of earthly treasure, so that he will follow the same unhappy road to grasping self-love as Heremod. If he does not withstand the temptation, he will find the jaws of the Dragon closing about him, as about Adam, who *se ori illius devorandum funditus præbuit* 'suffered himself to be wholly devoured by his mouth'.[1] I think it now becomes quite clear that though the general doctrine of Hrothgar's speech appears to be a generalization from the facts of Heremod's life, it is rather likely that the facts of his life were selected with the theme of the sermon in mind, the speech itself being a carefully planned conclusion to the story of Hrothgar's pride, persecution and humiliation, and a carefully directed forecast of the story of Beowulf's trial to come. The relative obscurity of the images in Hrothgar's speech compared with similar figures in homiletic writers I attribute to the poet's fondness for allusive statement, observable throughout the poem, and also to his desire to avoid markedly ecclesiastical language in order to maintain the fiction that the old Danish king is speaking out of his natural wisdom.

The more extended metaphorical passage about a devil's attacks in *Juliana* reveals that in *Beowulf* there is a conflation of two homiletic images, the one being that of the poorly-defended stronghold—in *Juliana*, lines 399–409—and the other that of the ineffective warrior, the *cempa sænra* of lines 395 ff.[2] A contrast is made in Cynewulf's poem between the soldier of God, invincible in his spiritual armour (382 ff.), and the weaker man who is the target of the Devil's arrows (403 ff.). In *Beowulf* the image of the unguarded soul precedes the image of the ineffective soldier, who though accoutred for battle (*under helm*, 1745), is unable to defend himself (1746) from the enemy shafts, which are perverse suggestions—the *bitre geþoncas* of *Juliana* (405).[3] The emphasis on the sins is slightly different in *Beowulf* because the poet is primarily interested in the effect of this inner corruption upon the man's conduct as king; the public manifestations are his hostility to his fellow men and his increasing

---

[1] cp. Gregory, ibid. [2] *Juliana, ASPR* III, 124.

[3] The adjective *biter* is related by Klaeber (*Angl.* 1912, 130) to *amarus* in Ps. 63: 4, but this is not a true parallel. This verse refers to 'bitter words' hurled by the wicked at those they envy (cp. *Vainglory*, 34 f.). *Biter* is too common in battle-phrases to be specially significant, but one might perhaps note that it is used also of sin (cp. *Rhym. Poem*, 81) and Adam's 'cup of death' (cp. *Guthlac* B, 985).

covetousness (1749 f.). He no longer shares his wealth, for all that he can acquire seems too little,[1] thus he piles up gold until the day of his death, when it falls to another to distribute it.

The anonymity of the man who inherits the treasure (1755) recalls to my mind the psalm-verse (38: 7) which I have already quoted in relation to the patristic view of man's nature,[2] as designed to find its true place only in God, because it was made in God's image, yet as perversely seeking lesser satisfactions. The psalm in question seemed to religious writers to epitomize the tragic situation of fallen man, busy about his short-lived concerns and gathering together possessions which would soon, upon his death, fall into other hands. The last line of the verse is a particular favourite with writers upon cupidity; I quote as an example Aldhelm's use of it in his verse *De Virginitate* as part of the battle with Avarice:

> Ut psalmista canit lacrymans delicta reorum
> Semper avaritiae nummi servire volentum
> 'Thesaurizat et ignorat, cui congregat illa'.
> Paulus apostolico promulgat famine doctor
> Cunctorum causam contestans esse malorum.[3]

As the psalmist sings, lamenting the sins of the guilty who are the willing slaves of Avarice's wealth: *he stores up treasures and he does not know for whom he gathers them.* Paul the teacher with apostolic voice makes his pronouncement, affirming that this is the cause of all evils.

Aldhelm is writing about those who serve Mammon, but in patristic thinking any man who puts temporal advantage before eternal reward *vane conturbabitur* 'will be disquieted in vain'.[4]

---

[1] cp. Gregory, *Moralia, PL* 75, 1093: *Avaritia obtentis bonis desideratis crescit, non extinguitur* 'Avarice grows as the good things desired are obtained, it is not quenched'.

[2] There are a number of slightly different versions of Ps. 38: 7, but all contain the three thoughts: (i) that man as he lives and moves is an image of God (only *Ps. Romanum* has *in imagine Dei*, but the commentators interpret the *in imagine* of the other texts in this sense), (ii) that disquiet about earthly things is vain, (iii) that piled-up wealth will pass into unknown hands. Apart from Augustine's quotation of it, quoted on p. 152, above, I have noted its use in warnings against avarice by Columban, Boniface and Nithhard. Another psalm-verse on the leaving of wealth to others (Ps. 48: 12) is discussed on p. 240, below.

[3] Aldhelm, *De Virginitate, MGH AA* xv, 458, 2581 ff. (Some mss read *congreget* for *congregat* in *Ps. Romanum*; the Vulgate reads *congregabit*.)

[4] *Vane conturbabitur, vl. frustra conturbatur.*

Hrothgar's speech applies to everyman, not only to misers. The whole of human life is a series of temptations by the Devil to prefer the vanities of earth to the *bona æternæ patriæ*, and the contemplation of death and the transience of life is considered a saving antidote to the Devil's poisoned suggestions. Gregory quotes the same psalm-verse in a context of the temptations and vanity of life (cp. Ps. 38: 6) linking it with *Tentatio est vita humana super terram* 'Human life upon earth is a temptation' (Job. 7: 1).[1] He finds no occasion to make reference at this point to the alternative reading of this verse which he himself had used in his commentary on Job. 7: 1, namely *Militia est vita hominis super terram* 'The life of man upon earth is a warfare'. Obviously the equation of the figures was so familiar to him that it needed no comment, and I suppose that it was also familiar to the Anglo-Saxon poets who followed him: the whole of *Beowulf* seems to me informed with this idea. Gregory's earlier observations on the verse begin thus:

Hoc in loco translatione veteri nequaquam militia vita hominis, sed tentatio vocatur. Sed si utriusque verbi sensus aspicitur, diversum quidem est quod exterius resonat, sed unum eumdemque concorditer intellectum format. Quid enim nisi pugna contra malignos spiritus, nomine tentationis exprimitur? Et quid appellatione militiæ, nisi contra hostes exercitium designatur? Tentatio itaque ipsa militia est, quia dum contra malignorum spirituum insidias vigilat, in bellorum procinctu procul dubio exsudat.[2]

At this place in the old translation the life of man is not called a warfare, but a temptation. However, if the sense of both words is considered, there is indeed a difference in the exterior sound, but it forms one and the same harmonious meaning. For what is expressed by the word temptation if not the fight against the malicious spirits? And what is intended by the name of warfare if not exercise against the enemy? Thus temptation is the warfare itself, since while a man is keeping watch against the secret attacks of the malicious spirits, he is undoubtedly toiling in readiness for battle.

Such thinking underlies the central part of Hrothgar's speech (1735 ff.) and provides the links between the pride and disregard of death of the fortunate but foolish man, the need for vigilance in the battle with the Enemy, and the growth of

---

[1] Gregory, *Moralia, PL* 76, 276.   [2] ibid., *PL* 75, 805 ff.

cupidity in the negligent warrior. When Hrothgar then pointedly addresses Beowulf with the words,

> Bebeorh þe þone bealonið, Beowulf leofa,
> secg betsta, ond þe þæt selre geceos,
> ece rædas; oferhyda ne gym,
> mære cempa

there is no longer any doubt of the import of his words. The *bealonið* 'evil enmity' which he urges Beowulf to guard against is the temptation to bask in the glory and fine living which his rank and his exploits have brought with them, a temptation figured as a military assault upon an unguarded position. If he becomes proud of his achievements and ascribes them to his own strength, he will become spiritually vulnerable. The best prophylactic for this spiritual ill is meditation upon man's weakness and the certainty of death, hence the content of lines 1761 ff.

The parallel phrases *þæt selre* and *ece rædas* take for granted the hearer's participation in this view of human life; by implication Hrothgar's speech has presented two ways of life, the one governed by the desire *adipisci terrenam gloriam, et multiplicari rebus temporalibus,*[1] the other governed by wisdom, which guides a man towards his Creator and eternal life. The 'better way' is urged upon Beowulf, who, in the successful future that Hrothgar foresees for him, will be more and more tempted to look for satisfaction in his own glory and his great wealth. If he chooses the better way, he will place the observance of God's law above every other consideration, directing his life towards *ece rædas*, not to *eorðan dreamas.*[2] The much-disputed phrase *ece rædas* occurs in two other Old English poems, in passages which leave no doubt that the meaning I have just suggested is required. In *Daniel*, the joys of the world are plainly contrasted with *ece ræd*, and wisdom (*snytro*) is similarly contrasted with desire (*langung*); the Hebrews, says the poet, often fell into unrighteous ways through pride (*wlenco*, 17), and God sent them wise teachers who persuaded them to amend for a time:

> Hie þære snytro soð gelyfdon
> lytle hwile oð þæt hie langung beswac

---

[1] cp. Gregory's words quoted on p. 194, above.
[2] On *ece ræd*, see also pp. 92 and 169, above.

eorðan dreamas   eces rædes,
þæt hie æt siðestan   sylfe forleton
drihtnes domas,   curon deofles cræft.   (*Daniel*, 28–32)[1]

In *Exodus* (516) the plural phrase *ece rædas* is used of the words of Moses to the Israelites after the crossing of the Red Sea: the contents of the speech are not given, but are reasonably referred to the laws given in the Book of Deuteronomy, among which occurs the passage I quoted earlier in this chapter.[2] With *þæt selre* in Hrothgar's speech may be compared

nu us boceras   beteran secgað
lengran lifwynna.   þis is læne dream
wommum awyrged,   wreccum alyfed
earmra anbid.   (*Exodus*, 531–4)[3]

I see no reason to dissociate these ideas in *Daniel* and *Exodus* from the thought of Hrothgar's sermon. Each of these poets is using the same complex of patristic teaching about the brief and delusive life of the world compared with the lasting joys of eternal life. There is no need to suppose that any one of these passages is directly influenced by another, as used to be thought;[4] the treatment is not very similar. I conclude that when each of these poets uses the phrase *ece ræd*, or the plural *ece rædas*, he is thinking of attitudes, decisions, or acts which will profit the soul in the perspective of eternity.

Before I leave the subject of *ece rædas*, I should perhaps take some account of the different construction placed on this phrase by Donahue, who has discussed its contextual meaning rather fully. He argues that in Hrothgar's philosophy fame is eternal, and that the phrase as used by him has reference to posthumous good repute:

Hrothgar, who wants the best of all things for his adopted son, advises him to follow the heroic code, be generous as a king, and thus assure for himself eternal *dom* as a generous lord. Such are Hrothgar's *ece rædas*, his 'counsels valid for eternity'. Hrothgar is not without hope in God. But his *hyht* has been solely concerned with matters of this world. ... He is grateful to God and determined to

---

[1] *Daniel*, ASPR I, 111.
[2] See p. 195, above.
[3] *Exodus*, ASPR I, 105 f.
[4] See Klaeber, *Beowulf*, p. cxi and n. 4.

reward Beowulf. His *dom* after death is assured, and he hopes for nothing else beyond the funeral pyre.[1]

Up to a point I can concur with what is said here. Hrothgar certainly advises Beowulf to be a generous lord. I believe that the poet means to show that the kingly ideals of the old order—loving and protective care for dependants, and generosity in giving—are also the ideals of the Christian order. The wish to leave a good name in the world is not un-Christian, and fame may be a gift of God.[2] Nevertheless, the pursuit of *dom* may easily become the desire for vainglory, unless the hero sets his thoughts upon God.

Recognizing this fact, the poet adds to the story of Heremod, which urges the prince to shun the moral vices that make a man despised upon earth, a further *exemplum* which has even more pertinence to Beowulf's situation, since it shows how the character of any man can become degraded through the machinations of the Devil. Hrothgar's counsels include at their heart the injunction to be on guard against the *bana*, a point overlooked in Donahue's argument. The mention of the *sawele hyrde* and the *bana* with his *wundorbebod* requires in the speaker some belief in the separate existence of soul and body, leading inescapably to thoughts of life after death. Nothing in the text warrants Donahue's conclusion that Hrothgar 'hopes for nothing else beyond the funeral pyre'. Moreover, the unprejudiced reader will find a great deal about morality and death, and nothing specific about the endurance of fame, in this speech. In fact, when Hrothgar's admonition is interpreted in purely secular terms, it is somewhat incoherent and substantially impertinent, as many commentators have thought. Only in terms of the king's right relation with his Creator and the evils that will follow if he errs from this does the sermon hold together and fit into the story of Beowulf.

The homiletic part of the speech concludes with a passage

[1] Donahue, *Traditio*, 1965, p. 82. In the lines I have omitted, Donahue conjectures that Hrothgar 'has obeyed his conscience. God has rewarded him by sending Beowulf.' This interpretation does not at all account for the twelve years of tribulation *before* God 'rewarded him'.

[2] As in the *Vita S. Antonii*; the Lord promises Antony, *faciam te in omni orbe nominari* 'I will make your name known throughout the world' (*PG* 26, 859); cp. p. 264, below.

upon *yldo oððe ærdeað*.[1] The purpose of these lines is to oppose man's incipient arrogance with a reminder that even a strong man like Beowulf must succumb to wounds or disease, or old age. The catalogue of ways of dying has analogues in other Old English poems, namely in *The Fortunes of Men* (10–57),[2] *Juliana* (468–94),[3] and in summary form in *The Seafarer* (68–71).[4] Of these, the brief passage in *The Seafarer* is closest to *Beowulf* in its purpose as a reminder of the transience of *eorðan dreamas* compared with *ecan lifes blæd*. The means of death in *Beowulf* are restricted to those which a hero is most likely to meet; such contingencies as starvation or the gallows are obviously not to be envisaged for Beowulf.[5] Of the various bodily infirmities which might render him helpless, Hrothgar specifies only one, the loss of sight. It is possible that the poet is thinking also of spiritual blindness, which is associated by Gregory with the arrogant wealthy man, following the speech of the angel in The Apocalypse of St John (3: 17) to the man *qui habet aurum* 'who possesses gold'.[6]

In the last section of his speech, Hrothgar relates what he has been saying to his own personal experience. He himself ruled prosperously for fifty years, and thought that he had no enemy left (172 f.), like the fortunate man of his *exemplum* (cp. 1735–9). He does not accuse himself of the pride and spiritual sloth which he has spoken of as the successful king's weaknesses, but the implication can hardly be avoided. In his own case, the violent intrusion of Grendel upon his peace brought a reversal of fortune (1774 ff.). The disciple of Augustine would infer from this that the temporal affliction came in time to turn Hrothgar's thoughts from their complacent dwelling upon his success and wealth towards *ece rædas*. In *De civitate Dei* Augustine teaches that temporal disasters and losses may be spiritually beneficial, in teaching the right use of earthly goods.[7]

Perhaps it will be granted that the sermon is not unsuitable as a piece of moralizing in the mouth of a rather sententious old

---

[1] cp. *Exodus*, 540; *ASPR* I, 106.   [2] *The Fortunes of Men*, *ASPR* III, 154 ff.
[3] *Juliana*, *ASPR* III, 113 ff.   [4] *The Seafarer*, *ASPR* III, 143 ff.
[5] cp. *The Fortunes of Men*, 15 and 33 ff.
[6] Gregory, *Moralia*, *PL* 76, 259; it is to be noted that this chapter is on the subject of arrogance. The darkness of sin is a commonplace; cp. p. 156, above.
[7] Augustine, *De civ. Dei*, *CCSL* 47, pp. 12, 65–9.

man, and yet it may be argued that Beowulf is not another Heremod, and bears no resemblance to the unnamed king in *The Rhyming Poem,* so that the sermon remains dramatically inappropriate. Hrothgar praises Beowulf for moral as well as physical excellence: why should he seek to warn the prince he so much admires against becoming arrogant? Two quotations from Gregory will demonstrate the pertinence of Hrothgar's fears; the first is from a letter written by the Pope to the Visigothic King of Spain, Rechared, which begins like Hrothgar's speech to Beowulf with commendation for deeds well done, and proceeds with a very similar warning. Rechared had done much to strengthen the Church in his kingdom, and for this Gregory praises him highly. But he continues:

Sed inter hæc vigilanti sunt studio antiqui hostis insidiæ cavendæ; qui quanto maiora in hominibus dona conspicit, tanto hæc auferre suptilioribus insidiis exquirit. Neque enim latrunculi in via capere viatores vacuos expetunt, sed eos qui auri vascula vel argenti ferunt. Via quippe est vita præsens. Et tanto quisque necesse est ut insidiantes spiritus caveat quanto maiora sunt dona quæ portat ... Sæpe namque malignus spiritus, ut bona destruat, quibus prius adversari non valuit, ad operantis mentem post peractam operationem venit eamque tacitis cogitationibus in quibusdam suis laudibus excutit ita, ut decepta mens ammiretur ipsa, quam sint magna quæ fecit. Quæ dum per occultum tumorem apud semetipsam extollitur, eius qui donum tribuit gratia privatur.[1]

But in the midst of these things one must be on one's guard with unremitting vigilance against the secret attacks of the Ancient Enemy, who, the greater the gifts he perceives among men, uses the more subtle snares in seeking to take them away. For petty robbers on the road do not try to capture empty-handed travellers, but those who are carrying vessels of gold or silver. This present life is a road indeed. And each man needs to be on his guard against the lurking spirits in proportion to the gifts he carries. For often the malicious spirit, in order to destroy those good things which previously he was not strong enough to oppose, comes into the mind of the man who has just performed some good act and disquiets it with silent thoughts of self-praise, so that the deluded mind admires itself for the great things it has done. And while he is puffed up within himself by the hidden swelling, he is robbed of the grace of him who bestowed the gift.

[1] Gregory, *Ep. ad Reccharedum, MGH Ep.* II, pp. 223 f.

From this letter it will be seen that Gregory believes that the more gifted the man, the greater the danger of attack upon him by the envious spirits of evil. Moreover, his early successes against the Devil's forces will make him the target of more strenuous assaults. The same thought is expressed through a different figure in the *Moralia*. Discussing Job 3: 8, *Qui parati sunt suscitare Leviathan* 'who are ready to raise up Leviathan', Gregory says,

Diabolum contra se suscitant qui ejus tyrannidem despiciunt.— Omnes enim qui ea quæ mundi sunt mente calcant, et ea quæ Dei sunt plena intentione desiderant, Leviathan contra se suscitant, quia ejus malitiam instigatione suæ conversionis inflammant.[1]

They raise up the Devil against themselves who show contempt for his tyranny. For all those who mentally spurn the things of the world and desire the things of God with all their hearts, raise up Leviathan against themselves, because they excite his malice by the goad of their good life.

According to this doctrine, if Beowulf, gifted and virtuous as he is, continues along the better path which Hrothgar urges him to follow, despising the rewards of the world and seeking to obey the law of God, he will find an enraged Leviathan in his path. The Devil's purpose will be to snare him with thoughts of self-praise which will lead to arrogance. As his life leads to further prosperity and freedom from earthly hardship, his mind will be less vigilant to repel such thoughts, and in course of time he may, like the Israelites in Moses's forecast,[2] forget that he owes everything to the Creator, so that even in his righteous acts *non conditoris laudem dilatari appetit, sed suæ opinionis gloriam requirit*[3] 'he does not seek to magnify the praise of his Creator, but looks for the glory of his own reputation'. As Adam was, Beowulf will be subject to the promptings of the Enemy towards vainglory and cupidity. By means of Hrothgar's admonitory speech, the poet creates an expectation in his hearers that in the second part of the poem they will be shown the contest between an older and more vulnerable Beowulf and the enraged Leviathan, and the hero's meeting with death.

[1] Gregory, *Moralia*, PL 75, 645.   [2] See p. 195, above.
[3] cp. Gregory, *Ep. ad Reccharedum*, p. 224.

7 *The Nature of the Hero*

The last voyage of Ulysses, as Dante describes it,[1] is a great
triumph of the human will. Ulysses dares to use his powers to
the uttermost without regard for safety or policy, pressing on
into unknown waters until 'death closes all'. The modern reader
responds with admiration to the magnificent gesture, finding
it difficult to understand how Dante could imaginatively conceive this great hero and yet present him as a lost soul shrouded
in everlasting flame. Ulysses, like Satan in *Paradise Lost*, and also,
I would say, like Beowulf, embodies his author's impulse to defy
his destiny. Yet in these poets themselves the impulse is subdued,
as they follow what they believe to be a nobler ideal. There is
something of this defiant spirit in Beowulf as he goes upon his
last adventure; the decision to fight alone is foolish and splendid
at once, like Ulysses's decision to press on into the uninhabited
world. The comparison of these heroes suggests that modern
interpreters of *Beowulf* may be misled by the poet's evident
admiration of the hero's unfaltering courage into the supposition
that he is drawn as a pattern of conduct to the end. In the case
of Ulysses, the portrait is of a noble lost soul; in the case of
Beowulf, the portrait is somewhat enigmatic and the manner of
his death a paradox of defeat in victory. Hrothgar's admonition,
as we have seen, prepares the audience for a conflict between the
hero and the Devil. If he becomes spiritually negligent, the
Enemy will have an initial advantage, as happened at Heorot
when Grendel attacked the Danish king. Whether or not Beowulf becomes arrogant in later life, the conflict is inescapable.
The appearance of the Dragon is prepared for, but the kind
of retaliation the old king will make is left uncertain, and when
he fights his motives and his spiritual strength are in doubt. For
this reason, those who read the poem may disagree about the
poet's attitude to his hero's end.

Both Ulysses and Beowulf are epic heroes inherited by a poet

[1] *Inferno*, 26, 112–20.

whose values are very different from those of the warrior society which brought the hero into being. The traditional hero both entertained and exhilarated the community whose admirable qualities he epitomized. He was remembered for his military successes and for his adherence to a code of honour which opposed certain loyalties to self-interest and a system of donation to personal greed. A Christian society could still admire the loyalty and generosity of such a hero, but could not accept him as the epitome of all the manly virtues. As the social symbols of the community were transformed, so the symbolic persons had to change their allegiances[1] or cease to be the source of inspiration they had been during their legendary life. Could Beowulf be a source of inspiration for a Christian prince?

It will be useful to examine the degree to which Beowulf is given personality, and in what areas of human activity he has his being. There is a prevalent opinion that the poet created in him a mirror of kingship,[2] but I think it can be shown that the kinds of royal behaviour which interested this author are narrowly circumscribed, and even a conflation of all the kingly acts described in the stories would not make a rounded portrait.

It is not difficult to demonstrate that the poet gives scant attention to Beowulf's private personal relationships. The hero does not speak of his parents, and his marriage is not mentioned, though it is inferred from the presence of a mourning woman at his funeral (3150). As he is dying he briefly regrets that he has no son and heir (2729 ff.); he gives his personal possessions to Wiglaf; to whom he uses the affectionate form of address *Wiglaf leofa* (2745), but it is hard to estimate what kind of feeling the word *leofa* implies. It is used by Hrothgar (1758, 1854), Wealhtheow (1216), and Hygelac (1987) in addressing the hero, by Beowulf towards Hrothgar (1483) and Wiglaf (2745), and by Wiglaf to Beowulf in his peril (2663). Hrothgar is filled with strong fatherly affection for the young champion who has delivered him from the destroyers; he kisses and embraces him and weeps at his departure (1870 ff.), but Beowulf gives no sign

---

[1] A prince's change of aim in life is clear-cut in the OE *Guthlac* A; and even more explicit in the *Vita Guthlaci*, c. 16–19 (ed. cit., pp. 80 ff.).

[2] See particularly Levin L. Schücking, 'Das Königsideal in *Beowulf*', and also J. Leyerle, 'Beowulf the Hero and the King'.

of reciprocal grief. Brodeur has made much of the mutual love of Beowulf and his uncle Hygelac:[1]

The demonstration of this love through Beowulf's words and acts gives warmth and depth to the hero's personality, and an additional dimension to his actions. It is his strongest and most enduring emotion, and exerts its influence as long as he lives. In Part I, Hygelac is the center of Beowulf's world; in Part II, the recollection of Hygelac remains, a living, moving force, in his heart.[2]

There follows a good deal more in the same vein, but the text does not wholly support it. Loyalty and trust between uncle and nephew are indeed mentioned more than once, the relationship of these two is held up as an example (2166 ff.), and a strong feeling of kinship warms the words with which Beowulf hands his rewards to his king (2148 ff.). This is the expression of an ideal relationship between man and lord, strengthened by the family tie.[3] Much or little may be made of Beowulf's *Hygelac min* (2434) in his recollections of youth. To Brodeur it means that Beowulf is 'thinking first and always of Hygelac',[4] but it might only imply that Beowulf took up arms in Hygelac's service. If Brodeur's reading were valid, some expression of sorrow at Hygelac's death would surely be demanded? Beowulf served faithfully, and avenged his lord's death, an action which according to his own philosophy was better than much mourning (cp. 1384 f.); nevertheless, Beowulf's last reminiscences, which include a sympathetic account of Hrethel's grief for Herebeald (2444 ff.), do not mention Beowulf's own early loss of Hygelac as such, though there is an oblique reference to the battle in which he died (2501 ff.). Brodeur reads between the lines a 'passionate resolve (lines 2497 ff.) to be worthy, in his last fight, of his beloved Hygelac'.[5] I do not find this personal element in the speech; it seems to me a recollection of past victories meant to hearten the great warrior,[6] countering the 'dark thoughts' (cp. 2332) which fill his breast:

---

[1] Brodeur, *Art*, pp. 80 ff.   [2] ibid., p. 83.
[3] cp. *The Battle of Maldon*, 223 f., *ASPR* vi, 13.   [4] Brodeur, *Art*, p. 85.
[5] ibid.
[6] The four references to Hygelac's last battle are of some structural importance in the poem; the event is a pivotal point in the history of the Geats, and this fact rather than interest in Hygelac as a person accounts for the repetition of it.

beotwordum spræc
niehstan siðe: 'Ic geneðde fela
guða on geogoðe;   gyt ic wylle,
frod folces weard,   fæhðe secan,
mærðu fremman ... (2510–14)

It could be argued that Beowulf's reticence about his personal
bereavements (cp. 2150 f.) is fitting for a martial hero, in whom
the softer emotions are cloaked. But the truth is that Beowulf, in
spite of his recollection of so many battles in the speech just
quoted, is not actually presented as a campaigner. No battle in
which he took part is fully narrated. One is particularly conscious of an opportunity missed in the account of Hygelac's last
battle, in which Beowulf's part is a feat of swimming bearing in
his arms thirty trophies of war (2359 ff.) and a wrestling with
Dæghrefn the Frankish champion, briefly mentioned in his
reminiscences (2501 ff.); there is no display of Beowulf's valour
against great odds on the banks of the Rhine. He provides no
model here for a royal commander or for a swordsman.

In what activities could Beowulf be considered a pattern of
princely behaviour? First I would place his courteous speech
and behaviour at court, which provide a counterbalance to the
savagery of the wrestling with Grendel, assuring the audience
that though he can at need match ferocity with merciless
violence, he is himself neither aggressive nor uncouth. His con-
trolled rejoinder to Unferth's scornful mockery, which might
have brought a challenge or a blow from an irascible man,[1] and
his reported forbearance with his drunken retainers (2179 f.)
consorts well with the brief statement that the Geatish warriors
thought him *sleac* and *unfrom* in his youth.[2] As his courage is
never in question, their poor estimation of him as a young
warrior is most reasonably taken as a sign that his temperament
was equable and peace-loving; his anger and the full use of his
strength were reserved for retaliation against aggressors (cp.
423 f.).

His motives for fighting are important. He is more the knight

[1] Schücking (op. cit., p. 153) suggests that the Unferth digression was introduced
principally to show Beowulf *continens in ira*. I think this is one among several functions of this episode.

[2] No doubt the trait was traditional, but it need not have been included by the
poet in his eulogy of the hero.

213

than the adventurer in his early exploits, first fighting the giants and *niceras* who attacked the Geats (420 ff.), and then sailing to the help of the Danish king, *þa him wæs manna þearf* (201). When he and his men arrive in Denmark, Wulfgar guesses from their bearing that they have come *for wlenco, nalles for wræcsiðum, ac for higeþrymmum* (338 f.). Hrothgar gives other reasons than these for Beowulf's appearance at his court; the first, unfortunately, is in some doubt, because of textual corruption, but the second lays to Beowulf's credit an unselfish desire to help: *for arstafum* (458). This bears out the laconic indication of line 201, and implies that Beowulf's great adventure at Heorot was not begun in a spirit of self-glorification as Wulfgar's words suggest, but to put his services at the disposal of the unfortunate Hrothgar. The other phrase used by Hrothgar about Beowulf's intentions reads in the manuscript *fere fyhtum* (457); the editors are divided in their choice of emendation; some read *for were-fyhtum* 'for defensive fighting',[1] which is palæographically probable and semantically in accord with what has been said above concerning Beowulf's successes as a deliverer of the afflicted. Klaeber, Dobbie and others adopt Trautmann's proposal *for gewyrhtum* 'because of deeds wrought in the past', an allusion to Hrothgar's generosity towards Beowulf's exiled father, now to be repaid by the son.[2] Though this reading is harder to defend on palæographical grounds, I think it undoubtedly makes better sense in the context. In a rather similar way, Beowulf's own generosity is repaid when he in his turn is in danger from a monster, as Wiglaf remembers all that he owes to his lord (2606 ff.) and urges his companions to think of Beowulf's deserts (*ealdgewyrht* 2657).[3] Whichever interpretation of Hrothgar's words is preferred, this speech ascribes honourable and unselfish motives to Beowulf. He certainly also desires to win fame at Heorot, but less for self-glorification than to deserve well of his king and reflect honour upon him[4] (cp. 435 f.). He does not set out for Denmark to enrich himself: he receives the

[1] So Grundtvig, Wrenn, and von Schaubert.

[2] For other less likely suggestions, see Dobbie's note, *Beowulf*, p. 140.

[3] I follow Klaeber and Wrenn in the interpretation of *ealdgewyrht*; for other possibilities, see Dobbie's note, *Beowulf*, p. 253.

[4] The warrior's duty to ascribe his own successes to his lord is an often-quoted feature of Germanic life as Tacitus records it (cp. *Germania*, c. 14).

great rewards Hrothgar offers him with natural pleasure, but he shuns the treasure he finds in the giants' hall (1612 f.), and on his return home he presents the costly gifts to King Hygelac and Queen Hygd (2145 ff.). His motives for fighting the dragon are more complex and I will defer consideration of them to later in the chapter.

The hero's relations with his followers are treated in the most general terms. His companions in the first adventure are a shadowy band, among whom he has no particular friend; he betrays no grief for Hondscioh as Hrothgar does for Æschere in similar circumstances.[1] The Geat warriors are not created as individuals; they share a corporate sorrow at the thought of never seeing their homes again (691 ff.), and an equal keenness to protect their lord's life (794 ff.). The death of one of them emphasizes both Grendel's savagery and, by contrast, Beowulf's extraordinary prowess; if the man had been introduced to the hearers as a living person, Beowulf's failure to try to save him would be intolerable.[2] The hero is conscious of his duty towards his men collectively (1480 f.) and he shows some magnanimity in sharing the honours of victory with them in his report to Hrothgar (958 ff.)[3] In these relationships, therefore, he worthily fills the office of a leader of men, but no private feeling is described.

This limited private portrait is consonant with the portrayal of an ideal ruler, but when the poem is scrutinized it becomes clear that the poet is silent about all the public duties of a king relating to law-making and the administration of justice. It is said that he ruled well, but there are no instances to show how he protected the helpless or kept peace within the land. It would seem, therefore, that the poet did not use the opportunities provided by the story to show Beowulf's private loves or friendships, or to create a complete portrait of an able commander or a just king. Apart from the monster-fights, few of the hero's specific deeds are mentioned. His goodness and success as a king are

---

[1] In his report to Hygelac, Beowulf does indeed speak briefly of him in terms of esteem and affection, but without mention of personal sorrow (2076 ff.).

[2] For further comment on this incident, see p. 264, below.

[3] His generous distortion of what actually happened may be compared with Wiglaf's equally honourable distortion of the end of the dragon-fight in his report of it (cp. 2875 f.).

215

stated rather than illustrated, and one must turn to what he says and what is said about him to discover more of his character.

I have already discussed Hrothgar's estimation of him in the great admonitory speech. I now turn to the summing-up of his character at the end of the first part of the poem (2177 ff.), in which he is praised for self-control (2179 f.),[1] as by Hrothgar. The first sentence of the passage reads,

> Swa bealdode   bearn Ecgðeowes,
> guma guðum cuð   godum dædum,
> dreah æfter dome.   (2177–9)

The phrase *godum dædum*[2] appears to be in strange company if the rest of the sentence is interpreted in purely secular terms. But it is to be remembered that the battles in which Beowulf has shown bravery up to this point in the story are not the campaigns of his king, but early combats against *eotenas* and *niceras* and the exploits at Heorot for which he is being honoured by Hygelac. *Dom* no doubt means the good estimation of his king and his fellows, but it also has connotations of righteousness, as in the compound *domfæst*.[3] I interpret this sentence, in accord with what follows, as an allusion to Beowulf's use of his strength in the service of God and man, never in brawling or in aggressive fighting. This is the only eulogy of Beowulf in the poet's own voice, but two other passages enumerate his virtues. One is his own appraisal of his life as he lies dying, the other is his followers' praise of him in their funeral lament. Neither of these can be assumed to present objectively the poet's estimation of the hero, since the former may also disclose the limitations of a pagan moral philosophy, and the latter will present the dead king in the best possible light according to the *ethos* attributed to that time and country. As these important passages come at the end of the hero's life, I will postpone discussion of them until after I

---

[1] One trait included in this speech has already been mentioned, namely, his forebearance towards his retainers in their cups.

[2] Klaeber's note, *Beowulf*, Suppl. pp. 457 f., suggests that this is a Christian phrase (cp. *bona opera*) which has here undergone what Tolkien calls 're-paganization'. I should prefer to look upon it as a nodal point where secular story and moral allegory meet.

[3] Note the use in the OE *Genesis* of *domfæst* (1510) and *godum dædum* (1507) of Noah.

have considered the actions and speeches which precede them in the narrative.

A useful starting-point is offered by Kaske's study of the heroic ideal in the poem, which he relates to a traditional formula *sapientia et fortitudo* 'wisdom and bravery'.[1] No one will deny that Beowulf is conceived as wise as well as brave; Kaske examines, among other things, the nature of Beowulf's wisdom:

With regard to *sapientia*, we seem to have in *Beowulf* a general eclectic concept including such diverse qualities as practical cleverness, skill in words and works, knowledge of the past, ability to predict accurately, prudence, understanding, and the ability to choose and direct one's conduct rightly; in this respect it contrasts noticeably with the *sapientia* of the religious heroic poems, which seems more strictly Augustinian.[2]

I believe this contrast to be over-stated, and the eclectic concept to be partly the critic's invention.

For an example of Kaske's method, one might take his 'key allusion' to the *sapientia et fortitudo* of Beowulf.[3] The first, *snotor ond swyðferhð* (825 f.), is unobjectionable. The second is Wealhtheow's admonition to Beowulf:

> cen þec mid cræfte   ond þyssum cnyhtum wes
> lara liðe.   (1219 f.)

Kaske does not translate this sentence, but it is evident from the reference to the 'formula' that *cen þec mid cræfte* is interpreted as an allusion to bravery.[4] There follow two quotations from Hrothgar's praise of Beowulf as strong and wise (1705 f., 1841 f.). The fifth 'key allusion' is part of the poet's eulogy of Beowulf which includes the phrase *mæste cræfte* (2181); Kaske here translates 'by means of the highest power, that is, *sapientia*'.[5] It appears, therefore, that *cræft* in Wealhtheow's speech (1219) refers to *fortitudo*, but *cræft* in the last quotation (2181) refers to

---

[1] See also p. 187, above.   [2] Kaske, op. cit., pp. 425 f.
[3] ibid., pp. 427 f.

[4] I would translate 'Declare yourself in strength and be kind in counsel to these boys', i.e. 'openly offer your strong support to these princes, and give them the benefit of your advice'.

[5] It seems to me better to assume with Hoops, Wrenn and von Schaubert that *cræfte* is here f. acc. sg. parallel to *ginfæstan gife*: 'and yet he, the brave in battle, of all mankind held the greatest strength, the massive gift which God had given him'.

sapientia. The range of meanings recorded for *cræft* does not preclude this, but the uncertainty of the rendering casts doubt upon the 'formula'. In the same quotation, *nealles druncne slog heorð-geneatas* (2179 f.) is called 'his avoidance of Germanic crime', but the phrase *hreoh sefa* which follows and surely refers to the same kind of cruelty, Kaske takes to be 'a description of *malitia*'.[1] In general, as we have seen, the poet presents Beowulf as a man who controls his passions with his reason and does not misuse his strength. This seems to me wholly in accord with the Augustinian teaching adduced in my previous chapter.[2] If *sapientia* is so elastically interpreted that any reasonable act or intelligent speech is included within it, it would be difficult to find any hero who did not possess the virtue. Beowulf's *sapientia* is analysed by Kaske into the skills of a warrior and a persuasive speaker, a competent diplomat and a philosopher. Some of these qualities are questionably present.

The first quality in Kaske's enumeration, quoted above, is 'practical cleverness'. I do not recognize this attribute in Beowulf at all. His preparations for the great fights are symbolic gestures rather than practical arrangements, as is evident if one compares them with the preparations of other heroes in similar predicaments: Grettir preparing his escape rope, Sigurð digging pits to give him access to the dragon's belly, Frotho making protective clothing against the flames, are all instances of practical cleverness.[3] In comparison, Beowulf's sole invention, the great iron shield, is cumbersome, and in the event not completely successful in its protection of the hero. Since Beowulf has least difficulty in overcoming his opponent in the contest for which he makes no practical preparation at all, the poet can

---

[1] Kaske, op. cit., pp. 428 f. *Hreoh sefa* seems to me more specific than *malitia*; if referred to violent wrath it makes excellent sense in the context and in contrast with Heremod. The reference to the more general concept *malitia* seems to be brought in to create a polarity with the *sapientia*-theme Kaske is emphasizing. In contrast, the comment about 'Germanic crime' is too limiting: one could quote, for example, Martin of Braga, whose moral instruction to his king includes this apophthegm: *Qui in servos irascitur et crudelis est, satis ostendit potestatem adversus alienos sibi defuisse* 'He who shows wrath and is cruel to his servants shows well enough that he has lacked authority in face of men outside his household'. (*Formula honestæ vitæ, PL* 72, 32.)

[2] See p. 187, above.

[3] See Chambers, *Beowulf: An Introduction*, pp. 160 and 93 f.

hardly wish to praise this faculty very highly. Of the other qualities named by Kaske, prudence is difficult to associate with the man who decided to face Grendel without a weapon; and Kaske's example 'their prudence in carrying weapons', as 'part of Beowulf's defence of his *sapientia*' in recounting the youthful swimming contest, does not convince the reader.

Skill in using words one readily grants to Beowulf. His speeches are thoughtful and courteous, and wholly deserving of Hrothgar's praise of them:

> þe þa wordcwydas   wigtig drihten
> on sefan sende;   ne hyrde ic snotorlicor
> on swa geongum feore   guman þingian.
> þu eart mægenes strang   ond on mode frod,
> wis wordcwida.   (1841–5)

In quoting this passage, Kaske omits the first clause, which puts a different complexion on Beowulf's wisdom as manifested in his speeches. His offer on Hygelac's behalf of military support for Hrothgar or his son, which elicits this praise from the Danish king, evinces, says Kaske, 'a subtle grasp of situation and innuendo and some skill in intertribal affairs', and he calls Beowulf 'a competent diplomat'.[1] These comments seem to me inapposite. It needs no very subtle understanding to take the import of Wealhtheow's open request for friendship to her sons. Beowulf offers unconditional help; no diplomacy is displayed here or in his report to Hygelac. The kind of wisdom revealed is an aspect of Augustinian *sapientia*, which is very close to Kaske's description 'the ability to choose and direct one's conduct rightly'.

Kaske's list of qualities includes one other which this same speech exemplifies: it is 'the ability to predict accurately', which appears in a more startling fashion in the hero's report to Hygelac. Such an ability could be a sign of political wisdom, but it has to be admitted that in Beowulf's case the predictions have no practical effects. His assurances that Hygelac will back him with encouragement and troops if Hrothgar needs his help again, and that Hrethric will find friends if he comes to Hygelac's court, though described by Brodeur as 'predictions',[2]

[1] Kaske, op. cit., p. 429.
[2] cp. Brodeur, *Art*, p. 160. Brodeur points out (p. 178) that the Heaðobard attack on Hrothgar which follows the breaking of the truce could be of importance to

are actually assumptions based on his knowledge of Hygelac's generous nature, just as his 'prediction' that Unferth will go to hell is an inference anyone might make who knew of his reputation for fratricide. These confident statements about the future show no special powers. In fact though Beowulf accurately assesses Hygelac's chivalrous nature—as far as we can tell—he does not see into the future, or he would know that Hygelac's early death will prevent the Geats from coming to aid Hrothgar. There is no support from this or any other speech to warrant the belief that he had powers of prophecy,[1] like a saint, though he seems to have had a vague premonition of his death, which is a rather different matter. Brodeur makes a very good case for regarding Beowulf's circumstantial account of what will happen to Ingeld and Freawaru as a conjecture about a possible contingency:

Accordingly, he represents his hero, not as predicting what the audience knew had happened between the Danes and Heaðobards but as seeing clearly the nature of the dangers which must threaten Hrothgar's hazardous policy, and as suggesting how unforeseen contingencies might bring disaster.[2]

The speech, according to Brodeur, illustrates Beowulf's 'wisdom and political insight'.[3] Again, one feels slightly uneasy about the introduction of politics, since Beowulf suggests no other, less hazardous, course of action for Hrothgar to pursue. The insight which Beowulf demonstrates is understanding of the consequences of human hatred and violence; it is not expressly revealed as a practical quality.

The evidence in my opinion shows that Beowulf's wisdom manifests itself in speeches rather than in actions and that it is neither so political nor so practical as Kaske and Brodeur would have it; I believe that the poet wished to portray a just and righteous man rather than a shrewd and competent governor. The underlying philosophy of the poem seems to me that the

Hygelac, whose aid Beowulf has promised: this justifies the inclusion of the long forecast in his speech to Hygelac. Nonetheless, the poet does not allow Beowulf any sagacious observations on the intertribal consequences, or even a diplomatic hint that Hygelac may be involved.

[1] Lawrence, *Beowulf and Epic Tradition*, p. 80, uses the verb 'prophesy' about Beowulf's account of Ingeld's wedding. For a survey of critical opinions on this point, see Brodeur, *Art*, pp. 159 f.   [2] Brodeur, *Art*, p. 178.   [3] ibid.

moral and spiritual health of those in high places is of paramount importance: a thoroughly Augustinian point of view. It takes for granted that God will steer human affairs through the wise ruler, whose wisdom consists in obeying God's law, both in ordering his own turbulent passions and in taking the morally right course in his public actions. A good example of Beowulf's 'wisdom' in operation is his refusal to supplant the boy Heardred. Politically, it was inexpedient for the boy to rule, for he was no match for Onela, but the poet clearly approves Beowulf's self-effacing regency, in spite of the practical consequences—a military setback and the premature death of Heardred.

Of evidence concerning the character of Beowulf there remain to be considered his own review of his life made just before his death (2732 ff.), and the reputation given him by his own people at his graveside (3180 ff.). The former speech may seem a strangely complacent one for the dying words of the hero of a Christian poem. Like many features of the account of Beowulf's last day it seems capable of more than one explanation. It may be thought to be self-praise, an illustration of the hero's pride. On the other hand, it might be an imitation of Job's speech of self-exculpation, made when the signs that God's favour had been withdrawn from him could have made him despair (cp. Job 31: 1–40). Gregory says of Job's review of his own just actions: *Ad cavendam desperationem, licet recte a se gestorum recordari* 'To avoid despair, it is rightly lawful to recall one's deeds'.[1] If this was Beowulf's motive also, the speech is not reprehensible in itself. There is, however, a decided difference in the content of the speeches, and it is significant that Job expressly absolves himself from having made gold his strength or having rejoiced over his great riches (Job 31: 24 f.),[2] whereas Beowulf's speech ends with his command to Wiglaf to bring him some of the treasure quickly, so that he may die the more happily for having looked upon it.

Beowulf's recollections cover fifty years in which all his enemies were kept at bay. These words naturally recall Hrothgar's similar experience before Grendel came, and bring

[1] Gregory, *Moralia, PL* 76, 214.

[2] Gregory comments upon this verse, *Prius itaque curandum est ne quis temporalia diligat* (ibid., 214) 'First, therefore, care must be taken not to love temporal things'.

Hrothgar's observations about his life back into mind (cp. 1769 ff.). The rather vague lines,

> Ic on earde bad
> mælgesceafta, heold min tela, (2736 f.)

perhaps suggest that King Beowulf did not journey abroad like Hygelac, leaving his people unprotected. A similar thought—that he did not engage in aggressive fighting—might lie behind *ne sohte searoniðas* (2738), but it is rather more likely that the poet's mind has turned to domestic affairs; Beowulf was not drawn into intrigue or treachery such as marred the lives of Unferth, Finn and Ingeld, for he speaks of false oaths, and as the climax of the list of evil acts eschewed he puts the murder of kinsmen.

It appears from this speech that Beowulf's life as ruler has fulfilled its promise. He has not fallen into the evil ways of Heremod or any of those other kings in the stories who came to violent ends. Kaske says that this speech 'illustrates his *sapientia* by his avoidance of the major forms of Germanic wrongdoing (2736–43), all of them Christian sins as well'.[1] If so, it is a curiously limited sort of *sapientia*. As Augustine said of another such list of negative virtues, the qualities of the just man in Psalm 14: *ista non sunt magna* 'these are not great'.[2] Augustine was not disposed to believe that it was enough to avoid certain kinds of malicious or dishonest dealing to reach God's holy hill; these must be the prerequisites to the attainment of higher virtues. Both the psalm and Beowulf's speech include rather universally-admired personal and social virtues; the form of the speech readily evokes remembrance of the psalm, which would seem to the Anglo-Saxon Christian more pertinent to Beowulf's situation than it does today, since the *tabernaculum* of the first verse suggested a military tent in which God's soldiers went campaigning with him. The Pseudo-Bede commentary on the psalm therefore calls the list of the just man's good qualities *nobilium militum descriptio* 'a description of noble soldiers'.[3] Moreover, the fourth verse of the psalm: *ad nihilum deductus est in conspectu eius malignus* 'in his sight the malignant one is brought to nothing'—is referred by the commentator (following Augus-

[1] Kaske, op. cit., p. 446. [2] Augustine, *Enarr. in Ps.*, *CCSL* 38, 89.
[3] Ps. Bede, *In Ps. Lib. Exegesis*, *PL* 93, 556.

tine) to the Evil One, who can establish no hold over a man unless the rational soul *Creatorem neglegit ... et terrena appetit* 'disregards the Creator ... and desires earthly things'.[1] Thus the underthought of Psalm 14 has the same tenor as Hrothgar's sermon and concerns the conquest of the Enemy by the just soul. It seems to me that Beowulf's enumeration of these lesser virtues was meant to call up such thoughts as underlie the description of God's soldier in the psalm, harking back to Hrothgar's admonitory speech and thus bringing the allegorical significance of the dragon-fight to the fore. But before I turn to the allegory, I must complete the secular portrait.

The last lines of the poem praise the dead king in the words of his followers: as kind and gentle to all men, and as *lofgeornost*. That final controversial word leaves the hearers with a tacit question: did Beowulf do right to challenge the dragon alone? Apart from this doubt, the picture is highly favourable. The nearest analogue I have found is the eulogy of the Emperor Constantine in the Life by Eusebius, which shows a similar combination of warlike fierceness towards the enemy and gentle benevolence of nature.[2] I do not know whether this Life was available to the *Beowulf* poet as a model, but it is interesting to find an earlier example of a kind but terrifying ruler in Christian literature. In other respects the eulogy notably lacks mention of Christian qualities, such as humility, piety, righteousness, justice for the weak and sternness towards the malefactor.[3] Some of these virtues would come strangely from the mouths of a pagan *heorðwerod*, and the poet shows a sense of artistic propriety in allowing the funeral itself to be the last word upon the hero. Granting this, one may still note that the poet's praise in his own voice is of Beowulf as prince, at the end of the first part of the

---

[1] ibid., 557.

[2] Eusebius, *The Life of Constantine*, trans. A. C. McGiffert, Bk. I, ch. 46, p. 495. It may also be noted that ch. 45 praises Constantine's forbearance with those who were exasperated with him.

[3] These qualities all occur in Ælfric's eulogy of the martyr-king Edmund, which is quoted by Schücking (op. cit., pp. 148 f.) without any indication that the portrait of Beowulf is substantially different. Schücking also speaks of 'das ideal eines milden Friedensfürsten' (p. 149) though there are no instances at all of Beowulf in the rôle of peace-maker; he terrifies his enemies into quiescence, but that is hardly the same thing; he also seems to have a poor estimation of Hrothgar's attempts to make peace by compact.

poem (2177–99), so that there is in fact no complete eulogy of Beowulf as king.

It has sometimes been argued that the word *lofgeornost* carries implications of excess,[1] but one would not expect the king's followers to review his faults in their lament for him. This consideration, and the parallelism of the other superlative expressions, make the translation 'too eager for fame' inappropriate. Nevertheless, the word is double-edged, and may well be meant as dramatic irony, in view of Wiglaf's earlier censure of Beowulf's decision to go after the dragon (3077 ff.) and the forecast of a wretched future for the Geats as a consequence of his fatal combat (3018 ff.). Beowulf's zeal for fame quite evidently proved calamitous to his people, and it may reasonably be thought an example of *desmesure*, the opposite of the ideal of *mensura* which Schücking rightly recognized to be present in the poem.[2] Strangely, Schücking did not consider the possibility that Beowulf in the end fell short of the ideal. Yet the hero was at the best tragically wrong to suppose that his single combat with the dragon would benefit his people. If a worse construction is placed on his decision to fight alone for the treasure, it may be said that his heroic desire for glory was selfish and imprudent. The poet does not say this, nor does he praise him unequivocally for this act of heroism. In this way he brings the code of personal heroism into question.[3]

In the first part of the poem no questioning of ethical ideals is apparent. It is said to Beowulf's credit, *dreah æfter dome* (2179). But his early fame was won in willing service of his fellow-men, accompanied by trust in God, so that his heroic deeds did not contravene God's law. If he endangered his own life, he harmed no other person by so doing. After fifty years, he is in the very different situation of a man with power and responsibility. In secular terms, the heroic gesture may prove detrimental to his subjects.[4] From a religious point of view, the search for fame

---

[1] See Tolkien's observations on '*Ofermod*', printed as an appendix to 'The Homecoming of Beorhtnoth Beorhthelm's Son', *Essays and Studies* (1953), 13–18. Leyerle, who states his indebtedness to Tolkien (op. cit., p. 97), translates *lofgeornost* 'too eager for praise' (p. 101). [2] Schücking, op. cit., pp. 151 f.

[3] The word *wyruldcyning* has the same double-edged significance as *lofgeornost*; see also my earlier comments on this word in *Neophil.*, 1964, 71, n. 21.

[4] Leyerle, op. cit., pp. 98 ff. stresses this aspect of the poem.

which in the young prince was a part of loyal service to God and king, has become in the old ruler a much more selfish quest in which God is not acknowledged as the author of his strength and upholder of his power. Following this train of thought, one can see that the heroic gesture and its calamitous effects are what one would expect to stem from the spiritual deterioration described by Hrothgar. The unrecking challenge *per se* is a symptom of arrogant self-confidence, and if there is added to it a desire for gain, the hero's bold action is spirtually perilous.[1]

I said at the opening of this chapter that the symbolic persons in the old legends had to change their allegiances or cease to act as sources of inspiration. Some critics who have realized this fact have themselves read into the poem a change from the traditional hero's motives of eagerness for personal glory and gold to an eagerness to serve the people even at the risk of death. However, the text places an obstacle in the way of this interpretation, in that Beowulf's expressed motives as he goes to meet the dragon do not mention the people at all, though he says plainly enough that he means to win the gold or die (2532–7) and utters a great *beotword* (cp. 2510) ending,

> Nu sceall billes ecg
> hond ond heardsweord ymb hord wigan.   (2508 f.)

His concern for the people has to be inferred from what is said after the fatal combat. His own last words about the treasure are a thanksgiving

> þæs ðe ic moste minum leodum
> ær swyltdæge swylc gestrynan.   (2797 f.)

Wiglaf later attributes to him the intention of fighting alone for his men's sake:

> þeah ðe hlaford us
> þis ellenweorc ana aðohte
> to gefremmanne, folces hyrde

---

[1] Note that the Carolingian writers on kingship quoted by Leyerle (ibid., pp. 98 f.) are more concerned with 'the consequence of pride as damnation of the soul' than 'the destruction of the nation'. He quotes Sedulius Scottus, *Non ergo fortis glorietur in fortitudine sua nec dives in divitiis suis* 'Let not the strong man glory in his strength, and let not the rich man glory in his riches', but fails to point out that Sedulius is quoting Jer. 9: 23 (which resembles Ps. 48: 7) and that *both* parts of the quotation have possible relevance to Beowulf.

> forðam he manna mæst   mærða gefremede
> dæda dollicra.   (2642–6)

However, Wiglaf's words to the followers are mitigating the
sting of their lord's earlier words to them—*nis ðæt eower sið* (2532)
—as the purpose of his harangue requires, and the impression
it leaves of Beowulf's care for the men's welfare is much
weakened by the same man's later speech regretting the misery
which Beowulf's action will cause the people; one might note
also the possible connotations of foolhardiness carried by *mæst* ...
dæda dollicra (2645 f.):

> Oft sceall eorl monig   anes willan
> wræc adreogan,   swa us geworden is.
> Ne meahton we gelæran   leofne þeoden
> rices hyrde   ræd ænigne
> þæt he ne grette   goldweard þone ... (3077 ff.)

Both of Wiglaf's speeches are conditioned by the immediate
rhetorical aim; the author himself does not make any objective
pronouncement about the rightness of Beowulf's action or the
true nature of his motives. But he goes out of his way to tell us
that Beowulf saw the dragon's attack as a sign of God's anger
upon himself (2329 f.). It is difficult not to conclude that Beowulf's *beotword* (2532 ff.), his sense of God's anger, and his
eagerness to set eyes on the treasure (2743 ff.) are signs of a more
worldly outlook in the old king than in the young champion
whom Hrothgar praised so highly. I would add to these indications the fact that he does not mention God before or during his
last fight.

   To ask whether Beowulf did right to challenge the dragon
alone is to assume that the poem treats of moral choice; some
critics, however, maintain that Beowulf's course is charted, and
any other response to the dragon's invasion out of the question.[1]
Professor S. B. Greenfield links him with Roland, whose refusal
to diminish his personal reputation by blowing his horn to
summon Charlemagne's army brought about his own heroic
death and the massacre of those under his command: 'The

---

[1] See, for example, B. Mitchell, 'Until the Dragon Comes ... Some Thoughts on
Beowulf', *Neophil.* 1963, pp. 126–38; also S. B. Greenfield, '*Beowulf* and Epic
Tragedy', *Brodeur Studies*, pp. 91–105.

consequences of Roland's choice are clear; he and his epic fellow-travellers act in the light of their societies' ethical patterns.'[1] Greenfield contends that the old Geatish king faced no dilemma; the code by which he lived could admit no other kind of action. This would be true if Beowulf exemplified only the ancient loyalties of the pagan warrior tribe. But because he has been re-created as the central figure in a history in which God himself intervenes, he must, like every human being, be held responsible to God for what he does. He does not act in ignorance of his duty to God, for Hrothgar has enlarged his natural understanding of the issues which he faces. The ethical pattern upon which the king's life is shaped is duplex, but its main elements can be kept in rough accord up to this point, at which the acceptance of excessive pride as a noble fault in the traditional hero is seen to be incompatible with the Christian belief that excessive pride, which separates man from God, is the greatest sin. It is possible for a Christian poet to pardon this *desmesure* in a hero, as *The Song of Roland* testifies, but not, I think, when he specifically brings into his composition a warning against pride as rendering a man defenceless against the Devil, or when he couples the *desmesure* of his fictional character with the pursuit of treasure.

It could be contended that the heroic fault is necessary to the plot. Only Beowulf's disastrous self-sufficiency can account for his death and the affliction of the people in a world governed by an all-seeing and beneficent Lord who has twice preserved him from death in similar contests. Even so, *desmesure* could have been an element in a story of the killing of the dragon without the motive of treasure-winning. I cannot see that Beowulf's boast that he would obtain the treasure, or his dying wish to set eyes upon it, were necessary ingredients of the plot. It would have been becoming in the old king to seek to rid the land of the dragon, as he had rid Denmark of Grendel, and he might have been forgiven an excess of valour in attempting the task alone. The proud gesture at the end of his life is not, as in Roland's case, the expected culmination of an arrogant career, and the story could have been as fittingly concluded with a death of self-sacrifice. Some readers have found a selfless motive

[1] Greenfield, op. cit., p. 99.

in Beowulf's decision to fight the dragon; obviously, therefore, the poet has not said very plainly that Beowulf went to his death because he was lured by thoughts of fame and the treasure. Even those who ascribe arrogance to him are loath to think of him as infected by cupidity. Nevertheless, it must be conceded that he shows great eagerness to see the treasure in his last hour, and the audience has been warned of the corruption of wealth as well as the spiritual dangers of power. His involvement with the treasure therefore asks for close scrutiny. It will be as well to begin with the one passage which has sometimes been translated so as to exonerate him from all covetousness.

The passage in question forms a kind of epilogue to Beowulf's death. The poet surveys, through the eyes of the bereaved people, Beowulf's corpse, the dragon's huge carcase, and the pile of rusted treasure; he then muses on the evil consequences that followed the burial of the hoard (3030 ff.). There follow some thoughts upon the mystery of death and its agents (3062 ff.), and a description of the protective incantation sung over the buried treasure, with its provisions,[1] leading to the final highly obscure lines:

> næs he goldhwæte gearwor hæfde
> agendes est ær gesceawod. (3074–5)

The terms of the curse are that the man who robs the hoard will be guilty of sin and will suffer torment as a prisoner in hell-bonds (3071–3).[2] Since the thief who did steal from the hoard was earlier described as *secg synbysig* (2226), there might seem to be little to say about the curse itself. Like Piers Plowman's pardon, it tells the hearer what he knew all along: that coveting the gold is wrong, that stealing it is sinful, and that, short of a special dispensation from God himself, the sinful thief will end in hell. What makes the curse interesting and enigmatic is the uncertainty whether or not Beowulf, or the Geats generally, suffer because of it. Certainly, it is introduced in a passage about Beowulf's death, but it is altogether unclear whether the thief's act caused Beowulf's death by rousing avidity for the gold

---

[1] For the burial of the hoard and the curse upon it, see p. 95, above.

[2] I follow Klaeber in taking *hergum* and *hellbendum* as practically synonymous. See his note, *Beowulf*, p. 227.

within him, or whether the last two lines exempt him from the curse and its consequences—so making the curse itself inoperative. I cannot myself believe that the intention was to say that Beowulf, though innocent of covetousness,[1] was not exempted by God from the consequences of tampering with the hoard. Such unmerited damnation has no place in the Christian poem.

My considered opinion of the probable meaning to be attached to the disputed lines 3074–5 was published in 1964.[2] I repeat my conclusions here with some added reflections. I interpret the phrase *goldhwæte ... agendes est* as 'the treasure-bestowing munificence of God',[3] and relate the comparative adverb *gearwor* to the two kinds of treasure, the earthly and the heavenly, implied in Hrothgar's sermon; heavenly treasure must be 'more eagerly' sought if a man is to escape the dangerous power of earthly treasure. If the lines are not emended, a reasonable translation would be, 'He had by no means more eagerly regarded the treasure-bestowing munificence of God'; that is, the despoiler of the hoard faced hell-bonds because he had preferred the pursuit of tangible gold to the service of the munificent Lord. However, the sense is much improved by Klaeber's simple emendation to *næfne* (for *næs he*), which makes a proviso that the curse would not harm a man who had preferred God's service to worldly wealth. I should therefore translate the whole curse: 'that the man who plundered that place would be guilty of sin, confined in heathen haunts, bound with fetters of hell, cruelly punished, unless he had beforehand more eagerly regarded the treasure-bestowing munificence of God'.[4] If it should be objected that this is no

---

[1] Klaeber considers that the lines are 'a declaration of Beowulf's virtual innocence', *Beowulf*, p. 227.

[2] 'The Choice in *Beowulf*', *Neophil.* 1964, pp. 68 ff.; in this discussion I withdrew my earlier suggestion (*MÆ* 1960) that *agendes est* refers to the dragon's cup, but see also p. 230, n. 1, below.

[3] For the concept of God as treasure-giver, cp. *sincgiefa* in *Christ* (460), *ASPR* III, 15, and *fæder ælmihtig ... heah hordes weard*, in *The Order of the World*, (38 f.), *ASPR* III, 164.

[4] The thought of the lines, so translated, would be rather similar to that in *An Exhortation to Christian Living* (37–40), *ASPR* VI, 68:

> Hit bið swiðe yfel
> manna gehwilcum   þæt he micel age
> gif he him god ne ondræt
> swiðor micle   þonne his sylfes gewil.

heathen curse, I would agree; but the mention of *domes dæg, synnum scildig,* and *hellbend* shows that the poet is not really thinking in heathen terms, quite apart from the disputed last lines. The translation I have offered has the advantage of agreeing with lines 3054–7, in which a similar *nefne* clause admits that God's servant could touch the hoard with impunity. It also leaves open—like lines 2329 ff.—the question of Beowulf's fault, but with a strong hint that cupidity might have led him into the dragon's power. Wiglaf's words, coming immediately after, reinforce the impression that Beowulf had been enticed (cp. *ontyhte,* 3086) from his proper duty when he gave his life for the gold.

It seems rather unlikely that a consensus of scholarly opinion will settle upon a single translation of these highly ambiguous lines.[1] It is therefore difficult to use them in any discussion of the hero's motives. I would however contend that the least substantial of the offered theories is that which interprets *næs he goldhwæte* as 'he was not gold-greedy', and a plain statement of innocence such as this is the only one among current interpretations which would call for some modification of my general argument. If Beowulf and the Geats were intended to be shown as the victims of an impersonal malediction, one would have expected further mention of the curse when the mound was ransacked under Wiglaf's orders, but nothing more is heard of it.

I return now to the matter of the hero's state of mind and spirit in his last hours, and to the allegorical significance of the dragon fight. I interpret this combat as an allegory of the temptation forecast in Hrothgar's warning speech. Like the earlier monster-fights this contest figures the hero's interior battle with the Devil. This time, the Enemy uses the gold to entice him away from *ece rædas,* and the hero, unguarded for the reasons Hrothgar describes, is almost conquered.

Kaske, in the last part of the article quoted above, speaks of

[1] For a summary of recent opinions, see E. G. Stanley, *Hæthenra Hyht* in *Beowulf', Brodeur Studies,* pp. 143 ff. He argues that *agendes est* (3075) means 'the gold-bestowing munificence of the owner' (i.e. the dragon), though he admits that *est* 'most frequently appears in such phrases as *Godes est, Metodes est*'. I am tempted to think that we have here a deliberate and fruitful ambiguity: unless the man who gained the treasure had very clearly seen (*hæfde ... gearwor gesceawod*) the Dragon's 'munificence' for what it is (an enticement to ruin) he would fall victim to its evil potency. This would be the obverse of the meaning I have suggested as the most likely.

the significance of the dragon. He thinks that the last adversary 'represents the greatest of internal ills, the perversion of the mind and will, *malitia* ... as a universal, and so comes a long step nearer allegory than any other figure in the poem'.[1] This is a cautious step towards what I believe to be the truth, that the dragon who invades Beowulf's land is a figure of the Ancient Dragon who is the source of *malitia*. The 'long step into allegory' was surely taken before Hrothgar's sermon was composed. That speech prepared the listeners for a growth of self-sufficiency in the prosperous king which could be his undoing when the *bana* made an attack upon his soul. In the light of that warning, Beowulf's decision to engage the dragon alone is seen to be the crucial point of his life. When he fought Grendel he put his faith not only in his might, but in *Metodes hyldo* (670); in his last hour his trust is in himself:

> strengo getruwode
> anes mannes.   Ne bið swylc earges sið.   (2540 f.)

At this juncture, a man familiar with the Psalms could hardly fail to remember *qui confidunt in uirtute sua, quique in abundantia suarum gloriantur* 'They that trust in their own strength, and glory in the multitude of their riches' (Ps. 48: 7).[2] Augustine, using the image of life as a fight with the Adversary, is obviously thinking of this psalm when he writes,

Ille autem vincit, qui et quod ferit, non de viribus suis præsumit, sed de protectatore Deo. Solus diabolus adversum nos pugnat. Nos si cum Deo sumus, diabolum vincimus: nam et si tu solus cum diabolo pugnaveris vinceris.[3]

But he conquers in the blows that he strikes who does not presume in his own strength, but in God as protector. The Devil fights alone against us. If we are with God we conquer the Devil, but if you should fight alone against the Devil, you will be conquered.

Beowulf receives no help from God in his last struggle, because he trusts his own strength. It is pertinent to read what Augustine has to say on *Qui habitat in adiutorio Altissimi* (Ps. 90: 1), a psalm interpreted as referring to temptation:

[1] Kaske, op. cit., p. 450.

[2] cp. the quotation from Sedulius Scottus, p. 225, n. 1, above.

[3] Augustine, *In Ep. Joan. ad Parthos, Tract.* IV, *PL* 35, 2006. For *protectatore* some MSS read *hortatore*, which has been preferred by Migne.

Quis est *qui habitat in adiutorio Altissimi?* Qui non habitat in adiutorio suo. ... Qui non est superbus, quomodo illi qui manducauerunt ut essent quasi dii et perdiderunt quod erant facti homines immortales. In adiutorio enim suo habitare uoluerunt, non in adiutorio Altissimi; ideo suggestionem serpentis audierunt, praeceptum Dei contempserunt; et inueuerunt hoc euenisse in se quod minatus est Deus, non quod promisit diabolus.[1]

Who is it *that dwells in the aid of the Most High?* He who does not dwell in his own aid ... who is not proud, like those who ate that they might be like gods and lost the human immortality created in them. They wanted to live in their own aid, not in the aid of the most High; because of this they listened to the Serpent's promptings and disregarded God's commandment; and they discovered that what happened to them was what God had threatened, not what the Devil had promised.

Even more significant for the understanding of Beowulf's fight is the same writer's discourse on Psalm 103, in which he quotes Psalm 90, again identifying the Dragon in these psalms with the Serpent who overcame Eve and now intends to destroy mankind. The scriptural source for the doctrine of the continuing feud between the Serpent and man is Genesis 3: 15; for Augustine's train of thought—and for the allegory in *Beowulf*—it is important to know that Augustine's version[2] of God's words to the Serpent in this verse is not, as in the Vulgate, *ipsa conteret caput tuum* 'she shall crush thy head', but *illa observat caput eius* 'she heeds his head' or, as he gives it in this discourse, *ipsa tuum observabit caput* 'she shall heed thy head'. The feminine pronoun addressed to Eve is understood to refer prophetically to *Ecclesia*. Augustine therefore implores his hearers to 'heed the Serpent's head', explaining the figure as follows:

Quod est caput serpentis? Prima peccati suggestio ... Contemne quod suggessit. Sed magnum aurum suggessit. Et quid prodest homini, si totum mundum lucretur, animæ suæ detrimentum patiatur. Pereat mundi lucrum, ne fiat animæ damnum.[3]

What is the Serpent's head? The first prompting to sin ... Spurn what he suggests. But he suggests much gold. And what will it

---

[1] Augustine, *Enarr. in Ps.*, CCSL 39, 1256.
[2] Augustine follows an Old Latin translation of the Septuagint.
[3] Augustine, *Enarr. in Ps.* 103, CCSL 40, 1525 f.; cp. p. 138, above.

profit a man if he gain the whole world and suffer the loss of his own soul? Let the world's riches be lost, that they may not become the soul's damnation.

It will be remembered that after Beowulf has struck vainly at the dragon's head, Wiglaf comes to help him, and *ne hedde he þæs heafolan* (2697a). I have no doubt that the phrase *observat caput eius* was running in the poet's head; whether the line could act as a signpost to the audience—like line 2323[1]—would depend on their familiarity with this version of the text. Those who knew the *Moralia* or sermons derived from it might have met the figure used in this way in a context which further illuminates the allegory of the dragon-fight. Gregory quotes Genesis 3: 15 in the *observabit caput* version and interprets it as Augustine does, as an injunction to be vigilant against the Devil's *suggestio*:

Caput quippe serpentis observare, est initia suggestionis ejus aspicere et manu sollicitæ considerationis a cordis aditu funditus extirpare ... ergo summa cura vigilandum est, ne vel bonis operibus serviens mens, reproba intentione polluatur.[2]

Of course, to heed the Serpent's head is to descry the beginnings of his prompting and totally root them out from the entrance to the heart with the hand of careful self-examination. Therefore, unremitting vigilance is needed, lest the mind, while keeping watch over its good deeds, be polluted by an evil intention.

In view of the different metaphor found in Hrothgar's sermon for vigilance against the temptation to cupidity, it is interesting to find that Augustine combines the two figures in the discourse quoted above, in describing Job's repulse of the Serpent:

Repulsus est tentator, obseruatum est caput eius, penetrare non potuit in cor. Muratam ciuitatem forinsecus oppugnauit, sed non expugnauit.[3]

The tempter was repulsed, his head was heeded, he could not invade the heart. He attacked the walled city from outside, but he could not storm it.

---

[1] See p. 142, above.

[2] Gregory, *Moralia, PL* 75, 552. In the same paragraph he refers to the fruit of a man's good works being carried off by the Serpent, who spoils the tree at its roots *veneni dente* 'with venomous tooth'. I suppose that in the allegory line 2697 means that the warrior strikes at the heart of the covetous thoughts raging within him; the burnt hand could signify some yielding to covetousness, the hand standing for liberality. (cp. p. 237, below.)   [3] Augustine, op. cit., 1527.

Gregory takes up and expands the allegory of temptation in his explanation of Job's contest with the Enemy, as I have already indicated in Chapter 4,[1] identifying the Serpent with Leviathan, the fire-breathing Beast. Similarly, in the *Vita S. Antonii*, the demons who represent the temptations of the hermit are described as appearing to him in this guise:

Crebro denique Antonius talem a se visum diabolum asserabat, qualem at beatus Job, Domino revelante, cognoverat. *Oculi ejus ac si species luciferi, ex ore ejus procedunt lampades incensæ, crines quoque incendiis sparguntur, et ex naribus ejus fumus egreditur, quasi fornacis æstuantis ardore carbonum: anima ejus ut pruna, flamma vero ex ore ejus glomeratur.* ... Nam si non mendacia cuncta loqueretur, quomodo talia et tam infinita promittens hamo crucis ut draco aduncatus a Domino est?[2]

In short, Antony declared that the Devil had been seen by him in the same form that blessed Job had recognized through the Lord's revelation. *His eyes are like the morning star, from his mouth come forth burning torches, his hair also is spread with flames, and from his nostrils comes smoke like a furnace burning with a fire of coals; his breath is like a live coal, flame rolls from his very mouth.* ... If his words were not all lies, how, making such great and boundless threats, was he caught by the hook of the Cross like a dragon by the Lord?

Expanding the passage about the fire-breathing Adversary in his *Moralia*, Gregory describes how the fire and smoke breathed by him create disturbance in the minds of the good and blind the eyes of the wicked. Moreover, the smoke rouses illicit desires, the fiery breath *prunas ardere facit* (Job 41: 12), that is, it inflames the mind already kindling with cupidity.[3] Once again the Devil's *suggestio* appears in a figure, this time as the fiery breath of Leviathan:

Quid enim prunas nisi succensas in terrenis concupiscentiis reproborum hominum mentes appellat? ... Toties igitur Leviathan halitus prunas accendit, quoties ejus occulta suggestio humanas mentes ad delectiones illicitas pertrahit.[4]

For what is called *coals* if not the minds of reprobate men inflamed with desire for earthly things? ... Thus the breath of Leviathan *sets*

---

[1] See p. 143 above.

[2] Athanasius, *Vita S. Antonii, versio Evagrii, PG* 26, 878 f. For further comment upon this passage, see p. 261, below.

[3] Gregory, *Moralia, PL* 76, 714.   [4] ibid., 716.

fire to the coals as often as his secret prompting entices human minds towards illicit delights.

The significance which men familiar with these patristic figures for temptation would be apt to find in Beowulf's contest with the dragon may now be discerned.

I would interpret the allegory like this: the rifling of the hoard, by exhibiting the dragon's costly cup to Beowulf and his men, lets loose the fiery breath of Leviathan through the kingdom. Beowulf suffers unwonted disturbance of mind and a sense of estrangement from God (2329 ff.).[1] He is enticed by thought of the treasure and the fame that will accrue to him if he wins it. His challenge to the dragon allegorically presents his attempts to repulse this thought, but he is already spiritually weakened by the feeling of self-sufficiency which long years of success have bred. Hence he goes into the fight foolishly trusting in his own strength, looking neither to man nor to God for help. He makes provision for the fight with a great iron shield, when what he needs is the shield of faith. On the historical level, this is simply making physical rather than spiritual preparation;[2] allegorically, Beowulf's defence is his own justice.[3] The iron

---

[1] cp. Gregory's observation:
Quid diabolus fumo pestiferi halitus, in humanis cordibus operetur. Deus nisi a tranquillo corde cognosci non potest ... Quasi enim flatu narium caliginem emittit, quia in reproborum cordibus insidiarum suarum aspirationis ex amore vitæ temporalis æstum congerit multiplicium cogitationum. (*PL* 76, 713 f.).
What the Devil performs in human hearts with the smoke of his noxious breath. God cannot be known except by a tranquil heart ... As if with the breath of his nostrils he sends forth a dark vapour, because with the exhalations of his artifices he builds up in the hearts of the reprobate out of love of temporal life a glow of devious thoughts. He also quotes Ps. 37: 11, which Augustine (*Enarr. in Ps.* 37, *CCSL* 38. 393) links with Adam's separation from God and also with Ps. 18: 12, *ab occultis meis munda me* (ibid., 393 f.). All these quotations give deeper significance to the description of Beowulf's spiritual state in 2329 ff. Though Gregory's words quoted above apply to the *reprobi* he also says (loc. cit.): *Iste fumus ex ejus naribus prodiens aliquando ad tempus etiam electorum oculos tangit* 'This smoke emitted from his nostrils sometimes even reaches the eyes of the chosen'.

[2] Ambrose (*Exp. in Luc, PL* 15, 1898 f.), discussing the wars which the Christian must sustain, says that the humble man, like David, casts off the earthly armour of the king and takes up the lighter weapons of faith.

[3] cp. John Chrysostom (*Comm. in Ps., PG* 55, 176, Latin version) *Tu quoque, quando adversus diabolum bellum geris, dic ita: Non confido meis armis, hoc est, non meæ virtuti nec meæ justitiæ, sed Dei misericordiæ* 'And you also, when you make war against the Devil, say this: I do not trust in my arms, that is, neither in my strength nor my justice, but in the mercy of God'.

shield protects him all too short a time; what saves him from utter defeat is the intervention of Wiglaf.

How can the young kinsman fit into an allegory of the interior battle? I am inclined to think that the poet was inspired here by a passage in Ecclesiasticus which is about the right use of treasure and the value of charitable giving. Wealth not buried but given away, says the writer, will fight for a man in his need, and prove a better defence than a shield or a lance.[1] Beowulf's weapon breaks and his shield does not protect him from the dragon's teeth, but because of his former love and generosity, Wiglaf comes in his extreme need to fight for him.

As the hero strikes vainly at the dragon, he suffers torment from its fiery breath and realizes that he is near to death. In Gregory's allegorical language, the breath of Leviathan is inflaming a mind already smouldering *in terrenis concupiscentiis*, increasing his desire to cling to the world he must leave. This, I believe, explains the lines which have given the commentators so much trouble:

> Ne wæs þæt eðe sið,
> þæt se mæra maga Ecgðeowes
> grundwong þone ofgyfan wolde;
> sceolde ofer willan wic eardian
> elles hwergen; swa sceal æghwylc mon
> alætan lændagas.[2] (2586–91)

He is quite solitary as he faces death; his men have left him, and we may suppose that Leviathan's blinding smoke has cut him off from that light which saved him when he was in perilous straits in Grendel's lair.[3] He faces not only death, but final defeat, until he is given fresh heart and an access of strength by the young man Wiglaf.

In the historical story, Wiglaf is to Beowulf what the hero himself had been to Hrothgar. As Beowulf repaid Hrothgar's

---

[1] Ecclus. 29: 13–16. The *Glossa Ordinaria* follows Hrabanus Maurus in relating the fight alluded to here to that *contra ignita tela nequissimi* 'against all the fiery darts of the wicked one' (cp. *PL* 109, 976); no doubt earlier scholars made the same association; cp. also p. 54, above.

[2] There is an implied contrast with the servant of God who is happy to go to his eternal home. See also my comments in 'The Christian Perspective in *Beowulf*', *Brodeur Studies*, p. 86.

[3] His mind is darkened; cp. *breost innan weoll þeostrum geþoncum* (2331 f.).

earlier generosity and goodness to his father Ecgðeow by risking his life in Hrothgar's time of need, so Wiglaf repays Beowulf's earlier love and liberality. In the moral allegory, I suggest, he stands for the timely recollection of the hero's earlier deeds of brotherly love and charitableness, which counter the temptation to cupidity. It will be noted that Wiglaf calls to him,

> 'Leofa Biowulf, læst eal tela,
> swa ðu on geoguðfeore geara gecwæde
> þæt ðu ne alæte be ðe lifigendum
> dom gedreosan. (2663–6)

He thus reminds him of his youthful resolve always to act nobly,[1] and implores him to do well to the end. Beowulf *m(ærða) gemunde* (2678), and made fresh resistance. When Wiglaf stood beside him, and diminished the dragon's fire,

> þa gen sylf cyning
> geweold his gewitte. (2702 f.)

Both *læst eal tela* and *geweold his gewitte* have satisfactory secular meaning in their contexts as referring respectively to bravery and a return to full consciousness, but they also have connotations of Christian goodness and recovery from demonic possession to a state where reason is once again in control.[2] In the *Psychomachia* of Prudentius, *Avaritia* is stupefied, overthrown and killed by *Operatio*, 'Good Deeds'.[3] In composing an allegory from a quasi-historical story, the *Beowulf* poet would find it difficult to make use of this kind of personification, but it seems to me that he indicates through Wiglaf's words and the action at this point that Beowulf is saved from spiritual destruction through remembrance of his former victories against evil, which are recalled—as in the review of his life which follows later (2732 ff.) —not to excite vainglory, but to counteract despair. The death of the monster naturally signifies the temporary overthrow of

---

[1] It will be recalled that *dom* is joined with *godum dædum* (2178); cp. p. 216, above.

[2] For examples of religious use, especially in Bede, see Bosworth-Toller, *AS Dict.*, sv. *tela* and *gewit*.

[3] Prudentius, *Carmina, CCSL* 126, 170, *Psychomachia*, 571–606. It will be noted also that *bona opera* have an important place in Gregory's commentary upon *observabit caput eius* (*PL* 75, 552) which I have suggested as part of the source-material of the allegory, though there is no personification of Good Deeds by Gregory in relation to the contest with the Serpent.

237

the Enemy, Beowulf's overcoming of his last temptation; compare what was said of the killing of Grendel:

> ðy he þone feond ofercwom,
> gehnægde helle gast.   (1273 f.)

The Dragon is quelled, but not before Beowulf has been wounded in the neck by its venomous teeth.

Beowulf dies of the poison from this wound. The Dragon does not suffocate or devour him, which would signify that he was swallowed into hell. Instead he suffers a wound in the neck—a part of the body often associated with pride—and from this the slow poison spreads through him.

Adam dente serpentis est vulneratus et obnoxiam hereditatem successionis humanæ suo vulnere dereliquit, ut omnes illo vulnere claudicemus.[1]

Adam was wounded by the tooth of the Serpent, and from his wound has left a heritage of guilt in his human posterity, so that we all go stumblingly because of that wound.

The likeness of Beowulf to Adam is hinted by Wiglaf's words after his death,

> Oft sceall eorl monig   anes willan
> wræc adreogan   swa us geworden is.
> (3076 f.)

These words remind the audience of St Paul's words about Adam, through whose desire for vainglory and more possessions his people were enslaved and brought to death.[2]

---

[1] Ambrose, *Explanatio Psalmorum* XII, *CSEL* 64, 365. (Adam's wound was in the foot with which he spurned the Devil.) A clear example of the use of the dragon's venomous tooth and the effect of its poison occurs in the temptation-scene dramatized by Augustine (*Enarr. in Ps.* 39, *CCSL* 38, 424) in which the Dragon tempts a man to deny Christ through heresy:

Et ille mirabili uoce percussus, si nondum ueneno penetratus est respondet: Plane christianus sum. Si autem mouetur, et dente draconis captus est, respondet: Quare mihi dicis: Est christianus? quid enim, non sum christianus?

And he, struck by the strange voice, if he has not been penetrated by the poison, answers: Certainly I am a Christian. But if he is affected, and held by the Dragon's tooth, he answers, Why do you say to me, Is he a Christian? Why, am I not a Christian?

cp. also p. 135, n. 5, above.

[2] cp. Rom. 5: 18: *Igitur sicut per unius delictum in omnes homines in condemnationem ...* 'Therefore, as by the offence of one, unto all men to condemnation...' The OE

It is thus reasonable to regard Beowulf as a just man who has fought the good fight during his lifetime, but who is in the end brought to death by the flaws in his human nature, the legacy of Adam's sin, in trying to fight the Dragon alone. He acts as a moral example in his early life, but in his last days he presents to the Christian audience the tragedy of fallen man, harassed by the Enemy and wanting in the supernatural strength of the *miles Christi*.

Through cupidity, Adam and his sons exchanged eternal life for brief possession of earthly goods. Christian writers used the image of barter in writing of the contrary exchange which the Christian must make: to sell all that he has to buy the treasure of eternal life.[1] When one reads Beowulf's words.

> Nu ic on maðma hord   mine bebohte
> frode feorhlege,   (2799 f.)

it is difficult not to think that the poet has chosen this form of words to emphasize the poverty of Beowulf's barter, his life the price of a mouldering hoard which brings no good to anyone in the story.[2] This is the very antithesis of the Christian exchange of worldly wealth for everlasting life, memorably expressed in Paulinus of Nola's poem *Verbum crucis*:

> Et res magna putatur
> mercari propriam de re pereunte salutem?
> perpetuis mutare caduca et vendere terram,
> cælum emere?[3]

Do you think it great hardship to buy your eternal salvation with goods that perish, to exchange transitory for lasting possessions, to sell earth to buy heaven?

---

willa is not, of course, synonymous with *delictum*, but it has connotations of cupidity in religious use (cp. Ps. 77 : 29 in the Paris Psalter, *ASPR* v, 41, where *a desiderio suo* is rendered *sceattes willan*).

[1] See the further illustrations of this idea in Goldsmith, *Brodeur Studies*, pp. 87 f., and add: *An Exhortation to Christian Living*, *ASPR* vi, 68: *Ceapa þe mid æhtum eces leohtes* (35); cp. also p. 258 and p. 265, below.

[2] The metaphor was obviously not coined for the occasion (cp. 2482), but the poet has given it great prominence in relation to Beowulf's death; cp. also lines 2415 f., 2843, 3012.

[3] Paulinus of Nola, *Opera*, *CSEL* 30, 275; *Carmen* 27, 301 ff.; cp. also Augustine's comment on Paulinus, who had himself given up great wealth to store up treasure in heaven (*De civ. Dei*, *CCSL* 47, pp. 11 f.).

No part of Beowulf brings out so clearly the difference between Christian and non-Christian values as the hero's dying speeches.[1] Though he is a righteous man, Beowulf's mind is occupied with *terrena*. In spite of this fact, the nearest analogue known to me of his parting from the world is the passing of St Antony, who also leaves the world without a prayer, after giving directions for the disposal of his possessions and the burial of his body. Yet this is not so strange, if I am right about the poet's mode of working, for Antony was a fighter against the Enemy and likely to be in the author's mind. When he knew himself to be dying, Antony spoke to his two followers, using a form of words echoing the Old Testament and recalling the deaths of Joshua and David: *Patrum gradior viam* 'I go the way of the fathers'.[2] Beowulf's words about following his dead kinsmen, *ic him æfter sceal* (2816), have a similar pre-Christian ring, and may bring to mind Psalm 48, already quoted above, the general subject of which is the worthlessness of riches and worldly honours in the day of death, the folly of decorating a tomb and perpetuating a name upon the earth. For the rich and honoured man *introibit usque in progeniem patrum suorum et usque in aeternum non videbit lumen*[3] 'shall go in to the generations of his fathers;

---

[1] Schücking, op. cit., p. 144, recognized the un-Christian nature of Beowulf's death, but nevertheless maintained that Beowulf was the poet's ideal king.

[2] *Vita S. Antonii, PG* 26, 970. For further discussion of the similarities between the *Vita* and *Beowulf*, see pp. 259 ff., below.

[3] Donahue, *Traditio*, 1965, 109, unreasonably singles out Hrethel, who *Godes leoht geceas*, as the kinsman Beowulf expects to follow, ignoring the fact that his nearest kinsman Hygelac and Hygelac's son died violent deaths. Beowulf's rich ornaments and the treasure-hoard are bequeathed to his kinsman Wiglaf and his people, who use them to adorn his tomb: it seems likely that the poet would think of this psalm, especially *et relinquent alienis divitias suas*; Ps-Bede comments (*PL* 93, 737):

Nam et si reliquent nepotibus vel filiis relinquent tamen eis ut *alienis*, id est nihil sibi proficientibus... *Relinquent* quidem *alienis*, et nullam utilitatem habebunt inde, nisi quod *sepulchra eorum* marmorea sunt, *domus illorum in æternum*, id est, ita ornantur ab illis alienis sepulchra illorum, quasi credant eos æternaliter ibi mansuros.

For even if they leave them to kinsmen or sons, they still leave them to these as to *strangers*, that is, to those who cannot do them any good ... Indeed, *they leave them to strangers*, and will have no usefulness from them, save only that *their tombs* are marble, *their houses for ever*; that is their tombs are adorned by those strangers as if they believe that they are to remain there eternally.

With this last sentence, cp. *Beowulf* 3167 f., and Wiglaf's speech about carrying Beowulf's corpse to the grave:

ond þonne geferian   frean userne
leofne mannan   þær he longe sceal
on ðæs waldendes   wære geþolian.   (3107 ff.).

and he shall never see light' (Ps. 48: 20). Thus the description of Beowulf's passing is designed both to celebrate the valour and nobility of a great hero of the past and to look with compassion upon the limited horizons and misdirected aims of the unregenerate sons of Adam. As Dante with Ulysses, so our poet with Beowulf admired the unbending spirit of the old king and yet acknowledged that without divine aid the hero could not win eternal life.

I have reserved until last the controversial question whether Beowulf was portrayed by the poet as *figura Christi*, which requires more consideration than the bare denial I gave in an earlier chapter.[1] The theory that Beowulf was a Christ-figure was cautiously implied by Earle in 1884,[2] and given authority by Klaeber's extension of the idea in 1912.[3] His last observations on the subject are guarded but unchanged:

> But it is not deemed a reckless supposition that in recounting the life and portraying the character of the exemplary leader, whom he conceived as a fighter against the demon of darkness and a deliverer from evil, he was almost inevitably reminded of the person of the Savior, the self-sacrificing King, the prototype of supreme perfection.[4]

Nevertheless, Klaeber remains unwilling to look upon the poem as an allegory with Christ as its true hero. Others have not been so hesitant, and several critics have treated the poem as an allegory of salvation.[5] These critics lean heavily upon the occasional verbal echoes of the gospel which Klaeber found in the poem, and those who would disagree with their theories must find some other explanation of these echoes.

The echoes collected by Klaeber are in lines 942 ff., 1707 ff., 1273 f., 2799 f., in reference to the Saviour; 2598, 2602 ff., 2694 ff.

These words appear to imply that Beowulf will remain in that place, though (like the dead Scyld) still in the Lord's keeping.

[1] See pp. 72 f., above.

[2] J. Earle, *Anglo-Saxon Literature*, p. 135.

[3] Klaeber, *Angl.* 1912, 190 ff.

[4] Klaeber, *Beowulf*, pp. cxx f.

[5] The most notable are G. G. Walsh, *Medieval Humanism* (New York, 1942), p. 45; A. Cabaniss, '*Beowulf* and the Liturgy'; M. B. McNamee, '*Beowulf*—An Allegory of Salvation'; Donahue takes a curious position in which he regards Beowulf as *figura Christi* but also maintains that the poem is not an allegory, *Traditio*, 1965, see especially p. 116.

in reference to his followers; 2419, 2529 in reference to the scene in the Garden of Gethsemane.[1]

Of these resemblances, the first three are natural enough in their contexts to have arisen spontaneously; none of them is an exact repetition of the gospel phrases. The desertion of the followers seems likely to have been a motif in pagan heroic verse—Wiglaf's condemnation of their disloyalty has a traditional ring—and was obviously required by the plot, as was the presence of one faithful man to listen to the king's dying words. Only Beowulf's choice of eleven companions, with the thief as the thirteenth man,[2] is at all like the situation of Christ and his followers. But there is no attempt to make the thief act the part of a Judas; his forced and unwilling guidance of the party is in marked contrast to the behaviour of the betrayer.

Among the speeches of Beowulf only one supposed resemblance to the words of Christ need be examined (2799 f.). Klaeber noted the similarity of the gospel phrase *ponere animam* 'lay down one's life' (Joan. 1: 17) to the Old English *feorh alecgan*,[3] but it would be unsafe to deduce that the Old English phrase necessarily has similar connotations of a willing or self-sacrificial death; it is sufficient to note that the same phrase is used of Grendel's death (851). Donahue's attempt to find undertones of self-sacrifice in *feorhlegu* (2800), which he translates 'a laying down of life',[4] depends principally upon the similarity which Klaeber noted, and must be rejected. It is true that *ealdorlegu* in *Guthlac* B (1260) has the meaning Donahue postulates, implying a willing (though not a sacrificial) death, but such a meaning does not fit the *Beowulf* line, in which *feorhlegu* is qualified by the adjective *frod*, a normal accompaniment of synonyms for 'life'. Klaeber is undoubtedly right to compare the use of *aldorlege* in *Daniel* (139), where it means 'the remainder of (the king's) life'

---

[1] Klaeber, *Angl.* 1912, 190 ff.

[2] I have already expressed the view that secular associations of ill-fortune already clung to the number thirteen, which would account for the use of it here (cp. 'The Choice in *Beowulf*', *Neophil.* 1964, p. 68). My opinion of the gospel echoes generally is that they serve as incidental reminders that the life of Christ is beyond the horizon of the story; they do not make a connected narrative; cp. the remarks of Tuve quoted above, p. 74.

[3] Klaeber, *Angl.* 1912, 463.   [4] Donahue, *Traditio*, 1965, 108.

—as revealed to him in his dream.[1] The meaning required for Donahue's argument that Beowulf is a saviour cannot be substantiated. Donahue further changes the emphasis of Beowulf's dying speech by translating *fremmað gena leoda þearfe* (2800 f.) 'Those treasures will hereafter serve the people's need', supplying the plural subject from the genitival phrase *maðma hord* in the previous line; this has no support from the editors. Unless these dubious translations are accepted, it is difficult to find in Beowulf's thanksgiving for the treasure 'an act of charity'.[2] Without the explicit element of self-sacrifice, Beowulf's death does not greatly resemble that of the Saviour. The subsequent events, the re-burial of the treasure and the people's apprehensions of an overwhelming onslaught of their enemies, seem completely inappropriate to an allegory of redemption.

The other critics who have regarded the poem as an allegory with Christ as its true hero have concentrated principally on incident rather than phrase in detecting resemblances. Earle's original approach was more reasonable:

The material is mythical and heathen; but it is clarified by natural filtration through the Christian mind of the poet. Not only are the heathen myths inoffensive, but they are positively favourable to a train of Christian thought. Beowulf's descent into the abyss to extirpate the scourge is suggestive of that Article in the Apostles Creed which had a peculiar fascination for the mind of the Dark and Middle Ages; the fight with the dragon; the victory that cost the victor his life; the one faithful friend while the rest are fearful—these incidents seem almost like reflections of evangelical history.[3]

Earle's statement that the myths are 'favourable to a train of Christian thought' seems to me essentially right. Whether this characteristic is part of the conscious design of the poem or whether it springs from inculcated habits of thought in the poet is a question we cannot answer. Certainly the author of *Beowulf* cannot have been unaware of the 'recollections of evangelical history' which are discernible in his poem. But he does not use the incidents Earle mentions to mirror the story of the redeeming of the captive souls. Such hints as there are seem to me

---

[1] Klaeber, *Beowulf*, p. 329; cp. also von Schaubert's translation 'mein altes Leben', *Beowulf*, Glossar, p. 69.

[2] Donahue, loc. cit. [3] Earle, op. cit., p. 135.

to remind the hearer of what is lacking in Beowulf's world. They remind him that the strength of the second Adam upholds the Christian who faces the Dragon or any demonically-inspired enemy. As Prudentius says of Judith's killing of Holofernes, though she fought 'under the shadow of the Law' she was a prophetic example to those who live in the new era, when strength to 'cut off the Enemy's head' is given even to the weak:

> At fortasse parum fortis matrona sub umbra
> legis adhuc pugnans, dum tempora nostra figurat,
> uera quibus uirtus terrena in corpora fluxit,
> grande per infirmos caput excisura ministros.[1]

It may be that a woman still at that time fighting under the shadow of the Law was hardly strong enough, though she prefigures our era, in which the true strength has flowed into earthly bodies, working through frail servants to cut off the great head.

[1] Prudentius, *CCSL* 126, 153 f., *Psychomachia*, 66 ff.

8 Structure and Meaning

The Emperor Constantine, according to his biographer Euse-bius,[1] commissioned the painting of a great picture which was placed prominently on the portico of his palace. It allegorically presented the conquest of the Devil by Constantine and his children. Above their portraits stretched the cross, and below their feet, a dragon, pierced with a dart, was shown falling headlong into the sea. The fame of this picture could have reached the *Beowulf* poet; the matter is one of speculation only. What is more important for our purposes is the implication of Constantine's act. He wished to proclaim, in a language men of all races could read, that God had chosen him as a champion against the Enemy of mankind and that in God's strength he was victorious. The symbols in the picture must have been comprehensible to large numbers of people, or there would have been no purpose in putting it on public display. The symbol of the overthrow of the Ancient Dragon, as I have tried to show, remained an important element in Christian teaching up to and throughout the period of our study. The poem of *Beowulf*, though much less crudely political, seems to me to present to its public a message which has something in common with Con-stantine's picture. It does so through the medium of contrastive allusion, as I indicated at the end of the last chapter in my comments upon the *Psychomachia*. The philosophy which lies behind both picture and poem is that a man's greatest source of power is his pious dependence upon God.

Beowulf, as I have said in my previous chapter, is portrayed

---

[1] Eusebius, *The Life of Constantine*, trans. McGiffert, ed. cit., Book 3, ch. 3, p. 520. The inspiration of the picture is said by Eusebius to have been Isa. 27: 1, which speaks prophetically of the Devil spiritually slain by Christ:

In illa die visitabit Dominus in gladio suo duro, et grandi et forti, super Leviathan, serpentem vectem, et super Leviathan, serpentem tortuosum, et occidet cetum qui in mari est.

In that day the Lord with his hard, and great, and strong sword shall visit Leviathan the bar serpent, and Leviathan the crooked serpent, and shall slay the whale that is in the sea.

first and foremost as a just man who nobly fought a losing battle against the evil powers. Because he was also a king with responsibility to defend and protect a people, the consequences of his overthrow brought sorrow to a whole nation. God might pardon Beowulf's fault ultimately, but the temporal effects of his fatal fight could not be undone. The king's interior struggle was vital not only to himself, but to all those whose lives came into contact with his. The setting of actual wars and feuds was necessary to give Beowulf solidity and to present the truth, as the poet understood it, that the miseries of earthly life were caused by the subjection of mankind to the Devil.

The very influential study of the subsidiary stories and digressive elements in Beowulf by Professor Bonjour[1] shows, I think, a characteristically modern attitude to the relation of the historical to the symbolic fighting in the poem. I quote his general view of the value and function of the digressions:

First, the very number and variety of the episodes renders the background of the poem extraordinarily alive; they maintain a constant interest and curiosity in the setting and, by keeping continuously in touch with 'historical' events, represent the realistic note serving as a highly appropriate foil to the transcendental interest of the main theme with its highly significant symbolic value. The way in which many digressions are presented, the allusive manner that so often suggests rather than describes, the light and subtle undercurrent of implications and connotations that runs beneath the vivid pageantry of many scenes, all contribute to create that 'impression of depth' which, as pointed out by Professor Tolkien, justifies the use of episodes and makes them so appealing.[2]

With Bonjour's general valuation of the episodes in themselves I warmly concur, but I cannot accept that they 'represent the realistic note, serving as a highly appropriate foil to the transcendental interest of the main theme'. The word 'foil' implies opposition and contrast, but in the thought-world of the poem the meaning of life lies in the interpenetration of the visible and the supernatural worlds. Unless Beowulf were a 'real' man im-

[1] A. Bonjour, *The Digressions in 'Beowulf'*. Bonjour uses the terms 'episode' and 'digression' indifferently in his general study and I have followed the same practice in this chapter.

[2] Bonjour, ibid., p. 71. See also the perceptive comment upon the significance of the digressions by J. Blomfield quoted by him on the same page.

plicated in the affairs of nations the 'highly significant symbolic value' of the central action would not be shown to have relevance to other men in positions of authority. The 'historical' digressions which do not directly impinge on Beowulf's life I take to be examples which are chosen to point and elaborate certain elements in the central story, to make them more prominent and memorable. These elements have to do with human feuds and the motives which cause and perpetuate them. The motives are the Devil's own motives which he was thought to have insinuated into human nature, his daily business being to stir them into activity, to the detriment of the individuals concerned and the progress of mankind at large. The view of human nature in the stories is pessimistic, in accord no doubt with some of the author's own experience and his knowledge of history, but also in accord with his philosophy, in that the people of the stories had ordinarily no means of grace and were easily dominated by the unruly impulses which Adam's sons inherited.

The Christian historians from Eusebius onward taught that God governed human life, but that the Devil and his cohorts, including those human beings whom he had suborned, were permitted to cause strife and suffering, for reasons which remained inscrutable:[1]

Hæc plane Deus unus et uerus regit et gubernat, ut placet; et si occultis causis, numquid iniustis?
Sic etiam tempora ipsa bellorum, sicut in eius arbitrio est iustoque iudicio et misericordia uel adterere uel consolari genus humanum, ut alia citius, alia tardius finiantur.[2]

Manifestly the one true God rules and governs these things as he pleases; and if his motives are hidden, are they therefore unjust? So it is, even with the duration of wars, as it is in his will and just judgment and mercy either to afflict or to console the human race, so that some wars come to an end sooner, some later.

Augustine and his disciple Orosius[3] also believed that in the pre-Christian era the world was even more unhappily riven with contention than in their own troubled times. It is small

---

[1] See R. L. P. Milburn, *Early Christian Interpretations of History* (London, 1954), especially Chapters 4 and 5.

[2] Augustine, *De civitate Dei*, CCSL 47, 158.

[3] Paulus Orosius, *Historiarum adversum paganos libri VII*, CSEL 5, passim.

wonder that an Anglo-Saxon Christian poet, who received besides in his native poetry a memorial to the legendary past of feuds and violent deaths, should himself portray the imagined world of his ancestors in a rather one-sided fashion. Like Augustine, he was able to believe that a beneficent Creator had ordered the universe and still watched over it, though men were given the freedom to act against the eternal law and cause suffering to themselves and others, even as Cain was permitted to kill his innocent brother. A Christian poet of that period would certainly not have expected to find in existence in the unregenerate world the *ordinata concordia* which was, as Schücking says, the ideal of a Christian state in its internal and external relations.[1] The world which Beowulf is imagined as inhabiting had no pattern of brotherly love to oppose to the spirit of self-interest which haunted it, and in it the natural goodness of the wise was all too easily marred by the Devil's persistent attempts to make men more like himself.

The history of the world according to the Christian historians began with a brother-murder and the building of a city.[2] The central story of *Beowulf* begins with the building of Heorot, which shelters the fratricide Unferth and is taken over by the posterity of Cain. These things and the foreshadowing of the destruction of the place by fire are signs that the poet wished his hearers to see in his history a microcosm of the story of carnal man, his technical achievements, his destructive antagonisms and his ultimate ruin. He portrays the ruthless ferocity of the forces of evil, opposed and for a time held off by the power of natural goodness in one man, and the way in which the corruption of the race itself nullifies the effects of that victory. He then shows, with more terrifying effect, how the evil powers sap the hero's strength from within, so that he too follows Adam's errant steps to the way of all the earth, leaving the people once more in the power of the forces of destruction.

One of the effects of the incidental stories is to illustrate the lasting and ever-widening misery which springs from single acts

[1] cp. Schücking, 'Das Königsideal im *Beowulf*', p. 147. He finds this to be Hrothgar's ideal of conduct, but fails to observe that Hrothgar's peacemaking all comes to nought and that Beowulf himself has no confidence in such treaties. (cp. 2029 ff. and the discussion of these lines on p. 251, below.)

[2] cp. Augustine, *De civitate Dei*, CCSL 48, 457–65.

of violence—*ne wæs þæt andæge nið*—and from offences against
truth,[1] particularly oath-breaking and disloyalty. Some of these
stories have been handled incidentally in my earlier chapters in
their pertinence to the central narrative.[2] Those that have not
must now be shown to bear out what I have just said.

The episodes which present piecemeal the course of the feuds
that bring down the royal houses of Scyld and Hrethel need
little explanation.[3] The saga of the feuds covers a period of
three generations, but the poet with admirable artistry keeps
Beowulf in the foreground, so that the relevance of these earlier
events to the story of his cleansing of Heorot and his pacification of
the Swedes, Franks and Frisians is not lost from sight. I have already remarked[4] that Beowulf's part in the tribal wars is played
off-stage, as it were, so that the hacking and wrestling on
the battlefield appear relatively unimportant in his life-story.

Among the tales of feuds, the episodes involving Finn and
Ingeld respectively are outstanding for their dramatic quality.
Lawrence is the forerunner of most modern critics—Sisam
notably dissenting—in suggesting that in the former the story of
Queen Hildeburh was designedly brought into connection with
the tragedy in store for Queen Wealhtheow.[5] Bonjour thinks the
parallel is unmistakable, and finds in 'the theme of the precarious peace' the 'actual *trait d'union*' between the episodes of
Finn and Ingeld.[6] I fully agree with Bonjour in this, in spite of

---

[1] It will be remembered that among the wicked whom St John in his vision saw
excluded from the heavenly city were *homicidæ ... et omnis qui amat et facit mendacium*
'murderers ... and everyone that loveth and maketh a lie' (Apoc. 22: 15). For Cain
as the source of strife, cp. *Maxims* I, 192–20, *ASPR* III, 163.

[2] For Sigemund and Heremod, see pp. 139 f., 188 ff. I take these two princes
to represent the opposite poles of the secular heroic life: they received their rewards
in this world.

[3] Bonjour (op. cit., Ch. 2 and 3) most successfully draws together the separate
incidents in the feuds and comments (p. 43 and pp. 62 f.) upon their cumulative
effect. I disagree with his detailed findings upon them in minor respects only, but I
think he is mistaken to stress 'the inexorability of fate' in the progress of the feuds
(pp. 33 f.); it is rather a matter of the sins of the fathers being visited on the children
(cp. Exod. 20: 5). Only to the deluded pagan participants does it seem that a blind
force controls their lives. An instructive parallel is Chaucer's treatment of pre-
destination in his *Troilus and Criseyde*, in which the hero sees only one side of the
Boethian argument. (cp. C. A. Owen, 'The Significance of Chaucer's Revisions of
Troilus and Criseyde', *MP* 55 (1957), 1 ff.)

[4] See p. 213, above.   [5] Lawrence, *Beowulf and Epic Tradition*, p. 126.
[6] Bonjour, op. cit., p. 61.

Sisam's more recent objections. I cannot find any reason for the inclusion of lines 1163–8 if the scene is intended, as Sisam argues, as entirely one of national rejoicing in which ominous notes are not detected.[1] Wealhtheow's request for Beowulf's support and his departing offer of friendship to Hrethric are most naturally taken as hints of the dangerous position of a child heir to the throne. Sisam endeavours to restore Hrothulf's reputation as a great man, citing Saxo's presentation of him as a hero who did well to kill the niggardly weakling Røric.[2] Even if Hrethric was known to have turned into an undesirable ruler, I cannot see that Wealhtheow's unhappy presentiments in his childhood or her fear of Hrothulf are affected thereby. As for Hrothulf himself, as Sisam remarks, 'in *Beowulf* he says and does nothing'. Sisam infers that the poet 'carefully ... shields him from competition or reproach.'[3] It may equally well be inferred that he shields him from attention: no one could guess from the poem that he was one of the most renowned of Danish heroes. There are two sound reasons why the Hrothulf of the poem has to be given an unheroic role. As a warrior of renown, he could not remain inactive while a stranger challenged Grendel; it is therefore essential to the plot that he should be given a very minor part. Similarly, his failure to appear on the scene when Ingeld came to burn Heorot would need explaining if he were both brave and loyal to Hrothgar. Sisam's attempt to deny the irony of this scene is unconvincing.[4]

The treatment of the Finn story brings out very clearly the poet's interest in the queen's sorrow, the troth-breaking, the resurgence of hatred and violence, and above all the futile loss on both sides, which he makes the dominant feature of the story through his description of the spectacular funeral pyre on which the enemy kinsmen were laid side by side.[5] The Danes come off best in the feud, but only through perfidy of their own. Hengest, who is the central character as the story is told, is completely enmeshed in the obligations of the feud; he breaks

---

[1] Sisam, *Structure*, p. 39.   [2] ibid., pp. 35 ff.   [3] ibid., p. 36.

[4] Of the praise of Hrothulf and Hrothgar (1163 f.) he says 'Irony will not serve to reverse the plain meaning here, since Hrothgar is involved' (p. 36); but cp. *renweardas* (770) which couples Beowulf and Grendel, the latter with irony. Sisam's translation of *þeawum lyfde* (2144) as 'Hrothgar lived the good life' (p. 42) is tendentious.   [5] cp. p. 92, above.

his oath to Finn and kills him, even though he and his men have been treated well.[1] The poet himself does not speak either to commend or to condemn; the only general observation about 'the precarious peace' comes from Beowulf:

> Oft seldan hwær
> æfter leodhryre   lytle hwile
> bongar bugeð,   þeah seo bryd duge.   (2029–31)

This reflection on the unquenchable destructive force of hate is not contradicted by any of the stories; but it need not therefore be taken for granted that the poet gave his approbation to Hengest or Ingeld. It is precisely because '*Quid Hinieldus cum Christo?*' 'What has Ingeld to do with Christ?' can admit only one answer that Ingeld can put aside the claims of his wife and his given word and attack his father-in-law. Indeed, it may be observed of Ingeld, as of Hrothulf, that the poem itself gives no inkling of his reputation as a great hero. The transference of interest to a nameless warrior who reopens the feud may, as Brodeur argues, be a sign that Beowulf was merely conjecturing how events might turn out;[2] it also has the effect of diminishing Ingeld's stature.

These two parallel stories thus remain in the memory as stories of perfidy and needless slaughter rather than as celebrations of the ancient heroes.

Of the other incidental stories, the fratricidal act which brings King Hrethel to the grave is interesting for the reintroduction of the Cain theme. The story is given considerable prominence by the elegy which follows it, and it is noteworthy that Hæthcynn's slaying of his brother is said to have been *fyrenum gesyngad* (2441), as if some malicious intent was present in his mind, hinting perhaps that the accident was staged, or simply that he had wished his brother dead. The incident is used to introduce the moving passage upon a bereaved father's impotent grief when his son is taken from him. This man has no consolation, either secular or religious. Like the elegy upon the treasure-hoard (2246 ff.), the passage reveals that possessions cease to be important when

---

[1] Bonjour goes too far in saying that Hengest's 'dilemma had to be made particularly hard to solve' (op. cit., p. 59); no scruples on Hengest's part are mentioned.
[2] cp. p. 220, above.

they cannot be shared (cp. 2451 ff.). It also shows that even the palliative for grief which Beowulf's world administers to the bereaved (cp. 1384 f.) is not a universal balm for the one left alone. As in *The Wanderer*,[1] the human consolations help only a little; the true consolation is hinted in the choice of a phrase for the end of Hrethel's grief: *Godes leoht geceas* (2469).

The slaying of Ongentheow and the fierce battle at Ravenswood (2922 ff.) I take to be a crowning manifestation of the ruthless cruelty and the fortitude which the feuds have bred; it is a thematic, though not of course a chronological, climax to the violent enmities which have harassed Beowulf's people and now menace them on the day of his death. This one battlefield brought to life in the poem bears a name which betokens a place of foreboding, violent death, and the reprobate among human kind. Like the raven at Heorot, the ravens of *Hrefnesholt* herald a day of death; they and the wolves come off best in the whole unhappy vendetta (3024 ff.).

There remains to be considered the puzzling story of Offa's wife (1931 ff.), which has proved a stumbling-block to every interpreter of the poem. Bonjour makes an attempt to justify it on æsthetic grounds, recognizing that the likely guess that there were topical reasons for mentioning Offa does not really explain the curious way he was introduced. Bonjour's explanation of the treatment of Offa's wife is rather desperate:

If we compare the respective careers of Heremod and Modthrytho, it immediately appears that they ran an opposite course ... (the contrast) stresses the problem of the 'use of power'. Heremod's failure after such brilliant promise and Modthrytho's success after the worst beginnings are themselves implicitly contrasted with Offa, whose whole career ... may give us a kind of prefiguration of Beowulf's own successful leadership.[2]

I do not find this at all convincing. The mere alternation, the deterioration of the man and the improvement of the woman, does not seem interesting or edifying without more explanation than the story of Offa's queen gives. As for prefiguration, Offa's career resembles Beowulf's in no particular feature.

---

[1] I follow J. E. Cross, 'On the Genre of *The Wanderer*', *Neophil.* 45 (1960), 63–75, in interpreting that poem as a *consolatio*.

[2] Bonjour, op. cit., p. 55.

Since Bonjour wrote, Professor N. E. Eliason has published a detailed discussion of the episode.[1] In a highly original argument, he disposes of Thryth (Modthrytho) completely, offering the explanation that Hygd was in fact the wife of Offa, and mother of Eomer, before she married Hygelac. He demonstrates that no satisfactory documentary evidence exists for 'Thryth' as the name of King Offa's wife.[2] This part of the paper is more acceptable than the theory he then propounds, that Hygd as a young widow married Hygelac, uniting the Angle and Geatish lines. The details of her life simply do not fit this explanation. The proud princess was married to Offa when he was young (1945); it is said that he *wisdome heold eðel sinne* (1959 f.), without mention of his death, which must have been early if Hygd had remarried and raised sons before she welcomed Beowulf back to Geatland, when she was still *swiðe geong* (1926).[3] The unqualified praise of Offa would surely have included mention of the tragic shortness of his life if this sequence of events had taken place. I find it easier to accept the view of Sisam[4] and Wrenn[5] that the 'froward queen' is not named because of a substantial scribal fault at this place.

I therefore attempt to glean something from what is expressly said about this woman. Diffidently translating *modþryþo wæg* (1931) as 'she showed a violent temper', I note that she is charged with imprisoning and putting to death any man who dared to look at her. Offa put a stop to her cruel ways, apparently without earning her resentment; she became his loving and renowned queen (1954 f.). Perhaps one could describe this as an example of inordinate self-love yielding before lawful love.

---

[1] N. E. Eliason, 'The Thryth-Offa Digression in *Beowulf*'. In the crux of 1931b, he reads *modþryþ o wæg* 'she ever possessed haughtiness'. For objections to this reading, see Klaeber's note, *Beowulf*, p. 199, and Dobbie, *Beowulf*, pp. 214 f.

[2] Eliason, ibid., pp. 128 f. He shows that the queen of Offa II was actually called *Cynethryth*, the name *Drida* being a misunderstanding of the Latinized form of her name, *Quendrida*. (cp. Klaeber, *Beowulf*, p. 196.)

[3] Eliason brushes aside the age difficulty (p. 127), but the discrepancy concerning Hygelac's age which he adduces is rather different, as the passages involved are widely separated. The postulated widowhood of Hygd is so vital to the allusion Eliason detects that one cannot suppose that the poet forgot about it when he called Hygd *swiðe geong*.

[4] K. Sisam, 'Notes on OE poetry', *RES* 22 (1946), 266.

[5] Wrenn, *Beowulf*, p. 215, and Glossary, p. 275, sv. *mōd-þrȳðo*, 'arrogance, violence of character'.

The mention of the lady's beauty (1941) points to a reason for her arrogance. I think it possible that in this rather inadequate look at the duties of womankind the poet illustrates the misuse of God's gifts of beauty and power, these being the female counterparts of the male strength and authority misused by Heremod: the end of the story indicates the poet's belief that woman's proper subjection to man will prevent such wickedness. Both Eve and Job's wife were classic examples of women's inability to withstand the Devil's promptings; their hope therefore lay in obeying the wise counsels of their husbands. The poet is obviously not interested in exploring the special virtues and vices of woman, but he may have felt that his universal theme required some observations on womanly conduct, for which the dramatic story of Offa's queen gave him a sufficient opportunity.

The digressions and episodes of the poem are divided by Bonjour into two main groups: those which concern the background and those which are connected with the main theme.[1] The division is an artificial one, as Bonjour himself reveals by putting the Finnsburg and Heathobard episodes in both groups, and by separating the Swedish-Geatish wars (in the second group) from the Danish wars involving the destruction of Heorot (placed in the first group). These peripheral parts of the poem all reinforce the central theme, which Bonjour has conceived too narrowly. He follows Tolkien in defining the main theme, quoting the latter's statement 'In its simplest terms it is a contrasted description of two moments in a great life'.[2] This definition goes some way to explain the structure of the poem, but it leaves out a great deal, notably the part played by the treasure-winning in Beowulf's life and the importance given to the hero's death. In another place, Tolkien over-emphasizes the theme of death: the author, he says, 'is still concerned primarily with *man on earth*, rehandling in a new perspective an ancient theme: that man, each man and all men, and all their works shall die'.[3] Again it is a partial truth. Bonjour, accepting Tolkien's theories, is driven to speak of a 'main theme' and a

---

[1] Bonjour, *Digressions*, pp. 72 f.
[2] Tolkien, *Monsters*, p. 29; quoted by Bonjour, op. cit., p. 70.
[3] Tolkien, *Monsters*, p. 265.

'fundamental theme', the latter being 'the transience of all earthly things, even the most beautiful'.[1] Both scholars miss the significance of Beowulf's involvement with the dragon's hoard. This is the point where these themes meet: man chooses the things that must die, and he must die with them.

The beauty of the earth and man's handiwork is deeply felt by the poet, as Bonjour's phrase implies, but it would be a great mistake to infer on this account that his preference for the *invisibilia* is spurious. The conflict within Beowulf externalized in the fight with the dragon is one which the poet can present poignantly because he himself knows the delight of the eyes. Augustine too shows the same keen sense of the beauty of physical things, and the same confidence that what he sees gives only an inkling of the beauty of the immaculate eternal world. Like the *Beowulf* poet, far from disparaging the wonderful work of the craftsman, he can describe it in all its burnished elegance:

Si vobis ostenderetur aliquod vasculum anaglyphum, inauratum, operose factum, et liceret oculos vestros, et duceret in se intentionem cordis vestri, et placeret vobis manus artificis, et pondus argenti, et splendor metalli; nonne unusquisque vestrum diceret, O si haberem vasculum istud?[2]

If someone were to show you a decorated vessel, overlaid with gold, delicately wrought, and you were free to gaze at it, and the desire of your heart were drawn towards it, and the skill of the craftsman, the weight of the silver and the lustre of the metal delighted you— would not every one of you say, if only I might possess that vessel?

This passage leads to a contrast with *charitas*, a more desirable possession and free to all men. The *Beowulf* poet, I suggest, has the same attitude towards the dragon's *dryncfæt deore*. It is beautiful, and any man might wish to buy or steal it, but it is a poor exchange for the chalice of God. The golden cup symbolized all the satisfactions the world can offer, not simply material wealth, as my quotations from Gregory's interpretation of the *calix aureus Babylon* showed.[3] There could be no more fitting object to signify the *temporalia* for which the aged Beowulf was willing to sell his life; in the allegory of mankind it merges

[1] Bonjour, *Digressions*, p. 70 and p. 74.
[2] Augustine, *In Ep. Joan. ad Parthos, Tract.* 7, *c.* 4, *PL* 35, 2034.
[3] cp. p. 144, above.

with Adam's *poculum mortis*[1] as the Dragon merges with the Serpent.

Here, unmistakably, in the dragon's cup and pile of gold is the missing link between the themes of glory, transience and death. The opposition between the two halves of *Beowulf* is that between life and death: life imagined as a campaign against the foes of God, or, in other language, as a series of temptations —*tentatio itaque ipsa militia est*[2]—and death imagined as the final battle with the *bana*, the death-bringer, who tempts men to grasp the things that perish.

It can be seen that for the pagan Beowulf there could be only limited victory in life and at best partial defeat in death, because he inherited Adam's spiritual vulnerability. The historical story makes a satisfying moral allegory in terms of the beliefs of the author's time, but he wanted, I believe, to make it both particularly relevant to his audience and also spiritually significant to all men. For the first purpose, he had chosen a story localized in a time just beyond the compass of living memory and in a place associated with ancestral heroes of the English kings. For the second purpose, he enriched each half of his composition with a tangential theme which is not kept within the progress of the narrative but leads off from it. The theme of life in the first half has as its upward tangent the life-giving contest of Christ with the Devil, hence the hints of the harrowing of hell and of baptism. The theme of death has a downward tangent in Adam's delusion by the Dragon and his drinking of the bitter cup, the poisoning of his race and the captivity of his people.[3] The poem ends, as Tolkien perceived 'looking back into the pit'.[4] The story was all in the past: Heorot and Beowulf and their gold had been swallowed up in the fire. But

---

[1] cp. p. 86 and p. 201, above. For the literary use of the symbol see Carleton Brown, '*Poculum mortis* in Old English' *Speculum* 15 (1940), 389–99.

[2] cp. p. 203, above.

[3] The curious lines upon the thief (2291–3) imply that he was one *se ðe Waldendes hyldo gehealdeþ*, in spite of his sinfulness (cp. 2226); they have reference to the tangential theme, as a reminder of the penitent thief upon the cross who, in spite of a life of cupidity, was wholly pardoned and released from the sentence of eternal death placed upon mankind after Adam's sin: the Dragon could not harm him. Since Adam's losing contest with the Adversary was a contrastive figure for the coming victorious contest of Christ, the images even in the second half are not wholly dark. (cp. p. 269, below.)   [4] Tolkien, *Monsters*, p. 265.

in the perspective of eternity the great cosmic war still raged and could only end in a universal conflagration; God still had need of heroes who would fight in his service.

The breadth of vision of *Beowulf* is quite unmatched in our early literature, but the personal allegory at the heart of the poem has an analogue in the poetic sequence upon Saint Guthlac.[1] Again one discerns the two-part structure, of life and death, and the theme of driving out the evil powers from God's world; the drama is played in this case upon a small stage, the tiny island of Croyland, with only two human actors, but with the great hosts of heaven and hell joining the battle for the man's soul. It is, I believe, a treatment in contemporary terms of the essential theme of *Beowulf*, shorn of its social and political periphery. It has been the fashion to treat *Guthlac* A and B as if they were separate poems[2] placed together by an anthologist, though E. V. Gordon many years ago remarked upon the similarity of the pattern of early victory and final death to that in *Beowulf*.[3] This is not the place to examine the supposed differences between A and B; I believe with Gordon that they are designed to be read as a sequence, whether or not more than one author had a hand in the composition. Some comparison of *Beowulf* and *Guthlac* will support my interpretation of the greater poem, since it demonstrates, I believe, that there is some relationship between the two: at the least a shared thought-world, at the most a dependence of *Guthlac* upon *Beowulf* as a model.

First to be noted is the general structural resemblance of *Guthlac* A to the first part of *Beowulf*. The saint survives a series

---

[1] *ASPR* III, 49–88. Dr B. Colgrave remarked in 1958 (*PBA*, vol. 44, pp. 35–60) that certain features were common to 'the heroic poem of the *Beowulf* type' and the saint's Life, mentioning both 'Antony in the desert and Guthlac in the fens', who were 'fighting against devils little less material' than Grendel and his dam; but he ascribed the resemblance to the fact that both types of composition 'were concerned with the cult of the hero-warrior' (p. 36), and did not pursue the comparison. No doubt there was interaction between secular and religious hero-stories, but the warrior-saint was a well-developed concept even before the time of Prudentius which must have been fully endowed with traditional features when introduced to the English.

[2] ed. cit., Introduction, xxx. See also Wrenn, *OE Literature*, pp. 130 f.

[3] See the note upon Beowulf in his edition of *The Battle of Maldon*, London, 1937, p. 24: 'A very similar structure is used also to present an ecclesiastical hero in the poem on Saint Guthlac'.

of contests, in which the demons try to drive him from Croyland while he is equally determined to cleanse the land of their presence.[1] In one of these he is dragged down *niþer under næssas* (563), to the mouth of hell. There is a double triumphant return after his victories, first to the place he has freed from the demons, and then to his home in heaven, where he is given his reward and a throne. Guthlac fights, like Beowulf, to serve and please his king; there is an arresting correspondence between *Guthlac* A 302 ff. and *Beowulf* 435 ff. The saint repudiates the usual reward for such service on earth (319 f.). In these two passages appears the important contrast between earthly hero and spiritual warrior which is implied in the treatment of Beowulf's fights: Guthlac will not bear *worulde wæpen* and he does not wish for *eorðwelan*. The prologue to *Guthlac* A explicitly states the contrast of the two lives and the need for the exchange of earthly for heavenly treasure.[2] It is noteworthy that Guthlac's death is not treated *as such* in this part of the sequence, though he is taken up to heaven.

In *Guthlac* B the struggle with death is not externalized as in *Beowulf*; the similarity with the latter appears chiefly in the solitary mourning servant who shares his master's agony and then conveys the news of his death. There is no contest with the Dragon; the saint has chosen *ece rædas*, he trusts in divine aid and the angels minister to him. In spite of these major differences (which are just those which my theory would predict) the close of *Guthlac* B is much more like *Beowulf* than like any conventional hagiographical poem. There is, moreover, in the image of death as a clutching *wiga wælgifre* who bursts through the door under the shadow of night to seize the hapless man (*Guthlac* B, 901 ff.) a very striking similarity to the description of Grendel's entry into Heorot and his grasping of Hondscioh (720 ff.).[3]

It is possible that this general structural resemblance between

---

[1] cp. Cuthbert's driving of the demons from Farne, p. 54, above.

[2] *Guthlac* A, 1–80; note especially 70 ff.:

> Swa þas woruldgestreon
> on þa mæran god   bimutad weorþað,
> ðonne þæt gegyrnað   þa þe him godes egsa
> hleonaþ ofer heafdum.

[3] It will be noted also that the author of *Guthlac* B later makes use of the symbol of Adam's bitter cup (980–91).

the poems and the similar details can be explained as due to the same Christian source-materials and the same secular heroic motifs. It is even possible that *Beowulf* was influenced by *Guthlac*. These alternatives, however, seem to me less probable. The incidents have a good deal more point in *Beowulf* than in *Guthlac*, and the heroic language is more in place in Denmark than in Croyland. It is not my intention to rest any part of my case upon this uncertain relationship, but I would draw from it the inference that the authors of both compositions could count upon the same sort of Christian knowledge in their hearers. An audience which could enter into the spirit of *Guthlac* could, I am sure, respond to the tacit contrasts which I have postulated to be part of the meaning of *Beowulf*.

Both *Beowulf* and *Guthlac* belong to the Antonian tradition. In the case of *Guthlac* this has long been recognized;[1] in the case of *Beowulf* it may yet be disputed, but I think it can be shown that *Beowulf* of the two has rather more in common with the *Vita S. Antonii*.[2] It is my belief that this Life gave the poet the ideas that he needed to retell the Grendel story as a temptation allegory, and that some of the more puzzling features of the poem can be explained by reference to it. I shall therefore attempt a conjectural reconstruction of the genesis of the poem, showing the part which the *Vita S. Antonii* could have had in determining the structure and the allegorical mode of the Old English composition.

Antony, as is well known, fought with demons in the desert. It may not be generally realized that not all his foes were insubstantial. He is much more like Beowulf when he passes through a river full of crocodiles and water-beasts,[3] and even more interestingly so when he confronts a creature who is part-man, part-beast—a kind of satyr—indubitably one of Cain's monstrous progeny. This latter is not one of Antony's great

---

[1] See R. Woolf, 'Saints' Lives', in *Continuations*, pp. 54 f.

[2] *Vita S. Antonii, versio Evagrii, PG* 26, 837–976.

[3] The water-beasts are Evagrius's own addition to the scene:

cum ... rivulum Nili, qui crocodilis et multis ejus fluminis bestiis plenus erat, transvadare esset necesse, tam cum comitibus suis transivit illæsus, quam inde rediit incolumis (*PG* 26, 865, f., cap. 15).

When ... it was necessary to ford a tributary of the Nile, which was full of crocodiles and many other river beasts, he crossed unscathed with his companions and returned equally unharmed.

struggles, which may account for the general neglect of its significance for *Beowulf* studies. In the *Vita* the creature approaches menacingly; Antony arms himself with the sign of the Cross and stands his ground. The encounter is brief. Antony puts the monster to flight with the name of Christ and his own courage:

'Christi servus sum, si ad me missa es, non fugio.' Nullum in medio spatium, et statim informe prodigium dicto ocius cum satellitum turba fugit, et in medio cursu ruens extinctum est. Ista autem explosi mors atque enecatio prodigii dæmonum erat communis interitus.[1]

'I am the servant of Christ. If you are sent against me, I shall not flee.' Without waiting any time at all, forthwith the misshapen monster fled with the throng of attendant demons more quickly than it can be said, and as it ran it died in mid-course. And this death and destruction of the monster thus exterminated was the general overthrow of the demons.

It will be remembered that when Grendel approached Beowulf and encountered his strong resistance, he at once tried to run away, though Beowulf's grip prevented him:

> Hyge wæs him hinfus, wolde on heolster fleon,
> secan deofla gedræg. (755 f.)

I am inclined to think that in the *satellitum turba* of the Antonian incident we have the source of the unexpected *deofla gedræg* whose company Beowulf's monster wanted as he ran, dying, from Heorot. More significantly still, the physical death of Antony's man-monster is expressly said to involve the overthrow of the demons—*dæmonum erat communis interitus*. Since the demonic attacks of the *Vita* are unquestionably the external accompaniment of the inner conflict of the saint, their overthrow represents a temptation repulsed. The association of the physical monster with this inner conflict provides, it seems to me, a sufficient hint to an allegorically-minded poet that the death of Grendel could be used as part of an allegory of temptation. The minor incident in the *Vita* leaps out at the reader who has

---

[1] *PG* 26, 919 f. *cap.* 53. I have emended the *prodigit* of the edition *to prodigii*, in accordance with the reading given in Teubner's *Thesaurus Linguæ Latinæ* (Leipzig, 1931–53), *s.v. explōdo*. The meaning *exanimis* is there suggested for *explosi* in this sentence, but perhaps it implies no more than 'driven off'.

the story of Grendel fresh in mind, and the same is true of another quite different kind of passage, one of two horrifying visions of the Devil which Antony describes. It is of an enormous giant reaching up into the sky, who stretches out clutching hands to seize the souls of men as they leave the earth.[1]

The other vision of the Devil mentioned is the one I have already quoted with reference to Beowulf's dragon: the by now familiar figure of flame-breathing Leviathan, described in the words of the Book of Job.[2] If our poet already had in his head a dragon-killing story in conjunction with the giant story, the *Vita S. Antonii* could offer him a suggestion for the second part to his purposed composition: a fire-breathing dragon to figure the Ancient Enemy who waits to devour men on the day of their death. As the Dragon traditionally has association with death and the end of the world, the dragon combat would make a natural conclusion to the story.

I have already remarked upon the strange similarity between the death of Antony and the death of Beowulf, but there is some likeness in their lives also. Antony's life as a man of God began with three great temptations, the first two figured by contests with demons, the third taking the form of the delusive silver and gold already mentioned in my discussion of the dragon's hoard.[3] The correspondence with Beowulf's three combats might be put down to coincidence, were it not for the remarkable circumstance that in the second contest, which lasts two days, Antony is brought prostrate to the ground by the physical battering given him by the demons, and in his great need is rescued by a miraculous light. It is hard not to believe that Beowulf's three great fights owe something to this model. Before I turn to some features of this particular Antonian contest and some other points in the *Vita* which may prove illuminating, I have one further comment to make upon the general structure of the poem.

I have supposed that the design of the poem was in two parts, one concerning Beowulf's life, conceived as a combat with evil

---

[1] *PG* 26, 937 f., *cap.* 66. On another occasion, Satan appears to him as a giant man (903 f. *cap.* 41) but not in this frightening fashion.

[2] ibid., 878 f., *cap.* 24., cp. p. 234, above.

[3] ibid., 845–62. The first contest, *cc.* 5–7; the second, *cc.* 8–10; the third, *cc.* 11–12. See also p. 96, above.

presences in the land—figuring the repulse of temptations in the hero's soul—and the other concerning his death, conceived similarly, but with the difference that as an unregenerate man he would find the Devil too strong for him; the traditional association of the dragon with gold, the fact that Antony's third temptation was by gold, and the rather curious association of Leviathan with gold[1] would combine to determine the form of that final contest. But, as many critics of Beowulf have observed with distaste, the poem is not symmetrical; there is also the long recapitulation scene which obtrudes in the middle. There is, of course, sound reason for the poet to bring his hero home, and I have already discussed his device of forecast which rounds off the story of Heorot.[2] Nevertheless, the hero's long speech to Hygelac has seemed to most readers to ask for some further explanation. The *Vita* suggests a possible reason why the poet took this course: Athanasius similarly follows his narrative of Antony's early combats with a section in which Antony makes a long speech in his own person, including among much homiletic matter some account of his earlier contests with the demons.[3]

Antony's speech does not contain a forecast as Beowulf's does, but there is in it a long disquisition upon the demons' claims to know the future, and on predictions generally.[4] The saint sets no great value on the capacity to foretell the future; he points out that farmers and pilots, for example, can use their experience to make forecasts; but he also says that a pure soul can see further than the demons. As Antony discusses both intelligent guesswork and clairvoyance, it is not possible to use this speech as a guide to the nature of Beowulf's look into the future, but I think it is a reasonable surmise that this passage about forecasts gave the *Beowulf* poet the answer to his technical problem of finishing off the story of Heorot without displacing Beowulf as the centre of interest.

It is quite possible, therefore, that the two-part structure of

[1] The cryptic scriptural text has been quoted above on p. 143, n. 2. Gregory's commentary suggests that he is nonplussed; he takes the line completely allegorically, as a reference to good souls whom Leviathan corrupts (*PL* 76, 732 f.). In a preamble to this idea he uses the symbol of the *calix aureus*, as quoted above (p. 144). See also my discussion of Leviathan's temptations to cupidity, p. 234, above.

[2] cp. pp. 219 f., above.   [3] *PG* 26, 899–904, *cc*. 39–41.

[4] ibid., 893–6, *cc*. 31–4.

Beowulf, with its curious recapitulation in the middle, owes its inception to the *Vita S. Antonii*. Antony's references to Job and Leviathan would be apt to turn the reader's thoughts to the *Moralia*, and these two works, together with Augustine's *Enarrationes in Psalmos* or some other Augustinan commentary upon the Psalms, would bring together most of the Christian doctrine and symbolism I have discerned in the poem. I would, however, reiterate that the possibility of intermediary works or oral teaching as the source of these ideas is not ruled out, though in the case of the *Vita* the correspondences are of such a kind as to make me believe that the poet knew it well. I now turn to certain features of the *Vita* which shed some light on matters in *Beowulf* sometimes misunderstood.

The first and most important of these concerns the ending of the second contest with the demons in both works, to which I have already referred. Three points of dispute in Beowulf's underwater wrestling seem to me to be cleared up by reference to the *Vita*. These are: the significance of the miraculous light, the part played by the hero's own fortitude, and the delayed intervention of the hand of God. This last point also bears some relevance to the swimming match of Beowulf's youth and the death of Hondscioh. It will be useful to note first how the light appears above the prostrate Antony, and then the words of the Lord to the saint:

Non oblitus Jesus colluctationis servi sui, eidem protector factus est: denique cum elevaret oculos, vidit desuper culmen aperiri, et deductis tenebris, radium ad se lucis influere. Post cujus spendoris adventum nec dæmonum aliquis apparuit, et corporis dolor extemplo deletus est.[1]

Jesus, not unmindful of his servant's wrestling, became his protector; now at last, when he raised his eyes, he saw the roof above him open, and a ray of light dispersing the darkness, streaming in upon him. After the coming of the light not a demon appeared and the pain in his body was taken away at once.

---

[1] *PG* 26, 859 f., *cap.* 10. An interesting but minor resemblance to the Grendel affair is that the demons had wrecked the building in their attacks upon Antony; the passage continues: *ædificium quoque quod paulo ante dissolutum erat, instauratum est.* 'all the building, which shortly before had been broken up, was restored' (cp. *Beowulf* 770 ff. and 997 ff., and also Klaeber's note, *Beowulf*, p. 156).

Antony addressed the ray of light, asking in a very human fashion where the Lord had been while the demons were assaulting him. A voice from the light replied:

Antoni, hic eram; sed expectabam videre certamen tuum; hunc autem quia dimicando viriliter non cessisti, semper auxiliabor tibi, et faciam te in omni orbe nominari.[1]

Antony, I was here, but I was waiting to see your combat, and because you did not cease to fight manfully, I will always aid you, and I will make your name known throughout the world.

I think it will be evident that the situation in *Beowulf* is not dissimilar, when it is remembered that Grendel's dam, having a physical body, cannot disappear. The resurgence of strength in the hero enables him to rise to his feet in both cases. As I have already remarked in discussing the religion of the characters, there is no direct colloquy with God in the poem, so nothing there corresponds with the two speeches: nevertheless the thought that God waits for a hero to prove himself is integral to *Beowulf*. It is implied in the swimming match, in which Beowulf's long endurance test is brought to an end with the coming of a peaceful dawn.[2]

The phrase *þonne his ellen deah* (573) expresses an idea very close to *quia dimicando viriliter non cessisti*. It may be concluded that Beowulf's reliance on both his *mægen* and *Metodes hyldo* is not a half-pagan compromise but a traditional Christian feature of demonic contests: Beowulf's *mægen* manifests itself in a more physical form because his adversaries are Cain's kin and giant serpents, who are diabolical but fleshly.

At another point in the poem, a helpless man is killed while the hero looks on and does nothing (739 ff.). Some critics have tried to explain this away by talking of earlier folk-tale elements incompletely worked into the composition. It is certainly hard to justify by ordinary human standards. I therefore find it extremely interesting that Antony's biographer had to deal with an incident in which Antony's slowness to act might seem to the reader the cause of a man's death. Athanasius feels obliged to exonerate his hero, by ascribing the man's death to God's judgment, and by warning his readers to think of God's mercy

[1] *PG* 26, 859 f.   [2] cp. p. 167, above.

in saving one of the two men concerned rather than question why the other died.[1] The Beowulf poet's observations on the death of Hondscioh (1055 ff.) have the same tendency.

My last observation upon the *Vita S. Antonii* is that the saint in his oration has much to say about the great exchange which God's servant must make; his earthly wealth is the price of eternal life. He uses the language of trade:

In præsenti hac vita æqualia sunt pro rerum commutatione commercia, nec majora recipit ab emente qui vendit: promissio autem vitæ sempiternæ vili pretio comparatur.[2]

In this present life, equal goods are exchanged in course of trade and the seller receives from the buyer no more than he gives, but the promise of eternal life is set against a paltry price.

He can use the phrase *vili pretio*, because in his eyes the wealth of the whole world is worth little in comparison with the promise of heaven. He reminds his followers that, *lege mortis* 'by the law of death', their treasure will one day be taken from them. If one recalls the circumstances of Beowulf's death and his satisfaction at sight of the the dragon's treasure, the price paid being his life, the ironic contrast is inescapable.

There were among the Anglo-Saxon kings a few who gave away their crowns and their possessions to embrace monastic poverty; it is by no means impossible that *Beowulf* encouraged one or other of them to make this choice, but I do not think the author's purpose was to turn his king into a monk. He appears to have been anxious for the welfare of both the king and the people, a welfare which in his philosophy depended essentially upon the spiritual health of the ruler. He therefore composed

---

[1] Antony had been granted a vision of two travellers dying of thirst; he sent water, but one man had already died. Athanasius comments:

Fortasse aliquis quærit, cur non antequam moreretur, Antonius dixerit; incongruo prorsus est Christianis argumento, quia non Antonii, sed Dei judicium fuit, qui et de recedente quam voluit, sententiam tulit, et de sitiente revelatus est. (*PG* 26, 927 f.).

Possibly someone will ask why Antony did not speak before the man died; this is an utterly irrelevant argument for Christians, because the decision lay not with Antony but with God, who both passed sentence upon the dying man according to his will and also revealed the state of the thirsting man.

[2] *PG* 26, 867; cp. p. 239, above.

Beowulf, as I believe, both as a fitting entertainment for a Christian court and as a prophylactic for the souls of men, especially those in high places.

It is no longer necessary to ask, 'Why was *Beowulf* preserved?'[1] In its large compass, its parables touch upon all the great questions which troubled that age, and succeeding ages: it speaks of God's ordering of the world and the causes of wars and violence, the relation of destiny and human responsibility, the inheritance of sin and its consequences, and, above all, of the dependence of the human being, however great, upon his Creator. It considers the right and the wrong use of power and wealth, reminding the listeners that these things are lent, not given. It sounds a battle-call, *memento belli*, to a society beginning to exchange the arts of war for the arts of peace, because the poet believes that the invisible hosts will take possession of an unguarded city and that the king is deceived who thinks he has no enemy.

If I have been right in interpreting *Beowulf* as a historical epic with both moral and allegorical significance, the poem clearly has much more importance in the history of literature than has been supposed. It becomes the precursor of the medieval allegorized romance and of the allegorical epic. In it are foreshadowed the two chivalries, the earthly and the celestial, and even, though faintly indeed, the quest of the Grail. Beowulf is not a Christian knight, but he is born of an imagination moving towards such a concept. It is because the poet has chosen to work with a thematic irony that he has been so generally misunderstood: but only by irony could the great figures of earthly heroism be presented to a Christian world in all their magnificence and their misdirection. As Rosemond Tuve says of Launcelot, Perceval and Bohort in the *Queste del saint Graal*,

The usefulness of irony is apparent in figures like these large fictional images where the persons are unaware or only half-aware,

---

[1] The argument was advanced by K. Brunner, *Études Anglaises*, 1954, 1 ff., in an article under this title, that *Beowulf* was preserved for its moral teaching. He pointed to the strong Christian bent of the four great codices, and thought that the *Beowulf* codex was 'one primarily devoted to Christian heroes'. My findings vindicate and go beyond his argument: it will be seen that *Beowulf* has something in common with *Judith* and even with *The Passion of St Christopher*.

or at least less aware than are we of what happens to them. Irony is native to the figures, and where significances are so quickly grasped that the mind moves with real freedom (as here), this must have been an important part of the pleasure taken by medieval audiences in such works.[1]

The modern mind has certainly not moved with real freedom in *Beowulf*, and for this faults of craftsmanship in the poem are partly responsible.

The potential of the ambitious design is not fully realized; the poet, brilliantly successful as he is at the great moments, does not always correlate his 'historical' material and his many-faceted allegory. Readers today may judge this a serious blemish, but the audience he wrote for probably did not, used as they were to similar handling of Old Testament history. Like the biblical commentators, he is content to enlarge single features of a story, paying small regard to possible discord between the allegorical meaning imparted to these features and the drift of the surrounding narrative. He combines, as they did, associative and contrastive principles to link story with story and to give new significance to events. No doubt when the religious symbols were more generally familiar and the incidental secular stories well known, the trend of his thinking and imagining was readily followed, but for the majority of modern readers—even those who have tried to acquaint themselves with these matters—there are barriers. It is very difficult in our times to take Beowulf seriously as a historical person or to accept demons as real presences upon earth, but unless the reader's imagination can accept these things as given facts of the created world, their appearance in a religious context seems bizarre, the literal story merges with the allegorical, and the double texture of the poem is not discerned. I believe this to have been the cause of much twentieth-century misunderstanding.

The poet's plain moral and religious statements can also be a source of difficulty. To those unsympathetic to the poet's beliefs and deaf to the overtones of the evocative phrases I have discussed, these comments on the action seem to be there to restrain errant attitudes likely to be generated by the stories,

[1] Tuve, *Allegorical Imagery*, p. 53.

and as such to run counter to the spirit of the narrative. I hope I have shown that they are there to bring to the surface the underlying irony inherent in the images themselves. I would not wish to deny that Beowulf's monster-fights can speak directly, without gloss, of the primeval human struggle with the hostile and death-bearing creatures of the world, or to pretend that this is not the source of the poem's universal appeal. But we deceive ourselves if we think we can wipe away a Christian 'colouring' to reveal these archetypal images in their true nature. When the poem is read entire, they can be seen to be absorbed into the medieval Christian model of the universe. Far from being cramped and distorted in a framework of alien ideas, they are made more luminous as vehicles of the mystery of man made in the likeness of God and God once revealed in the likeness of man.

A reader who can imaginatively enter the thought-world I have been describing will, I am confident, find the large structure of the poem simple and satisfying. Both the literal narrative and the moral allegory are closely knit and well-balanced in the two parts,[1] though one will perhaps still concede with Hulbert that the composition is 'clumsy in some details of development and too compressed and allusive'.[2] On the level of what I have called the tangential themes, in which Beowulf becomes a type of mankind opposing the diabolical powers, there is not, nor could there be, a progress similar to the movement through the three stages of trial in the personal allegory of the hero. For this transcendental purpose, the natural sequence of time had to be reversed, to move backward from Christ to Adam. I do not think this regress could be avoided, since Beowulf as man victorious in God-given strength must bring to mind human nature made invincible in the incarnate Christ: hence the symbolic acts of the wrestling, going down into the water, cutting off the great head, and so on, which evoke remembrance

[1] The work of Brodeur and more recently of Carrigan has sufficiently shown that the historical stories are cleverly interlaced across both parts of the poem. Carrigan, however, still maintains that there is no proper balance between the two halves, following T. M. Gang, who argued that the dragon fight was 'an impersonal vision in which neither adversary is given a divinely appointed status', so that it could not be either a balance or an opposition to the themes of the Grendel fight. (cp. E. Carrigan, 'Structure and Thematic Development in *Beowulf*', *Proc. R. Irish Academy*, 66, Section C, No. 1 [1967], p. 2.)

[2] J. R. Hulbert, 'Beowulf and the Classical Epic', *MP* 44 (1946–7), p. 74.

of the divine warrior, belong naturally to the first part of the poem. But Beowulf as man deluded by the Dragon's gold, rashly striving for independence and greatness, and discovering death, carries our minds back to the beginning of human time and the myth of Adam's rebellion against the law of his being. Though the poet can and does take great liberties with chronological sequence in the story of Beowulf's life and the events which touch upon it, he would surely have found it impracticable to treat the hero's death in the first part and his crowning achievements retrospectively in the second. There could be no more fitting end to the poem than the interment of the hero's ashes together with the gold. From every point of view, Beowulf's death and burial, as an image of man's encounter with the *bana*—the cause, as was then believed, of the mutability and transience so movingly described at several places in the work —is a proper culmination of all that the poet has had to say about life on earth. It is a melancholy, but by no means a despairing conclusion to the work. For even here, because Adam's fatal contest with the Serpent-Dragon had a typological significance, the thoughts are once more turned forward. The second Adam, the divine warrior, is shadowily foreseen when the Dragon is struck down, as the Lord piercing Leviathan with his sword in the day of ultimate victory.

Select Bibliography

A. EDITIONS OF TEXTS

1. Old English Poetry

All quotations from Old English poetry are taken from *The Anglo-Saxon Poetic Records*, ed. G. P. Krapp and E. v. K. Dobbie, New York and London, 1931–54:

I. *The Junius Manuscript*, ed. G. P. Krapp.
II. *The Vercelli Book*, ed. G. P. Krapp.
III. *The Exeter Book*, ed. G. P. Krapp and E. v. K. Dobbie.
IV. *Beowulf and Judith*, ed. E. v. K. Dobbie.
V. *The Paris Psalter and the Meters of Boethius*, ed. G. P. Krapp.
VI. *The Anglo-Saxon Minor Poems*, ed. E. v. K. Dobbie.

In addition to the above edition and the unique manuscript, BM Cotton Vitellius AXV, the following texts of *Beowulf* have been consulted:

Beowulf reproduced in Facsimile, by J. Zupitza, 2nd ed. with an introductory note by Norman Davis, EETS, Oxford, 1959.

The Nowell Codex, Early English Manuscripts in Facsimile, vol. xii, ed. Kemp Malone, Copenhagen, Baltimore, and London, 1963.

Beowulf and the Fight at Finnsburg, ed. F. Klaeber, 3rd ed., repr. with supplement, Boston and London, 1950.

Beowulf, ed. E. von Schaubert, from the earlier edition of Heyne-Schücking, Paderborn, 1963.

Beowulf, ed. C. L. Wrenn, London, 1953, repr. 1961.

2. Other Texts Quoted and Cited

Note: Greek texts are quoted in translation, in English or Latin.

Acta Sanctorum, ed. J. Bollandus *et al.*, Antwerp and Brussels, 1643–.

(Adamnan) *Adomnan's Life of Columba*, ed. A. O. and M. O. Anderson, London, 1961.

Aldhelm. *Opera*, ed. R. Ehwald, *MGH AA*, vol. 15, Berlin, 1919.

— *The Riddles of Aldhelm*, ed. J. H. Pitman, Yale, 1925.

Alcuin. *Carmina*, *MGH Poet.*, ed. E. Duemmler, Berlin, 1880–1.

— *Epistulae*, *MGH Ep. Kar.*, vol. 2, ed. E. Duemmler, Berlin, 1895.

Ambrose. *Exameron*, *CSEL*, vol. 32, 1, ed. C. Schenkl, Vienna, 1887.

— *Explanatio Psalmorum XII*, *CSEL*, vol. 64, Vienna, 1919.

— *Expositionis Evangelii secundum Lucam Libri X*, *PL*, vol. 15, col. 1527 ff.

Athanasius. *Vita Sancti Antonii, versio Evagrii*, *PG*, vol. 26, col. 835 ff.

Augustine. *De catechizandis rudibus*, ed. G. Krüger, Tübingen, 3rd ed., 1934.

— *De civitate Dei*, ed. B. Dombart and A. Kalb, *CCSL*, vols. 47 and 48, Turnhout, 1955.

— *De doctrina christiana*, ed. W. M. Green, *CSEL*, vol. 80, Vienna, 1963.
— *Enarrationes in Psalmos*, *CCSL*, vols. 38–40, ed. E. Dekkers and I. Fraipont, Turnhout, 1956.
— *De libero arbitrio*, ed. W. M. Green, *CSEL*, vol. 74, Vienna, 1956.
— *De Trinitate*, ed. J. P. Migne, *PL*, vol. 42, col. 819 ff.
— *De utilitate credendi*, ed. J. Zycha, *CSEL*, vol. 25, 1, Vienna, 1886.
— *De vera religione*, ed. W. M. Green, *CSEL*, vol. 77, Vienna, 1961.
Bede. *Expositio in Epistolam I S. Joannis*, ed. J. P. Migne, *PL*, vol. 93, col. 85 ff.
— *Opera Historica*, ed. C. Plummer, 2 vols., Oxford, 1896
— *Opera Homiletica*, ed. D. Hurst and J. Fraipont, *CCSL*, vol. 122, Turnhout, 1955.
— *In Pentateuchum Commentarii*, ed. J. P. Migne, *PL*, vol. 91, col. 219 ff.
— *De schematibus et tropis sacrae scripturae*, ed. J. P. Migne, *PL*, vol. 90, col. 175 ff.
Blickling Homilies, The, ed. R. Morris, EETS, OS, vols. 58, 63, 73, London, 1880.
(Felix). *Felix's Life of Saith Guthlac*, ed. B. Colgrave, Cambridge, 1956.
Gregory I, the Great. *Dialogorum Libri IV*, *PL*, vol. 77, col. 149 ff.
— *Moralium Libri in Librum B. Job*, ed. J. P. Migne, *PL*, vol. 75, col. 509 ff. and vol. 76, col. 1 ff.
— *Registrum Epistolarum*, ed. P. Ewald and L. M. Hartmann, *MGH Ep.*, Berlin, 1891.
Irish Liber Hymnorum, The, ed. J. Bernard and R. Atkinson for the Henry Bradshaw Society, vols. 13 and 14, London, 1898.
Isidore of Seville. *Etymologiarum sive Originum Libri XX*, ed. W. M. Lindsay, Oxford, 1911.
Patrologia Graeca, ed. J. P. Migne, Paris, 1857–86.
Patrologia Latina, ed. J. P. Migne, Paris, 1844–64.
Psalterium Romanum. Le Psautier Romain et les autres anciens Psautiers latins, ed. R. Weber, Rome, 1953.
Phædrus. *Fabulæ Æsopiæ*, ed. G. H. Nall, London, 1895.
Prudentius. *Carmina*, ed. M. P. Cunningham, *CCSL*, vol. 126, Turnhout, 1966.
Sulpicius Severus. *Libri qui supersunt*, ed. C. Halm, *CSEL*, vol. 1, Vienna, 1866.
Tacitus. *Germania*, ed. J. C. G. Anderson, Oxford, 1938.

B. OTHER SCHOLARLY AND CRITICAL WORKS
PRINCIPALLY USED

Bessinger, J. B. and Creed, R. P., *Medieval and Linguistic Studies in honor of Francis P. Magoun, Jr.*, New York and London, 1965.
Blackburn, F. A., 'The Christian Coloring in the *Beowulf*', *PMLA*, vol. 12 (1897), pp. 205–25.
Brodeur, A. G., *The Art of Beowulf*, California, 1959.
Brodeur Studies. See Greenfield, S. B. ed.

Select Bibliography

Bonjour, Adrien, *The Digressions in 'Beowulf'*, Medium Ævum Monographs 5, Oxford, 1950, repr. 1965.

Brown, A. and Foote, P., ed., *Early English and Norse Studies presented to Hugh Smith*, London, 1963.

Cabaniss, Allen, *'Beowulf* and the Liturgy', *JEGP*, vol. 54 (1955), pp. 195–201.

Campbell, J. J., 'Learned Rhetoric and Old English Poetry', *MP*, vol. 43 (1966), pp. 189–201.

Carney, James, *Studies in Irish Literature and History*, Dublin, 1955.

Chadwick, Nora M., 'The Monsters and Beowulf', in *The Anglo-Saxons: Studies presented to Bruce Dickins*, ed. P. Clemoes, London, 1959, pp. 171–203.

Chambers, R. W., *Beowulf: an Introduction to the Study of the Poem*, 3rd ed. with a Supplement by C. L. Wrenn, Cambridge, 1959, repr. 1963.

Cope, Gilbert, *Symbolism in the Bible and the Church*, London, 1959.

Courcelle, Pierre, 'Les Pères de l'Église devant les Enfers Virgiliens', *Archives d'Histoire Doctrinale et Littéraire du Moyen Age*, vol. 22 (1955), pp. 1–70.

Cross, J. E. and Tucker, S. I., 'Allegorical Tradition and the Old English *Exodus*', *Neophil.*, vol. 45 (1960), pp. 122–7.

Curtius, E., *European Literature and the Latin Middle Ages*, London, 1953 (original German edition, Berne, 1948).

Daniélou, Jean, *Bible et Liturgie*, Paris, 1951.

Deanesly, Margaret, *The Pre-Conquest Church in England*, 2nd ed., London, 1963.

Dillistone, F. W., *Christianity and Symbolism*, London, 1955.

Donahue, Charles, *'Beowulf,* Ireland and the Natural Good', *Traditio*, vol. 7 (1949–51), pp. 263–77.

— *'Beowulf* and Christian Tradition: a reconsideration from a Celtic Stance', *Traditio*, vol. 21 (1965), pp. 55–116.

Du Bois, Arthur E., 'The Dragon in *Beowulf*—Symbol or Image?', *PMLA*, vol. 73 (1957), pp. 819 ff.

Earle, John, *Anglo-Saxon Literature*, London, 1884.

Ehrismann, G., 'Religionsgeschichtliche Beiträge zum Germanischen Frühchristentum', in P. und B. *Beiträge zur Geschichte der Deutschen Sprache und Literatur*, Band 35, Halle, 1909, pp. 209–39.

Eliason, Norman E., 'The Thryth-Offa Digression in *Beowulf'* in *Magoun Studies, q.v.*, pp. 120–33.

Emerson, O. F., 'Legends of Cain, especially in Old and Middle English', *PMLA*, vol. 21 (1906), pp. 831–929.

Eusebius. See McGiffert, A. C.

Fletcher, Angus, *Allegory: the Theory of a Symbolic Mode*, New York, 1964.

Gatch, Milton McC., 'Eschatology in the Anonymous Old English Homilies', *Traditio*, vol. 21 (1965), pp. 116–65.

Godfrey, J., *The Church in Anglo-Saxon England*, Cambridge, 1962.

Greenfield, S. B., ed., *Studies in Old English Literature in honor of Arthur G.*

272

Brodeur, Oregon, 1963. (Part 1, including articles 1–9, also appeared in *Comparative Literature*, Winter, 1962.)

— *A Critical History of Old English Literature*, New York, 1965, London, 1966.

Hamilton, Marie P., 'The Religious Principle in *Beowulf*', *PMLA*, vol. 61 (1946), pp. 309–31.

Jones, P. F., 'The Gregorian Mission and English Education', *Speculum*, vol. 3 (1928), pp. 335 ff.

Kaske, R. E., '*Sapientia et Fortitudo* as the Controlling Theme of *Beowulf*', *Studies in Philology*, vol. 55 (1958), pp. 423–57.

Kenney, James F., *The Sources for the Early History of Ireland*, vol. i, *Ecclesiastical*, Columbia University Records of Civilisation, New York, 1929.

Keiser, A., *The Influence of Christianity on the Vocabulary of Old English Poetry*, University of Illinois Studies in Language and Literature 5, 1919.

Klaeber, F., 'Die Christlichen Elemente im *Beowulf*', *Anglia*, vols. 35 and 36 (1912), pp. 111 ff.

Laistner, M. L. W., 'Bede as a Classical and a Patristic Scholar', *Transactions of the Royal Historical Society*, 4th series, vol. 16 (1933), pp. 69–94.

— *Thought and Letters in Western Europe A.D. 500–900*, 2nd ed., London, 1957.

Lawrence, W. W., *Beowulf and Epic Tradition*, Harvard U.P., Cambridge, 1928, repr. New York, 1961.

— 'Grendel's Lair', *JEGP*, vol. 38 (1939), pp. 477 ff.

Leake, Jane Acomb, *The Geats of 'Beowulf'*, Wisconsin, 1967.

Lewis, C. S., *The Allegory of Love: a study in Medieval Tradition*, Oxford, 1959.

— *The Discarded Image*, Cambridge, 1964.

Leyerle, J., 'Beowulf the Hero and the King', *MÆ*, vol. 34 (1965), pp. 89–102.

Magoun, F. P., Jr., '*Béowulf B:* a Folk-Poem on Beowulf's Death', in *Smith Studies, q.v.*, pp, 127–40.

— 'The Oral-Formulaic Character of Anglo-Saxon Narrative Poetry', *Speculum*, vol. 28 (1953), pp. 446–67.

Magoun Studies. See Bessinger, J. B., ed.

Malone, Kemp, 'Grendel's Abode', *Studia Philologica et Litteraria in honorem L. Spitzer*, Berne, 1958, pp. 297–308.

Morrell, M. C., *A Manual of Old English Biblical Materials*, Tennessee, 1965.

McGiffert, A. C., trans. Eusebius: *The Ecclesiastical History* and *The Life of Constantine*, in A Library of Nicene and Post-Nicene Fathers, vol. 1, Oxford and New York, 1890.

McNamee, M. B., '*Beowulf*—An Allegory of Salvation?', *JEGP*, vol. 59 (1960), pp. 190–207.

Nicholson, Lewis E., ed., *An Anthology of Beowulf Criticism*, Indiana, 1963.

Nowottny, Winifred, *The Language Poets Use*, London, 1962.

Ogilvy, J. D. A., *Books known to Anglo-Latin Writers from Aldhelm to Alcuin*, Cambridge, Mass., 1936.

Pope, J. C., 'Dramatic Voices in *The Wanderer* and *The Seafarer*' in *Magoun Studies, q.v.*, pp. 164–93.

Select Bibliography

Rankin, J. W., 'A Study of the Kennings in Anglo-Saxon Poetry', *JEGP*, vols. 8 (1909), pp. 357–422 and 9 (1910), pp. 49–84.

Robertson, D. W., Jr., 'The Doctrine of Charity in Medieval Literary Gardens: a Topical approach through Symbolism and Allegory', *Speculum*, vol. 26 (1951), pp. 24–49.

Schücking, Levin L., 'Das Königsideal im *Beowulf*', *MHRA* Bulletin 3, 1929, pp. 144–54; repr. in *Englische Studien*, vol. 67 (1932), pp. 1–14.

Sisam, Kenneth, *The Structure of Beowulf*, Oxford, 1965.

— *Studies in the History of Old English Literature*, Oxford, 1953.

Smith Studies. See Brown, A., ed.

Smithers, G. V., *The Making of Beowulf*, Inaugural Lecture, Durham, 1961.

—— 'The Meaning of *The Seafarer* and *The Wanderer*', *MÆ*, vol. 28 (1959), 1–22.

Stanley, E. G., ed., *Continuations and Beginnings: Studies in Old English Literature*, London, 1966.

— '*Hæthenra Hyht* in *Beowulf*', in *Brodeur Studies*, q.v., pp. 136–51.

Tolkien, J. R. R., '*Beowulf:* The Monsters and the Critics', *Proceedings of the British Academy*, vol. 22 (1936), pp. 245–95.

— 'The Homecoming of Beorhtnoth Beorhthelm's Son', *Essays and Studies*, 1953.

Tuve, Rosemond, *Allegorical Imagery*, Princeton, New Jersey, 1966.

Vansina, Jan, *De la Tradition Orale*, Tervuren, 1961.

Whallon, W., 'The Christianity of *Beowulf*', *MP*, vol. 60 (1962), pp. 81–94.

Whitelock, Dorothy, *The Audience of Beowulf*, Oxford, 1951, repr. 1958, 1964.

Wild, Friedrich, *Drachen im 'Beowulf' und andere Drachen*, Vienna, 1962.

Woolf, Rosemary, 'Saints' Lives', in *Continuations and Beginnings*, q.v. under Stanley, E. G., ed., pp. 37–66.

Wrenn, C. L., *A Study of Old English Literature*, London, 1967.

Index

Index

Behemoth, 51, 115n
Benedict Biscop, 36, 40, 72
Beowulf, hero of the poem, 3, 48, 67,
90, 186–8, 210–30; death of, 95,
163, 167, 175, 185, 210–11, 221,
228, 238, 240–3, 252, 254, 256,
261–2; dragon fight of, 103, 128–
129, 132, 143, 160–1, 166, 191,
195n, 210, 215, 223–4, 226, 228,
230–9, 243, 255, 268n; as *figura
Christi*, 72–3, 241–3; as God's
champion, 117, 124, 264; Grendel
fight of, 111, 115, 117, 158, 162–3,
213, 219, 268n; as king, 91, 211,
215–16, 221–7, 246; the memorial
of, 92; as pattern of princely
behaviour, 213–30; religion and
philosophy of, 42, 89, 146–7, 151–
152, 154, 161–70, 178, 212, 264;
reputation of, 92, 221, 223–4; as
type of mankind, 4, 185, 255, 268;
underwater fight of, 113, 116–19,
124, 137–8, 160n, 165–6, 261,
263–4; as winner of treasure, 92–
94, 254
Bible, the, 31, 36, 37, 49n, 130, 149,
154, 159
Blickling Homilies, The, 11, 115,
121, 164n
Boar figures in *Beowulf*, 87
Bonjour, A., 140n, 246, 249, 251n,
252, 254–5
Brodeur, A. G., 109n, 157n, 158n,
162–3, 167n, 171–6, 179, 212,
219–20, 251

Cædmon, 7, 8, 11, 12, 17, 40–1,
175
Cain, 3, 73, 104–12, 120–1, 144, 150–
151, 169n, 174, 181, 191, 248–9,
251
Cain's kin, 3, 101, 105–12, 115–16,
118, 122–3, 174, 248, 259, 264
Canterbury, 26, 36
Carney, J., 101, 137
Cassian, 31, 36
Cassiodorus, 36, 38, 56

De catechizandis rudibus, see Augustine,
St, of Hippo
Celtic Christianity, 22–9, 30–1, 35,
38, 56, 181
Chadwick, N., 100, 103, 110
Chambers, R. W., 113, 129n, 189n,
190n, 218n
Christ, 7, 12, 40, 51, 53, 56, 65, 69,
72, 74, 136, 148, 152, 173–6, 179–
180, 200, 241–5, 251, 256, 260,
268–9
'Christian Excursus', the, in *Beowulf*,
170–82
Christian teaching in Anglo-Saxon
England, 12, 22–6, 36, 38–41, 47–
48, 55, 58, 178
Christian vocabulary, the, in *Beo-
wulf*, 3, 7, 16–17, 20
De civitate Dei, see Augustine, St, of
Hippo
Clovesho, Council of, 10
Colman, 27–8
Columba, St, 27–8, 32, 42–3, 51, 57,
137, 182n. *See also* Saints' Lives
Columban, 32
Concupiscence, 77–8, 185, 236
Constantine, the Emperor, 223, 245;
Life of, *see* Eusebius
Creation Song, the, in *Beowulf*, 44,
52, 107, 114, 170, 175
Creation, the, 12, 41, 43–4, 52, 175
Cupidity, 90, 96, 118, 122–4, 141,
144, 184–5, 187, 196, 202, 204,
228–30, 233–4, 237, 239
Cup, the dragon's, 86, 144, 229n,
235, 255–6
Cura pastoralis, see Gregory, St, the
Great
Curse, the, on the hoard in *Beowulf*,
95, 228–30
Cuthbert, St, 24. *See also* Saints'
Lives
Cynewulf, 9, 19, 201

Danes, the, in *Beowulf*, 52, 80, 85,
89, 91, 94, 109, 112, 117, 159, 162,
170–7, 189, 214, 250, 254

276

Index

Fletcher, A., 70

Flood, the, 12, 46, 51, 73, 89, 102, 107–8, 121, 143, 186

Formulaic diction, 8, 10, 62–3, 79

Fourfold interpretation in Scriptural exegesis, 33, 69, 71–2

Fulgentius, 75; *Expositio Virgilianae continentiae*, 75

Geats, the, in *Beowulf*, 86, 90, 93, 95, 149, 160, 177, 188, 212n, 213–15, 220, 228, 230, 254

Genesis, The Book of, 51–2, 106, 111–12, 125, 150, 232–3

Giants, 45–6, 48, 73, 86, 88–9, 97, 107, 116, 118, 120–1, 123, 139, 140n, 144, 186, 190, 214, 216, 261

gifstol, 86, 109, 253

Gildas, 38

Gnomic Verses, The OE, 97, 128, 141, 249

God the Creator, 34, 38, 44, 45, 49, 51–2, 66, 80, 89, 107, 109, 114, 149–50, 154, 167, 170, 175, 194, 206, 209, 223, 248, 266; as governor of life, 80–2, 147, 157–9, 162, 170, 177, 221, 227, 247, 266; as judge, 13, 47, 155, 158, 163, 165, 174, 181, 264; as Lord of retribution, 51, 59, 89, 108, 163, 232; as Lord of victory, 50, 52, 59, 81n, 161, 247; man's natural knowledge of, 52, 149–53, 172–4, 184; as protector, 89, 95, 117, 158–9, 231, 235, 263; as provider, 40, 81, 157, 188, 192, 206, 229; wrath of, 155–6, 177, 226

Godfrey, J., 24, 25n, 27, 38

Gospels, echoes of the, in *Beowulf*, 241–3

Greek, knowledge of, in Anglo-Saxon England, 37, 108

Greenfield, S. B., 226n, 227

'Gregorian' foundations, 23, 25, 36, 37n

Gregory of Tours, 38

Gregory, St, the Great, 23, 31, 34, 35, 36, 38, 42, 43, 48, 50, 56, 71, 148–9, 151, 180, 186, 188, 196–204, 207, 236, 237n, 255, 262n; *Dialogues*, 67, 133n, 136; Homilies, 133n, 197; Letter to Rechared, 208–9; *Moralia in Job*, 34, 38, 46, 48, 51, 58, 71, 112, 115n, 119, 122–3, 141n, 142–4, 149n, 151n, 152, 158n, 180, 182, 186n, 188n, 192n, 193–4, 196n, 197–204, 207, 210, 221, 233–5, 263

Grendel, 80, 84–5, 88–9, 94, 97–100, 104–12, 114–17, 136, 140n, 147, 151, 162, 165, 167, 176, 179, 186, 188, 190–1, 207, 210, 213, 215, 221, 227, 231, 238, 242, 250, 257n, 258–61

Grendel's dam, 98, 104, 110–11, 257n, 264

Grendel's lair, 112–16, 118, 121–3 236

Grendel's mere, 48, 75, 97, 113–15, 121–3, 137

Grettissaga, 100, 113, 218

Guthlac, 9, 91, 116–18, 120, 168, 178n, 201n, 211n, 242, 257–9

Guthlac, St, 105, 117–18, 257. *See also* Saints' Lives, *Vita S. Guthlaci*

hæðenra hyht, 177, 205, 230

Hagiography, 11, 30–1, 54, 130–1, 182n, 258

Hama, 80, 91–2, 169

Hamilton, M. P., 111–12, 122, 153n, 179, 181

Hart, the, 83–4

Hell, 45, 114–16, 120–1, 124, 133, 136, 138, 144, 147, 149, 163, 165, 171, 179–80; the harrowing of, 243, 256

Hengest, 82, 88, 250–1

Heorot, 52, 72n, 83–6, 88–92, 96, 97, 100, 103, 108–9, 112, 116–17, 123, 144, 172, 174, 176–7, 210, 214, 216, 248–50, 252, 254, 256, 260, 262

Hercules, 60, 132, 134

Index

Index

PR 1585 .G6
GOLDSMITH, MARGARET
MODE AND MEANING OF
BEOWULF

DATE DUE

MA

MONTGOMERY COLLEGE LIBRARIES
germ, circ   The mode and   PR 1585.G6

0 0000 00033597 6